Cistercian Fathers and Forefathers

Essays and Conferences

Published by New City Press of the Focolare
202 Comforter Blvd.,
Hyde Park, NY 12538
www.newcitypress.com

Cover design & book layout by Miguel Tejerina

Cistercian Fathers and Forefathers
by Thomas Merton

Library of Congress Control Number: 2018950350

ISBN: 978-1-56548-671-3 paperback
ISBN: 978-1-56548-672-0 e-book

Printed in the United States of America

Cistercian Fathers and Forefathers
Essays and Conferences

by

Thomas Merton

Edited with an Introduction by

Patrick F. O'Connell

Foreword by

Michael Casagram, OCSO

New City Press
Hyde Park, New York

Table of Contents

Foreword

Reading the essays and conferences collected in the present volume will be a rewarding experience for any person who has a desire to enter more deeply into the mind and heart of Thomas Merton and to share the wisdom of a tradition he loved. One will only fully appreciate Merton, his ongoing contribution to monastic and secular life today, if one has a real sense of his continuous immersion in the thought of the monastic and Church fathers, and of his willingness to draw on his own study and reflection to share their wisdom with others: with the novices to whom the conferences transcribed here were first presented, with the original readers of various journals in which the published articles initially appeared, and now with those who encounter these previously uncollected pieces on the early Cistercians and their immediate predecessors that have been brought together here for the first time.

The gathering of this material, ably edited and introduced by Patrick F. O'Connell, is a wise selection. O'Connell's headnotes are especially helpful in unravelling the context in which these pieces were written or presented. Delving into what Fr. Louis is seeking to convey to his novices and his readers in this series of conferences and essays makes possible a new appreciation of Merton and of his ability to penetrate and to communicate the thought of the masters of the spiritual life. Some readers may be familiar with parts of this volume from acquaintance with earlier periodical publication, but considering all the pieces together as a unified whole has left me with a fresh awareness both of Merton's avid search for wisdom and of the tradition represented by the persons whose insights he seeks to pass on to future generations. Anyone who has read much of Merton finds himself or herself amazed at his ability to articulate an author's message and above all, to make this message new and readily accessible for the people of today. To grow in our self-understanding, to grow in our grasp of the wisdom of the past, is to come ever closer to what God is seeking to bring about in our often conflicted society or in the life of the Church itself. Merton has a special gift for exploring both the ideas and the deep inner longing of the writers he consults in his pursuit of transformation and authenticity.

One recognizes this gift right away in the opening selection on St. Peter Damian. Merton tells his audience that "Damian insisted that the only justification for penance and penitential works was a deep and sincere love for God. He speaks of this love in accents that are unmistakably real, and he insists that unless penance proceeds from an *experience* of such love, it will be sterile to say the least" (33). Though St. Peter Damian was famous for his penitential life and his efforts to call the monks, clerics and laity of his time to live such a life, Merton presents him as well-grounded in a living sense of divine initiative.

Again and again these essays and conferences are revelatory of Merton's own inner life and journey. Fr. Louis himself struggled long and hard with his vow of stability, which is often the greatest challenge for monks because of the way it exposes a monk to his own and his community's limitations. It is a struggle not unfamiliar to many in our world today as we look at what is happening among married couples and with family life in general. In his conferences on St. Anselm, Merton highlights the way the great monastic thinker warns his monks against falling into false forms of reasoning. It is all too easy for a monk to develop an attitude that starts "to suggest that he was foolish or imprudent to undertake [a monastic vocation] under such superiors, or among such companions, or in such a place" (77). Only when our thinking is grounded in faith will we be able to resolve these inner conflicts. Merton sees St. Anselm as immersed in a contemplative experience that allowed him to explore the power of human reasoning like no other of his time, leading Merton to identify him as "one of the most prominent existentialists of all history." He goes on to tell us that the great Protestant theologian Karl Barth "loves this man," and "understands him better than anybody else in the twentieth century" (78). As we enter into Fr. Louis's reflections on Anselm we are exposed to an impressive response to this man's thinking, the insights of Étienne Gilson, Paul Evdokimov, R. W. Southern, David Knowles and others. One is impressed by the thoroughness of Merton's research, his capacity for scholarly work when this took him still further along the spiritual journey. This is one instance among many where we see how Merton's own horizons were ever widened while maintaining at the same time a depth of insight that reveals his own inner experience.

While the Bible, liturgy and reading of the Fathers are essential for the monastic life of contemplation, Merton tells us they are meant to bring us to "encounter the life-giving and creative Spirit who, in full continuity with the 'old,' is able to 'make all things new' and indeed to fuse the old and the new in an original and entirely creative unity" (113). Whether one is a monk, a lay member of the Church or a seeker responding to Merton's ever-broadening ecumenical outreach, he would have us open up to an ever-new and more living sense of the life of the Spirit in our world today. This invitation is as challenging now as it ever was.

Fr. Louis' treatment of the little-known figure of Guigo the Carthusian is particularly intriguing and revealing. Here is someone dedicated to the solitary life, a life for which Merton himself had a great longing and desire. He writes: "To love solitude is to love truth, for in solitude one is compelled to grapple with illusion. The solitary life is a battle with subjectivity in which victory is to be gained not by the subject, but by Truth" (158). And isn't this the desire and often desperate search of every human heart?

Turning to the early Cistercians, as he presents the sermons of Blessed Guerric of Igny and the life and thought of St. Aelred of Rievaulx, one does not have to be from Kentucky, the bourbon capital of the world, to appreciate the way Fr. Louis is able to distill what is most precious and invigorating from these authors so as to give his readers ready access to their wisdom. We receive fresh insight into the early Cistercian love for the mystery of the Incarnation, filling them, and us, with gratitude for God's immeasurable love for humanity, as revealed in Guerric's sermons. Then in Aelred we are given the opportunity to explore this mystery as it touches on every aspect of our life together in community or as members of the human family. Merton's study of Aelred's life and particularly his commitment to serving his brethren as Abbot of Rievaulx makes real for us the transformative power of God's taking on our human flesh. Though Aelred was influenced by the teaching of St. Bernard, he takes us to a whole new level of hope for what can take place in the human family by his loving witness to the power of spiritual friendship when it is fully explored and experienced. True to the Cistercian charism, Aelred lived the Christ-life to the full as "poor and obscure, a life of suffering and labor and hardship, embraced … for the love of God" (260). In the final selections, on Isaac of Stella and Adam of Perseigne, we see Merton's ability to be formative not only of the monks he instructed but of all those who will take the time to read his works. We find in the tradition they exemplify not only a literature rich in biblical culture, but "a genuine theology and a humanism full of psychological insight with plenty of relevance for our own day" (394), a real "feast of freedom" (447).

The lives of all of us are being continually formed with each new day. Walking in the path of wisdom of these great masters, as Fr. Louis would have us do, will affirm us in our ability to continually grow into that freedom for which we were created. This rich collection of essays and conferences, marked by Merton's own deep wisdom and perceptive insights, helps to make such a journey possible.

Michael Casagram, OCSO
Prior, Abbey of Gethsemani

Introduction

From January 1963 through early August 1964, Thomas Merton gave a series of conferences to the novices and newly professed monks at the Abbey of Gethsemani entitled *The Cistercian Fathers and Their Monastic Theology*.[1] Despite the title, however, the focus of this course presented by the novice master was almost exclusively the life and teaching of the greatest of these early Cistercians, St. Bernard of Clairvaux. The series was a revision and expansion of a set of conferences delivered earlier under the title "The Life, Works and Doctrine of St. Bernard," and while the new title, along with the fact that it opens with the subheading "Part I: Saint Bernard," strongly suggests that Merton's intention was to include substantial discussion of the work of Bernard's significant Cistercian contemporaries and immediate successors, in the event the revised version of these lectures developed in a different direction, adding extensive discussion of Abbot Peter the Venerable of Cluny, the Carthusian Prior Guigo I and the controversial theologian Peter Abelard, in the context of their relationships to Bernard and his writings, as well as considerably expanded attention to the writings of the Abbot of Clairvaux himself, rather than material about his fellow Cistercian authors of the twelfth century. William of St. Thierry,[2] the most significant Cistercian theologian and spiritual writer after Bernard himself, appears in the text only as Bernard's biographer, composer of the first book of the *Vita Prima* of his friend (13-31), and as fellow antagonist of Abelard (173-83). Of the two other figures grouped as the so-called Four Cistercian Evangelists, Aelred of Rievaulx receives just a couple of brief mentions in passing, and Guerric of Igny appears only in the third of the seven appendices to the main text (313-20), in which his sermon

---

1. Thomas Merton, *The Cistercian Fathers and Their Monastic Theology: Initiation into the Monastic Tradition* 8, ed. Patrick F. O'Connell, Monastic Wisdom vol. 42 (Collegeville, MN: Cistercian Publications, 2016).
2. On William, see the biographical profile in Thomas Merton, *In the Valley of Wormwood: Cistercian Blessed and Saints of the Golden Age* edited by Patrick Hart, OCSO (Collegeville, MN: Cistercian Publications, 2013) 327-37.

on the Assumption is paired with a treatise by Baldwin, Abbot of the English Cistercian monastery of Ford and subsequently Archbishop of Canterbury, two texts that share a focus on the theme of spiritual rest. These appendices – the four longest of which consist in further discussion of Bernard – contain the only other substantial treatment of material by additional early Cistercian Fathers: a brief investigation of the theme of self-will and disobedience in a sermon of Abbot Isaac of Stella in Appendix II (311-13) and a set of extracts (in Latin) on silence by Abbot Adam of Perseigne (356-59).

This lack of attention given to early Cistercian writers other than Bernard should not be taken, however, as evidence of a disinterest on Merton's part in these other spiritual masters of the century following the foundation of the Order of Cîteaux in 1098. Throughout his monastic life, almost from the time of his entrance into the rural Kentucky monastery of Gethsemani on December 10, 1941 until his untimely death in Thailand on December 10, 1968, exactly twenty-seven years later, when Adam of Perseigne made a brief but significant appearance in his final talk, "Marxism and Monastic Perspectives," given on that very day,[3] Merton returned repeatedly to the writings of this Cistercian "Golden Age," as well as to works by other significant monastic authors of the period immediately preceding and overlapping the rise of this new expression of Benedictine life. Written for both popular and more scholarly audiences, for monastics and for laity, sometimes rather briefly and at other times at considerably greater length, in prefatory materials for volumes written or translated by others, in conferences given to his novices, these materials are generally little known, because whereas virtually all of Merton's writings on St. Bernard have been included in books,[4] none of his pieces on Bernard's fellow Cistercian Fathers and their immediate monastic predecessors has been available except in periodicals or books not by Merton himself. It could in fact be plausibly suggested that these articles on eleventh- and twelfth-century monastics constitute the most important group

---

3. See Thomas Merton, *The Asian Journal*, ed. Naomi Burton Stone, Brother Patrick Hart and James Laughlin (New York: New Directions, 1973) 333.

4. See the discussion in *Cistercian Fathers and Their Monastic Theology* xi-xliv, and the bibliographical information in Appendix A below.

of hitherto uncollected writings by Merton. Hence the present volume is intended to fill a significant lacuna in Merton's publications.

The thirteen pieces included in this volume, focused on seven authors, were composed by Merton over the course of nearly two decades, from the end of the 1940s, shortly after the publication of *The Seven Storey Mountain*,[5] the autobiography that made him one of the best known Catholic figures of the mid-twentieth century, until the very week before he left in August 1968 for the Asian pilgrimage from which he would not return. The three initial figures considered, the "forefathers" of the volume's title, were non-Cistercian predecessors or contemporaries of the first generation of the Order of Cîteaux; the other four were significant Cistercian authors from the mid- to late twelfth century. While a case could be made for arranging these essays sequentially according to their dates of composition, so as to highlight the development of Merton's own maturing response to his medieval monastic ancestors over the course of his career, the decision has been made instead to present them in an order corresponding to the chronology of the subjects themselves, a historical survey of these important figures that reflects some of the developments of monastic thought and practice during their own era.

The opening essay, on St. Peter Damian, the eleventh-century ascetic, monastic and ecclesiastical reformer and proponent of the solitary life, is the only piece written for a general audience, published in Merton's friend Edward Rice's monthly magazine *Jubilee* in August 1960. Though prompted by the appearance of a collection of Damian's spiritual writings, it is not simply a book review but a wide-ranging analysis of Damian's complex personality and important participation in the life of the Church of his time, including his significant if somewhat fraught relationship with Pope Gregory VII and his sweeping reforms. If Merton was more enthusiastic about the Introduction to this volume than about what he considered the rather timid selection of primary-source materials, he still welcomed the opportunity the book provided to make Peter Damian better known to an

5. Thomas Merton, *The Seven Storey Mountain* (New York: Harcourt, Brace, 1948).

English-speaking audience, even as he recognized that the medieval saint's firm endorsement of corporal penitential practices and his intransigent castigation of opponents would evoke at best an ambiguous response from contemporary readers. His own evaluation recognizes the challenging aspects of Damian's prickly character but also highlights some of its more positive features, and shows an appreciation of his love of solitude and championing of the eremitic life that Merton himself found particularly attractive.

The second figure considered, St. Anselm, is much better-known, though perhaps, Merton suggests, not much better understood, despite his reputation as an important philosopher and theologian, a major predecessor of the thirteenth-century scholastics. Merton's two published articles on Anselm, both appearing in monastic journals, are also review-essays that respond positively to current revaluations of some of Anselm's major work. In what are perhaps the most theologically sophisticated discussions he ever wrote, he strongly endorses recent revisionist analyses of two of Anselm's most celebrated and influential treatises. He adds his voice to those of theologians Karl Barth and Paul Evdokimov who argue that the so-called "ontological argument" for the existence of God in Anselm's *Proslogion* was not intended as an apologetic attempt to convince unbelievers but as a profoundly spiritual meditation to show the compatibility of faith and reason, an exemplification of Anselm's *ratio fidei*, his method of "faith seeking understanding." Likewise he endorses the rejection by contemporary scholars of a reductive understanding of the "satisfaction theory" of redemption presented by Anselm in his *Cur Deus Homo* that would interpret it as requiring an infinite sacrificial action by the God-man Jesus Christ to rectify the infinite affront offered to the divine majesty by human sin; such an interpretation, Merton notes, ignores key aspects of Anselm's position, especially his focus on the free decision of Christ to choose the way of powerlessness and self-emptying love to restore the right order of creation, rather than to placate an angry God. In both articles, drawing on a new biography of Anselm, Merton highlights the intrinsically monastic dimension of all of Anselm's work, much of it written during his time as prior and then abbot of the Norman Benedictine monastery of Bec, before becoming the embattled Archbishop of Canterbury at the end of the eleventh century.

This focus is particularly apparent, not surprisingly, in the five conferences on Anselm that Merton presented to his novices over the course of 1963, the period when he was working on these articles. Transcribed here for the first time, these informal talks touch on the better known writings of Anselm, but spend more time looking at his similitudes, the concrete anecdotes and examples presented to his monks to illustrate various aspects of monastic life, at his sermon on heaven with its emphasis on the fulfillment of the deepest level of earthly experience, and at his letter on monastic stability that considers an issue encountered by virtually all monks, and certainly one that Merton knew from repeated personal experience. In both public and private expositions of Anselm's life and work Merton's enthusiastic and rather unexpected appreciation of Anselm as both monk and thinker is readily apparent.

While the last period of Anselm's life, as Merton notes, overlapped with the early days of the new monastery of Cîteaux, founded in 1098 while Anselm was Archbishop of Canterbury, the final non-Cistercian figure included here, Guigo, the fifth prior of the monastery of the Grande Chartreuse, was a slightly older contemporary and influential friend of St. Bernard. Merton's translation of the brief letter of Guigo on solitude, prefaced by an equally brief introduction, reflected his continued admiration for the Carthusian Order, to which he had been strongly attracted in his early days at Gethsemani; his own close epistolary friendship with the Carthusian Procurator General Jean-Baptiste Porion, to whom he dedicated the little booklet containing this work; his immersion in the *Meditations* of Guigo as part of his preparation for the Cistercian Fathers conferences, in which he emphasizes the importance of this collection of aphorisms for Bernard's own teaching on the love of God as found in his letter to the Carthusians, written in response to Guigo's gift of a copy of his work and included as the last part of Bernard's famous treatise *De Diligendo Deo* (*On Loving God*); and the request from the Benedictine nuns of the English Abbey of Stanbrook to print some work of Merton on their press, which led to a warm relationship between Merton and some of the sisters there. Not widely known, this tribute to the Carthusian love of solitude as articulated by one of its greatest advocates has a kind of "hidden" quality particularly appropriate to its author and his subject. The fact that its recipient is unknown, as is his response to Guigo's urgent invitation to take up the solitary life, adds to its mysteriousness. His depiction of the monk as nonviolent warrior who shares the lot of his commander Christ by entering into the paschal pattern of dying and rising with the Lord, of sharing His suffering in order to share His glory, presents the solitary as a paradigm of the Christian experience, a "servant of the cross," as Guigo describes the members of his own community, whose vocation above all is "to live and to die for Christ."

The first of Merton's four Cistercian figures, Blessed Guerric of Igny, was already a mature teacher, probably some years older than St. Bernard, when he was drawn to the Cistercian life by an encounter with the Abbot of Clairvaux, as Merton notes in his introductory essay to the translation of Guerric's five Christmas sermons that he himself had commissioned and that was published at Gethsemani in 1959. This volume, as Merton also notes, was apparently the first to appear in English that was completely focused on Guerric. Though the only extant works of Guerric are the series of liturgical sermons presented to his monks after he became Abbot of Igny, a daughter house of Clairvaux, in the late 1130s, Merton emphasizes that Guerric was not merely a skillful homilist but a profound theologian, steeped in the doctrine as well as the imagery of St. Paul, reflecting in this set of sermons both the "objective character of the grace of Christmas" and also "its subjective reception" by individuals, specifically monks, and by the Christian community at large. Merton also stresses the abbot's challenge to a lugubrious spirituality that fails to respond unreservedly to the "great joy" of the Incarnation with its full participation of the Word made flesh in human experience that transforms the meaning of life, or rather of one's awareness of its meaning. He points out that for Guerric Mary is the perfect model of this transformation, and touches on the theme of the birth of Christ in the soul that is a participation in the maternal love of Mary for her Child.

Merton returns to Guerric and his sermons twice in his novitiate conferences of the 1960s, first in a pair of presentations on the Easter sermons in April 1963 and then in a set of three talks on the Advent sermons in November-December 1964. Even as he highlights Guerric's accessibility, both in thought and in language (his clear, readily translated Latin), he enjoys calling attention to

Guerric's provocative use of unexpected scripture texts as the basis for many of his homilies and his informal, good-humored responses to his listeners' putative objections to these seemingly unrelated texts – we want Jesus not Joseph, the Savior not the dreamer, he imagines them saying in response to their abbot's first Easter sermon, on a text from Genesis 45. But he proposes that it is Guerric's imaginative yet insightful reflections on the scriptures, rather than the ostensibly more "objective" approach of some of his contemporaries, that continue to be meaningful for present-day Christians. The abbot's focus on the experiential rather than the abstract dimension of scripture texts make him a kind of existentialist, who challenges his listeners to internalize the word of God and so respond to the transformative power of the Spirit not merely with the intellect but with the whole person. At the same time, Guerric's realistic appraisal of the process of spiritual development allows him to meet his listeners at their own level, without any expectation of extraordinary contemplative elevation as a prerequisite for a meaningful response to his message. One has an authentic encounter with the Lord in one's own way, at one's own level. While Merton seems unsure whether all his novices share his own positive response to Guerric, as some of them were arriving at the classes on the Advent sermons rather tardily, he continues to highlight in Guerric a sense of dynamism, of spiritual discovery, an awareness of the centrality of the "middle" advent of the present, between the Lord's first coming at Bethlehem and His final coming at the end of time. His appearance "in the secrecy and silence of grace" is the essence of contemplative realization, which Merton associates particularly with the desert experience; "the blessedness of the wilderness" that Guerric describes in his fourth Advent sermon, Merton's favorite, is characteristic of all genuine monasticism in one way or another, a lesson that Merton is eager to communicate to those in formation.

The best known of the Cistercian Fathers after St. Bernard himself, his younger contemporary, the English abbot Aelred of Rievaulx, receives extensive attention from Merton from the earliest days to the very end of his career as a writer. His ambitious plan from the late 1940s to assemble an anthology of key excerpts from Aelred's works was never realized, but his extensive introductory essay for this work, by far the longest piece in the present collection, survives in an almost completed form that was first published in a five-part series from the late 1980s. Here Merton situates Aelred (or Ailred, the variant form still widely used at the time of writing) in the context of early Cistercianism, of the new Norman order in England that had begun less than a half-century before Aelred's birth, and of the Scottish court where Aelred spent his early years and became a trusted servant and valued advisor to King David. Relying largely on the contemporary biography by Aelred's disciple Walter Daniel, not yet available in a complete text or in English translation at the time of writing, Merton surveys the main events of Aelred's life and influential career as abbot of the most important English Cistercian monastery, and provides a convincing portrait of Aelred's singularly attractive character and his profound pastoral sensitivity in serving as spiritual father for a community of hundreds, from simple, illiterate laybrothers to questing and often troubled intellectuals. While his most famous work, then and now, is the dialogue on *Spiritual Friendship*, Merton draws most extensively from Aelred's earliest treatise, the *Speculum Caritatis* (*Mirror of Charity*), written while he was still novice master at Rievaulx, which Merton calls "his longest and, on the whole, his most profound book … a memorial not only to Ailred's spiritual genius but also to his tireless energy.… the fruit of the years of meditation and silent reflection he had been able to enjoy since his entrance into the monastery."

As with his presentations on Guerric, the pair of conferences Merton gives to his novices on Aelred in mid-1964, transcribed here for the first time, are not intended mainly to provide information but to be part of the process of spiritual formation of the aspirants to monastic life for which Merton, like Aelred himself in his early role as novice master, was principally responsible. Aelred's discussion of the function of memory in the recovery of the divine likeness, as found in *The Mirror of Charity*, once again, as well as in his *Rule for Recluses* and two of his sermons, is connected to and integrated with more immediate contemporary elements: to the unusual cross hanging in the novitiate chapel, to a recent anonymous poem about entering religious life, to Merton's own memories of his first days in the monastery, to relevant aspects of Buddhist spirituality, to the feast of the Ascension being celebrated on the day of the second conference, which provides a vivid reminder of the deepest purpose of the memory: to "relive the mysteries of Christ," which "is much more than just recalling them to mind. In reliving them, our whole being enters into the mysteries."

Composed as a preface for a fellow Cistercian's book on the monastic theology of the Abbot of Rievaulx, Merton's final reflection on Aelred, written as he was in the last stages of preparation for his trip to Asia in 1968, is the shortest of the pieces included in this book, as the first Aelred essay was the longest. But it serves as an incisive witness to Merton's continued conviction at what turned out to be almost the very end of his life that the Cistercian Fathers had lost none of their relevance for contemporary Christians. Here the importance of Aelred's teaching on spiritual friendship becomes a central focus, as Merton identifies "monastic" theology not as a narrowly restricted analysis of life in a monastery, separated from "the world," but as "highly concrete, existential, biblical, imaginatively rich, full of esthetic as well as mystical intuitions, and deeply rooted in the everyday life of the time … concerned above all not with abstract ideas about God but with the living relationship of man with God in Christ." It is deeply relational, at once interpersonal on the human level and Trinitarian in its invitation to participate in the divine life of love which is imaged by authentic friendship. According to Aelred, "The Christian life is," Merton writes, "simply the full flowering of freedom and consent in the perfection of friendship. Friendship with other human beings as an epiphany of friendship with God.… Contemplation is not an individual gnostic exploit arrived at by turning away from everybody else to God: it is a sharing in the friendship of God." It is an experience of communion and community lost in the fall and recovered in the unification brought about by the incarnation, cross and resurrection of Christ. Such a perspective, Merton maintains, is "quite modern," and he concludes his brief meditation by demonstrating the validity of this claim, finding the same profoundly humanistic and intrinsically Christocentric perspective in the advocate of "a world come of age," the contemporary theologian and martyr Dietrich Bonhoeffer.

Like the first piece on Guerric included in this volume, Merton's essay on Isaac of Stella was originally intended to preface a selection of sermons, but in this case the volume was never published, despite Merton's own enthusiasm for the material, so that his introduction eventually appeared separately, the year before his death. An English-born contemporary of Aelred, Isaac evidently left his native land as a young man for studies in France and never returned. He entered the Order there and eventually became abbot of the monastery of Stella (or L'Étoile), though he spent at least part of his later life, for some unknown reason, at a small monastic foundation on the Isle of Ré off the French coast, where many of his extant sermons were preached. As Merton points out, Isaac "seems to stand somewhat apart from the others … a more independent thinker and less subject to the dominant influence of St. Bernard," with "a speculative mind trained perhaps in schools to which Bernard was not well-disposed." Yet in true Cistercian fashion Isaac's sermons are profoundly sapiential, imbued with the search for and the insights of divine wisdom, "a knowledge based on the experience of life and of love, which embraced the whole of life and indeed synthesized the whole of knowledge in transcendent religious experience, expressed in traditional symbols which were common currency in the monasteries and schools." Whereas Merton stressed in various ways the modernity of both Guerric and of Aelred, here he calls attention to the difference between the mechanistic Newtonian universe of modernity and the animate cosmos of the medievals, a "view of the world of nature and of grace as a vast system of affinities, sympathies, likenesses and loves" bound together by the Creator's love for creation and the invitation for a reciprocal response that discovers the true end of all that is made in a participation in the fullness of life, the fullness of reality, found only in God. It is this vision, at once ascetic and eschatological, that Merton sees exemplified in Isaac, in particular in those sermons in which he reflects with his community on their life of island solitude, poverty and exile, dependent totally on Christ, like the apostles in the stormy sea, subject to trials and fears, and yet brought like them as well into intimate contact with their Lord precisely in their deprivation. Summing up Isaac's character and his writing, Merton notes such elements, some "peculiarly Cistercian" and others uniquely his own, as exemplifying "a singular consistency, a coherence in variety, an austerity with sensitivity, a certain daring curiosity, an impatience with half-measures and an ardent poetic fervor, and above all a deep love for Jesus Christ."

It is clear, both from this introductory overview and from various other comments recorded in his journal and elsewhere, that Merton finds in Isaac a particularly bracing quality that makes him a personal favorite among these early Cistercian writers.

This is actually the fourth time that the final piece in this volume, Merton's detailed analysis of Adam of Perseigne's letters on spiritual formation, has appeared in print – the first time in French translation in the Order's journal in 1957, then in revised form in English in 1962, and posthumously in a slightly different text as the introduction to a volume of Adam's selected letters in 1976; the present text is an edited version of this last revision. Despite its multiple appearances, neither the essay nor its subject is widely known. Adam is the only one of the writers included here never to have a full-length published volume devoted to his work, and the forty-year-old collection of letters is the only primary source material available in English. Yet Merton himself clearly considered Adam, a couple of generations younger than the other major twelfth-century Cistercian authors, a significant contributor to the final phase of the Cistercian "Golden Age." Initially he was particularly enthused about Adam's Marian writings, which as a young monk he had proposed to translate into English (another unrealized project), but after becoming master of novices at Gethsemani in late 1955 he evidently turned to Adam, who held the same position at the Abbey of Perseigne before becoming abbot, as a model for his own work. Merton notes his psychological insight, his idea of the monastic life as having a therapeutic dimension, as a locus of healing from the deformities, even the craziness (*amentia*) of the world, and his emphasis on friendship, encouragement and pleasantness as well as challenge in dealing with new recruits to monastic life. He highlights Adam's evocative term "*spiritus fictionis*"– the life of illusion and self-deception that characterizes the typical person's perspective, a phrase that certainly has resemblances to Merton's classic descriptions of the false self throughout his writings. (The opposition of Truth and "falsity" recurs a number of times in the middle of the essay.) Merton finds typically Cistercian themes in Adam's emphases on the mediatorial role of Mary, the call to spiritual childhood in identification with the simplicity and innocence of the infant Jesus, the stress on humility, freedom and wisdom as essential components of monastic life, and the focus on spiritual development, "characteristically Cistercian in its concreteness and its positive emphasis on the happiness of our life in Christ." Largely missing from the earliest version of the text but the climactic section of the second as well as the third is Adam's teaching on the "*festivitas* of our new existence in Christ," the sevenfold feasting aligned with the traditional seven gifts of the Holy Spirit, beginning with holy fear and progressing to the feast of wisdom, each of them a deepening of the "feast of freedom" that culminates in contemplative union with the Lord. Here Adam is fully aligned with and expressive of the teaching of his own tradition: "His emphasis, as is usual in the Cistercian Fathers, is upon mystical union as a supreme manifestation of liberty: the liberty of God in choosing the soul for his spouse and the liberty of the soul in responding to the choice. Mystical union is then a feast of supreme freedom, the feast of Truth himself rejoicing in the soul whom he has made free with his own freedom." This mystical feast is genuine, Adam insists, only when it is shared with others. As he writes to a Benedictine friend and his community: "break your bread to your begging and hungry friend; for in this you will prove yourself a friend if you will allay your friend's hunger with your bread. Your bread is Christ. Your bread is your love. Your bread is your prayer. Your bread is your compunction of tears with which you wash away not only your own sins but also those of your friend." In these words Merton finds "a typical example of that frank, spontaneous and warm affection which is so often found among the medieval and early Christian saints and which seems to have vanished into oblivion in our day." He declares, "it is obvious that such friendship should exist as the normal fruit of our participation in the eucharistic banquet." Hence the title of the final version of the text, which can perhaps, following Merton's hint, be broadened to incorporate the teaching of the other Cistercian Fathers about whom he has eloquently written in these essays or discussed in these conferences, and even to include the "forefathers" whom he would surely recognize as sharing in the same banquet, the same feast of freedom.

* * * * * * *

Each of the thirteen pieces included in this collection is preceded by a headnote that provides information on the circumstances of its composition, significant connections with other writings by Merton, and a brief overview of key themes. Each item is also accompanied by supplementary annotations, distinguished from Merton's own notes in those essays that have them by the use of roman rather than arabic superscript numerals and by being gathered together as endnotes after each piece rather than appearing as footnotes at the bottom of the page where Merton's own notes are found. These additional notes include information on sources not already provided, on persons mentioned but not otherwise described, related citations or passages from Merton's writings or other relevant sources, literal translations of material quoted by Merton only in the original languages, or passages in the (generally Latin) originals given only in translation, and a variety of other material that the editor considered worth making available to interested readers. Unless otherwise noted, the texts of previously published essays are reproduced as they first appeared in print. The transcriptions of Merton's conferences do not add any non-authorial language, but do eliminate various repetitions, false starts, "filler" words without substantive meaning and occasional questions to the novices and their responses. If appropriate, quotations from secondary sources are sometimes modified to conform to the original passage being quoted. The text is followed by three appendices, the first providing bibliographical information on Merton's writings on St. Bernard, which of course complement the materials included in the present volume; the second listing all Merton publications, with complete bibliographical data, cited simply by title in the headnotes and supplementary annotations to the various essays and conferences; the third making available a list of significant primary and secondary resources for each of the seven authors featured in the present volume.

* * * * * * *

In conclusion I would like to express my gratitude to all those who have made this volume possible:

- to the Trustees of the Merton Legacy Trust, Peggy Fox, Anne McCormick and Mary Somerville, for permission to publish the *Cistercian Fathers and Forefathers* essays and conferences and for their consistent support in this and other projects;

- to Rev. Michael Casagram, OCSO, former student of Thomas Merton at the Abbey of Gethsemani and current prior of the Gethsemani community, for the insightful foreword in which he shares his own perspective on the significance of the materials included in this volume;
- to Paul M. Pearson, director and archivist of the Thomas Merton Center at Bellarmine University, Louisville, KY, for his invaluable assistance in providing needed print and audio materials found in this volume;
- to Claude Blanc and Gary Brandl of New City Press for their gracious willingness to publish this volume;
- to the Gannon University Research Committee, which has awarded a generous grant that allowed me to pursue research on this project at various libraries;
- to Mary Beth Earll of the interlibrary loan department of the Nash Library, Gannon University, for once again providing helpful assistance by locating and procuring various obscure materials;
- again and always to my wife Suzanne and our children for their continual love, support and encouragement in this and other projects.

St. Peter Damian
(c. 1007–1072)

St. Peter Damian and the Medieval Monk

In his 1963 conferences on Cistercian History (currently being prepared for publication), Merton called St. Peter Damian, identified as a cardinal, a doctor of the Church and a hermit, the "dominant figure of eleventh-century monastic spirituality." The monastic historian David Knowles, whom Merton references here, wrote that "alike in writings, words and actions [Peter Damian] stands in something of the same prophetical relation to his age as does St Bernard to the age that followed a century later" (*Monastic Order in England*, 2nd ed. [Cambridge: Cambridge University Press, 1963] 194). In March 1955 Merton had obtained a relic of St. Peter Damian from Dom Anselmo Giabbani, the Prior General of the Camaldolese, with whom at the time he was in correspondence about the possibility of transferring to this most eremitic branch of the Benedictines (see Donald Grayston, *Thomas Merton and the Noonday Demon: The Camaldoli Correspondence* [Eugene, OR: Cascade Books, 2015] 168-69); Peter Damian was an early supporter of this order and founder of the hermit colony of Fonte Avellana, later canonically united with the Camaldolese (Grayston 163-64). Merton expressed deep appreciation of this "magnificent" gift (along with a relic of Camaldolese founder St. Romuald) as a source of consolation and encouragement in his efforts to discern the appropriate form of his own vocation to solitude (Grayston 93, 109). In the section on the Camaldolese in his 1957 volume *The Silent Life*, Merton refers to Peter Damian as a figure "whom Camaldoli rightly claims as one of her great spokesmen and witnesses" (150), and goes on to quote the saint's assertion that someone living in solitude has not separated himself from his fellow members of the Body of Christ, but rather fully identifies with and indeed embodies the whole Christian community. This vision of spiritual unity would of course have been particularly meaningful to a person with aspirations to a solitary life such as Merton, who comments, "the whole Christ is present in each individual member of the Church. It is by virtue of these principles that St Peter Damian shows how the hermit priest, reciting the office alone in his mountain oratory, can and indeed must say 'Dominus vobiscum' [the Lord be with you] and answer himself 'Et cum spiritu tuo' [and with your spirit]. The whole Church is present in the cell where he is alone" (151). The appearance in 1960 of a collection of Peter Damian's spiritual writings prompted the article on Damian's life and work that Merton published in the monthly magazine edited by his friend and baptismal sponsor Edward Rice: "St. Peter Damian and the Medieval Monk," *Jubilee* 8 (August 1960) 39-44. Though disappointed in the "rather timid" selection of material provided by the anthology, Merton welcomed its publication as at least serving to make this influential if highly controversial figure better known to an English-speaking audience, especially through the "excellent introduction" that precedes the selections. Merton presents Damian both as a traditional spiritual theologian and as a fierce defender of ascetical practices that would certainly be considered extreme today. While recognizing his rigorism, and pointing out its exaggerations, as in his views on marriage, Merton also provides a historical and religious context that makes Damian's preaching and writing more comprehensible, stressing his recognition that penitential exercises, while necessary, were not sufficient in themselves but only as outward signs of interior compunction and *metanoia*, conversion of heart. "For all his excesses, St. Peter Damian was a balanced and healthy man: how else could he have played the vital and constructive role which he actually played in the world of his time?" Merton highlights his role as a reformer of both Church and society, and notes the contradiction between his apparent contempt for humanistic learning and his cultured and cultivated writing style that resulted from his own impressive literary gifts as well as his pre-monastic education. He concludes both by acknowledging Peter Damian's tendency toward intolerance and by pointing out his underlying humanity, marked by understanding and mercy, and, lest modern readers be too judgmental of Damian and his contemporaries, suggests a telling contrast between the saints of the Middle Ages who "were more often cruel to themselves and kind to others" and contemporary autocrats and oppressors who "have been rather kind to themselves and pitilessly, fiendishly cruel to everyone else."

St. Peter Damian, the Camaldolese hermit who became Cardinal Bishop of Ostia in the most turbulent age of the Church's history, the eleventh century, is generally portrayed, so I am told, with cardinal's robes and a scourge of knotted cords in his hand. The reason for the scourge is not, as one might imagine at first sight, that he strove to imitate Christ in cleansing the temple (which he did), but because he was a great propagator of the discipline as an instrument of corporal penance. Peter Damian was a vigorous and austere reformer, a man who feared no opposition, who was utterly immune to that moral disease known as human respect, and who, in the midst of robbers, sycophants, ecclesiastical grafters and decadent clergy could declare with all truth: "I seek the favor of no one, I fear no one, and I need only the witness of my own conscience!"[I] In a word, he is typical of the tough intransigence of those hard-headed popes and bishops who built up the Church's power in the early Middle Ages. He was a close friend and supporter of the monk Hildebrand, who was to become Gregory the Seventh, excommunicate the emperor, and maintain the doctrine the "two swords" which had been propounded by St. Peter Damian: the doctrine of the twofold power, temporal and spiritual, of the Christian "city." The temporal power in the hands of the emperor was to be subordinated to and guided by the spiritual power of the papacy. Scarcely a popular doctrine in twentieth-century America, and the subject is not raised in the recent book of Damian's *Selected Writings on the Spiritual Life* (Harper's, $5).[II]

This interesting, though rather slight volume, a very timid selection from the two well-packed tomes of Peter Damian's works in Migne's Latin Fathers,[III] presents English readers with the first opportunity to make the acquaintance of Damian in our language. There has been only one other full-length work in English about St. Peter Damian, and this is a doctoral dissertation published at the Catholic University of America in 1947.[IV] The present book, perhaps less satisfactory than most of the others in the same series of "Classics of the Contemplative Life," comes to us adorned with an ambiguous cliché which claims that it is "a comprehensive edition of the works of a leading medieval mystic." It is by no means comprehensive. In fact, it studiously avoids all but two of the really important works of the saint and there is very little of real mysticism in these pages, except in the excellent introduction of Patricia McNulty. This introduction is worthy of all praise. It is a very capable summation of Damian's life, work and spirituality, but it takes up over one-fourth of the pages of this volume.[V] One can imagine what St. Peter Damian, that honest and explosive enemy of greed (pardon me: I mean "good business"), might say if he were to hold this little volume in his hand, and take note of the price which is five dollars.

Since we are on this point, we might as well pause to ask just precisely what is a "leading medieval mystic"? The blurb on the jacket says with perfect justice that Damian "closes the hiatus" between St. Gregory the Great and St. Bernard of Clairvaux in the mystical tradition. However, this must not be interpreted to mean that there is anything particularly new or original in the mysticism of Peter Damian. I take it that, if the word "leading" means anything in this connection, it ought to mean "starting a new trend." I do not think that Damian does this precisely as a mystic. As an ascetic and religious reformer, a contemplative and devout solitary, as an ardent preacher of the Christian and monastic life, he certainly helped prepare the way for the great mystical revival of the twelfth century. Apart from that, he simply repeats what was said about contemplation by St. Augustine and St. Gregory the Great before him, with the accents of one who knows from experience what he is talking about.

There are also evidences of that "nuptial mysticism"[VI] characteristic of St. Bernard, but here too St. Peter Damian is no originator. He simply borrows from a tradition going back to Origen. And in any case the *amore langueo*[VII] of the Spouse in the Canticles is too feminine to be characteristic of this rugged and militant ascetic.

If, on the other hand, by "leading mystic" we mean one who is outstanding, who dominates the others in the Middle Ages, I think this can be questioned. Peter Damian is by no means superior to St. Bernard, St. Francis, Richard of St. Victor, St. Gertrude, St. Mechtilde, or even some of the less well-known contemplative writers like William of St. Thierry, Aelred of Rievaulx,[VIII] Guerric of Igny and Peter of Celles. He was indeed a mystic and a contemplative, but his importance is above all as an ascetic. And so we return to the scourge of small cords, and Peter Damian's book on the Praise of Scourges (*De Laude Flagellarum*[IX]) which editorial modesty has banned from the pages of this "comprehensive selection" along with so many other really characteristic works of Damian. For example, we look in vain for the "Gomhorra Book" (*Liber Gomhorranus*[X]) in which he attacks some vices of his time in very graphic language. Of course we must recognize that present policies of religious publishing would hardly make the inclusion of such works expedient. But the works of St. Peter Damian in Latin include at least sixty other *opuscula* of which our "comprehensive selection" contains exactly three. Among others that could have been included there are two very interesting tracts on the eremitical life[XI] as led by St. Peter Damian's own community at Fonte Avellana. There are important doctrinal treatises, though admittedly these are not exactly on the "spiritual life." But why not have included his nineteenth *opusculum*[XII] in which he pleads with Pope Nicholas II to be allowed to resign his episcopal dignity and return to the hermitage? Or the twentieth[XIII] in which he calls the future Pope and Saint Gregory the Seventh a "holy Satan" for opposing his resignation! This is an interesting, lively and humorous autobiographical document. How many other tracts were written by this energetic hermit – on avarice, on patience, on the religious state, on nuns, on Purgatory, on a dozen other topics! Everywhere we find curious anecdotes and original views, or the record of opinions that have long since been forgotten, like the peculiar notion once held in Italy that the souls in Purgatory do not suffer on Sundays!

The narrow selection given us in these pages comprises the interesting treatise on the *Dominus Vobiscum*,[XIV] which is really a tract on the unity of the Mystical Body of Christ and one of Damian's best and most original works. It also includes the best of his monastic *opuscula*, that on the Perfection of Monks,[XV] but there is precious little else.[XVI] The sermons are ingenious but trite mosaics of Scripture quotations in the familiar medieval style.[XVII] There is not one of Damian's many letters, not one of his two hundred and twenty-five poems nor of his meditative prayers, and his more fiery diatribes against the sins of his society have, as we notice, been excluded. So also have his biographical writings, those lives of saints which, being full of rather dubious miracles, would not be calculated to appeal to the modern reader. Yet the weird life of St. Dominic Loricatus,[XVIII] one of Damian's disciples, crazy as it is, might rightfully claim a place in a "comprehensive selection." Well, it is not there. And just as well, perhaps, because one hardly knows how the modern reader would react to the spectacle of a man with a scourge in each hand beating himself silly for the major part of the day, while reciting the psalter twice through from beginning to end.

The controversy about scourging came up when a Roman cardinal reproved the monks of Monte Cassino, disciples of the discreet St. Benedict, for scourging themselves frequently and publicly in chapter for long periods. St. Peter Damian flew to their defense, and said that by no means should any penitent be restricted to a mere hundred blows a day. Two hundred, three hundred, a thousand! Of course, a discipline is not a real whip, and it does not hurt as much as all that, unless you break the skin, which is not easy. The traditional measure is of course to take the discipline for the space of a psalm, notably the *Miserere*,[XIX] or two, or seven. Was there a limit? Well, Peter Damian thought that forty psalms ought to be about enough. This would take about three-quarters of an hour. Dominic Loricatus, scourging himself for the space of three hundred psalms a day was going a bit beyond the limits of Benedictine discretion, as even St. Peter Damian was willing to admit.

Seriously, what is the value of all this for our time? The editor has implicitly raised the question and answered it in his own way by excluding such material from the book.[XX] The fact that it is all mentioned in the introduction[XXI] suggests that perhaps the translator had originally planned to include "The Praise of Scourges" in her selection.

St. Peter Damian was not a fanatic, not an illuminist. He justified his stress on penance in the following terms. The whole society of his time was guilty of very grave sin. This was true. Five hundred years of ignorance, decadence, war, robbery, inhumanity, had reduced Christian society including priests and monks to a level of savagery and depravity for which most of them could scarcely be held responsible. It was the result of the calamities of those times, in which Europe had been overrun from end to end, repeatedly, by every kind of barbarian army. It is not for us to wonder at the evils of the day, but rather at the saints who reacted against the evil with such nobility, energy and purity of heart, like St. Odilo of Cluny, St. Romuald, the founder of Camaldoli, and many bishops who stemmed the tide of iniquity. And we can wonder too at the simplicity and generosity with which so many men responded to their call to do penance. In reforming the clergy and the monastic orders, St. Peter Damian knew that he was reforming the whole of society, for if monks and clerics became what they were supposed to be, the laity would follow.

His view of sin and the reparation due to sin may seem to us to be somewhat crude. But it is in the main quite just and quite in accordance with Christian tradition. Where there has been sin, there must be reparation, there must be penance. It is not enough to shrug off one's misdeeds and forget about them. The mercy of God is of course the only force that can destroy sin, but mercy is not granted to anyone who does not sincerely repent, and works of penance are a sign of sincerity. Damian's self-assured method of measuring the amount of penance required may strike us with consternation. But to him it was the most obvious and natural thing in the world. He was simply following the *penitentiaries* or penance-codes which had been drawn up in the Dark Ages. Here he found precise punishment listed for precise sins. What is to us a matter of astonishment was for Peter Damian nothing more than simple addition. Later on, the question of penance became still more abstract when it became possible in meet one's obligations in this regard with indulgences granted by the Church. Such things are not comprehensible at all unless we see them against the background of the times, and the mentality of an earlier age. And admittedly the practice lent itself to abuse. It led to the scandals which precipitated the revolt of Luther. In fact, it might be said that the mentality of a Peter Damian was categorically opposed to that of the Protestants of the sixteenth century, and that their reaction was precisely against such attitudes as his. Yet, strange to say, Peter Damian was "protesting" against much the same evils as the later Protestants criticized and deplored. But his viewpoint was totally different.

Here is how St. Peter Damian looks at the situation: a sinner who enters a monastery has gone there not to relax and live a quiet, harmless, contented life. He has gone there to make positive and physical reparation. This demands not only that he keep the Rule of his monastery faithfully, but even that he go beyond the Rule. Penance, in St. Peter Damian's eyes, means essentially something over and above the normal obligations of one's duty.

And here, perhaps, he is extreme. Not every theologian would agree with him, least of all in our day.

"How," asks Damian, "can he be sure that his offenses will be pardoned who, coming to a place of penitence, performs no penance?"[XXII] It is a good question. And he continues:

"A certain brother came to us from a monastery and he confessed to me the sins which he had committed as a layman. If I understood rightly, it seemed to me that according to the decrees[XXIII] of the holy canons he was bound to perform seventy years' penance. He had been wearing the habit of religion for almost seven years; but when I asked him how much penance he had already done for these sins he replied that he had confessed all these matters to the Lord Abbot, who had imposed on him no other penances over and above the common practice of the monastery, because he declared that his changed way of life was in itself enough to procure full absolution for all his sins. What can I say? I must admit that I was gravely displeased by all this, I looked down, I trembled, I cried that the man had been misled; for he had not even begun to do his penance, whereas if only he had imposed on himself certain mortifications, he could already have completed it!"[XXIV]

St. Peter Damian is certainly deeply sincere when he says he was shocked by this discovery. He could not conceive of such an attitude. It shook him to the very roots of his being. And we must not ascribe this to a morbid, pathological state of mind. For all his excesses, St. Peter Damian was a balanced and healthy man: how else could he have played the vital and constructive role which he actually played in the world of his time?

Damian insisted that the only justification for penance and penitential works was a deep and sincere love for God. He speaks of this love in accents that are unmistakably real, and he insists that unless penance proceeds from an *experience* of such love, it will be sterile to say the least. As St. John of the Cross would say, such flagellations, without inner charity and discretion, are nothing but "the penance of beasts."[XXV] Damian insists on compunction, the interior *metanoia* or change of heart without which exterior penance is a perversion of nature, and not a work of the spirit. This is the key to his doctrine. All its austerity is correlative to the love contained in it. Where there is no genuine love, austerities lead to simulation or even madness. Of this St. Peter Damian was clearly aware. Penance born of love leads to a growth of love, and ultimately it opens out into the peaceful paradise of solitude and contemplation. But no mistake must be made about it: solitude and the desire of contemplative experience are an illusion without self-denial, mortification, serious asceticism. And if asceticism is serious it must take a concrete, tangible form. St. Peter Damian would have nothing of a mortification that is purely in the will, because if it claims to be "purely in the will," it is very likely to be purely in the imagination.

It is not enough to make "acts of pure intention." If fasting is prescribed, one must fast and not just eat with more "pious dispositions," renouncing the dessert! One must feel hunger. And even if the regular prescribed fast is strict, one ought in certain cases to make it even stricter. Of course, he is writing for hermits, and there can no doubt in his mind that fasting is essential in the life of the hermit, just as essential as silence and solitude. "Priests," he says, "offer sacrifice, doctors teach and hermits rest in fasting and silence."[XXVI] Though his standards may seem a little extreme, and though in point of fact few religious in our day could keep the strict rule which he laid down for the hermits of Fonte Avellana (related to the Camaldolese who have recently made two foundations in the U.S.A.[XXVII]), we must admit that there is a salutary realism about his attitude. We need to recover this sense of realism in our own day when religious practice tends to become more and more abstract, more and more a matter of intention, so that it finally evaporates in pure sentimentality or formalism. The fashion today is to assume that the man who feels the need of exterior bodily practices of penance is somehow a "pharisee." But perhaps we ought to admit that pharisaism is even more likely to be on the side of these whose penance is entirely in the mind, a pleasant theory, an "act of will" that has no practical bearing on anything whatever, just an exercise of thought and volition in the void.

Of course, there must be discretion in one's fasting. But discretion for Peter Damian means that one is content with bread, water and salt once a day on fast days – this was the traditional menu of Nitria and Scete.[XXVIII] Even today in monasteries of strict observance there remains a vestige of the custom: the only items one is allowed to ask for, oneself, if they happen to be missing in the refectory, are bread, water and salt. However, one is generally provided with soup, vegetables, and even milk and cheese. Peter Damian admitted all these things,[XXIX] and even more: fish and eggs, on feast days. But there were three black fasts every week and often more.

The life of fasting and silence leads to the delightful "rest" of the solitary, the rest which is not an absence of fatigue and labor, but a spiritual repose (*quies*) which results from interior freedom – from indifference to desire, from the absence of care, the joy of the heart that is not dominated by the tyranny of multiple and harassing needs of body, mind and imagination. It is something much more than the quiet of the stoic who has become indifferent to material things and united his will with the impersonal, universal law. It is the mystical repose of the contemplative in the divine silence, the presence of God.

"You, o solitary cell, are the wonderful workshop of spiritual labor, in which the human soul restores to itself the likeness of the Creator and returns to its pristine purity, where the blunted senses regain their keenness and subtlety, and tainted natures are renewed in their sincerity by unleavened bread … The hermit's cell is the meeting place of God and man, a crossroads for those who dwell in the flesh, and heavenly things. For there the citizens of heaven hold intercourse with men, not in the language of the flesh, but by being made manifest, without any clamor of tongues, to the rich and secret places of the soul."[XXX]

And yet, when we have said all this in favor of St. Peter Damian's ideal, we are bound to admit that the reader is frequently jarred and appalled by an almost Manichaean note in his "contempt for creatures." This must certainly not be exaggerated, but when he says plainly in so many words, that "St. Peter (the Apostle) wiped out the *stain of his marriage* in the blood of martyrdom,"[XXXI] it is hard to elude the evidence that Damian considers marriage almost a kind of sin. Such obviously extreme statements as this warn us to be a little cautious in accepting some of his other excesses. His rigorist interpretation of the Rule of St. Benedict is certainly exaggerated, and will rightly be rejected as such by most theologians. It is one thing to admit the possibility of austere and solitary vocations *as exceptions* within the ordinary compass of the Benedictine Rule, but quite another to oblige all monks to do more than the Rule prescribes. The spirit of St. Peter Damian is not calculated to assist the average modern monk to find peace and balance in his vocation!

I would like in particular to mention one exaggeration which he shares with many of the more ascetic Fathers, and particularly with St. Jerome, to whom he has been compared: that is his utter contempt for humanistic learning.

"Moreover, (if I may speak angrily) those who follow the rabble of grammarians, who, forsaking spiritual studies, desire to learn all the follies of worldly skill, who, despising the Rule of St. Benedict, love to apply themselves to the rules of Donatus … these men are bored by the intricacies of ecclesiastical teaching and long for worldly knowledge; this is like deserting the chaste spouse lying upon the bridal couch of faith and consorting with the harlots of the stage."[XXXII]

Such tirades must be understood. As everyone who has ever made the acquaintance of St. Jerome well knows, Jerome's diatribes against Cicero and Virgil[XXXIII] were simply the expression of his guilty love for them: even in Lent, Jerome could refrain from food but not from Virgil. His anger against the classics was proportionate to his shame at being so weak as to love fine style even after he had given himself to God. In reading Damian one is almost reminded of the protestations of the faithful Communist against "Trotskyite mad-dogs and Bukharinist deviationists." There is all the furious intensity of the man who fully realizes how easily he himself might be accused of deviation. St. Peter Damian, like St. Bernard after him, may have reviled the classics, but still he quotes them. His anger is aroused, reasonably enough, by those monks who make classical studies a genuine evasion from the deeper realities of their life. Yet no matter how much basis of truth there may be behind his practical observations, his intemperate language must not lead us to contemn all humanistic learning. This is not the mind of the Church, and recent legislation has brought home to contemplative monks without any ambiguity that if they hope to live up to the obligations of their state without acquiring the appropriate foundation of humanistic learning, they will live in delusion. And this foundation of learning is not merely philosophy and theology. Scholastic theology and philosophy cannot be properly understood by an immature mind that has not been formed by the liberal arts and particularly the study of the classics. There is a certain tendency among ascetics to treat literature, psychology, history, natural science and other studies centered more or less on man and his world, as if they were unpardonable amusement, "curiosities" serving only to distract and entertain the mind which ought otherwise to apply itself to things more serious and more "spiritual." Unfortunately, those who know nothing of man and who have never become fully acquainted with human culture, tradition, history and, in short, with the living and human experience of their time, are not as well equipped as they imagine to learn about the things of God.[XXXIV] For the mystery of Christ is a mystery of Incarnation – of God's revelation of Himself in man and in history. Over and over again experience has taught us, in monasteries, that those who learn by rote the formulas of the dogma text book without a sufficient basis of liberal education can only with great difficulty become mature contemplatives or genuine theologians.

St. Peter Damian himself is by no means a boorish and uncultivated writer. He may have started life as a poor swineherd, but he did receive a good and thorough education in the schools of Parma and Faenza, famous for their faculties of Humanities and Law. His style is vivid and earnest: his thought is clear and direct: his imagination moves with agility and wit, and he has a fine though not always sympathetic eye for everything that is human. Like so many of the great mystics, Peter Damian is in contact with the realities of life on this earth, and there is nothing too small or too ordinary to escape his interest. His interest in men was intense and affectionate. He was genuinely concerned for what he believed to be the good of their souls, and his concern was not abstract and juridical only: it sprang from love. Of course, the kind of love he believed in did not hesitate to punish, and perhaps the ardor of his paternal zeal may at times have wounded where it strove to heal. A case in point is the story of his monastic secretary, Sylvester, who was so upset by the burning chapter on compunction he was copying for the Master that he had what we would call a breakdown. He began to weep uncontrollably, demanded to be sent to a hermitage, there mutilated a precious manuscript which he had borrowed, and defended himself with a knife when the brethren came to bring him home to the cenobium. This is told vividly in the fifteenth chapter of "The Perfection of Monks," just after the event had taken place.[XXXV]

St. Peter Damian and St. Gregory the Seventh, together with the lesser monastic saints of the age, were the creators of the Middle Ages as we know them. They represent the monolithic austerity, the sense of order and authority, the passionate devotion to the Church and to Christ which we now think of as characteristic of the "ages of faith." But for all his austerity Peter Damian is never inhuman, never without feeling, never without understanding. The power of his singleminded convictions may appall us at times with their potential intolerance – indeed he is the kind of Churchman who makes a virtue of rigid intolerance – but at least we know he was well acquainted with mercy.

Yet it is not always easy to reconcile ourselves with St. Peter Damian's violent and dominating aggressiveness when we have seen so many examples, in our time, of this spirit carried to inhuman, even diabolical extremes. Let us remember – if it is any comfort – that the violent saints of the Middle Ages were more often cruel to themselves and kind to others. In our time, the violent have not been saints. They have been rather kind to themselves and pitilessly, fiendishly cruel to everyone else: and they have had all the resources of modern science to aid them in their cruelty.

I. See *Epistola* 1.4 to Pope Leo IX (J. P. Migne, ed., *Patrologiae Cursus Completus, Series Latina* [*PL*], 221 vols. [Paris: Garnier, 1844-1865] vol. 144, col. 209AB): "*Verumtamen in his ad conscientiam redeo, ad mentis meae secreta recurro, certus quia nisi pro amore Christi, cuius ego malus servus sum, nullius mortalis hominis gratiam quaero, nullius iracundiam pertimesco. Quapropter ipsum conscientiae meae testem invoco*" ("Truly with regard to these matters I return to conscience, I turn back to the secrets of my mind, certain that except for the love of Christ, whose poor servant I am, I seek the favor of no mortal man, I fear the anger of no one. Therefore I call upon the witness of my conscience"); cf. 2 Cor. 1:12: "*nam gloria nostra haec est testimonium conscientiae nostrae*" ("For our glory is this: the testimony of our conscience").

II. *St. Peter Damian: Selected Writings on the Spiritual Life* translated with an introduction by Patricia McNulty (New York: Harper, 1959).

III. *PL* 144, 145.

IV. Owen J. Blum, *St. Peter Damian: His Teaching on the Spiritual Life* (Washington, DC: Catholic University of America Press, 1947).

V. *Selected Writings* 11-52 (of 187 total pages).

VI. McNulty refers to *Opusculum* 56.6 ("*De Fluxa Mundi Gloria et Saeculi Despectione*" [*PL* 145, col. 815BD]) and *Epistolae* 4.16 (*PL* 144, col. 333A).

VII. "I languish with love" (Canticles 2:5).

VIII. "Rievault" in original text.

IX. *Opusculum* 43 (*PL* 145, cols. 679A-686C).

X. *Opusculum* 7 (*PL* 145, cols. 159A-180C, where it is spelled "*Gomorrhianus*").

XI. *Opusculum* 14: "*De Ordine Eremitarum, et Facultatibus Eremi Fontis Avellani*" (*PL* 145, cols. 327D-336A); *Opusculum* 15: "*De Institutis Suae Congregationis*" (*PL* 145, cols. 335B-364D).

XII. "*De Abdicatione Episcopatus*" (*PL* 145, cols. 425A-442D).

XIII. "*Apologeticus ob Dimissum Episcopatum*" (*PL* 145, cols. 442D-455B).

XIV. *Opusculum* 11 (*PL* 145, cols. 231A-252B); *Selected Writings* 53-91.

XV. *Opusculum* 13 (*PL* 145, cols. 291A-328D); *Selected Writings* 82-136.

XVI. The other text included is the brief *Opusculum* 58, "Concerning True Happiness and Wisdom" (*PL* 145, cols. 831A-838A; *Selected Writings* 137-46).

XVII. Four are included, on the Epiphany, St. Benedict, the Finding of the Holy Cross and the Holy Spirit and grace (*Selected Writings* 147-81).

XVIII. Chapters 5-13 of *Vita SS. Rodulphi et Dominici Loricati* (*PL* 144, cols. 1012C-1024B).

XIX. "Have mercy [on me, O God]" (Ps. 50[51]).

XX. Merton apparently thought that the selection was made by the general editor of the series, S. S. Hussey; it seems more likely that the translator, Patricia McNulty, would have chosen what to include in the volume.

XXI. *Selected Writings* 38-39.

XXII. *Perfection of Monks*, c. 6 (*Selected Writings* 93).

XXIII. Text reads: "degrees."

XXIV. *Perfection of Monks*, c. 6 (*Selected Writings* 95-96, which reads: "… monastery, and confessed …. sins, he … imposed upon him … penances above and beyond the … monastery; because …. all this. I … imposed upon himself … it.").

XXV. *Dark Night* 1.6.2 (*The Complete Works of Saint John of the Cross*, ed. and trans. E. Allison Peers, 3 vols. [Westminster, MD: Newman Press, 1946] 1.365).

XXVI. *Opusculum* 15, "*De Institutis Suae Congregationis*," c. 5 (*PL* 145, col.

339D), quoted by McNulty in the Introduction, which reads: "as it is the duty of priests to offer sacrifice and of doctors to preach, so the task of the hermit is to rest in fasting and silence" (*Selected Writings* 36).

XXVII. New Camaldoli Hermitage in Big Sur, California was founded from Camaldoli in 1958; Holy Family Hermitage of the Congregation of Monte Corona in Bloomingdale, Ohio was founded in 1959.

XXVIII. Major sites of early Egyptian monasticism; for a brief description see *Cassian and the Fathers* 123-25.

XXIX. See McNulty's Introduction (*Selected Writings* 36-38).

XXX. *Liber Dominus Vobiscum*, c. 19 (*Selected Writings* 75, 77, which reads: "You, O solitary ... spiritual labour, in ... of its Creator .... meeting place ... cross-roads ... any clamour of ...").

XXXI. *Perfection of Monks*, c. 6 (*Selected Writings* 92; parenthesis and emphasis added by Merton).

XXXII. *Perfection of Monks*, c. 11 (*Selected Writings* 104, which reads: "... the rule of Benedict .... These men ..."); Donatus was a fourth-century grammarian and the teacher of St. Jerome (*Selected Writings* 16, n. 1).

XXXIII. See the famous Letter 22 of Jerome, in which he warns his disciple Eustochium against the attractions of secular literature, saying "What does Horace have in common with the Gospels, or Vergil with the Psalms, or Cicero with St. Paul?" and then goes on to recount his dream in which he is summoned to judgment and accused of being a Ciceronian rather than a Christian (*PL* 22, cols. 416-17).

XXXIV. See Merton's comment in *Life of the Vows* 285: "The reading of good literature, though not specifically religious, and enjoyment of good art, music etc., which may not necessarily be religious, are not to be considered 'worldly' and 'evil' if they contribute to the monk's formation and education in the humanities. It is to be remembered that a solid and deep cultural formation contributes much to the spiritual life."

XXXV. *Perfection of Monks*, c. 14 (*PL* 145, cols 311D-314C; *Selected Writings* 111-13).

St. Anselm of Canterbury

(c. 1033–1109)

St. Anselm the Monastic – Conferences

In a journal entry for June 26, 1963, Thomas Merton wrote: "Have read St. Anselm's *Proslogion* and having for the first time considered the ontological argument, have come under its peculiar spell. It is certainly much more than a mere illogical confusion of orders, or an illicit transition from the level of words to the level of being. On the contrary, it begins and ends in being. It has extraordinary faults, impossible to define and describe because of the underlying spiritual experience which it suggests. I talked of this to the novices on the F. of St. John Baptist, which was a beautiful day, with great East Anglian clouds over St. Theresa's field" (*Turning Toward the World* 333). The reference is to the first of five novitiate conferences on St. Anselm that Merton presented between June and December 1963 that are transcribed here for the first time. While he had first read the *Proslogion* with its famous ontological "proof" for the existence of God when he was teaching at St. Bonaventure College and studying medieval philosophy and theology with the Franciscan Philotheus Boehner (see his January 28, 1941 letter to Mark Van Doren [*Road to Joy* 9]), it evidently made little impression on him at the time. The impetus for this new interest in Anselm was his reading of *St. Anselm and His Biographer*, a recently published study by the medieval historian R. W. Southern. He writes of this "very fine book" to his British correspondent Etta Gullick on July 28, 1963: "I think he did a very good job. I took this occasion to get into St. Anselm a little, too. I had always been put off him by the standard philosophy textbooks, but I find him fascinating" (*Hidden Ground of Love* 361). Journal entries, some of them quite substantial, over the course of the next six months record his enthusiasm for Anselm as he progressed through most of his major and many of his minor works: *De Libero Arbitrio*, *De Veritate*, *Cur Deus Homo*, *De Casu Diaboli*, the prayers, meditations and letters (*Turning Toward the World* 337; *Dancing in the Water of Life* 3, 5, 12, 15, 16, 19, 28, 31, 36, 41, 42, 65, 74-75, 76-77), along with the study of the argument of the *Proslogion* by Karl Barth, whose rejection of an apologetic motive on Anselm's part Merton heartily endorses (*Dancing in the Water of Life* 17, 22; *Hidden Ground of Love* 586). His comments (a number of them included in revised form in the closing pages of *Conjectures of a Guilty Bystander*) highlight "the clarity and strength of his dialectic," "the mysterious, clear, contemplative" quality of his reasoning, the centrality of liberty in his thought (compared favorably to that of Sartre), his doctrine of human participation in divine creativity (*Dancing in the Water of Life* 3, 5, 12, 41). On January 19, 1964 he writes simply: "I love Anselm" (*Dancing in the Water of Life* 65). Over this same period he shares this love with his novices, though his focus in his conferences is principally on the monastic dimension of Anselm's life and thought as most relevant to the needs of his audience. In both his initial presentation (Gethsemani recording 58.4) and that which followed on July 16 (Gethsemani recording 65.2), he provides a broad background discussion of the monastic movements of the late eleventh century and the place of Anselm and his monastery of Bec in these reforms. In the June 24 conference he stresses the compatibility of Anselm's rigorously logical and capacious mind with his vocation as monk and later as abbot, then focuses on Anselm's insight into God as the fullness of Being, the basis of his argument for God's necessary existence, an illumination received in the context of the monastic *opus Dei*. Three weeks later he reiterates his conviction that no truths are intrinsically alien to monasticism when they are integrated into a holistic response to God by a mature monk, before going on to discuss, on a considerably lighter note, some of Anselm's much more accessible *similitudines* that he presented in his conferences to his own monks. He returns to Anselm on August 15 (Gethsemani recording 65.4), the Feast of the Assumption, in which, after devoting the first half of his hour-long conference period to a discussion of grace as prompted by the words of the angel at the Annunciation, he turns to the sermon on heaven given by Anselm at Cluny and other continental monasteries, in which the exiled Archbishop of Canterbury repeatedly asserts that nothing genuinely good in earthly existence is ever lost, that all true joys are incorporated into the everlasting joyful present of eternity. The two final conferences, on December 8 (another Marian feast) and December 22 (Gethsemani recordings 76.4, 77.1), consider Anselm's teaching on monastic stability and the joys and trials of fidelity to monastic community life – a topic that is certainly pertinent to Merton's own periodic crises over remaining at Gethsemani or finding a more eremitic form of monastic life elsewhere but is also particularly relevant to the inevitable struggles that his young charges will have to contend with in their own future religious lives. Anselm's wisdom on the topic is once again conveyed particularly in a style that is both rigorously logical and eminently practical, a synthesis that Merton strongly appreciates and recommends as salutary instruction for his audience of novices and recently professed monks. In a letter he had written on June 23, the day before his first conference on Anselm, to his former undermaster of novices Tarcisius Conner, then studying in Rome, Merton expressed his strong admiration for Southern's book and continued: "Anselm is very interesting, though not quite the pure monastic type that we are led to look for at the present moment. Yet in actual fact one of the greatest of monks: but with a definite eleventh-century character, I guess. But he is great" (*School of Charity* 175). While Merton was in the forefront of efforts to renew a focus on patristic and monastic theology as a central dimension of formation for Cistercians, rather than the more abstract scholastic theology that had dominated earlier generations, these conferences make clear that his was a vision that had room not only for "the last of the Fathers," St. Bernard, but for the first of the scholastics, or at least pre-scholastics, St. Anselm. In fact in his second conference he tells his novices that if he had to choose between Bernard and Anselm as his own abbot, it would be the latter that he would without hesitation prefer.

1

Now I want to get into this deal of St. Anselm. This is going to be a little hard, because his thinking is a bit tough. He thinks, so we're going to have to struggle a little bit now with the thought of St. Anselm. It's worth struggling with, though. First of all let's get St. Anselm situated. Yesterday we were talking about St. Pachomius;[1] today we're talking about St. Anselm. Where do they stand in relation to each other? Does St. Anselm live in a hut down the road, and St. Pachomius used to walk down and visit him every Sunday afternoon? Where do they stand in relation to each other? You've got to have at least some historical background to catch all this: Pachomius: fourth century; Anselm: eleventh century – that's a long time! That's almost as much as from the time of St. Bernard to our time – not quite: it's a hundred years short, but it's a long time. You look at how far back we look to St. Bernard. That's how far back he looked to St. Pachomius.

You've got to get something of this perspective when you start talking about these people, because St. Anselm lived in a totally different world from St. Pachomius. Bec is in Normandy, up in northern France. It's right near Lisieux. It's where all the fighting was in World War II and they landed and so forth. I don't know if Bec is still there. Normandy was a great place for Benedictine monasteries. So there's a great difference. Pachomius was this Coptic bird, living out in the desert, a Coptic peasant really, I suppose. What's a Copt? He's an Egyptian, a semi-oriental, practically speaking, what we would call an oriental. I don't know if you'd really call an Egyptian an oriental, but still. St. Anselm – what is he? Of course he was Italian, but he started out in Italy, went all the way up to France. When he was a boy in Italy, he said, "I want an intellectual life"; or "I want to be a hermit"; or "I want to be a cenobite" – one of those three. His dad said, "You're not going to have any one of them." He said, "Is that so?" and he took off and went to northern France, which people were frequently doing in those days. That's almost tantamount to leaving America now and going to Greece! It's a long way, a much longer journey than an ordinary journey from America to any part of the world now, if you go by plane. It took him several weeks. He got up into France and was looking around, and he found out that the best school that was going was the school at the monastery of Bec, where a man called Lanfranc was teaching.

Lanfranc was arguing at this point with a character called Berengarius[II] and this is very important. It's not important to your monastic life, but to get the situation about Anselm, because Berengarius was starting something quite new. What he was starting was the approach to philosophy and theology where you use reason rather than authority. Therefore in your eleventh century you've got a very important new step coming in the whole question of Christian thought: people beginning to say the authoritative arguments are all right, but let's use reason. Some people were pushing this – Berengarius was one of them – pushing things so far that he was saying, "If there's a contradiction between authority and my reason, my reason is going to be right, and I'll forget about the authority. If the Bible doesn't fit in with my reason, too bad about the Bible, and if the Fathers don't fit in with my reason, too bad about them." He was in a big fight with Lanfranc, who was taking the opposite view. Lanfranc was this Benedictine, and they were discussing especially the Blessed Sacrament, because Berengarius was taking the standpoint of reason to say that you couldn't hold transubstantiation because it didn't fit in with reason. (The term "transubstantiation" wasn't developed yet – I mean the concept, our idea of transubstantiation.) He was bringing up the question of reason, and saying this doesn't fit reason; therefore it can't be. Lanfranc was saying, yes; there's more to it than reason; there's a question of faith and authority and so forth.

Now this was the atmosphere in which St. Anselm appears. So right away you've got a whole new world. This is almost like a monk in our day suddenly getting involved in quantum physics! It's that much of a jump. It's a big step: a monastic life where people are tied up with the latest developments in thought. They're right in the forefront of it, and they're steering these latest developments in the direction of the Church and faith, so although they're going to tend to be conservative – Anselm is basically conservative in the sense that he does go back to the traditional Church teaching, but at the same time he's completely original. The thing that you want to understand about St. Anselm is his completely creative part that he plays in the thought of the Middle Ages. St. Anselm was one of those people who gets the whole thing around the corner, so that it develops toward St. Thomas. St. Anselm is one of the great pre-scholastics. When I say pre-scholastic, does it mean anything at all? What do the scholastics do? What was the difference between scholastic theology and patristic theology? Which was more developed, and how? The Fathers tend to discuss everything in the light of the Bible and tradition. It's more what they call positive theology. They simply say, "This is the way it's come down to us," and they simply develop that. They don't reason about it; they simply take the authorities and say what the authorities mean, and then they put one authority against another, and a lot of it is just simply applying it to the moral life or to the ascetical life. Sometimes they're very fanciful about this. St. Bernard is a patristic theologian. He'll take something that's been handed down and apply it to spiritual experience in a kind of literary way. Anselm doesn't do this. The scholastics don't do this. The scholastics use a critical scientific approach, with their reason. The real scholastics don't throw out authority. They keep the authority of the Bible; they keep the authority of the Fathers. But then they bring in the critical exercise of reason, critical intelligence. Why did Anselm use this? because this was a time when everybody suddenly discovers such a thing as logic. Logic is an instrument. It's like a knife in which you get in and dissect thought; you take it apart. The Fathers don't take things apart that way.

So Anselm comes along at a time where people are beginning to use reason critically in regard to the things of faith. He's one of the first. Right away we shrink. We say, this isn't good; this rings a bad bell. This fellow's dangerous! He's not dangerous at all. He's a very great monk. The thing you have to realize is that what he did was actually a very monastic thing. The reason why he's important for us right now is we're going to have a tendency to say the monastic party line is scripture and the Fathers. Stay away from these scholastics. They're all right when you get into theology, but there's bad stuff – it's not monastic. There's nothing that's not monastic, provided that it fits into a real monastic life. There is no such thing as a kind of exterior monastic party line, that says that it has to be just this particular kind of thing and no other. Einstein's relativity can be monastic if it's used by a monk. If it enters into the spiritual life of a monk, it's monastic. That's one of the things we have to come to realize today. We're not going to be archaic about this monastic thing. Of course you have to know how to use it, and you have to have a pretty good grounding in monastic tradition before you can sit around and start batting around some of the modern theories of nuclear physics or something like that. You have to have a good foundation to build on.

The important thing now is to get a little bit of this background of where St. Anselm fits in to Christian history. You've got to look at this eleventh century and look at the kind of people you've got in the eleventh century – the fact that Anselm took off from Italy and went to a monastery in northern France. At this time, in the eleventh century, people are very much alive.[III] This was a very original, creative period of Christian thought, just before the arrival of the Cistercians. They fitted into it in a certain sense. You had the beginning of this tremendous thing. Something we can really look back to and admire in the Middle Ages was this question of a Christian civilization. It's the kind of a civilization that we don't have any more. It was a super-national culture which was profoundly Christian, and which was filled with Christian wisdom and with Christian thought, in which a person who was really in the thing could be at home in any part of Europe, and could walk into any school and understand what was going on and participate in the thing or teach in it and so forth. You've got this tremendous movement of people from all over the place – some going to Ireland, some coming from Ireland; some going to Scotland, some going to Munich, some going to Hungary. A lot of them are on the road all the time. Later on this got to be a little bit too much because they were on the road all the time – people like Duns Scotus, a Scotchman, suddenly turns up in Paris, then turns up in Cologne. Thomas Aquinas, an Italian – Naples first, then Paris, then he's someplace else. Then you get these other fellows – all these different places where they can suddenly be, and they're at home in all these places. Everybody understands exactly what's going on. You've got this great intellectual elite, some of the best minds that you ever had, and some of the best thinking that you ever had.

A great deal of this is due to the monks. A lot of this is due to the ground that had been laid down by the monks in the time of Charlemagne. They kept on building it up quietly, without too much fuss, through the so-called dark ages, until around the beginning of the eleventh century things began to pop. You've got some very curious and very interesting people arising, people like Gerbert of Aurillac,[IV] who was Pope Sylvester II, who was quite a scientist. They thought that he was a magician. These people didn't know what the heck he was doing in the Vatican with all these astronomical instruments and stuff like that. They thought he was an astrologer and he was an alchemist. The pope's making gold! He was a man very much ahead of his time. Right in the middle of all this is Anselm, who was absolutely the best of the whole bunch. He is one of the great minds of the Middle Ages. He's one of the most original minds of the Middle Ages. Knowles says that from a certain point of view he was more original than St. Thomas.[V] In this real living and brilliant time, he appears in the middle of this as man who's got a great philosophical mind, and yet he's a great monk and a deeply spiritual man. The thing that's so wonderful about him is not that he is a monk who also happened to be a philosopher, as though a monk might be a monk and at the same time he might also be a great engineer or something like that on top of his monastic life, without figuring how they ever joined.

You've got this wonderful unity in St. Anselm. His philosophy is right in the heart of his life of prayer, so much so that this argument we're going to talk about was something that he was worrying about in the office. He gets the illumination of the thing at matins one day. The whole thing just dawns on him at matins. Now this sounds very bad, and right away somebody's going to say, "Now look, stay away from that kind of stuff. When you're in choir you're not thinking about philosophy. When you're in choir, you should be thinking about pious things and not philosophy." For Anselm there's no contradiction. He had a philosophical way of thinking about God, and at the same time it was not only philosophical but also deeply religious, and also mystical. This fact is one reason for the confusion about the quality of his philosophical thought, because philosophical thought is a whole lot easier to evaluate if it's just straight philosophy, not too much mixed up with mysticism. If a philosopher is at the same time a mystic, he's not only going to be a much better philosopher, but he's liable to not get through to professional philosophers, because professional philosophers don't fool with mysticism. If you get too much mysticism, if you've got a philosophical experience and a philosophical line which is based on a spiritual experience which you don't declare, and you're talking in philosophical terms, you're drawing at the same time on a spiritual experience underneath the philosophical terms, this is very fine for somebody like Dan[VI] or somebody like Maritain,[VII] and also somebody like Gilson.[VIII] But when Dan Walsh runs into some of these standard academic philosophers in a philosophers' meeting, they don't know what the dickens he's talking about. They haven't the faintest idea what he's after, because they have no contact with these deeper presuppositions, and that's the whole thing with St. Anselm.

People are completely lost on St. Anselm. He comes up with this ontological argument – it's stupid; it's meaningless. You can't do anything with it. You can't convince an atheist with this argument. Of course he's not trying to convince an atheist. The first thing that St. Anselm is not doing, he's not trying to convince anybody. All he's trying to do is to develop what he calls the *ratio fidei*; that is to say, he starts with faith and taking faith absolutely, totally, he adds to it the work of intelligence to clarify it more, not so that intelligence can clarify the faith, but so that intelligence can open up his mind to receive more light from God. His philosophical writing is at all times a prayer. It's like St. Augustine. That's why it's very good to read something like the *Proslogion*.[IX] The whole thing is a prayer from beginning to end. At the same time it's a meditation on the existence of God, with an attempt to produce necessary reasons why God must exist, necessary philosophical reasons. He's talking to God all the time. He's saying, "O my God, how does it happen …?" and so forth; and "I think this and this, and You tell me this, and that's right"; it goes on, this sort of a dialogue with God in which these necessary reasons keep coming out, and as he gets light he goes back to God in prayer and so forth. So here you've got a completely revolutionary kind of thing – except that St. Augustine had done it a little bit before. When he does this, he does like these other people: he says I'm not going to take the Bible and I'm not going to take anything from any authority. This is all going to be reason, but the catch about it is that the way he does it is absolutely saturated with the Bible and it's absolutely saturated with tradition.

He's using his reason in this supersaturated state, so that actually what you've got is a perfect synthesis of exactly the way a monk should think when he's thinking originally – which he seldom does. Here you've got a monk who actually made a creative use of not only the biblical revelation and tradition, but also of his reason. Here was a man who instead of simply tagging along after tradition – a long way after. (We're lucky if we do that. It's good to do that. At least if we're following after tradition we're going someplace. We're not following after some totally different tradition.) He's not following it. He's right in the vanguard of it, so that he becomes tradition. He becomes a very important person, and all through history now everybody simply keeps going back to St. Anselm because he's right in the middle of it. In philosophy, you have to negotiate some of Anselm's arguments.

Now let's get acquainted with this ontological thing.[X] We can't discuss it all in ten minutes, but we can get acquainted with it now. Once you get familiar with this argument then we'll go into the *Proslogion* and see the whole background of it. So what's the so-called ontological argument? What's it all about? This was this idea that he gets at matins one day, after struggling and struggling and struggling. He says, "I believe that God exists." He starts with faith in the existence of God. He starts with the concept of God that is given to us by faith, and then by a process of reasoning he arrives at the same conclusions that he arrives at by faith: that God necessarily exists. How does he arrive at this? We know by faith, we believe, that God exists, and that He necessarily exists. What do you mean, He necessarily exists? God is the one being who not only exists but must exist. He is the only being Who cannot not exist. His existence is necessary and not contingent; whereas all other beings besides God, their existence is contingent – that is to say, they can possibly not exist. In fact after a while they don't exist.

Now what is this ontological argument? He starts out, "The fool hath said in his heart, there is no God."[XI] Now God is that being than whom no greater can be conceived. Therefore what he wants to prove is that the being than whom no greater can be conceived has to exist. He necessarily exists. Once you just consider the existence of that being, it has to be an objective existence. It's not only an existence in the mind. Now what's the criticism of this? What he's saying is that if the being than which no greater can be conceived exists in your mind, He has to also exist in reality. This is true of Him; it's not true of any other being but it's true of Him. Once you conceive in your mind a being than whom no greater can be conceived, He has to exist necessarily outside you, because if He does not exist outside your mind, then the idea that you have in your mind of that than which no greater can be conceived is not the greatest, because there's a greater, which is the One that exists outside your mind. This is something you've got to chew on, you've got to fight with, because it's very hard to grasp. This isn't simple at all, and you never really get the thing in these particular terms. This guy had this cooking in his mind for days and days and days in the office. It's a very good thing to cook; it's a nice thing to think about during thanksgiving, for example, although that sounds like sheer heresy. But it is not. Absolutely it is not, because it gets you in contact with God as absolute being, as absolute reality, and anything that gets you in touch with reality, especially if it happens to be the reality of God, is extremely good for prayer.

If you think a little bit about this stuff, and don't think about it in the wrong way, and grasp the thing right, you get an awful lot of light out of it, but you don't know what kind of light you're getting. That's why it's so darn tantalizing. It's an extremely tantalizing thing. Maybe if I take a little time I can break it down on the board real quick. In your mind it is possible to conceive a being than which no greater can be conceived – that is to say, it has to have the fullness of being. So when you conceive in your mind a being which has the absolute fullness of being, that being must be real outside your mind. Otherwise it wouldn't have the fullness of being. Of course the objection to this was made, by another monk by the name of Gaunilo.[XII] He comes along and he says, "Look – the fact that something is real in your mind does not mean that it's real in reality. I can conceive in my mind a blue horse with ten legs." (He didn't say this – this is my example. It's funnier.) "I can conceive in my mind a blue horse with ten legs, but it doesn't mean that that blue horse with ten legs exists outside my mind." Is this a correct judgment of Anselm's argument? He's missed the point. Anselm is not just saying because this exists in my mind, therefore it exists outside my mind. He's talking about a very particular case – of the absolute fullness of being. If I conceive something than which there can be no greater fullness of being, it's got to be referring to a reality which exists objectively. Otherwise the concept is useless.

Let me try to get this on the board. I'm not going to have time. We're going to have to come back to this on Saturday[XIII] and start all over again, but it won't hurt to do it twice. Does anything exist? I conceive something that exists – two columns: in my mind / in reality. Something is. That's correct in all our minds, isn't it? Check that off. Is it correct in reality? Is there anything around here that has any being? You don't have to argue about it. This is self-evident. These are things that you don't argue about, or if you do you waste your time. You don't prove what's self-evident. Now something is not. Obviously it's in our mind. Is that correct? In reality, yes. It's possible to conceive something that is ceasing to exist, because everything that we know eventually is not. All contingent being is a mixture of "is" and "is not." Something is not, and therefore you can conceive beings which combine being and non-being. Now a being – all being and no non-being. This is the fullness of being – a being that has nothing but being, and no non-being can get into it. It cannot not exist. We can conceive this. Now the great point here is the question to get it from the mind to reality. If it is all being and no non-being, only in the mind, then outside the mind … [final words unrecorded].

2

So, St. Anselm – we've got some stuff on St. Anselm today. We'll talk about him a little bit – his monastic thought. There's a lot of it and it hasn't been studied. There's quite a lot there. You had to dig around to find it. First of all, to fit him in this, think a little of the personality of St. Anselm as a literary figure. Of the writers of the Middle Ages, he's really one of the most outstanding. He's quite an important person. He's got a terrific wholeness about him. He's one of those people who isn't divided up into compartments. When he writes about theology or when he's giving talks to the monks about the ascetic life and so forth, although there's a difference in style and difference in approach, nevertheless it's the same man all the time. He's consistent. He's always himself. He's always very individual, and his individuality is very distinct. He's a very original person. He's very striking as a person. St. Thomas is a great person alright, but you never see the person. All you see is the thought. You could say the thought is the person. It is, but nevertheless the thought of someone like St. Thomas is kind of disembodied. It gets a little away from St. Thomas, although he's there. But Anselm, he's always in it. He's always right there. There's always the person.[XIV]

That's what's characteristic of that proof we were talking about. It is a proof. Can it really be called a proof? Yes, it really can. It is a proof, yet when I say it isn't a proof, I mean he's not starting from something that he absolutely doesn't know at all, to arrive at certain knowledge, because he already has some certitude from before he starts, so in that sense, but it is a proof, certainly. It all depends on how you look at it to say how strictly it is a proof; there's a great deal of dispute about it. However what's really in it is Anselm. His experience is what comes through in this thing and in everything. This man's experience keeps coming through. The beauty of his mind and the beauty of his soul keeps coming through. That's what's so nice about him. At least that's what attracts me about him. He's got a lot more than most of these other people. Bernard's the same way. But when you get down to Bernard himself, if it was a choice between who I had to have as my abbot, Bernard or Anselm, I wouldn't have much doubt. I would have much preferred St. Anselm. I don't know why. I just would. I hope this doesn't get me under excommunication *ipso facto* or anything like that! I just would have preferred St. Anselm. He's more my speed, I think.

Anyway, the person keeps coming through all the time. He's got a love for the beauty of ideas. He loves the beauty of thought. He likes to think in a beautiful way and he likes to develop things beautifully. Also he likes examples. His monastic teaching was very entertaining. He was all the time dragging out quite interesting examples, very simple examples that obviously the monks of his time appreciated. Any of his monastic stuff is mostly not written, except in letters. His monastic talks (evidently he was giving talks all the time to these monks) are mostly reported by the monks. There's a big collection of what they call the *Simil-*

itudes of St. Anselm,[XV] taken down by some unknown monk or group of monks. These are all the things that he said, and all the examples that he gave come in these similitudes. They're very simple and original. He's got a lot of imagination and it isn't the kind of imagination that St. Bernard has, either. St. Bernard has this terrific scriptural imagination. He gets very flowery and so forth. Anselm is very simple and down-to-earth. These are the simplest possible kind of examples, as you'll see. He has a great love for ordinary experience of things. Because he's a man who goes at things with his whole being in all simplicity, what counts with him is experience of spiritual things. What you've got in St. Anselm always is this spiritual experience. Whether of high things or low things, it's always straight from his heart and from his own experience.

A fundamental principle with him, which you've already had in another form, is this: he says, "He who does not believe will not understand."[XVI] Of course you know that. "I believe in order to understand."[XVII] This is his basic principle. This sums up the thought of St. Anselm. If you never get any other idea about St. Anselm, get at least that, because that's him: "I believe in order to understand." Then he says, "He who does not believe cannot understand." That's never been fully explained. How do you suppose this is explained? "He who never believes cannot understand." A person, when he makes an act of faith, what does he do? He lets his guard down completely. He disposes himself to accept. He puts himself in an attitude of complete openness. He becomes receptive, and when a person becomes receptive to the things of God, in some way he begins to experience them, and when he experiences them, then he understands them. We all experience this in some way or other. You know very well that as you go through your life, you get into different corners and so forth, and you go through a lot of struggling, and when you finally give in, when you finally drop your guard and say, "All right, I quit. I give in. I will now do what you want," then all of a sudden the whole thing becomes very clear, and there is an experience of a difference. You feel different when you're fighting it and when you stop fighting it. After you stop fighting it there's a whole new attitude that you take, and so there is an experience there. So he says, "He who does not believe will not understand, for he who has not believed has not experienced anything, and he who has not experienced will not understand." So that's got quite a lot to it. This, I think, sums up his attitude toward the spiritual life. You believe, and therefore that leads into the realm of experience, and then on the basis of your experience, you understand. I think that's pretty good. I don't see any holes in that. Is anything wrong with that? That's pretty solid. It's the kind of thing that appeals to us, in our pragmatic way. We like to have concrete evidence for things, and this gives a certain evidence – the evidence of experience.

Let's look at Anselm as a monastic figure. It's the Feast of St. Stephen Harding.[XVIII] Anselm was a contemporary of Stephen Harding. They were living at the same time, and incidentally they formed part of the same monastic movement. One of the things that we need to remember about the eleventh century – Stephen Harding: what was he doing in the eleventh century? When did he go to Cîteaux? 1098 – that's the foundation of Cîteaux; 1098 – Anselm was Archbishop of Canterbury, and he had been for about eight years. He was in England. He used to go to the continent. He used to visit different abbeys. I don't know if he ever went to Cîteaux. He went to Cluny, and he might have gone to Cîteaux but he probably couldn't be bothered. Cîteaux was still very small. Anselm died about 1112, 1115 – something like that.[XIX] Cîteaux was just about getting started, so he probably didn't go. So this whole eleventh century – in Cistercian monasteries, people get the impression that there was one monastic reform in the twelfth century, and it was us. There just wasn't anything else. Everything else was completely lights out. They were all shot. There wasn't anybody doing anything any good except the Cistercians. This is absolutely wrong. The Cistercian reform was just one. It was probably the most successful one, but it was one out of a whole bunch of reforms. The eleventh century was full of monastic reforms. We could go through at least a dozen monastic reforms that took place in the eleventh century. What were the names of some of them? Camaldolese; Carthusians; Vallombrosans.

You should have a broad view of what each century stands for, at least roughly: twelfth century – St. Bernard and a couple of crusades. It's mostly St. Bernard and Cistercians; twelfth century is all Cistercian, practically speaking, with a few Benedictines around. Eleventh century is not yet Cistercian. It's the beginning of the Middle Ages. It's a big, important century. The great name of the eleventh century is Gregory VII, who reformed the whole Church, and Cluny is a big thing in the eleventh century: eleventh century – Cluny; twelfth century – Cîteaux. Thirteenth Century is the big century: there's your Franciscans, Dominicans, St. Thomas Aquinas, the big scholastics and so forth. The fourteenth century, they're starting to go down, but you still have a lot of great mystics, and then the fifteenth century, everything is in pretty bad shape – of course fourteenth century is also the black death and the end of the Middle Ages. The fifteenth century is one of the low ebbs, and the sixteenth century is the Reformation, of course; fifteenth century there's a preview of it. Seventeenth century, you're getting close to us now – people like Louis XIV; eighteenth century: French Revolution; nineteenth century, we're in the middle of the thing; twentieth century, that's us, the great achievement!

In this monastic movement, you've got all these different reforms, and Bec was really a monastic reform of sorts. One of the lively things in the eleventh century was Bec, and Anselm at Bec was very good. At Canterbury, he had this biographer, a fellow called Eadmer, and this biography of Anselm is very interesting because it's a new kind of biography.[XX] Very early biographies of the saints are all trying to make you see what great instruments of God they were, and consequently everything they do is very miraculous: emphasis on the miracles, emphasis on the spirit of prophecy, emphasis on the fact that this man is completely out of his world. He's an instrument of God. In Eadmer's *Life of Anselm*, it's quite different. As a matter of fact, you've got two people writing about Anselm. Several of his monks wrote about him.[XXI] There's an interesting contrast between one of them called Alexander, and another one called Eadmer, and the way they treat Anselm and his miracles. It's this funny thing that Eadmer, who's a much better biographer, just doesn't seem to be able to see these miracles. All these other guys see miracles all over the place. I'll just read a little bit in this book. It's interesting:

> We have only to compare the account, which Alexander gave, of the curing of the blind man at Lyons with Eadmer's own account of the curing of a mad woman on the road to Cluny, to

> see the difference. Alexander's account is quite crude and unsophisticated; a blind man begins making an uproar; Anselm sets out to find the reason, Alexander reports. Anselm tells the man to come forward; he makes the sign of the Cross and splashes holy water on the man's eyes; the man goes away seeing with perfect clarity. This is the kind of story which the credulity of the times demanded. But when Eadmer tells a story it follows a quite different pattern: while they are riding along towards Cluny a clerk approaches and asks Anselm to cure his mad sister; Anselm turns a deaf ear to his tearful entreaties and rides on; the man redoubles his plea, but Anselm repels him; then they come on a crowd holding the mad and gesticulating woman; the crowd gathers round and seizes Anselm's reins; they beg him to put his hands on her; he refuses; they revile him; at last he relents, makes the sign of the Cross and rides quickly away, drawing his cowl over his head weeping, leaving his companions. But was the woman cured? On this point Eadmer, who said so much, could only speak from hearsay. He believed what he heard, but he could not say he has seen a cure.[XXII]

In other words this is an exceptionally honest medieval biographer. Actually, what's more impressive to us? Obviously the second. Why? his humility. Instead of this business of "Okay," sign of the cross and they all go away cured, you can see that this constituted a problem for the man: all these people expecting him to work miracles, and in his heart he knows that he's not worthy to do anything like this, and he's struggling against it. He doesn't want any part of it: "Get away. Leave me alone. I can't work any miracles. Can't you see I'm not a saint?" They keep pestering him and bothering him and then he finally does what they want, and then he hates himself for giving in to them. He goes along weeping and hates the whole thing. "Why do I have to get into all this stuff?" It's really a very impressive biography. You see the man. You see the heart of this person. It's so much more impressive than some of these other biographies. In the *Life of St. Benedict*[XXIII] you've got the other kind – although that's very impressive too. St. Benedict just sits there and says: "Go get Placid out of the water" and Maurus just takes off and runs on the water and grabs him and says, "Gee, I was walking on water," and then comes back and says, "Why were you walking on water?" "It was the merit of your obedience, my child." You got the feeling that this was all sort of a put-up job beforehand between St. Benedict and the Heavenly Father. They're together in this thing. The human beings just don't understand.[XXIV]

Let's take a look at some of these so-called *Similitudes* of St. Anselm – just one or two. You've got a whole collection in Migne of these little examples that he gave in his talks. This is the kind of stuff that he was giving out in informal conferences to the monks. You've got a theology of the monastic life here, and it's a different kind of thing altogether from what we're talking about on Sundays.[XXV] It isn't at all like St. Pachomius; it isn't at all like Cassian. There's a whole new view of the thing. It's a much more modern view. What have you got in Cassian? You've got the ascetic life of the individual developing towards mystical contemplation. You've got this developing toward mystical contemplation too, I suppose, but what he is talking about is the religious life and the life of the vows. Here you've got a whole new thing because in the eleventh century that's one of the things they were talking about. There was a great deal of theological discussion about the life of the vows. There's one book of St. Bernard[XXVI] where some Benedictine monks were worried about the vows, and they asked him, "Give us some dope on the vows. We want to know." They ask him three or four questions about precise cases – about obedience. They ask him technical questions which modern theologians still debate – does the *Rule* bind under pain of sin? For Cassian, never in a million years would he worry about "does the *Rule* bind under pain of sin?" He didn't have a rule. But with Anselm in the eleventh century and the twelfth century, you begin to get this kind of theology – the theology of the vows. These similitudes of St. Anselm are mostly about the vows and about the practice of the vows. We're already over the line into a more modern theology, although it's still monastic. It fits in very nicely with the monastic life.

Here's one of his similitudes.[XXVII] This is about the monastic life, about the security of the monastic life. Of course everything that St. Anselm says, whether it's about the vows or about the monastic life or something, it's medieval. He's thinking in terms of his medieval surroundings and the relationship between the medieval people and their feudal lords. When he starts talking about the vows he's always talking about the relation of a servant and the lord in the castle and so forth. Of course this has stayed with spiritual literature right up to the last century. Now it's changing. Finally we're going to get out of the feudal relationship. All our spirituality of the vows is still in this feudal context, really, in terms of the service that's owed to a feudal lord, so if you don't have any feudal lords anymore, it's good to get out of this. But still, this is all familiar to you because we're brought up with this, or you are being brought up with it.

The monastic life is like a castle. Who else talked about the spiritual life like a castle? This is just like this other famous business of the castle – St. Teresa's *The Interior Castle*.[XXVIII] What's the set-up of the interior castle? How does it work? A castle is a series of concentric circles. You've got an outer wall, then you've got an inner wall, then you've got another one inside, and finally you've got this central tower, and in the central tower you've got the hidden room in the middle of it – or something like that. Now Anselm thinks in terms of castles. He says the monastic life is like a castle, and outside the castle you've got a village, and in the village you've got all these different houses. Some are pretty solid and some are kind of shaky. He says the village is Christianity at large; the whole Christian world is the village. What's going to happen is this castle is going to be attacked. When the castle is attacked, of course the attackers first of all get into the village, and they make a fine mess out of the village. Some houses in the village are pretty strong and they can't destroy them, but usually they find most of these houses are defenseless. They just break in and kill all the people and take all the stuff. The village hasn't got much of a chance. This is his view of the world. He doesn't take this strong view that Pachomius takes. He just says, "If you're out there in that village, you're going to have a rough time." Then he says, some of the houses of the village are defensible. They can't break into them, but the people have a pretty tough time, and if the enemy really wants to get rough about it, he can break in. Now there's the castle. He says the castle is the monastic life, and if you're inside the castle there's nothing they can do to you.

That's true. If you've ever seen any of these medieval castles, there simply wasn't a thing you could do. I used to live in a valley where there was one every ten miles. This was a narrow, rocky sort of a gorge, which in the eleventh and twelfth century every ten or so miles was a feudal baron who had his gang – it was really sort of a gangster proposition. It was very complicated later on, because the Albigensians were there, and some of them were Albigensians.[XXIX] They were not only robbers but also heretics. There was one place about twenty miles from where I lived. There was a cliff about 200 feet high, straight. Down at the bottom of this cliff was a river. On that side there wasn't anything you could do. On the other side it goes about three sides, like this. On the fourth side there was a sort of a very steep hill, and you could climb this steep hill and you'd come to the front door of the place. When you came to the front door you had a great big chasm dug here, with a drawbridge over it, and then high walls, so that this thing was absolutely isolated on top of this cliff. If you tried to take that place out just with bows and arrows (they didn't have cannons and they didn't have atomic bombs; what they had was bows and arrows; they had sort of big slingshots that threw huge rocks and that sort of thing) there just wasn't a thing you could do to a place like this. All you could do was starve the people out, and if the fellow got himself ensconced inside there with all his buddies and plenty of food and so forth, there just wasn't a thing you could do.

This was the monastic life, in Anselm's view. It was something absolutely impregnable. He says, inside the castle which was the monastic life, you've got all these people who are absolutely secure, and he says they will be perfectly secure as long as they stay inside. The trouble is, they get looking outside and they say, "Let's get out in the village and fight down in there. There's more fun down there. There's more going on." When they get out in the village, they're liable to get hit. Finally he says, inside the castle there's a central tower. This central tower he calls a dungeon. We usually think a dungeon is a kind of place underground; a dungeon originally is this central tower of the castle, which is the hardest place of all to get to, because you've got this great big tower rising up in the middle of this thing, surrounded by walls and on top of a cliff. Usually the boss gets up on the top of this big tower, and you can't even get him with an arrow. You can't even get that far with an arrow, but he can get you with an arrow because he's got gravity on his side. Of course they could have a few slingshots up there too, and lob huge rocks off the cliff. One of the things they used to do on these cliffs, if a lot of people were milling around at the bottom of the cliff, they just get a big vat of molten lead and empty it out on the whole bunch of them down below. In the center there is this dungeon, and the dungeon is not only absolutely impregnable but the people in the dungeon are so well set that they don't even want to go out into the castle, and still less the village. What are these three things? The village is the Christianity in the world; the castle is the monastic life. What's the dungeon? He says the dungeon is *angelica conversatio*[XXX] – angelic conversation, or monastic perfection. He says the man who's living in the dungeon, who's living in a state of monastic perfection, is so impregnable that he has no desire even to go out into the village. There's nothing can touch him whatever. He's in absolutely impregnable condition. So this he told to his monks and I'm sure the monks were very edified. This is a typical kind of a thing.

Now here's the stuff that's really good, that I like. It's on the vows, and I think it's very practical. Of course here again, you're in the Middle Ages. He's get two examples from medieval medicine – the potion[XXXI] and the operation[XXXII] – and they both apply to monastic vows. The potion: the man is real sick and so he calls in the doctor and the doctor gives him a potion. These medieval potions must have been pretty potent. He gives him this potion and it starts burning him inside, and he gets cramps and he gets furiously thirsty and he wants to drink. The doctor won't let him drink. He wants to go out into the air so he can breathe. The doctor says, "No, you can't go out in the air." He has to stay in this room in torment, with this potion burning his insides out, so he complains: "*Cur potionem hanc accepi?*" "Why did I take this potion?" "*Male mihi prius erat, et modo est pejus*."[XXXIII] "I was badly off before but now I am worse." Then he starts blaming all the persons who gave him the medicine. This is like the religious life. He says, "You come to the religious life. You're sick, and you say, 'Give me a potion. I'm sick.'" Then he says, "They give you the potion and it starts to burn, and you say 'Why did I ever take it?' 'Well, you took it, and if you'd be a little bit patient, it'll make you feel better after a while, but right now it's burning your insides out. You can't get a drink of water, you can't go out and run around and breathe and forget about it.'" He says the potion is the frustration of desires. It's the asceticism of the monastic life. We take this potion and we start burning inside, and then we say, "Before, I acted badly, but now I act much worse, because there are so many darn things ordered to me: *tot et tanta, quae mihi iubentur*.[XXXIV] I am ordered so many things, and I can't fulfill any of them, and furthermore I can only do a little bit of good, more or less unwillingly. Why did I ever enter this life in the first place? Why did I ever believe these people who counseled me to enter this place? I thought that all these people in here were going to be saints" blah, blah, blah. Finally he says, when he is purified of sin he will be happy and grateful. Just hang on and it'll get a lot better.

The operation is much better. This guy is real sick. He's sick again. Part of his body is rotting, so he says, "Doc, I'm falling apart. I'm rotting. You gotta fix me. Tie me up, get the knife, and start." The doctor says, "You really want it now? You want an operation?" He says, "Yes." The doctor says, "We haven't invented any anesthetics yet." "Okay, tie me up." What they did, they just tied these people up and went to work on them, so the doctor says, "All right, I'll tie you up and I'll work on you." So they tie him up securely, and the doc gets out the knife, and of course there's no anesthetic or anything like that. He just starts cutting. St. Anselm says, when they start cutting, the fellow starts to yell. After they cut about ten seconds, he's changed his mind. "I've changed my mind! Untie me! Let me out of here!" They say, "No, sir. Once you begin, we got to finish." The guy says, "Untie me or I'll kill you!" The doctor says, "You can't kill me. I've got you tied up to keep you there!" So this is the life of the vows, medieval style. So it goes on like this. This gets to a good little theological point that we could close with. What you do when you make vows, you realize that drastic treatment is necessary, and you have to be tied up, because you know you're not going to like it, but when the operation comes out successfully, all the putrid places cut away, he gets healed and then he's happy.

So he says that somebody will say that this isn't the right way to do it. This is a very modern question – in fact its ultra-modern. Someone will say you shouldn't make vows. You shouldn't bind yourself because your acts of virtue should be spontaneous. They should come freely from your heart at the moment. The way you feel at the moment, you should feel like it and do it, whereas if you're bound by vows, you're not spontaneous, and it's less meritorious. Anselm says no, it's much more meritorious, and he goes into a comparison between two people. On the contrary, this question of giving your whole life beforehand, and committing yourself beforehand and completely renouncing your will beforehand, so that they can just do what they want with you, is obviously much more meritorious. Then he comes up with a very interesting theological point about the faults of religious and the faults of laypeople.[XXXV] He says a religious who has given himself to God by vow, if he commits a sin, and a layman commits the same sin, God is going to be much more merciful to one of them than to the other, all things being equal. Which one is He going to be more merciful to? The monk, because the monk belongs to God. The monk is His property. He gets into a real long, complicated comparison that I haven't worked out here, but he just simply says that because the monk is God's property, if he repents of his fault, God will be much more merciful to him than to a layman, because He's much more concerned with him. This person belongs to Him, so he can always expect much more mercy. But if he doesn't repent, then he gets a much worse punishment. The monastic state in which one belongs to God is a state in which one can always count on much more mercy, provided that he's corresponding with the state, that he's living according to the state.

3

This being the Assumption we could say a little bit about Our Lady and a little bit about heaven.... Now about heaven: this is St. Anselm. This is this famous sermon on heaven[XXXVI] that he went around preaching all over the place. Some of the ideas in this are very interesting. It's very simple. It's very childlike in a way. This is a kind of a scholastic approach. But you'll find it has a deep biblical basis – as I say, very simple. He goes around to all these monks, especially Cluny and places like that. He's in exile from England, from Canterbury, and he's going around Benedictine monasteries preaching about heaven. He says, "I'm going to give you very simple ideas about heaven." A little child can't eat a whole apple. He hasn't got a big enough mouth, so his father has to cut the apple up and peel it and cut it up in little pieces and put it in his mouth piece by piece. He says, "That's what this sermon is. I can't give you the whole apple of heaven, but I cut it up and give you little pieces of what it's about." He goes at it in a kind of a logical way. His principle is this: consider all the things that we love most in this life and then transpose them to the order of heaven, and realize that we will get everything that we love in this life infinitely more in the next life. This sounds like a very naïve approach. This is definitely kid stuff. This is all very nice, and it's kind of quaint, but if you aren't too critical and too sophisticated about this, you'll find that there's a great deal in it. He starts with the goods of the body, and says, in a way that's really quite surprising, what goods of the body we will have in heaven.

He starts with this, but first of all what you've got to realize is that this is a very valid approach. It's one of the standard approaches in theodicy, the mystery of God. It's what philosophers call in Latin the *via eminentiae*, the way of eminence. It's mostly applied to the attributes of God. To arrive at a knowledge of God as He is in Himself, you have to take any created perfection, and then you transpose this into the divine order by saying that whatever this perfection is, you can make it as perfect as you like in the created order and it's still infinitely beyond that. Take anything you like – take being, for instance, which is the perfection of all beings, the fundamental perfection. The perfection of God's being has all the perfection of any being that we're capable of knowing, but infinitely more so. The beauty of God is infinitely more than any created beauty that we can see, and infinitely beyond that. Take the most beautiful thing you can imagine and then say, this is nothing compared to God. Compared to God, this is so far from the beauty of God that it is ugly. That's what St. John of the Cross says.[XXXVII] You don't have to say that – you don't have to be negative about it. So this is the way it's going to be, St. Anselm says, with regard to all the things that we love in this life. We'll have them in the next life in this extraordinary way.

Here's one point that I'd just like to make, I was thinking about this afternoon. In the order of grace, and in the order of our supernatural life, there has to be a quality called continuity. This is one of the things that you recognize in your life as you go along, and it's one of the things that's very important to be able to recognize. What do I mean when I say that there should be continuity in the life of grace? I mean to say you can trace a sort of a line, a sort of a kinship, between the graces that are in your life. After a while, if you have responded to grace, as everybody does to come to the monastery, and as everybody does to stay in the monastery, you have to respond to grace all along the line. You get into the habit of recognizing when you are on the road of grace and when you're not, because there's a continuity on the road of grace. I was just thinking this because this afternoon I was sitting on the edge of a field where I think I worked the first time we went out to work when I came to the monastery. The first day I got in, we went to work out there, and I was sitting there twenty-two years ago, pretty near – thinking of the continuity between that and now. It isn't only the same field and the same me, but there's been a continuity all the way through. You recognize this in your life. It has something to do with Bede Griffith – his title *The Golden String*:[XXXVIII] in his book there's a golden string that runs through your life, and when you're on this golden string, you know you're on the right track because of this continuity. Infidelity to grace and sin and so forth come in and break this continuity, and you can tell right away. It's like flying on a beam. As soon as you get off it, you know. You can tell right away. It isn't right. It's out of continuity. You're breaking the continuity, and this is a very important thing to know.

Therefore, applying this to St. Anselm, there's a continuity between the spiritual goods even of our bodily life, and the goods of heaven. This is a very important point. In the Greek idea of contemplation, for example, St. Maximus[XXXIX] (that Fr. Romanus[XL] was quoting) has this idea that there is such a continuity between the created order and our life in heaven that is to come, that everything around us is constantly speaking of what is to come, and everything is a symbol of what is to come, and everything is, so to speak, a sacrament of what is to come. Even the most ordinary bodily things in life have this sacramental quality because there is this continuity. Therefore think of the real happy moments of your life – the ones that you know at the same time are really human happiness and are really spiritual happiness. Those are the ones. They're the important ones, not the ones that you think are utterly, totally, purely spiritual and have no relation to humanity, because sooner or later you're going to find that they weren't connected with anything. All they were, were at the top of your head someplace, but there are real joys which are completely incarnate, so to speak. They're completely embedded in the human order of your life, and at the same time they're completely spiritual. Sometimes you don't recognize them at the moment. Sometimes they just seem to be an ordinary human event. Just think of some moments with your family or something like that. Some afternoons at work are like that, or some afternoon when you're doing some darn thing. There just are moments in your life that seem quite ordinary, then all of a sudden you find that they're really transfigured by grace. They're just ordinary human moments and yet God's grace is in them. Those things are not lost. St. Anselm says, "Right away, they're going to complain. I say they're going to be the goods of the body in the future life, and you're going to say, 'We're supposed to renounce all the goods of the body. We came to the monastery because we hate the body.'" (They don't say that – they were Benedictines! He was thinking there might be some Cistercians around the corner that would say this, although they wouldn't – not in those centuries; in that time period they wouldn't.)

It is definitely true that the purest joys of your life are those of your youth. There's something about the joys of youth that the joys of old age do not have, as I can tell you from experience about the joys of old age. The joys of youth have something that the joys later on don't have. There's a joy that you can never have again when you have been sort of messed up a little bit by life. The joys that a person has when he has been untouched by life have a very special beauty about them. This sort of runs under this whole idea of beatitude, because Anselm is thinking about this: what I get in heaven. Am I going to think back to the joys of my most innocent childhood? Am I going to say that those joys are more pure than my joy in heaven now? He's going to say, "No." There's a continuity there too. "I go to the altar of the God who rejoices my youth."[XLI] I've got experience of the joys that God gave me in my youth, and they seem to be getting away in my old age, with my gray hairs and that sort of stuff, all these things are going and there's nothing but sorrow, but then I remember that He gave me all these joys in my youth. We are aiming towards a fulfillment when all this will come back. Nothing has been lost.

We're heading for a time when everything that was ever any good is going to be recaptured completely as present, because you will go back into the presence, when these things were present, in eternity. We live in the dimension of time. We move along and things are left behind us, but anything that's good and anything that we ever did is present in eternity, and when we are in eternity, all this stuff is present to us the way it was then. What happens when we go to heaven is that anything that was ever any good at all in our life is all present there, and anything that was no good in our life is absent. It's gone. It's finished. All that we have in heaven is the hundredfold of all the good that was in our life, present eternally – plus the infinite joy of the vision of God. When the new heaven and the new earth are made, I suppose our part of the new heaven and the new earth will be this little section of Nelson County, all completely remade, with the association of all the graces that we had in this. All the grace that you had looking at these hills for all your monastic life, for all eternity you'll see the meaning of those. You'll see that what you were looking at when you thought you were looking at trees, you were looking at Christ. This will be for all eternity. You're going to see this, but you're going to see Him too. You'll see Him not only in creation but in Himself.

He says, what do you mean, that I should talk about the body in heaven. Aren't we supposed to leave the body behind? Isn't the body going to die – and good riddance – back to the worms, and that sort of stuff, and he says, "No." There's nothing the matter. In heaven, there's going to be beauty and pleasure of the body. This is medieval Anselm – nowadays if somebody got up and said this – he's really off. What's the matter with him? They're going to have pleasure in heaven? This is definitely Old Testament, and it's the Moslems too, if it comes to that. What are we singing all the time about heaven, every morning in lauds? The saints are in heaven lying around on their couches – *in cubiculis suis*.[XLII] They rejoice on their couches. Of course they're resting. They're not doing a lick of work! They don't have to move a limb! They're lying on their couches. As I understand it, lying *in cubiculis suis* is a banquet. At a banquet they lay around on couches. In heaven they're lying around, really enjoying life. This is a great eternal banquet, and the thing that St. Anselm brings out very clearly right away is that the pleasures of heaven will be among other things – the least of the pleasures of heaven – will be bodily pleasures, but they will be bodily pleasures (when we have a body there – it'll be a little while before we get the body; we'll have to do without for a bit). They will be bodily pleasures but there will be no satiety in them. The thing that ruins bodily pleasure in this world – how many of those cookie deals can you eat for breakfast? After about two, you quit. In heaven, it isn't that you have an infinite number of those things – one will be enough – but you will find in it all that you want without any satiety, without getting tired of it, and of course without being such a fool that you stuff yourself with the stuff.

The reason why all these things will be joyful in heaven is that there will be no disorder in the body and there will be no disorder in our taste. There will be beauty of body in heaven. This seems to be a very naïve and simple approach, but there's something rather fundamental about this, when you realize what will be the beauty of the bodies of the blessed in heaven. Where will this beauty come from? Will it just be their natural good looks? I suppose we'll all get back the same faces we had – there'll have to be a little bit of improvement if it's going to be heaven! But the beauty of heaven isn't going to be just the beauty of our features and our figure. (There'll have to be a little trimming done on some of us, I think.)

What will be the bodily beauty of the blessed in heaven? What's it going to consist of – not just the reflection of Christ but the actual glory of Christ. The beauty of all the blessed in heaven will come from the fact that they are the Body of Christ, and that in them shines the glory of the risen Christ. It will be the beauty of grace, but it will be more than the beauty of grace, it will be the beauty of glory. Grace is only the beginning. Glory is the full radiance of grace. All the idea we have here of the fullness of grace is infinitely more in glory. Our Lord, when he walked the earth, and Our Blessed Mother, when they walked the earth, were full of grace, but it wasn't as visible as in the transfiguration and after the resurrection. Our Lord was full of glory on the mountain of the transfiguration; He revealed the divine light that was in Him just a little bit – didn't reveal the whole thing because it couldn't be borne by the apostles. But in heaven we will all shine with the light. In fact some of the Fathers of the Church say that the actual beauty of the bodies of the risen saints in heaven will be the same light as shone in Our Lord in the transfiguration; that's our light in heaven. His light will be a million times more. Don't think of it in material terms, please – but light *is* a material thing, and this will be also a bodily glory, a visible glory. This is the teaching of the Church. This isn't purely and simply an imagination that somebody had. The thing that we have to remember is this is true, but it's only the beginning. The spiritual graces are far more than this.

Here's another one – you're going to think this is really ridiculous. He says we will have speed![XLIII] I don't know why he says we will have speed. We'll be able to get around with the speed of light. Now this is true. The question that arises: who cares? Why do you want to get around with the speed of light? The point that he's making is that the body will in no sense be an impediment to the mind. Supposing that you all of a sudden became a glorified body in choir and you had a distraction and you started thinking about Cape Town, South Africa. You'd be there! That's why I say it's a good thing we don't have this quality in this present life. We don't know where the dickens you'd be. You're liable to turn up almost anyplace! This will be possible in heaven, because we're going to have some kind of control over it. It won't control us. If the body has a good reason to be at Cape Town, it won't want to go to Cape Town unless it's the will of God. If it's the will of God and you want to think about Cape Town, the moment you think about it, you'll be there, just like an angel. That's the way the angels operate: the angel is present where he operates. The angel doesn't have any body at all. Where is an angel? As soon as an angel applies his mind – a guardian angel of your little sister – as soon as he thinks about your little sister he's there, right next to your little sister, right in her heart, so to speak. (I suppose an angel can get somewhat inside there.) He's there. As soon as he wants to do something, he thinks of it, and it's done. There are no obstacles to angels. Well, there'll be no obstacles to glorified bodies either. You've got that with Our Lord – all of a sudden He was there, and then He wasn't. There won't be any obstacles.

4

This is really a filler-inner. What this really is, is chapter 3 in how to avoid talking about St. Jerome![XLIV] I'm going to take a letter of St. Anselm on stability. This will fit in very nicely with what we're doing in the Wednesday class,[XLV] and will also be useful for these professed, because probably they're getting in the stage where they're all thinking, wouldn't it be so nice to be someplace else! Let's lay on the line here. This is a very fine letter of Anselm. It's Letter 37 in the new edition.[XLVI] We don't have the new edition yet, but it's ordered, so it's going to be here.[XLVII] This letter of St. Anselm on stability is very good. It's saying pretty much the same things that we've been saying on our Wednesdays, but what's interesting about it is the way he proceeds, and the way he thinks.

The great thing about St. Anselm, and the thing that's important about St. Anselm – St. Anselm's one of the unknown men in monastic thought because the monastic people aren't following him too much. He's all in the hands of people like Gilson, who's of course one of the best minds of the century, but he's in the hands of people who are studying medieval philosophy. The monastic folk don't pay too much attention to him, but he's very, very good for monasticism, because his great approach to the monastic life is the approach of reason. Now there's nothing wrong with reason. It's a very useful thing to have around. A little bit of reason doesn't hurt once in a while. So the thing that's interesting in his approach to stability is that it's the approach of reason to stability. Remember that when you say reason, what's the great thing that you have to remember about reason in St.

Anselm, as opposed to when you're talking about some eighteenth-century thinker talking about everything by reason? He always starts from faith. In Anselm, the reason that he's using is always to elucidate a truth of faith. So he always starts with faith. Don't get the idea that it's reason instead of faith. That's the thing that we usually run into when we say reason. Somebody is talking in terms of reason, reason, reason. Outside the Catholic context it means reason substituted for faith. At Cana they had these water jars and they were filled; there was wine in them already – that sort of a thing; or Jonah and the whale – it was really an ocean liner; they just said it was a whale because they didn't know what it was; they hadn't seen it – it was really the Cunard Line already working!

This letter is very good. It takes a reasonable approach to stability. It's called by Southern the most important of Anselm's monastic letters.[XLVIII] It's written to a fellow called Lanzo. (All his friends have funny names – one of his best friends is called Boso. The dialogue of *Why God Became Man*[XLIX] is all between Anselm and Boso.) Somebody said, write a letter to Lanzo. He's just got a job as prior in a monastery in England, the poor guy. Write him a letter.[L] So Anselm says, "What'll I write about?" "Oh, write him a letter." This is the sort of thing that happens to people. "Write him a letter, or write somebody a book." So Anselm writes this man a letter about stability, not because the person is being tempted against stability. He says it's good for everybody. I might as well give you this letter on stability because you're going to need it sometime. So here we go.

He starts from the assumption that all monks – this isn't the article of faith that he's elucidating, but it might as well be – that all monks at some time are going to need a letter on stability, and so this is it: the temptation against stability that happens to the fervent monk. This is the only one he's concerned with, so this is the only one that concerns us. What's the temptation that we're excluding? The temptation against stability which gets the unfervent monk. What's that? What's the difference? What's the temptation of the fervent monk and what's the temptation of the unfervent monk? The unfervent monk wants to get out and go back to the fleshpots. The fervent one, he's fervent, and so his very fervor is going to be enlisted in favor of the temptation, but the unfervent one: "There's no movies around here. This is very dull in this place. I'm bored. Let's face it – I want to go back and play pool!" This we exclude. This doesn't affect people like us! Actually it doesn't that much, really. How many people in this room really want to shoot pool? All I do is rip up the cloth and get everybody mad at me, so I'd rather not.

So this is the temptation of the fervent monk, who wants something better, and it's divided into three parts. We've got this letter, all quite logical. It starts out with a description of the temptation and how it occurs and what its signs are and what the effects of this temptation are. Then he goes along and says, how should one handle the thing? How should one resist it? Then he makes a personal application to Lanzo and says, the real purpose of this letter, the fruit of this letter, should be to get you to seek *quies mentis*[LI] – quiet of the heart, tranquility of heart – because the whole reason for stability is what? It's tranquility of heart. What's the purpose of tranquility of heart that stability gives? What is this for? Is this important or you're just supposed to be a prisoner here because this is a stunt that we're doing? Is stability essential to the contemplative life? One has to be peaceful, quiet inside. One should not be worrying about where he is any more. He should have settled the question of where he is. There should be a tranquility, an inner peace, which comes from having totally finished with the question of where do we go next. This question having been settled, a person then calms down and becomes quiet inside and then God speaks to him. Then that's it. His life enters this new dimension. This is the real point of this letter of Anselm.

Yesterday we were talking about silence.[LII] Today it's stability – both the same thing. The inner meaning of both these things is, these are necessary for a monk, not just because it's a stunt that a monk takes on, something that he does for the heck of it – other people do funny things and he does this. He just shuts up because it's a cute trick to do – just keep quiet all your life and people will know you're serious. It's for the sake of this inner tranquility, so that God can really work in our heart. There's a work that cannot be done in our heart until we have reached the point where we are no longer concerned with the question of where next. When that question is completely out of the way, then there's a work that begins, and until that question is out of the way, that work does not begin. It may begin in another form, but it doesn't really get underway until we've solved that. Of course there's a time and place for everything. This doesn't mean that everybody in the monastery should have solved this, even by the time of simple profession. You should have it solved by solemn profession, but if you don't, still don't worry about it. It'll get solved along the line somewhere. Somewhere along the line it should be solved. There should come a point in one's life where all these things are no longer relevant. There comes a point in a man's life that I would call – that particular point – a sign of maturity, of full maturity in the contemplative life for our kind of religious. Until we have reached that, we're not yet fully mature, on this particular point at least, because the fruit isn't ripe until one has made this kind of decision. You can't force it. It takes time. It may take 10–15 years, so don't worry about the time element.

Who is the person that is tempted against stability? Anselm uses all kinds of phrases. He uses the phrase *novitius* up in here somewhere, but he's writing, obviously, to a professed monk.[LIII] He doesn't mean *novitius* in the sense that we mean it. The sense we mean it is during the two-year period of probation. This is Order of Cluny. How long was the novitiate in Cluny?[LIV] Liable to be a month, if they were really getting strict! It was liable to be a month, liable to be a week, liable to be a few days. So he had to use the term *novitius* for somebody who was still maturing in the religious life. Even though he's made profession, he's still being formed. The fact that they made profession after a month didn't mean they were considered formed in a month. It just meant that they made their profession. But they continued to be formed, so the formation was going on. He was still a *novitius* although he'd made profession. He also uses phrases like *tiro Christi*, the recruit.[LV] He also says the *monachus professus*,[LVI] and he's talking about the man who has a *monachicum propositum*.[LVII] That word *propositum*, which would mean a proposal or a decision or something like that, actually is equivalent to what in all this literature? It's equivalent to profession. It's a Jerome word.[LVIII] Jerome uses it for the man who has made up his mind to be a monk and to remain one, so it is equivalent to profession even where there isn't a vow. Then later on, where there is a vow, they use it as equivalent to the vow.

Then he says the *monachus infelix*,[LIX] the unhappy monk, has this – and then the *ignarus monachus*.[LX] What's the *ignarus monachus*? a stupid monk, a silly monk. Of course the *ignarus monachus* is very important in Anselm because when you read Anselm, when you get to know his terminology, remember what the proof of the existence of God in the *Proslogion* is all about. Who's it addressed to? He's still giving it to somebody who presumably is going to be very recalcitrant for a certain reason. What does he call this person? the *insipiens*.[LXI] He's the fool. The *ignarus monachus* is related to the *insipiens*. He's his first cousin, at least. The *insipiens* is not just a fool in any ordinary sense – a stupid person. He's a person who does not know that by the very fact of saying that there is no God, you are saying there is a God. Now that's a particular kind of fool, of which the world is full, but to Anselm that's the beginning of all folly, because to Anselm, but not to most philosophers – they're fools according to Anselm. To Anselm it is obvious that the mere statement, the mere use of the name God, means that God is. You can't use the name God without implying God's existence because God means "He who is"; so the fool is one who says "God is not," thinking that this is a different sentence from "Is is not." The fool who says that there is no God is a person who thinks that it makes sense to go around saying "is equals is not." That's the way Anselm looks at it. Most people don't look at it that way.

The *ignarus monachus* – he's not quite as bad as the fool, but he's still a bit of a fool, because he is here and yet he isn't. What he's doing is that while being in one place, he is there only physically in one place, and he's living everyplace else in the world except where he is. So the *ignarus monachus* is the one who isn't where he is. All his energy goes into living another life than the one that he's living. This is important, because this is what the temptation is – this temptation against stability. What happens is that the devil, he says, comes up. This is the temptation that the devil gives to a person whom he cannot make turn against the monastic *propositum*. The man has his monastic *propositum* and he's clinging to this. He's not going to go back to the world. He's absolutely dead set – no going back to the world. "I'm going to be a monk. I'm a monk forever – I just want to be a better kind of monk than I can be here." This is the strict temptation. He's got his monastic *propositum* and the devil hands him a goblet of poisoned reasoning. What you're dealing with, then, is with poisoned reasoning. You're not dealing with an impulsion of the will or an impulsion of the emotions. You're dealing with poisoned reasoning. This is Anselm's approach. Most people regard it as dealing with a push of the will or something like that, but he says, "No. This is something you have to think out, and you have to know how to think it out." So it's the *prudens monachus*[LXII] who rejects this cup of poisoned reasoning.

Personally I think this is a very, very good approach. This is an intelligent and virile approach to problems of monastic life, the approach of intelligibility. To what extent is this thing intelligible? To what extent does this thing make sense? But the point is also that not everybody can handle this all by himself, and so it implies somebody else in the picture. Most people, when they try to figure something like this out, if they get in a real bind and they try to figure it out, figuring it out just makes it worse. Basically, there is this question of learning how to reject reasoning that has poison in it by substituting a reasoning that has true intelligibility in it, which is the reasoning of a *verus monachus* – a true monk – the *prudens monachus*. What is the devil trying to do? He says the devil appears to be willing to grant that the monk must be loyal to the monastic profession, but he never ceases in all kinds of ingenious ways to suggest that he was foolish or imprudent to undertake it under such superiors, or among such companions, or in such a place. A great deal of analysis could go into this. What he does is gets it down to a question of reasoning about a very particular case. I haven't got this thing figured out yet, because it's extremely subtle, but what I think he's doing is that the devil is making you try to reason about a particular case in a way in which you can't do it. I think that's behind this. I haven't got the whole thing absolutely lined up yet, but I think that this is pretty much what he's getting at. He's putting you in a place where your thinking is going to be useless. He's trying to make you think about a situation in a way that's plausible, but which actually leads to no solution. This is the proposition: a person says, "My monastic vows are fine. I love the monastic life, but I'm in the wrong place. I made a mistake to make the vows here." Most of us aren't worried about going and shooting pool, but a lot of people are worried about this. This is the thing that you've got to fix in order to arrive at maturity and stability in the monastic life. Before this you have to have made vows. Before you make the vows, it has another form, but after you've made the vows, it takes this form.

"I should have made my vows someplace else." There is in that a deep fallacy somewhere, but I don't know what it is.

What are the effects of this? The effects of this are being persuaded into ingratitude for the benefits which God had begun towards him. The first thing is ingratitude for the real graces that are there. Again Anselm is talking in very realistic spiritual terms. I think that as usual when Anselm talks about these things, there's much more in it than meets the eye. Anselm is a man who seems on the surface to be an essentialist, and under the surface is one of the most prominent existentialists of all history. That's why people like Barth are nuts about him. Karl Barth loves this man.[LXIII] Karl Barth is the person who said the best things about Anselm in the twentieth century, understands him better than anybody else in the twentieth century. The person who after Barth likes Anselm and understands him best is Evdokimov,[LXIV] who is one of the best Orthodox existentialists that's floating around, an Orthodox and an existentialist, and also a very deep contemplative person. What Anselm is really starting from is this fact. You have been given this particular grace by God. The grace of having vows in this place is a special gift of God.

If you know Anselm well enough, you can see parallels between this and the kind of reasoning in the *Proslogion*. He starts from the concrete fact of God in the *Proslogion*. He doesn't just start from the name of God, although he seems to; he says he is. He says, "When I talk about God, I say the name God."[LXV] But he's starting from a religious experience of God; and here he's starting from an experience which he has of the fact that one has vows here is not at all one case out of a possible five thousand. It's possibly the one and only case where God has granted me this grace. The way the *insipiens* approaches it, he says, "Well, I've got vows here, therefore I could also have vows at Montserrat, at Grande Chartreuse, La Grande Trappe, Monte Cassino, Mount Athos" – pick the best. But that's not it. The mere fact that I have vows in one place does not imply, in this particular setting, that I could have vows anyplace else. It means that God has given me the grace to make my vows here, whereas there's no indication whatever that I would have made vows any place else. This is a funny sort of approach to things, but it's something that you get when reasoning is based on religious experience.

The next thing he says is, with this ingratitude, what happens is that all progress immediately stops, because the person stops making any effort to progress, all the effort that should go into making progress. He puts all his effort into figuring why it was a mistake that he made vows here, the reasons why this is the wrong place for him to be, and how much better he could be doing someplace else. This can take a great deal of time. A person can put a great deal of ingenuity and mental effort into this syndrome. A person could really work hard on that. A person can put enough work into that to crack some of the toughest Fathers, for example. If the amount of energy that went off in figuring out why we made a mistake to be here were harnessed and channeled, we could produce something equivalent to the *Encyclopedia Britannica* in about one week flat! We could sell so much cheese that we could put cheese from here to New York, and give it out free! We could do a lot of things. The other thing that happens is that the final result is that one may lose the result, the vocation that he has, simply by failing to give rather the kind of thought to his vocation, and to give all this thought to something else, and to lose what he's got, or else to remain in one's vocation fruitlessly. It tends to be fruitless and kind of stupid. The whole thing gets to be a little inane. He gets into this fine example, a standard example. First he says this: he gets down to the root of this thing. He says, "While his mind is perpetually occupied with thoughts of removal, or if he cannot remove, with dissatisfied reflections on the beginning he has made, he gives up all attempts to reach the goal of perfection. While he is displeased with the foundation he has laid, no superstructure of a good life can be built upon it."[LXVI] This is important. Your beginning is the foundation on which you're building. If the devil makes you dissatisfied with this beginning, your life ceases to have continuity.

There has to be continuity in our life. I think this is one of the great principles of the religious life – that there is a continuity of grace throughout a man's life, from your earliest turning to God right up to your coming to religion and on through religion. If you think deeply on this question of temptation, of substituting something better, you will find that it's something that breaks the continuity. You could make it seem to be part of the continuity if you work hard enough on it; it takes a great deal of effort, but you can do it, but if you're sincere about it, you'll see that you're breaking the continuity, and one of the most obvious ways in which you break this continuity – this is a whole new initiative of our own that gets in. If the continuity is there, it's going to be obvious to everybody. It's going to be obvious to those who are supposed to understand those things. They'll see it. Anselm admits the possibility of going someplace else. He doesn't exclude the possibility. He says the basic theological principle in all this: this has to be entirely under the sway of grace. It has nothing to do with this kind of thinking. We should train ourselves to see immediately. It takes time, but after a little experience with this kind of horsing around, you can tell. We should know when we are fooling with something that we shouldn't fool with, and when we are inserting something in there out of our own will, we have to learn this. We have to also know how to recognize when God is doing it, and this requires somebody else's approval and intervention to a great extent. The further we get, the more we get involved in this life, with vows and that sort of thing, the more one's own initiative is meaningless. The moment I've made vows, I've excluded my initiative. If I've made a vow of stability, the last thing that counts after I've made a vow of stability is an initiative on my part to change. I've practically excluded an initiative on my part by making a vow of stability. That's what I really have done. In other religious orders, they do take into account possibilities of moving much more than we do. In our life, it's much more essential to stay put in one place than it is in theirs, because they're not living the contemplative life, most of them, and we are.

Just one more point – it's this idea of roots.[LXVII] This gets it back again to the contemplative meaning of the vow of stability, which is the important thing. Once we grasp the contemplative implications of the vow of stability, as well as the contemplative implications of silence and so forth, you really get the meaning of it, there's no problem any more. You can't take a plant and plant it here this year, and then plant it there next year. If you take some of these trees that they've planted outside the waterworks, if in March they suddenly transplanted them to another part of the field, and then next fall they transplanted them out to Dom Frederic's Lake, and then after that down to St. Bernard's Field, those trees aren't going to survive. He also applies this to the tree that's staying put and won't grow roots. What does he mean by that? A monk can be in the monastery and not being transplanted, but refuse to sink his roots into the monastery. This is very important. What does he mean by that? How do you sink your roots into the monastery, and how does one refuse to? What's the key word? Love. Love implies involvement. To sink roots into the place where I am means to become involved in that place. It means to commit myself to some extent.

Now wait. Here you've got to make a distinction. Don't commit yourself to the nonsense of which there is plenty. We're under no obligation to get involved in the nonsense that's in the community, but we have an obligation to get involved in all the good, in the right sense of the word, which means that one of the sources of trouble about stability is not so much that a person lacks love, but he can't handle the question of how far one is involved with all these brethren. One of the things about stability in the monastery is that one has to know how to be rightly concerned about your brothers without them becoming a total distraction. There's really no conflict, but there seems to be. How one can be deeply involved in the problems of all the other people in the monastery to some extent and to care for one's brother and to care for the community in the right sense of the word, without caring about the nonsense – this is extremely difficult. It takes years. It's one of the root problems with stability. You're not going to have a serious spirit of stability if you just have this idea of me and God in the community and the devil take the hindmost. The idea that these confreres don't exist – they are as if they weren't there – obviously they're there, and obviously if I try to kid myself that my brothers have no effect on my life and I have no effect in their life, this is pure nonsense. It's unthinkable. Even when I make that decision, that is a way of being involved with people, and the thing that's wrong with it is the wrong way to be involved with the community – but it is a way of being involved. Every reaction that a person has with regard to the people in the community is a way of being involved. The only question is, can I be involved or not involved – not that. It's can I be involved rightly. What is the right way to be involved and what are the wrong ways to be involved? There's one word for the right way to be involved in my community, and that's charity, which means to say that I am to some extent vulnerable with regard to these people. If I'm seriously involved with my brothers, it means to say that if one of my brothers is unhappy, I'm going to be to some extent unhappy. If he's really unhappy, and it's a real serious unhappiness, it's liable to be to some extent a distraction. All right, this is necessary. It is part of this business of having one's roots in one's community. He also says about the branches, but I guess we'll take that next time.

5

Let's get down to St. Anselm and his stability thing and get a few good points on this too. Where we left off last time was this idea you had to have roots, and then you also had to have branches. The monk is like a tree planted in the soil of his monastery. He's got to take root in his monastery, and the roots he has to have in the monastery are the roots of love. He's got to love his monastic community, and to take roots in it like that. What do roots do? Roots hold you in the ground, and roots nourish you – roots in this sense. If you look at stability purely from a juridical point of view, it doesn't get very far, but if you look at it from the point of view of having roots of love in your community, you find that you are involved with the people in your community, not just with the buildings or with the landscape or something like that – although that's important too – but over a period of years what happens? What is the history of an individual and the history of a community? It's made up of its decisions and as we live together over a period of years, we make crucial decisions that involve not only ourselves personally but also others and we are woven together by these decisions. If you ever dig around under a tree in the woods out there where you've got a whole bunch of small trees living together under a big tree or something like that, then you sort of dig in there, you see to what extent their roots are all tangled up together, and you don't know which root is which, and if you go in there and you dig out one of those trees, you're liable to tear out the roots of five or six other smaller ones, because the roots are all tied up together. Sometimes it'll happen that you dig out a tree and then you prune the roots of the others.

That can happen too, but this idea of being rooted together with one another by virtue of the decisions which we have made with one another – this is the heart of stability. The things that we've accepted and the things that we've determined to put up with and the things that we've determined to help one another get along with – this is the real root of stability, and the people who don't handle their stability properly one way or another haven't been able to make this kind of decision and get involved with people in this particular way. It takes a great deal of time.

Now there is also the question of branches. The branches have to grow. This isn't a problem of stability, but it's typical of St. Anselm. Let me read this chapter.[LXVIII] It's a fine chapter, an excellent chapter, on education in general and monastic education.

> On one occasion a certain abbot, who was considered to be a sufficiently religious man, was talking with St. Anselm about matters of monastic discipline, and among other things he said something about the boys brought up in the cloister, adding, "What, I ask you, is to be done with them? They are incorrigible ruffians. We never give over beating them day and night, and they only get worse and worse." Anselm replied with astonishment: "You never give over beating them? And what are they like when they grow up?" "Stupid brutes," to which Anselm retorted, "You have spent your energies in rearing them to no good purpose: from men you have reared beasts." "But what can we do about it," said the abbot. "We use every means to force them to get better, but without success." "You force them?" said Anselm. "Now tell me, my lord abbot, if you plant a tree-shoot in your garden, and straightway shut it in on every side so that it has no space to put out its branches, what kind of a tree will you have in after years when you let it out of its confinement?" "A useless one, certainly," said the abbot, "with its branches all twisted and knotted." "And whose fault would this be,

except your own for shutting it in so unnaturally? Without doubt, this is what you do with your boys. At their oblation they are planted in the garden of the Church, to grow and bring forth fruit for God. But you so terrify them and hem them in on all sides with threats and blows that they are utterly deprived of their liberty. And being thus injudiciously oppressed, they harbour and welcome and nurse within themselves evil and crooked thoughts like thorns, and cherish these thoughts so passionately that they doggedly reject everything which could minister to their correction. Hence, feeling no love or pity, good will or tenderness in your attitude toward them [this is very important], they have in future no faith in your goodness, but believe that in all your actions you are proceeding from hatred and malice against them. The deplorable result is that as they grow in body so their hatred increases, together with their apprehension of evil, and they are forward in all crookedness and vice. They have been brought up in no true charity towards anyone, so they regard everyone with suspicion and jealousy. But, in God's name, I would have you tell me why are you so incensed against them. Are they not human? Are they not flesh and blood like you? Would you like to have been treated as you treat them, and to have become what they are now? Consider this. You wish to form them in good habits by blows and chastisement alone. Have you ever seen a goldsmith form his leaves of gold or silver into a beautiful figure with blows alone? I think not. How then does he work? In order to mould his leaf into a suitable form he now presses it and strikes it gently with the tool, and now even more gently raises it with careful pressure and gives it shape. So, if you want your boys to be adorned with good habits, you too, besides the pressure of blows, must apply the encouragement and help

> of fatherly sympathy and gentleness." To which the abbot replied: "What encouragement? what help? We do all we can to force them into sober and manly habits." "Good," said Anselm, "just as bread and all kinds of solid food [he's always full of these comparisons he comes out with – there's a whole book called the *Comparisons* of St. Anselm[LXIX]] – just as bread and all kinds of solid food are good and wholesome to those that can digest them; but feed a suckling infant on such food, take away its milk, and he will strangle rather than be strengthened by his diet. The reason for this is too obvious to need explanation, but this is the lesson to remember: just as weak and strong bodies have each their own food appropriate to their condition, so weak and strong souls need to be fed according to their capacity …."[LXX]

This is just the *Rule*.[LXXI] Then he goes on like this, and finally the abbot says, "When he heard this, he was sorrowful, and he said, 'We have indeed wandered from the way of truth, and the light of discretion has not lighted our way.' And he fell on the ground at Anselm's feet confessing himself a miserable sinner, seeking pardon for the past, and promising emendment for the future."[LXXII]

This is a very fine indication of what Anselm understood about education. Of course this indirectly has something to do with the question of stability too, obviously. But the thing is that if we're going to have roots in the community of love, there has to be also trust there, and a person has to have enough confidence. One of the things that throws people with regard to stability is this sort of a standard approach, a feeling of: "Here I am in this place. I don't fit in here. Nobody loves me. Nobody likes me. I don't get along with anybody. Nobody gets along with me. What am I doing here anyway? I'm wasting my time in the place." That's not the way to look at it. Generally speaking, this is up to you. This is up to the person who's speaking. If a person comes to me and says, "Nobody loves me in this community," translate that into plain English and what does it mean? He doesn't love anybody in the community. That's the acceptable way of putting it. I can't go around saying, "I hate everybody in the community," but I could say, "Everybody in the community hates me." There's a big difference, because this way I'm giving myself a reason to start with. I've got myself whitewashed, and everything's fine, and then here I am treated unfairly, so now if it happens that I don't like anybody in the community, I'm in the clear. I've got a reason. They all hate me, but the point is that this is a two-sided thing. We're not in this kind of thing all by ourselves. Everybody has mixed feelings about everybody. The amount of love that's in the community is the amount of love that people want to put into the community. Of course up to a point it's up to the person and there are things that one can't control. There are providential events. There are all sorts of things. But we have to see that the love that we can put into our community is not something you're supposed to just press a button and it comes out of the stars or something. God has brought us together here because He knew what kind of people we were going to be, and He knew the kind of a situation we were going to get into, and the question of loving our community and loving the people in it is simply the question of corresponding with God's grace, with the historical, factual grace that He's given us in our vocation. This is what we have to live up to. It's not automatic. We have to be constantly measuring up to this. It's a grace and a challenge. It's a challenge which we can meet or not meet every day. If we're in the habit of meeting it, then we develop roots; if we're in the habit of not meeting the challenge, we don't have the roots, and then when the wind comes, we haven't got anything to stand on.

The background of Anselm's stuff on stability has a very interesting basis in a tract of his on *The Fall of the Devil*.[LXXIII] This is a very interesting correspondence, because he's concerned very much, as all the people of that time, concerned with how did Adam sin. How did the devil sin? Could they have avoided the sin? Were they free in sinning, or were they compelled to sin? Then it's tied up with predestination. Did God refuse them the grace, and that sort of thing. Without going into all the details, we could take some of these ideas some other time, but what the devil was supposed to do, says Anselm, what all the angels were supposed to do, what Adam was supposed to do, where they fell, was, strictly speaking, what was expected of them by God, was *stare in veritate*[LXXIV] – to stand in the truth. Adam and the devil failed in their stability, from a certain point of view. They did not stand in the truth. Now what does he mean by truth? This ties in with the Anselm idea of rectitude.[LXXV] Truth is not only just truth in the abstract and absolute truth, but the truth of each one's own life, and the basic truth that everybody has to stand in isn't just general truth but it's the particular truth of our own life, our own history and our own vocation. Of course the basic truth for all beings outside of God, the first truth that they have to stand in, is that they're creatures. Anselm develops this to some extent. The sin of Adam and the sin of the devil were both, from a certain point of view, a refusal to stand in the truth that they were creatures. They willed to act as God. The temptation of Eve was: "You shall be as gods,"[LXXVI] and of course he analyzes this and explains that what this sin of attempting to be like God was, was simply putting their own will in a position of absolute primacy, so that if there's something that they want, the fact that they want it comes first, and everything else follows from that. Everything else has to fit with the fact that they want such and such a thing.

But it's much more subtle than that. It isn't just a question that these were self-willed beings, and so forth. He goes into the question of how did they not stand in the truth. Were they capable of standing in the truth? How do you stand in the truth? You stand in the truth by using your freedom, which is willing the truth for its own sake – because it's true. Your freedom conforms you to the truth because it's true. This is the way it is. This is the way I want it because this is the way it is. That sounds very obvious and very silly and so forth, but if you go right down into it, you find that that's where all sin starts. All sin starts with a refusal to accept the way things are, the way things are in some way or other. All sin is a refusal to accept things as they are and an insistence on having them other than they are. Of course things are bound to change, but taking the initiative in changing them, rather than let God change them. Why the devil didn't stand in the truth wasn't that he didn't have the grace to stand. He had the grace to stand in the truth and he had the will to stand in the truth and his will was changed, but only by himself. What he did then was, instead of willing the truth, he willed something else: "*voluit aliud.*"[LXXVII] He wanted something else and what was this something else? It was "*aliud ad quod crescere potuerit*"[LXXVIII] –

"something else to which he could grow." This is the thing that's very interesting that Anselm brings in: that the devil and Eve both fell not by willing something that they weren't supposed to have, but by willing something that they weren't supposed to have at that moment.[LXXIX] He emphasizes the fact that they willed – because Anselm presupposes that they're supposed to be like gods. Both the devil and Adam and Eve were supposed to have this godlikeness. They willed it simply in a way that God didn't will it. That's the thing that's extremely interesting. This ties in with his treatment of stability, as we'll see in a minute. Simply willing it because he willed it, rather than because God willed it, the devil got out of the order of truth, and Eve got out of the order of truth, whereas if he had simply waited, he would have got what he wanted. It is something to which he would have grown anyway. If he had allowed God to lead him, he would have received it anyway. Where he fell was in wanting to have it by his own power, wanting to have by his own power something that God alone could give.

Now flash back to the question of stability. This is exactly how Anselm treats the whole problem of stability. He says you have a temptation against stability. This presents itself. This is the fervent monk – he's looking for a better life. A better life is something that he could have – *ad quod crescere potest*. It is something to which he can grow, so therefore it's not totally a delusion. He can have a better life. Anybody can have a better life, but the point is that instead of a better life in the way that God wills it, which we don't know, he determines that it's going to be a better life in this particular way – namely by leaving here and going some other place. What does Anselm say about this? How should this be met? He goes at it very logically. This temptation for the greater good is either true or it's false. Either you're right or you're wrong – that covers everything. Supposing that you're wrong, supposing that you're not called to a greater good, then the answer is quite simple: put the whole thing aside, because it's dangerous to try to go to something that you're not called to. Supposing that you are called to it, maybe you have to examine whether this is the time for it or not, and whether this is the way for it or not. If there is no strong evidence that this is the time and this is the way, you have to put aside too, and you have to tell yourself, "Either I don't deserve this better good yet, or if I will trust in God He will give it to me later." Well I think that's a pretty rational sort of approach. He covers the whole field, and he puts a person in a position where what's the final option on that? Is this a bad position to be in? Supposing the person comes to this conclusion, what should he really worry about? If he's worked it out this way, how does he stand? Is there anything wrong with this position, anything the matter with it, except that he can't have what he wants right now? What he is doing is putting the whole thing completely in the hands of God. He is saying, "Okay, either I'm right or I'm wrong. If I'm wrong, I'll be a fool to make a move, because if I make a move, what's going to happen is that the whole thing's going to collapse. If I'm right, the question arises, is it right to do this thing now." We presume the case that Anselm has set up is that we shouldn't do it now or we don't know where to go, or we don't know what to do. It's not clear, so what the person has to say is: "Okay, if I've put myself completely in God's hands, He knows what He's going to do. If He wants something better for me, when I am ready for it I will get it, and if I'm not going to be ready for it, I'll never get it."

Here's where the problem of stability usually comes in. Supposing somebody wants this better life and he gets it down to this particular point. You see what happens to him when he makes the wrong judgment. What's the judgment that he makes? What does he say? He says, "I should go because I *am* ready and I *am* worthy." The position he puts himself in is of being the only one that thinks this. He puts himself in the position of maintaining his readiness and his worthiness against the world, against everybody else. Theoretically you could say a man may be right – he may be so right he should say this. Maybe he should be Athanasius against the world[LXXX] and stand up against it and bowl everybody over. What's the answer to that? On the face of it, what does it look like? Does it look prudent? Prudence comes in here, doesn't it? What is at stake here? It isn't just a question of "Shall I be here or shall I be there?" The whole purpose of God in that man's life may be at stake. A man's entire vocation may be at stake. The thing you have to remember with this stability stuff with us is that it's not just a question of "Can I do this? Can I go from here to there?" Usually there's much more involved than that. Usually these stability questions are all-or-nothing questions, because if a person makes his move at the wrong time, if he makes a wrong move, there are real possibilities that the whole thing will collapse on him. How do you know this? You know this from experience. This is the way it goes. Watching the thing for twenty-two years, there are so many people that have done this on this basis of the greater good and so forth, and where are they today? They're walking the baby up and down in the middle of the night! It could be perhaps for those people that that was the greater good that God had in store for them, and that they didn't know how to choose for themselves, and He had to get them to it by devious ways. There may be something to that, but the point is, it's a kind of a silly way to do it. If you want to get married, why waste time in a Trappist monastery? Just go get married! But there have been plenty of people that have left here for the higher, the more contemplative, the more silent, and like I say – the fifth, the sixth, the seventh baby. Bear this in mind if the temptation arises.

God doesn't change, but we do, and God's will in our life to some extent does evolve in a way. There is no such thing as absolute inertia. We mustn't look at our life as a sort of inertia. It is staying with the will of God as it evolves within the particular field that He has offered to us to evolve in. We go along with God's will through the years that are coming. Now of course one of the things that's involved here too, one of the great problems in this question of stability – this is the one for the problem of stability that comes when you're about 45 (I'm now nearly fifty) – one of the ones that comes when you're in middle life (of course it's the same all through your life but especially in middle life) is the great question as to how willing you are to completely abandon your future into the hands of God, or how much you want to maintain control over your own future. This is one of the most crucial trials in the life of a monk, because there comes a time in the life of a monk where he has to absolutely abandon control over his future. You know what Our Lord said to St. Peter: "When you were young you girt yourself up and you went where you wanted to go. When you're an old man, somebody else is going to gird you up and you're going to have to go where you don't want to go."[LXXXI] This is the sacrifice that is asked of a man in middle life, because in middle life everything starts to get away from you. You become decrepit – hair, teeth, all that sort of stuff. They chop little pieces out of you and so forth. (I saw the x-ray of this neck. You ought to see the seventh vertebra – it looks like somebody bit a chunk out of it!) As you go along, things get away from you. One of the things that a man in middle life wants to do, he wants to hang onto what's getting away from him. One of the things he wants to hang onto is control over his life, the ability to make a plan that's going to cover the rest of his life. You've got to give that up, but if you can suddenly tell yourself, "I'm getting out of here and I'm going to start all over again in another place," what you're doing is that you're planning your life again; you're taking your life out of God's hands and you're saying, "Hey, listen. I'm going to run this thing for the next twenty years. I'm going to start in on a new track, and I'm going to control it, so that it goes more the way I'd like to have it go." This is one of the things that a person has to give up. He's got to simply accept the fact that his life is going to be governed by God, and he's got to take it blindly, on faith, and for this he has to accept the fact that it's going to be a plan of love, and wherever you are in the life, this is the purpose of stability. Among other things in the monastic life is that you have to make that sacrifice somewhere along the line. If you can make it at solemn profession, fine; but if you just make your solemn profession as best you can, and then have to do the interior thing later, well do it whichever way you can.

Incidentally, before I go any further, there's a beautiful thing here on Socrates,[LXXXII] a tremendous thing on Socrates. Socrates is a very good man to read and study and to know about. Who was he? What did he do? What's this Socrates and why do we bring him in here? What's he got to do with stability? Fifth century BC (399), he drank the hemlock. He stayed in Athens – that was the thing. Socrates was a philosopher. He never wrote a book about anything. He just went around Athens talking to people. His great thing was to walk around the marketplace asking people questions and making them realize that the certitudes which they thought were certain were not certain. He got the whole of Athens realizing – this was the golden age of Athens, when everything was absolutely on top and Athens was the top place in the world, practically, and Socrates went around and got everybody to realize that all this wonderful situation that he had was something that they didn't know what it was all about, and the certitudes on which it was built were not certain, and that the thing that people had to do was to find the truth by questioning, and having found the truth by questioning, to stick to it, to adhere to it, with all the force of their will when they were convinced that it was the truth, and not to adhere with all the force of their will to any truth of which they were not convinced. This involved believing that there was such a thing as a truth that one could find out by questioning, and not a truth that was just handed down by somebody else. This is where he got in trouble. The Athenians felt that Socrates ought to just shut up and take the truth that was given out by the rulers of the people but Socrates also believed in Athens, and he believed that it was his job to be in Athens, and the time came when they said to Socrates, "Now look, Socrates, you are becoming a great nuisance in this town. You're going all around the town asking people if they're certain about all these things which are certain, and you know darn well that they're certain, and you're just being cussed about it. You've got all these people mixed up so that they're no longer certain, and we don't want this kind of thing. When we say something is certain we don't want it questioned. We want you just to shut up. So now Socrates, you're going to do one of the following things. You're going to either get out of Athens or you're going to take a drink of what we're going to give you in this cup, which is hemlock" – which was their way of executing an Athenian citizen. So Socrates said, "Well, I've lived all my life in Athens, and this is the place where I have obviously" – he didn't say it in these words – "where I have been called to be, and my life is a continuity which is rooted in this city," and he said, "it would be foolish for me at my age to go running around to these other cities, so consequently I will stay here and drink the hemlock."[LXXXIII] This made them all very mad, because they wanted to get rid of him; they didn't want to make him drink the hemlock.

The point that's interesting is what he says toward the end of this business, in the *Apology*. You remember that he was guided to some extent by this inner voice. He had his little spiritual voice, which would tell him when he was doing wrong. It never told him to do something positively, but when he was doing something that was wrong it told him not to do it. Now this is a very moving thing here, because it has to do with his stability in Athens. "This voice always forbids but never commands me to do anything I am going to do."[LXXXIV] The voice for example said

"No" whenever he thought of going into political life. During his trial, the voice was silent, and this he found strange and encouraging. He said, "Recently the divine faculty has constantly been opposing me even about trifles if I was going to make a slip or error in any matter; and now as you see there has come upon me that which may be thought the last and worst evil [the death sentence]. But the divine voice made no sign of opposition, either when I was leaving my house in the morning, or when I was on my way to the court, or when I was speaking … the customary sign would surely have opposed me had I been going to evil and not to good."[LXXXV] I think that's one of the most tremendous things that's ever been said – this idea that here was a man who felt that he was called to stick with Athens until he died at the place.

This is really something tremendous and I think it's something that we really ought to meditate on, because I think it's the deepest possible expression of what monastic stability is. You're called to the monastery not necessarily because you're going to be happy in the monastery, and not necessarily because you're going to do anything special in the monastery, but you're called to the monastery to really die in it – not to die in it in any particular way that you have planned, but to die in it according to God's plan. I'm not saying that the monastery is going to feed you some hemlock (although watch the coffee – that might have the same effect!) but you really have to see it in this light. It's not at all a question just of being here. If you look at it from this other point of view – "I've come to this place to be a mystic and I've been here ten years and I'm not a mystic so I've got a right to clear out and go some other place where I'm going to be a mystic" – this has got absolutely nothing to do with the whole shooting match. It's not the problem at all. What I've come here for is to give my life to God. When the moment comes when you're not able to give your life to God, then the question of changing stability becomes relevant and only then. That's the only time. If it becomes clear that you can no longer give your life to God in this place, then you not only may leave, you should leave, and you should leave as fast as possible, and if necessary, without permission, because it's absolutely clear. If it were absolutely clear that I couldn't in any sense give my life to God here, I would walk out immediately and gladly. But on the other hand, as long as it's not clear, and as long as there's no indication that this is not a place where you could give your life to God, then you have to stay.

We have put ourselves in the position of Socrates, where we don't move unless there is some definite certain thing that says, "You've got to do the other thing or you're doing wrong." If it is clear that a person is wrong in staying, then he shouldn't stay, but if it's not clear, then he should stay. It doesn't matter how confused it is. It doesn't matter how silly it is. He really should see that this is the only thing that makes any kind of sense out of our life. We're not here for anything else. If we don't see the meaning of it, that doesn't matter. That's not part of the contract – that we're supposed to see how it's working out. If we do, fine; but if we don't, it doesn't matter. We're not supposed to see the fruits because the basic thing that we're doing is that we're giving ourselves to God, and this is the way we do it. I think that's the real kernel of this St. Anselm thing, and you see it in Socrates and you see it everywhere. What does he finally say: "Let him patiently undergo the divine judgment. God will not defraud him of a just desire."[LXXXVI] You see, the greatest good in the life of Socrates was the fact that he laid down his life in the way that he did. Supposing he had said to himself, "It's a much greater good. Let's go to Corinth, a new city. Everything is booming there. We'll be able to start things over, start a new school of philosophy, and really make something go there"; or "Let's go to Sparta. That's a real tough place." Actually, if Socrates hadn't died the way he died, we probably wouldn't be paying nearly so much attention to what he said. His life would have much less meaning to us. We have to believe that by following God we are actually being led to the greatest good and we're being led to a good that we can't imagine, and we have to see it in that way, and we have to want this good that we can't see and we have to want it in such a way that we're going to be absolutely faithful to any indication of God's will that's going to lead us in that direction.

I. On June 2, 1963, Merton began his discussion of Pachomius in his Pre-Benedictine Monasticism conferences, and on June 23 (Gethsemani recording 57.4) he was focusing on the Egyptian monk's *Catechesis I* (see *Pre-Benedictine Monasticism* 81-82).

II. In his treatise *De Corpore et Sanguine Domini* (J. P. Migne, ed., *Patrologiae Cursus Completus, Series Latina* [*PL*], 221 vols. [Paris: Garnier, 1844-1865] vol. 150, cols. 407-42), Lanfranc affirmed the real presence of Christ in the Eucharist against the theories of Berengar of Tours. Merton is clearly relying on the discussion by David Knowles, *The Evolution of Medieval Thought* (New York: Vintage, 1962) 94-96 (c. 8: "The Revival of Dialectic: Berengar, Lanfranc and Anselm").

III. Here Merton is following Knowles, *Evolution* 79-92 (c. 7: "The Awakening of Western Europe").

IV. Knowles calls Gerbert "The first great name in the history of medieval thought" (*Evolution* 93).

V. See Knowles, *Evolution* 99: "There is nothing in Anselm's greatest work that derives from his own age or from his teacher; in this he is more original than Abelard or Aquinas.… It is his achievement to stand forth as absolutely great in an age when others were only feeling their way towards thought and expression."

VI. Daniel Walsh had taught philosophy at Columbia and had been the one who first brought the Trappists to Merton's attention (see *Seven Storey Mountain* 218-21, 259-65, 275-310). After retiring, Walsh moved to Kentucky, lived in the monastery guest house and at this time was teaching philosophy to the young monks and to nuns in formation at the nearby motherhouse of the Sisters of Loretto.

VII. See Merton's letters to the great French neo-scholastic philosopher in *Courage for Truth* (22-53).

VIII. Reading Étienne Gilson's *The Spirit of Mediaeval Philosophy* began the process of Merton's conversion in 1938 (see *Seven Storey Mountain* 271-75); Gilson had been Daniel Walsh's teacher (*Seven Storey Mountain* 220). Merton's October 1, 1962 letter to Gilson is included in *School of Charity* (148-49).

IX. *PL* 158, cols. 223A-248C; *S. Anselmi Cantuariensis Archiepiscopi Opera Omnia*, ed. F. S. Schmitt, OSB, 6 vols. (Edinburgh: Thomas Nelson, 1946-1961) 1.93-122.

X. One important source for Merton's discussion here is Knowles, *Evolution* 100-106.

XI. Psalm 13[14]:1.

XII. *Liber pro Insipiente* (*PL* 158, cols. 243A-248C) and Anselm's response: *Liber Apologeticus contra Gaunilonem* (*PL* 158, cols. 249A-260B).

XIII. There is no indication that Merton did return to this material on the following Saturday, June 29, for which no recording exists.

XIV. See Knowles, *Evolution* 99: "Among all the host of medieval philosophers and theologians perhaps only Aquinas and Bonaventure are in his company as thinkers who have put into currency, so to say, ideas which may again and again provoke controversy and meet with contradiction, but which cannot with impunity be despised, for they will again and again make their appeal to another generation in the future. In addition to this, Anselm, surpassing in this respect his two rivals of the later century, succeeded in putting into all his writings, and so in transmitting to us, that charm of personality, that supremely winning and compelling charm, which, as he himself tells us, none of his contemporaries could resist save through conscious hostility."

XV. *PL* 159, cols. 605A-708D.

XVI. *Proslogion* 1: "*Nam et hoc credo quia nisi credidero, non intelligam*" (*PL* 158, col. 227C) ("For I also believe that unless I believed, I would not understand").

XVII. "*Credo ut intelligam*" (*Proslogion* 1 [col. 227C]).

XVIII. July 16; for a biographical sketch of this third abbot of Cîteaux (c. 1156-1234), see *Valley of Wormwood* 262-77.

XIX. Anselm actually became archbishop in 1093 and died in 1109.

XX. *The Life of St. Anselm, Archbishop of Canterbury by Eadmer*, edited and translated with an Introduction by R. W. Southern (New York: Thomas Nelson, 1962).

XXI. Actually Alexander did not write stories about Anselm himself but passed on his reminiscences to Eadmer: see R. W. Southern, *St. Anselm and His Biographer: A Study of Monastic Life and Thought, 1059-c. 1130* (Cambridge: Cambridge University Press, 1963) 330: "But between Eadmer and those who were nearest to him in the friendship of Anselm there was an important distinction. His two rivals for Anselm's regard, the monks Baldwin and Alexander, saw miracles more frequently and more clearly than Eadmer was able to do. It is not a hazardous suggestion that if either of them had been writing Anselm's life there would have been many more, and more striking, miracles than Eadmer reports. Baldwin and Alexander both told him stories which were a good deal more bluntly miraculous than anything that Eadmer himself saw."

XXII. Southern, *St. Anselm and His Biographer* 331, which reads: "… gave him, of … which the eager credulity …"

XXIII. *PL* 66, cols. 125A-294C.

XXIV. *PL* 66, col. 146AC. See Merton's summary of this story from chapter 7 of the *Life*: "the famous rescue of St. Placid by St. Maur. St. Benedict sees the accident in {a} vision. St. Maur asks a blessing – then *runs*, and keeps on running, even over the water. St. Benedict attributes everything to the merit of obedience. St. Placid says he saw the Abbot's *melotes* (cowl?) over him" (*Rule of St. Benedict* 29).

XXV. These were the Pre-Benedictine Monasticism conferences, which ran from February 3, 1963 through August 15, 1965 (see *Pre-Benedictine*

Monasticism xvi-xvii, 359-62).

XXVI. *De Praecepto et Dispensatione* (*PL* 182, cots. 859D-894C): for Merton's discussion of this work see *Cistercian Fathers and Their Monastic Theology* lxiv-lxvii, xciii-xciv, 214-24, 405-12.

XXVII. C. 26: "*De Regno, et Villa, et Castello, et Dungeone*" (*PL* 159, cols. 647A-648B).

XXVIII. For Merton's discussion of this famous work, see *Introduction to Christian Mysticism* 229, 237-45, 249, 295-301, 303.

XXIX. The Albigensians were the heretical dualistic sect that was very popular especially in southern France in the twelfth and thirteenth centuries.

XXX. Col. 647C, which reads: "*conversationem ... angelorum*".

XXXI. C. 76: "*Similitudo inter Monachum et Potionem, et Abbatem et Medicum*" (*PL* 159, cols. 648B-649B).

XXXII. C. 81: "*Quod Monacho Prosit, si Aliquod Bonum Invitus Faciat*" ("What Happens to a Monk if He Does Something Good Unwillingly") (*PL* 159, cols. 652A-653B).

XXXIII. Col. 648C.

XXXIV. Col. 649B.

XXXV. C. 83: "*Similitudo inter Monachum Peccantem et Laicum*" ("Comparison between a Sinful Monk and a Sinful Layperson") (*PL* 159, cols. 654B-655B).

XXXVI. This is the "*Liber de Beatitudine Coelestis Patriae*," or (as it is entitled in Eadmer's own manuscript copy) the "*Scriptum Quoddam de Beatitudine Perennis Vitae*," originally preached by Anselm at Cluny, evidently without a written text, that Eadmer reconstructed from memory, apparently augmented with further material from other occasions, and sent to a monk of Cluny some time after it had been preached. It is printed in *PL* 159, cols. 587-606, found in another form under the name of Guigo the Carthusian in *PL* 184, cols. 353-64. See Southern's Appendix II in *St. Anselm and His Biographer* (362-64) for details of its various forms; see also chapter 14, "Les écrits spirituels des deux Guigues," in André Wilmart, OSB, *Auteurs Spirituels et Textes Dévots du Moyen Âge Latin: Études d'Histoire Littéraire* (Paris: Bloud et Gay. 1932) 248-59 for the history of its misattribution and its eventual recognition as Anselm's.

XXXVII. "And, coming down in detail to certain examples, all the beauty of the creatures, compared with the infinite beauty of God, is the height of deformity.... and all the grace and beauty of the creatures, compared with the grace of God, is the height of misery and of unattractiveness" (St. John of the Cross, *Ascent of Mount Carmel* 1.4.4 [*The Complete Works of Saint John of the Cross*, ed. and trans. E. Allison Peers, 3 vols. (Westminster, MD: Newman Press, 1949) 1.25-26]).

XXXVIII. Bede Griffiths, OSB, *The Golden String* (London: Harvill Press, 1954); this is the autobiography of the British convert and Benedictine monk who subsequently moved to India where he was a founder of a Christian ashram, Kurisumala, in Kerala. The title is taken from William Blake's famous lyric "To the Christians," often called "Jerusalem," that begins: "I give you the end of a golden string, / Only wind it into a ball, / It will lead you in at heaven's gate, / Built in Jerusalem's wall" (William Blake, *Complete Writings*, ed. Geoffrey Keynes [Oxford: Oxford University Press, 1966] 716). Griffiths visited Gethsemani the very next week after this conference (see *Dancing in the Water of Life* 13); he spoke to the novices on August 23 and to the whole monastic community on August 24 (Gethsemani recordings 66.2, 66.3).

XXXIX. For an overview of St. Maximus the Confessor and his contemplative doctrine, see the section entitled "Contemplation and the Cosmos" in *Introduction to Christian Mysticism* 121-36; Merton also wrote an article entitled "St. Maximus the Confessor on Non-Violence" (*Passion for Peace* 242-47), which first appeared in *The Catholic Worker* 32.1 (Sept. 1965) 1-2.

XL. Romanus Ginn, OCSO was a monk of Gethsemani who was sent to Rome for biblical studies and upon his return to the monastery after finishing his degree took over the teaching of scripture to the novices. He later lived for many years as a hermit, both in Latin America and on the grounds of the abbey.

XLI. Psalm 42[43]:4; this psalm was part of the "prayers at the foot of the altar" at the beginning of the Tridentine Mass.

XLII. See Psalm 149:5: "*exultabunt sancti in gloria; laudabunt in cubilibus suis*" ("The saints shall rejoice in glory: they shall be joyful in their beds").

XLIII. C. 2: "*De Velocitate*" (*PL* 159, cols. 589C-590A).

XLIV. Merton had discussed Jerome's monastic doctrine on December 1, the previous Sunday, as part of his Pre-Benedictine Monasticism conferences (Gethsemani recording 76.3) (see *Pre-Benedictine Monasticism* 159-69).

XLV. Merton had been discussing the vow of stability in his conferences on the monastic vows between August 21 and December 11, 1963 (see *Life of the Vows* 447-78).

XLVI. *S. Anselmi Opera Omnia* 3.144-48; also *PL* 158, cols. 1093A-1101D (1.29).

XLVII. In fact Merton records in his journal on January 18, 1964: "Unable to buy Schmitt's edition of Anselm. We have two volumes on interlibrary loan from West Baden – I have them until Easter" (*Dancing in the Water of Life* 64).

XLVIII. Eadmer, *Life of Anselm* 32, n. 1.

XLIX. *Cur Deus Homo* (*S. Anselmi Opera Omnia* 2.37-133; *PL* 158, cols. 339C-4328).

L. Merton is mistaken here: the title of the chapter in which Eadmer quotes much of this letter is "The letter which he wrote to Lanzo who was afterwards prior of St Pancras at Lewes" (*Life of Anselm* 32); as Southern points out in his note, Lanzo became the first prior of this English monastery in 1077, but the letter was probably written four or five years earlier. Eadmer himself writes: "I have taken care to insert in this work a letter of advice which he sent to a certain Lanzo when he had recently become a monk at Cluny" (32). In a later reference to this letter, Anselm himself said it was written "to Lanzo when he was a novice" (*"Lanzoni quando novitius erat"*) (*Ep.* 336 [Schmitt 3.103]).

LI. *S. Anselmi Opera Omnia* 3.147.78 [*PL* 158, col. 1101B], which reads: "*quieti mentis*."

LII. Merton had been discussing silence in a number of conferences at this time, both in his vows class and in other presentations: see Gethsemani recordings 86.4, 86.3, 89.1, 89.2 (December 4, 7, 11, 14, 1963).

LIII. The title of the letter in Schmitt is "*Ad Lanzonem novitium*" (3.144); again, Merton is misunderstanding the context of the letter – Lanzo could well have been a novice canonically at the time of its composition.

LIV. For St. Bernard's objections to the briefness of the novitiate at Cluny and Abbot Peter the Venerable's response, see *Cistercian Fathers and Their Monastic Theology* 134-35, 138, 160.

LV. *S. Anselmi Opera Omnia* 3.145.23 [*PL* 158, col. 1095B], which reads: "*tironem Christi*."

LVI. *S. Anselmi Opera Omnia* 3.145.26 [*PL* 158, col. 1095B].

LVII. *S. Anselmi Opera Omnia* 3.145.27 [*PL* 158, col. 1095C].

LVIII. See *Pre-Benedictine Monasticism* 163, which refers to *Epistola* 39.3 (*PL* 22, col. 468) among other sources.

LIX. *S. Anselmi Opera Omnia* 3.146.39 [*PL* 158, col. 1096A], which reads: "*infelix monachus*."

LX. *S. Anselmi Opera Omnia* 3.147.74-75 [*PL* 158, col. 1101B], which reads: "*ignarum monachum*."

LXI. *S. Anselmi Opera Omnia* 1.93 [*PL* 158, col. 227C and *passim*].

LXII. *S. Anselmi Opera Omnia* 3.147.76 [*PL* 158, col. 1101B].

LXIII. See Karl Barth, *Anselm: Fides Quaerens Intellectum: Anselm's Proof of the Existence of God in the Context of His Theological Scheme*, trans. Ian Robertson (London: SCM Press, 1960).

LXIV. See Merton's November 12, 1966 letter to Hans Urs von Balthasar: "I have just published an article on St. Anselm where I speak much of

Barth. It seems to me that, of all those who have been discussing Anselm these past few years, Barth and the Orthodox P. Evdokimov have appreciated him the best" (*School of Charity* 312); Merton is referring particularly to Paul Evdokimov, "L'Aspect Apophatique de l'Argument de Saint Anselme," *Spicilegium Beccense: Congrès International du IXe Centenaire de l'Arrivée d'Anselme au Bec* (Paris: J. Vrin, 1959) 233-58, which he will cite in his published articles on Anselm (see below, 120-21 and 139-40). On Barth and Merton see Rowan Williams, "'Not Being Serious': Thomas Merton and Karl Barth," in Rowan Williams, *A Silent Action: Engagements with Thomas Merton* (Louisville, KY: Fons Vitae, 2011) 69-82; and Ryan L. Scruggs, "Encountering the Word: A Dialogue between Merton and Barth on the Bible," *The Merton Seasonal* 33.3 (Fall 2008) 18-33. On Evdokimov and Merton see Rowan Williams, "Bread in the Wilderness: The Monastic Ideal in Thomas Merton and Paul Evdokimov" (*Silent Action* 21-39) and Michael Plekon, "God's Mercy and Foolish Love: Thomas Merton and Paul Evdokimov," *The Merton Annual* 30 (2017) 145-55.

LXV. I.e. his apparent starting point is a common definition or understanding of the term "God" as "that than which no greater can be conceived," which is agreed upon by both the believer and the non-believer. Merton makes a similar point in *Conjectures of a Guilty Bystander*: "Anselm does not start from a notion of God, though in the *Proslogion* he seems to. He starts from the direct awareness of God as the ground of being that cannot-not-be. To love God 'for His own sake' is therefore not just to love the notion of an omnipotent and all-good Father. It is, on the contrary, to love Him who is *without knowing really who or what He is* simply because He *is* and because His Being is existentially present to us as the ground of all existence, all knowledge, all freedom, and all love" (299). See also his distinction in his article "St. Anselm and His Argument" between a definition of God and the "Name" of God, which implies a relational dimension, as in the paradigmatic encounter of Exodus 3:14 where God reveals Himself as "the One who Is" (see below, page 110).

LXVI. *S. Anselmi Opera Omnia* 3.146.32-35 [*PL* 158, col. 1096A].

LXVII. *S. Anselmi Opera Omnia* 3.147.36-45 [*PL* 158, col. 1096AB].

LXVIII. Eadmer, *Life of Anselm* c. 22: "Concerning the discretion which he taught a certain abbot to practice towards boys who were being educated in his school" (37-39).

LXIX. Southern points out that in fact the passage from "Now tell me" through "crookedness and vice" and that from "Have you ever seen a goldsmith" through "sympathy and gentleness" are included with slight alterations as chapters 178 and 179 of *De Similitudinibus* (Eadmer, *Life of Anselm* 39, n. 1).

LXX. The original text reads: "On one occasion, then, a certain … with him about ….'Stupid brutes,' he said, 'To which …. about it,' said the abbot. 'We … force them? Now tell me … certainly, with its …. that all your actions proceed .... they now are? Now consider this .... with his tool, and now .... wholesome for those who ... and you will see him strangled rather than strengthened ....'"

LXXl. Actually chapter 30 of the *Rule* of St. Benedict, on dealing with faults of children, focuses on penalties of fasting and corporal punishment for infractions. But chapter 37, on care of the elderly and the young, stresses kindly consideration in making allowances for the needs of old and young. Chapter 64, on electing an abbot, emphasizes the need for prudence and love, and for avoiding extremes in disciplining members of the community, quoting James 2:13 that mercy should triumph over judgment (*The Rule of St. Benedict in Latin and English*, ed. and trans. Justin McCann, OSB [London: Burns, Oates, 1952] 80/81, 92/93, 146/147).

LXXII. The original text reads: "When the abbot heard this, he was sorrowful, and said ... emendment for the future."

LXXIII. *De Casu Diaboli* (*PL* 158, cols 325B-360C).

LXXIV. See *PL* 158, cols. 328A, 328B, 352B, 352C. 354C, 356C: the Master seeks to show the disciple why the devil's failure to stand or persevere in the truth is not due to God's refusal to provide him with the grace to do so, even though the good angel's perseverance is due to the gift of God. See also his journal entry for December 3, 1963: "I finished *De Casu Diaboli*. If a first reading can be said to finish such a book. Must go through it again. Especially for the difference between real freedom and mere determination. Perhaps the devil's sin was after all merely to substitute (arbitrarily and out of his own will) one for the other. Freedom is God's. He wills us to share it by *rectitudo* – willing according to the principle that is in reality itself – but the devil willed to have it regardless of *rectitudo* and reality, by his own arbitrary fiat. Hence he willed to be like God on his own (arbitrary and willful) terms – and by this he understood that the use of power in any way he chose was Godlikeness. Yet it was not. The devil's sin was then to put his own power against all contingencies and ultimately against all principles, too – so that the final word was open purely and simply to power. That this was not 'Godlikeness' is shown by the Incarnation and Redemption, works not of power but of justice and mercy" (*Dancing in the Water of Life* 42).

LXXV. In his journal entry for August 11, 1965, Merton links "Anselm's *rectitudo* [with] *stare in veritate*" and identifies them with "seeking nothing but to do God's will in everything, to please Him alone, to be perfectly united to Him in love by the renunciation of our own will" (*Dancing in the Water of Life* 279). See also his discussion of *rectitudo* in *Conjectures of a Guilty Bystander*: "For St. Anselm *rectitudo* is not merely the 'uprightness' of a will that takes a self-complacent pleasure in its own moral exercise knowing that it is 'right' and is 'doing its duty.' *Rectitudo* is in fact the right and authentic use of freedom: and this means spontaneous love of God for His own sake....

[T]he Anselmian *rectitudo* ... is really a much more existentialist concept than one would imagine (it corresponds to 'authenticity')."

LXXVI. Genesis 3:5.

LXXVII. "*Sed quaero quid aliud voluit, quam quod habebat*" (c. 4 [*PL* 158, col. 332D]) ("I seek what it was that he willed other than what he had").

LXXVIII. C. 6 (*PL* 158, col. 334D, which reads: "*aliquid ad quod crescere potuerunt*").

LXXIX. See c. 4: "*Voluit igitur aliquid quod non habebat, nec tunc velle debebat, sicut Eva similis voluit esse diis prius quam Deus hoc vellet.... At cum hoc voluit, quod Deus illum velle nolebat, voluit inordinate similis esse Deo.... Non solum autem voluit esse aequalis Deo, quia praesumpsit habere propriam voluntatem; sed etiam maior voluit esse, volendo quod Deus illum velle nolebat, quoniam voluntatem suam supra voluntatem Dei posuit*" (*PL* 158, cols. 332C-333C) ("Therefore he willed something that he did not have, and that he should not will at that time, just as Eve willed to be like gods before God willed this.... But when he willed this, because God did not wish him to will it, he willed to be like God in an inordinate way. Not only did he will to be equal to God, because he presumed to have an autonomous will; but he even willed to be greater than God, by willing what God did not will him to will, because he placed his own will above the will of God").

LXXX. St. Athanasius seemed to be standing alone in defending the Nicene doctrine of the Son as consubstantial (*homoousios*) with the Father against Arian subordinationism.

LXXXI. John 21:18.

LXXXII. Karl Jaspers, *The Great Philosophers*, trans. Ralph Manheim (New York: Harcourt, Brace & World, 1962) 15-31.

LXXXIII. "Socrates, when offered the choice between exile and death, chooses death: 'A fine life that would be for me at my age, to leave my country and wander from one city to another for the rest of my days'" (Jaspers 19).

LXXXIV. Jaspers 20.

LXXXV. Jaspers 21.

LXXXVI. "*Si autem vere meliora illis quae in promptu sunt nondum meritus optat, patienter toleret divinum iudicium, quod ulli aliquid iniuste non denegat*" (*S. Anselmi Opera Omnia* 3.147.62-64 [*PL* 158, cols. 1101A]) ("If, however, he truly hopes for better things than those which are presently his, but which are not yet merited, let him patiently undergo the divine judgment, because God will not defraud him of a just desire").

St. Anselm and His Argument

Though Merton's article on the ontological argument was the second of his two scholarly studies of St. Anselm to be published, it was the first to be written. On July 5, 1963, less than two weeks after he had presented his first conference on Anselm to the novices, he notes in his journal: "I finished my article on St. Anselm and the ontological argument" (*Turning Toward the World* 334). While it seems clear that this version of the article underwent further development in the coming months, as it incorporates material on Karl Barth's discussion of the argument that Merton was reading while in the hospital in mid-September (*Dancing in the Water of Life* 17), as well as on R. W. Southern's edition of Eadmer's *Life of Anselm* that he comments on appreciatively in a journal entry for November 5 (*Dancing in the Water of Life* 31, included in revised form in *Conjectures of a Guilty Bystander* 313-14), much of the material on the personality of Anselm, on the eleventh-century monastic background of the argument and on its basis in Anselm's profoundly spiritual intuition of absolute Being bears a close resemblance to his presentation to the novices, though on a much more intellectually sophisticated level. It is clear that Merton has done his homework here, investigating and evaluating the argument itself, the milieu in which it arose, and the controversy that it prompted both in its own time and subsequently. Merton draws on and engages with a wide variety of thinkers in the course of his discussion of the true methodology of this "proof," emphasizing that Anselm's dialectic takes place in the context of faith, and agreeing with Barth that "The designation of God as 'that than which no greater can be conceived' is not a definition but a 'Name' in the Old Testament sense of a presence and epiphany of God Revealed and Revealing. It designates Him as a hidden and transcendent One who is beyond all concepts. Yet He can nevertheless be 'reached' by a necessary conclusion of reason, which confirms and expresses the certitude contained in the 'Name' that reveals Him." He endorses David Knowles' position "that the ontological argument has 'no apologetic design,'" and considers Southern's statement in his edition of Eadmer's *Life* that Anselm's biographer "evidently did not look on the work primarily as a proof of the *existence* of God but as a proof that the attributes of God are such as the Christian faith holds them to be" as "a much more accurate exposition of Anselm's thought" than Southern's tendency in his own biography to consider the argument "both as a meditation for the believer and as a proof for the unbeliever." He also has recourse to the massive collection *Spicilegium Beccense*, proceedings of a conference held to commemorate the ninth centenary of the arrival of Anselm at the Monastery of Bec, highlighting in particular the discussion of the apophatic element of Anselm's approach in the argument as presented by Paul Evdokimov, the exiled Orthodox theologian whose religious outlook especially resonated with Merton. As Merton himself expresses this perspective later in his essay: "the very fact that any concept at all exists, even in the mind, is a witness to the being of that supreme self-existing Nature beyond the reach of concepts, and by which all beings and even mental acts, have existence." His own evaluation of the argument, which goes a long way to explain his attraction not only to Anselm as a person but to his basic orientation, may be summed up in his statement that "It was Anselm's mission to show that any thought that conceives God as 'an existence' on a par with 'other existences' is actually conceiving Him as a non-being. Either He alone is, in which case no other 'existence' can be compared with His being *quo major cogitari nequit*, or else He does not exist and in that case nothing has any meaning." The issue in Merton's view is anything but theoretical or merely abstract: "In raising the question of God's being and existence, Anselm is raising the question of *existence itself* in order to find it saturated with religious and spiritual meaning." Sometime before the end of the year, Merton had evidently sent the article to *The American Benedictine Review*, as he writes to Killian McDonnell, OSB on December 20: "I have read a little Barth this year and like him very much indeed. You will, I hope, see an article of mine on Anselm in the ABR, which deals with Barth's study among other things" (*School of Charity* 189-90). Periodically the article is mentioned in correspondence as forthcoming: on July 3, 1964 Merton writes to Hans Urs von Balthasar: "I am very fond of your neighbor Karl Barth and have written on his book on Anselm (which is wonderful I think). I mean to send him the essay when it gets printed" (*School of Charity* 219); almost a year later, on June 2, 1965, he writes to the British scholar Nora Chadwick: "I have done a little work on St. Anselm lately … I am quite fond of him too. I have a long essay on his 'argument' coming out. I think it is not appreciated" (*School of Charity* 283). It was, however, not until another year had passed that the article finally appeared: "St. Anselm and His Argument," *American Benedictine Review* 17 (June 1966) 238-62.

The indisputable importance of St. Anselm has long been acknowledged by historians of Christian thought, and his "ontological argument," whether one agrees with it or not (perhaps better, whether or not one *understands* it), must always be recognized as one of the great landmarks in western thought.[1] Unfortunately the fact that philosophical manuals have been in the habit of summarily dismissing this argument as "invalid" has meant that only a minority of students have gained access to the profoundly religious intelligence of this Doctor of the Church.

It cannot be said that the full scope of Anselm's argument is appreciated until Anselm himself is really known in all his wholeness. He certainly cannot be said to be known to those who are acquainted only with one or two theses from the *Monologion* and the *Proslogion*, or even his great theological exposition of the Redemption in the *Cur Deus Homo*. His other dialogues – for instance, the *De Veritate* or the *De Casu Diaboli*, even the *De Grammatico*[1] – must also be read, studied and meditated. Nor is it sufficient to complete this acquaintance by excursions into his meditations and meditative prayers, or into his numerous letters.

It is essential to see Anselm in the monastic and pre-scholastic background of the eleventh century. But one must not make the fatal mistake of regarding him simply as a "pre-scholastic." One must realize his remarkable creative contribution to the age of William the Conqueror, St. Gregory VII, St. Peter Damian, the age of the great Eucharistic controversies which accompanied the re-awakening of dialectic and served as prelude to the rediscovery of the complete *Organon* of Aristotle. Yet we must also see to what extent he transcends his age and speaks to our own. He has frequently been recognized as a genius without equal between Augustine and Aquinas. He is, in point of fact, one of the noblest and most original of Christian thinkers.

1. This review article is occasioned by the appearance of two important books: Dom David Knowles, *The Evolution of Medieval Thought* (Baltimore, 1962) and R. W. Southern, *St. Anselm and His Biographer* (Cambridge, 1963); see also Karl Barth's *Fides Quaerens Intellectum*, the English Edition of which appeared in 1960 (London and Richmond, Va.). Constant reference will also be made to the remarkable collection of conferences given at Bec in 1959 and published as the *Spicilegium Beccense*, Vol. I (Abbaye du Bec and Librairie Vrin, Paris, 1959).

In the twentieth century, when Anselm has been to a great extent taken for granted by Catholics, a powerful stimulus to the study of his thought was given by Karl Barth in a book on "the Argument" which continues to be much discussed and which amounts to a real rediscovery of the profound religious dimensions of Anselm's thought.[2] He has also been appreciated by modern philosophers as various as Bertrand Russell and Maurice Blondel, Louis Lavelle[3] and Maurice Nédoncelle.[4]

Anselm is not only a thinker. He played an important and active part in the history of his time. It is important to know him as Abbot of Bec, that brilliant center of learning created in Normandy by Lanfranc. And he was no ordinary Abbot. David Knowles has said of him that he was "perhaps the nearest approach to the ideal abbot that the Benedictines ever saw."[5] It is important also

---

2. Karl Barth, *Fides Quaerens Intellectum, Anselms Beweis der Existenz Gottes* (Munich, 1931). French translation, *La Preuve de l'Existence de Dieu* by Jean Carrère appeared at Neuchâtel and Paris (published by Delachaux et Niestlé, 1958). English translation by Ian W. Robertson, *Anselm: Fides Quaerens Intellectum* (Richmond, Va., 1960). On Karl Barth's study of Anselm see also Henri Bouillard, "La Preuve de l'existence de Dieu dans le 'Proslogion' et son Interprétation par Karl Barth" in *Spicilegium Beccense*, pp. 191-207. Reference may likewise be made to H. Bouillard's monumental study of *Karl Barth*, Paris, 1957, Vol. I. pp. 144-147; vol. III. pp. 143-173. Barth's study of Anselm is "the book that Barth declared that he wrote with the greatest love." It is "the key to Barth's *Dogmatik*." Bouillard concludes: "The Barthian interpretation of the theological program of St. Anselm is one of the most profound that can be read today" (Vol. I., p. 147).
3. See A. Forest, "Argument de S. Anselme et philosophie réflexive" in *Spicilegium Beccense*, pp. 273-294.
4. M. Nédoncelle, "La Notion de Personne dans l'Oeuvre de S. Anselme," *ibid.*, pp. 31-43.
5. *Evolution of Medieval Thought*, p. 347.[II] It would be interesting to know exactly what Knowles meant by this. As Archbishop of Canterbury, Anselm was Abbot of the Cathedral monastery and was absent for many years in exile, in which he took care of the community by letter. His policy was to leave the monks the greatest amount of autonomy so that they could manage their own affairs. In general St. Anselm was an extremely understanding and sympathetic father and teacher, solicitous for the genuine growth of the minds entrusted to him by God, generously endowed with patience and empathy, much more concerned with souls than with material administration. Southern says of him, "On no issue is he more remote from his own age than in his opposition to the insensate

to know Anselm the Archbishop, sent to Canterbury to succeed Lanfranc and to carry on the work of Norman "stabilization" after the conquest of England. His conflicts with the Norman kings over the rights of the Church give us important insights into his theology.

With all this it is essential to encounter the warmth and originality of Anselm's mind as it was manifested in his "table talk" and informal conferences among the monks of Canterbury, Bec and Cluny. All this is recorded not only in his letters and his life but in the writings and compilations of disciples such as his biographer Eadmer, Alexander of Canterbury, and the anonymous redactor of Anselm's *Similitudines* (which we might almost dare to translate as "parables").

Anselm's Personality

What we meet in Anselm is not only a "mind" and not only an "achievement." Still less do we run into a mere "system" of thought. Rather we meet in him the fullness of a totally integrated and extraordinary person, gifted in every possible way, and manifesting his gifts in what has been called the "Anselmian experience." This is of course not reducible to one flash of light; the thought of Anselm, and the experience in which it was incarnate, were the fruits of a lifetime of monastic study, contemplation and action. Without this life and this experience, the Middle Ages would not have been quite what they were, and Christian civilization, indeed the whole development of western thought, would have been less brilliant, less spiritual and less profound. Hence David Knowles has said of Anselm: "Like Bernard in the next generation, and like Theresa and John of the Cross in a later epoch, (he) has a significance in the history of the Church quite apart from his actions and achievements in his own age; he remains in perpetuity a living doctor from whom intelligence and spirit draw light and warmth."[6]

---

brutality with which the monastic authorities – not doubting their imitation of the rest of the world in this – treated the children under their care."

6. *Monastic Order in England*, p. 92.[III]

In St. Anselm we can admire all that was best and greatest in Medieval Christendom: that extraordinary break-through of culture, philosophy, and mysticism, transcending all national boundaries and bringing into being a Catholic elite of the intelligence and a genuinely Catholic civilization which doubtless must not be idealized, but which was nevertheless a considerable achievement.

In St. Anselm we must above all recognize the extraordinary *unity* that raises his thought and experience above the conventional divisions between "mystical and dogmatic," "philosophical and theological," or "active and contemplative." Indeed, we will find Anselm's peculiarly Catholic genius for unity endowed him with a spirit that in our times, would be called in the highest degree "ecumenical." That this should be true of a contemporary of Gregory VII and of the first Crusade is certainly something that should make us wary of clichés and generalizations about the Middle Ages.

God, the Unique Being

The Anselmian experience was first of all completely personal, and yet it was of a kind to galvanize the intellectual world of his time, which had been prepared for it by the previous "experience" of the great Augustine. Anselm, whom John of Salisbury called the "lesser Augustine" (*Augustinus minor*),[IV] rediscovered the truth that man, when he is able to recover a sufficient sense of who he really is, finds himself confronted with the inexpressible reality of a God whom he cannot comprehend and yet cannot ignore. This apophatic sense of "presence" and of transcendent being was not without obscure torment, as also it was not without moments of joy beyond articulation: but it made impossible a comfortable and narcissistic kind of contemplation that could be content with glossing the allegories and etymologies of the minor western Fathers. It was also incompatible with the religious banality of those whose thought is capable of equating "the existence of God" with any other existence, as if God were merely one of many existing beings, part of a series of causes and effects. Such thought feels no such passionate need as Anselm's to understand the unique necessity of that Being "than whom no greater can be conceived." It is in reality unconcerned with the divine Being except as a convenient concept serving as a cornerstone for a structure of other such concepts.

It was Anselm's mission to show that any thought that conceives God as "an existence" on a par with "other existences" is actually conceiving Him as a non-being. Either He alone is, in which case no other "existence" can be compared with His being *quo maius cogitari nequit*,[V] or else He does not exist and in that case nothing has any meaning. If God is merely an existent who may or may not *be*, then there is no point in even speaking of Him, for concepts of Him cease to have any serious content. The real import of Anselm's argument is, as Barth saw, that it is aimed not against the unbeliever only, but against the unbelief of believers whose God is only a concept and not a transcendent, revealed and intimately personal reality. The tension generated by the need to find reasons for what was beyond reason produced Anselm's dialectical meditation on the *ratio fidei*, the "quest of faith for understanding"[VI] by which the Abbot of Bec heralded the awakening of Scholastic and critical investigation. But there is much more in his thought than this. In actual fact, it is the *ontology* and the *theology* of Anselm's thought that is important, and not its dialectic.

In raising the question of God's being and existence, Anselm is raising the question of *existence itself* in order to find it saturated with religious and spiritual meaning. The "intelligibility" which Anselm seeks in his meditation on being is by no means merely logical. On the contrary, the domain of mere logic, of pure reason, is the domain of the "*insipiens*" who says that God is not. The light of understanding which shines through being is an epiphany of the God who reveals Himself as the Source of all the intelligibility in all the being created by Him.

The Dialectical Pursuit of Truth

Anselm's enthusiasm for the dialectical pursuit of truth was not restricted to the privacy of his own cell. He was a magnificent educator, and "Few in the whole history of education can have equaled him as a teacher whose influence covered every activity of mind and will, and for whom his pupils never failed to feel a love which was greater even than their admiration."[7] Orderic Vital called Bec, under Anselm, "a community in which all the monks were philosophers."[VII]

Yet it can never be said that Anselm was less of a monk, or that his contemplation was less monastic, indeed less mystical, than that of St. Bernard. The devout meditations of Anselm are so much in the monastic vein of the time (following Augustine's Soliloquies) that a great proportion of the meditations assigned to Anselm in Migne are in fact by others of his contemporaries, including such disciples as the monks Ralph and Elmer of Canterbury. Dom Wilmart,[VIII] forty years ago, devoted many painstaking articles in the *Revue Bénédictine* to unravelling the complex threads of authorship and identification running through this collection. Out of seventy-four prayers, twenty-one meditations, and sixteen homilies attributed to Anselm, Dom Wilmart finally concluded that only nineteen prayers and three meditations were genuine. However, it is not the intense, fervent, and supple rhetoric of these impassioned meditations that marks Anselm as a monk. This abundance of fervent affections makes him at best a child of his own time and of Augustine. We must rather say that Anselm is often most a monk where some monks might be inclined to think of him as least monastic: that is to say in his moments of greatest dialectical originality. Anselm the pre-Scholastic and Anselm the monk are not to be divided.

The later debates between different Orders of monks and between different schools of theology accentuated divisions which never existed at all in one like Anselm. It is true that later on, in the decadence of Scholasticism, a dry and cerebral theology was the enemy of mysticism and spiritual elevation. It is equally true that a decadent and sentimental spirituality drove men to technical theology in search of intellectual substance. But in Anselm there is no divorce between intelligence and mysticism. They are one and the same thing. Intelligence springs from mystical intuition and seeks to deepen its religious meaning in an act of homage to the truth. For Anselm reason serves adoration, and is not mere logic-chopping. The "argument for the existence of God" is itself an act of worship that takes place in the presence of God

7. *Ibid.*, p. 97.

who reveals Himself to the contemplative as the One beyond all comparison, whose Being is absolutely necessary. Hence the monk would have no valid reason to view with suspicion the dialectical intuitions with which Anselm struggled during Matins and which resulted in "the argument."

Monastic Spirituality

The *Proslogion* is a monastic meditation born of a profoundly monastic experience. The mind of Anselm was, in fact, entirely monastic because his heart was entirely so. Few saints can give proof of a purer, deeper, simpler and more complete love for the monastic life and for their own cenobitic family than Anselm. If, when he set about writing the *Monologion* at the request of his own monks, as an example of meditation (*exemplum meditandi*[IX]) he deliberately excluded all "arguments from Scripture" and "from the Fathers" in order to clarify the truth of faith by the investigation of reason, he was not, as one might suppose, departing from monastic tradition and dealing the spirit of monastic prayer a deadly blow. Whatever may have been the effects of later dialectical thought, such as that of Abelard which did, we must confess, have a distinct flavor of rationalism, we have to recognize above all that Anselm's thought is steeped in faith, and that his thought, even when he is most absorbed in dialectic, is profoundly biblical and patristic. The Prologue of the *Monologion* reminds us that there is nothing in Anselm's theodicy that cannot find support in Augustine, and what is the "ontological argument" of the *Proslogion* if not a meditation on the "I am who am" of Exodus 3:14? This biblical text is the foundation of all Christian theodicy and indeed the starting point of Scholastic metaphysics.

However, Anselm's insistence on preceding *sola ratione* is not merely justified by a general background of scriptural and traditional suppositions. The paradox is that in Anselm this mode of meditation is itself completely religious, and is by no means a rationalistic method inserted by force into a traditionally religious context. If anyone would be expected to protest against a supposed "rationalism" in Anselm, it would be Karl Barth. And yet it is precisely Barth who has most forcefully insisted that Anselm's "*intellectus*" is a spiritual understanding of the "inner

Text" of the Bible, and indeed a *more validly theological penetration* of Biblical revelation than that of the typologists and allegorists who had so far arrogated to themselves a kind of religious and mystical monopoly on theological investigation. Anselm's thought is not a mere *lectio* of the biblical text, but an *intellectus* (*intus legere*) of the inner theological content of revelation or in Barth's words, the apprehension "of sanctifying truth in all its fullness." Anselm is not content to "recite articles of faith" with a quotation of chapter and verse, he seeks to understand the *ratio fidei*, and this ratio is not mere logical reasoning but theological and ontological truth, it is the *ratio veritatis* revealed in the Incarnate Word.

Contribution to Monastic Theology

It would therefore be not only superficial but actually false to assume that because Anselm substituted dialectical speculation for allegorical and literary typology he was departing from monastic tradition. Certainly there is a rich mine of material in the marvelous literature inspired by the Origenist and Alexandrian sources.[8] There is also an immense value in the ascetical and psychological reflections handed down by the followers of Augustine, Cassian, and Gregory the Great. But we must not on that account exclude the totally new and original contribution made by Anselm to monastic theology by his dialectical quest for objective theological truth in the *ratio fidei*.

Monastic writers are not bound to restrict themselves to one very narrowly defined sphere of thought which must not only be "purely spiritual" but which must moreover conform to standards

8. H. De Lubac, in his Essay, "Sur le Chapitre XIV du Proslogion" in *Spicilegium Beccense*, pp. 294-312, exaggerates what he calls the spiritual "frustration" (*échec*) of Anselm's *ratio fidei*. He perhaps misinterprets the Anselmian rhetoric of aspirations and desire as representing a kind of "fracture" between "extreme rationality" and "spiritual dissatisfaction." He then proceeds to contrast the "modern" dissociation of theology and spirituality (of which he accuses Anselm of being an originator) and the unity of "spiritual intelligence" found in Origen. One may excuse De Lubac as a professional Origenist for this failure to understand the real genius of St. Anselm. Karl Barth has better appreciated the religious and spiritual unity of Anselm's thought.

of spirituality set by the sixth and twelfth century. Monastic spirituality is not a pure withdrawal into the past or a resolute refusal to give any attention to anything later than 1153.[X] The Bible, the liturgy, and the Fathers are, by all means, absolutely essential for the monastic life of contemplation. But the monk who enters by these means into the mystery of Christ should learn something more than a knack of repeating late patristic allegories and applying them, somewhat arbitrarily, to the ups and downs of the ascetic life. He should rather, encounter the life-giving and creative Spirit who, in full continuity with the "old," is able to "make all things new" and indeed to fuse the old and the new in an original and entirely creative unity.

This was what St. Anselm did. His theology was at once traditional and original: conservative without being archaic, creative without rash innovation. It was neither his conservatism that made him a monk, nor his originality, but the fusion of both in the ardor of prayer and fidelity to the Holy Spirit in the earnest quest for truth. So Gilson says of him: "The conflict which arose (in the eleventh century) between the defenders of a strictly monastic ideal of Christian life and those of a wise use of secular culture found its first satisfactory solution between the walls of a monastery, in the writings of St. Anselm of Canterbury."[9] Such solutions are a proof of the vitality of monasticism, and where they cease to be possible, monasticism, however well organized, is a body without a soul.

New Study of St. Anselm

We are now in a position to appreciate R. W. Southern's admirable new study of *St. Anselm and His Biographer*. To say this book "fills a need" is to put it mildly. It is the best and most authoritative biography of St. Anselm in English or any other language.

---

9. Remarking on the contrast between the splendor of the architecture and liturgical art encouraged at Canterbury by Anselm, and the "intimacy" of his personal meditations, Southern says, "There is of course no formal contradiction here; but the difference illustrates Anselm's poise between the old and the new, between Cluny and Citeaux. It is not the poise of compromise, but of standing where extremes meet, and of embracing both" (*op. cit.*, p. 261).

Such a book is essential, as it gives a proper perspective to all the various and controversial studies of diverse aspects of Anselm's thought. Besides, it rescues Anselm from the inevitable distortion that must follow when his thought is seen through the thought and experience of so many powerful modern minds. Our view of Anselm can easily become purely Barthian, Gilsonian or Blondelian if we are not kept in contact with the *person* of the second abbot of Bec himself.

R. W. Southern, who is professor of history at Oxford, examines Anselm's thought as an historian rather than as a technical philosopher or theologian. Perhaps that is one reason why the outlines he gives are particularly readable and satisfactory. They are entirely free of controversy, clear, perceptive, and sympathetic, and they enable us to enter into the spiritual and intellectual climate in which Anselm's great theses were conceived and written. Although it is true that the ontological argument of the *Proslogion* aroused the protest of another monk, Gaunilo of Marmoutier, Anselm was essentially a non-controversial writer. As Professor Southern points out, his early treatises were the product of the "monastic peace" of the cloister at Bec. He says:

> All the writings of this period are the witnesses of this peace: his intimate correspondence with his friends at Canterbury and elsewhere, his prayers and meditations, his *Proslogion* and *Monologion* – themselves meditations on the nature of God – are his philosophical and theological dialogues, which were the product of his teaching in the cloister. The only controversy was with the remarkable Gaunilo over the argument of the *Proslogion* and it was conducted with such regard and identity of purpose that it is hard to realize that a new philosophical issue had suddenly sprung into existence. Nothing could be more peaceful or more withdrawn from the storms and controversies, which in the realm of government, were rending the Empire and Papacy of Henry IV and Gregory VII, or which in the realm of theology, in 1079, produced the final condemnation of Berengar of Tours (p. 48).

It was the very depth of his faith that gave Anselm, as Gilson has said, a "practically unlimited confidence" in the power of reason.[XI] Whatever is revealed has meaning and this meaning is, by God's grace, accessible to the understanding of the believer who seeks light. Anselm finds "necessary arguments" even for the Trinity. Anselm is therefore convinced that questions about the meaning of revelation can and must be asked.

There is good reason to write a book in answer to the question: Why Did God Become Man? (*Cur Deus Homo?*) Reason and intelligence can discover evidence which is concealed from simple faith. But is this "revelation of evidence" the same as what we would, today, call an "apologetic argument"?

Anselm's Dialectical Meditations

In the *Monologion* (Chapter 1) Anselm clearly says that one who does not know God by faith can arrive at the knowledge of His existence by reason, at least *ex magna parte* if he has a moderate intelligence (*si vel mediocris ingenii est*[XII]). In other words, for one who is well-disposed, reason alone can be an apt instrument for arriving at a knowledge of God. However Anselm himself never starts from "reason alone" in order to arrive at faith. It is with faith as his starting point that he embarks on his dialectical and metaphysical meditations upon the content of revealed truth. He does not reason in order to believe. He believes in order to understand. And the understanding at which he aims is not a mere matter of logical conclusions. He seeks the light of metaphysical intuition and, beyond that, of spiritual (mystical) contemplation.

Anselm's argument is situated in a very special context – that of man's quest for beatitude in the Vision of God the Supreme Truth. His investigation is not that of dispassionate and scientific detachment, but of total spiritual commitment. It is the quest of one "striving to raise his mind to the contemplation of God and seeking to understand what he believes." As Barth says: "Anselm thinks and proves in prayer and therefore not on logical presuppositions, but by acceptance in practice of the One whose existence he undertakes to think out and prove. The point of the proof … would be missed … were the fact to be ignored that Anselm speaks *about* God while speaking *to* Him" (English Translation,

p. 101). Hence there is no question that a "proof" for the existence of God is, for Anselm, simply the affirmation of "necessary reasons" for what he already accepts and "knows" in so far as it is revealed by God to the Church.

The "Anselmian experience" in the *Proslogion* is, then, not a logical maneuver which starts with an essential definition of God and proceeds to "deduce" God's existence from His essence. On the contrary, this is where those who fail to understand his argument usually go wrong. Barth says that the Anselmian experience has a "prophetic" character. The designation of God as "that than which no greater can be conceived" is not a definition but a "Name" in the Old Testament sense of a presence and epiphany of God Revealed and Revealing. It designates Him as a hidden and transcendent One who is beyond all concepts. Yet He can nevertheless be "reached" by a necessary conclusion of reason, which confirms and expresses the certitude contained in the "Name" that reveals Him. It is true that our mind's eye cannot gaze directly on the sun, but it can view the light which comes from the sun, and in that light the sun can be said to be "visible." So too with the intelligible light diffused by this infinite Being of God.

Anselm is therefore never afflicted with uncertainty or doubt. He does not wonder whether or not "God is." The being of God is, for him, no "problem." His quest is for the new and additional light of intelligence, and for the beauty and harmony of necessary reasons which supplement and clarify the loving acceptance of faith. He is not using reason to show that the existence of God is credible, but to show how the proposition that "God is" must be necessarily true and evident even to reason alone.

Understanding the Argument

We may perhaps complain that he does not clearly distinguish the light of supernatural or infused understanding, or indeed the light of mystical wisdom, from the ordinary light of the human intelligence fortified by the habit of theological science. This is why the apparent conclusiveness of his dialectic sometimes leaves us hanging in the air, as if we felt that he had left the most important point unsaid. And often he has done just this; he has expressed everything but his ontological and spiritual *experience* of a truth that dialectic is not really capable of grasping. His evidence is therefore in some sense "loaded" by the unformulated implications of a religious experience which guides and enlightens the dialectical progress of his thought.

His argument is "prophetic" rather than "apologetic" and one who, by reason of obscure and personal diffidence or repugnance, rejects these spiritual overtones and refuses to attune himself to them, cannot easily accept Anselm's "proof." Anselm however refuses to speak to those who do not come at least part of the way to meet him on this spiritual ground. Hence the clear distinction he makes between "the fool" (*insipiens*) and the "unbeliever" (*infidelis*). The fool is one who refuses to believe what is not immediately evident to his mind here and now. He is a "fool" precisely because he does not seek any truth beyond what conforms to his present prejudices. He mocks all that he does not understand.[10] The *infidelis* however is seeking the truth, but by reason alone, without faith. He is not a fool, because he seeks the truth, and it is not his fault that he has not received the gift of faith. Anselm will therefore enter into dialogue with the "unbeliever" who seeks the truth by reason. He will *share* with this unbeliever the understanding of the *ratio fidei* which he himself has acquired in theological meditation. Those who are, so to speak, on the same "wave-length" will, without difficulty, admit his reasons as necessary. Those who are not will never be able to see what Anselm is talking about.

Southern's Interpretation

While Knowles declares that the ontological argument has "no apologetic design," Southern is perhaps too ready to consider the argument as a "proof for the unbeliever." We must remember however that the *Proslogion* deals not with the infidel but with the "fool" (*insipiens*) with whom no argument is possible. However, Southern has some interesting things to say about the "argument."

---

10. See *Cur Deus Homo*, I. 25. (*Sources Chrétiennes*, p. 344; Schmitt, p. 95).

> The *Proslogion* is intended both as a meditation for the believer and as a proof for the unbeliever. The proof for the unbeliever does not, as has sometimes been thought, depend upon the previous acceptance of certain theological truths, but it does depend on a previous acceptance of certain philosophical principles which appear, on analysis, to commit the unbeliever to a view of knowledge which necessitates the existence of God. A proof which demands, in however subtle and roundabout a way, assent to its conclusion before it begins, will rightly be thought to be no proof in the ordinary sense of the word (p. 63).

One feels that this judgment is based on a slightly anachronistic conception of what St. Anselm was really trying to do, and that R. W. Southern has neglected the primary importance, here, of the *ratio fidei* and of Anselm's characteristic striving to advance from faith to understanding, which he clearly acknowledges and describes elsewhere. The "previous philosophical principles" are certainly implied as a basis for the argument, but are they addressed, with polemical intent, to a hypothetical antagonist who cannot accept them? "I desire in some measure to understand the truth which my heart believes and loves. I do not seek to understand in order to believe but I believe in order to understand. And this too I believe, for unless I believe, I shall not understand" (*Proslogion*, Chapter 1). Karl Barth, who rejects the idea that the *Proslogion* is a "proof for unbelievers," rightly asserts that the whole argument must be seen in the context of the opening prayer of chapter one.

Barth certainly admits that there is in Anselm a "will to convince" a hypothetical interlocutor who does not understand. But Anselm enters no apologetic debate with one who refuses to seek the truth. He is, in the *Proslogion*, talking only to the Believer who seeks to understand the "necessary reasons" implicit in his belief. This is therefore not an apologetic approach at all. It does not seek to prove the existence of God *credible*, but to show that His Being is *intelligible*.

From Faith to Understanding

By apologetics, we must understand an appeal to arguments and a way of reasoning which goes out to meet the *insipiens* on his own ground. It is quite true that Anselm proceeds *sola ratione* as if there were no revealed explanations. But he never proceeds as if revelation as such were to be temporarily set aside as irrelevant. Yet this is what he would have to do to meet the "*insipiens*" on his own ground and bring him by logical, historical and other arguments to admit the relevance and credibility of revelation. This Anselm never does. He starts from the fact of revealed truth, and then goes on to show that *if his imaginary interlocutor were really consistent* he would be able to recognize that he already held some truths which implicitly point to the evidence which Anselm is trying to show him.[11] Now this is exactly the case in the *Proslogion*, and so Southern's criticism obviously does not apply. The unbeliever is not brought into the picture as an adversary to be "effectively reduced to silence." Anselm is not concerned with "silencing" the objector (to whom he barely accords the most transient and indirect attention) as with showing *believers* (his monks) that the very proposition "God is not" is self-contradictory to anyone who is fully aware of the meaning of *God* – that is to say to anyone who has a "sense of God" which preserves him from being "*insipiens*."

In his recent critical edition of the *Vita Anselmi*,[12] commenting on the Chapter (1:19) in which Eadmer describes the genesis of the "argument," Southern says: "Eadmer evidently did not look on the work primarily as a proof of the *existence* of God but as a proof that the attributes of God are such as the Christian faith holds them to be. In a sense he was justified in this because Anselm's philosophical outlook, strictly speaking, excluded the possibility of God's non-existence." This is a much more accurate exposition of Anselm's thought.

---

11. See J. McIntyre, "Premises and Conclusions in the System of St. Anselm's Theology" in *Spicilegium Beccense*, pp. 95-101. "There is an 'Anselmian method' which consists in getting the interlocutor to see that he is refusing to accept a conclusion that follows necessarily from his own premises" (p. 96).

12. *The Life of St. Anselm by Eadmer*, edited with introduction; notes and translation by R. W. Southern, Edinburgh, and N.Y., 1962.

After all, as Southern himself remarks, the fool is *by definition* the man who lacks wisdom (*insipiens*), and therefore the one who is incapable, in his present condition of realizing that the Name God is the Name of "The One Who Is," and that therefore to say "God is not" is meaningless. Anselm's "pastoral" approach to the *insipiens* would not have been the ontological argument but rather an urgent invitation to compunction and to hunger for truth awakened by the consideration of the wretchedness and the inner contradictions of a life deprived of both faith and reason and reduced to aimlessness and confusion. This is suggested by the fact that the *insipiens* is described as one who is quite content with a completely unthinkable thought, not realizing that it makes all his thinking and consequently his whole life totally meaningless – so meaningless and so confused that one cannot even talk to him intelligently about God. The only possibility would be to make him realize, if possible, his own confusion. The sense of error, of disorientation, of emptiness is the necessary prelude to a search for truth. Without this the *insipiens* will remain established in complacency and solipsism.

The first chapter of the *Proslogion* says this as clearly as anyone could desire and of course, in doing so, it echoes the classical lines of Augustine:

> I sought rest in the secrecy of my conscience and I found tribulation and anguish in my inmost heart.... Lord, I am bowed down and am able to look only downward. Straighten me, so that I may be able to look up. My sins have become so deep that I sink in them over my head, they completely imprison me, they crush me with their burden. Liberate me, unburden me, do not let their abyss yawn at me.... *Teach me to seek You because I cannot seek You unless You teach me to find You, nor find You unless You show Yourself.*

No Utilitarian Purpose

In Anselm's mind, therefore, dialectic does not precede conversion, but follows it. However, he did evidently hold that the "necessary reasons" provided by dialectic ought to be capable of convincing a man who had no faith, provided his faithlessness were not the product of stupidity or ill-will. Still the sharp new toy of logic was as yet too marvelous a novelty to be used in the practical affairs of pastoral life, where there were perfectly good traditional instruments of which Anselm was master and with which he was content.

In short Anselm does not use his dialectic merely to confute opponents of the faith, though his arguments are such that he feels they ought *also* to convince a reasonable unbeliever.

Nor does he use dialectic to *strengthen* his own faith and that of his monks. Actually, the Anselmian method is not a method "for" anything. He is not seeking to prevail in any argument, and the word "*probare*" must not generally be taken to imply "putting over" his point and "winning" the argument. The Anselmian proof has no utilitarian purpose: it merely adds to the joy and serenity of belief the further joy and clarity of understanding the evident truth. *Non ut me in fide confirmes, sed ut confirmatum veritatis ipsius intellectu laetifices.*[13]

A Russian Theologian's Insight

The Russian Orthodox theologian Evdokimov has contributed a no less interesting and provocative insight into the "Anselmian experience" in his essay on the apophatic implications of the argument.[14]

In many ways Father[XIV] Evdokimov's approach resembles that of Karl Barth, and he is no less capable than Barth of penetrating the deep religious implications of the "argument." Like Barth, Evdokimov stresses the difference between the theological contemplation of "evidence" and the apologetic manipulation of "proofs." For Evdokimov Anselm is much more an "Apostle and witness" than he is a logician, and the Russian theologian

---

13. *Cur Deus Homo*, II.15, *Sources Chrétiennes*, p.408, Schmitt, p. 116.[XIII]
14. P. Evdokimov, "L'Aspect Apophatique de l'Argument de Saint Anselme" in *Spicilegium Beccense*, pp. 233-258. This essay is a welcome contrast to that of H. De Lubac (see footnote #8) and explains the apparent "échec" of *Proslogion* XIV.

protests even more strongly than Barth against the "religious banality" of Kant's discussion of what he called the "ontological proof." Evdokimov and Barth are far more acute than Gaunilo, Descartes, and Kant in pointing out that the "one than whom no greater can be conceived" (in the *Proslogion*) is a different and far deeper designation of God than the "greatest that can be conceived" (in the *Monologion*).[XV] The difference *is* important, for in the second case the statement does *not* necessarily imply that God exists.

Evdokimov shows how the God of the *Proslogion* is not "a purely logical God," not one being among all others, not a first cause in a series of causes and effects. If God is only a logical concept, then the *insipiens* is right. No bond between God and His existence can be established by a purely human concept of His essence. We cannot start from a concept of God in order to arrive at His reality – we start from Him in order to arrive at a concept not only of Him, but of any being whatever. God is the *norm* of our thought about being, and we are able to "know" Him in proportion as our minds are conformed to His reality and His truth in spiritual likeness. Hence the Anselmian argument is a "mystical experience of the living and religious content of the word *God*" because "the Name of God is a theophany and the place of His Presence." Thus God Who is "totally apophatic in His essence" is "totally and immediately perceived as being."

Evdokimov concludes by pointing to Anselm as the "last witness" to the theological unity of East and West, writing precisely at the time of the fatal schism.

Ecumenical Quality of Anselm's Thought

One of the most impressive features of these studies by Barth and Evdokimov is their recognition of the ecumenical quality of Anselm's thought. This is true precisely because Anselm is *not* an apologist and is not simply trying to confute all the arguments of those who do not share his faith. In a word, Anselm is a truly ecumenical thinker precisely because he does not demand that his interlocutor share his faith before communicating to him the deepest and most personal insights of his theological contemplation. For Anselm there is not one doctrine for friends and another for foes – the one tenderly devotional, the other efficient and unyielding. All that concerns him is the *ratio fidei*, which is found in the "true light that enlightens every man coming into this world."[XVI]

Anselm's argument cannot be grasped unless one understands and accepts what he means by the "thought of that than which no greater can be conceived," and the "thought of that which cannot be thought not to be." What does Anselm mean by "thought" here? In the *Monologion* (chap. 10) he says: "In a word of the mind or of the reason (i.e., a thought) I understand here not simply the awareness of sounds signifying things, but *things themselves* whether future or now existing, seen by the light of thought in the mind." Clearly, the underlying principle upon which his thinking depends is an *intuition of being*, and beyond that, the empirical fact that *beings are unequal in perfection*. He is deeply conscious of the reality of being, and aware at the same time that all beings are not equally real. This of course implies a relation between concept and being. In this relationship, the concept has a lesser degree of reality than the being itself which it represents, and *it derives its reality from the reality which it represents*. However, it is entirely possible to occupy oneself with concepts as pure abstractions, unrelated to anything. But this, for Anselm, is thought without understanding. (It is the thought of a "fool.") Genuine thought, thought *which understands*, can only exist where the relation of the concept with the being from which it derives its reality, is apprehended.

At the same time, we must also consider that beings which exist in reality, "outside the mind," have different degrees of reality, and all owe their reality to the fact that they participate, to a greater or lesser degree, in one single principle of Being which is Pure and Absolute Reality. And this is the Being "than which no greater can be thought." Further, God is the *only* Being who cannot be thought not to be. All other beings offer to our minds a reality that *can cease to be* or that *came into being* and consequently can be thought of as not being, however real it may be here and now.

Obviously, since the fool hath said in his heart "there is no God," there is some sense in which even God can be thought not to be. But that is when God is considered *merely as a concept*, or worse, *merely as a word, unrelated even to its own content*. In such a case, one is not really fulfilling the condition of *thinking* about that than which no greater can be thought. One is really thinking a self-contradiction. In fact, here the word and name of God, through verbalism or confabulation, come to stand in the way of the light of truth which leads the mind to a hidden God. How? Either by diverting the mind from the experiential *intuition of being as such* which is demanded by the very nature of Anselm's argument, or rather by blinding the mind to the religious implications of the Name of God, in which, as Barth says so well, "God manifests Himself (not by revealing His essence but) *by forbidding us to think of a greater than Himself.*"

The Act of Understanding

In either case the "thought" of the *insipiens* is really not thought at all. Instead of uttering "in his heart" that "Good Word" which is filled with significance because it expresses an intuition of our being in a Being infinitely greater than can be conceived, he simply plays with words and concepts as if they were mere noises without significance. His folly consists above all in the fact that though he does not understand it, the reality of God is all the time present to his intelligence! But what Barth calls "the Christian event" of recognition (*intellectus*) has failed to take place, and God is not known as the sole and supreme reality. The Name of God has therefore been announced but the *insipiens* has not really heard it, since for him it is nothing more than a sound, or at best a concept among other concepts. He has not perceived the "interdiction" that forbids us to fabricate a concept of the inconceivable, and he has not perceived the summons to go forth and meet his God who is evidently present because He cannot not be present. This meeting takes place in an "event" which is a supernatural gift – the act of understanding.

Gaunilo objected that "God" is simply a word indicating a reality we do not and cannot know and that since we know nothing whatever that is "like God," then the concept of God in our understanding is really nothing at all. Hence we cannot proceed from such a concept to the affirmation of His necessary being. Anselm replies that though reason does not know God as He is in Himself, it does know *being* and it does know the differences that give some beings a greater reality than others. Therefore the notion of "a being than which no greater can be conceived" is itself quite understandable though it points to a Being beyond our comprehension. Anselm nowhere asserts that the essence of God is fully comprehensible, but only that His *Name* designates Him in a relevant and intelligible manner, so that once we recognize His Name we can also recognize His necessary Being.

Anselm is really not saying that "God exists because we can conceive of Him as existing," rather he is saying, "we recognize His Being because He reveals Himself to us as He-Who-Is." And He reveals Himself to us in the deepest act of intuition and reflexion in which we are aware of our capacity to meditate on reality, and to reach out beyond the limits of the reality that can be circumscribed in our concepts. Indeed, the very fact that any concept at all exists, even in the mind, is a witness to the being of that supreme self-existing Nature beyond the reach of concepts, and by which all beings and even mental acts, have existence. The Being of God is "in all and through all. It is that from which, by which and in which all things are" (*Monologion*, ch. 14). Further, if a concept is true, there is but one truth by which all else is true, and that truth is God. Such is the theme of Anselm's *De Veritate*.

Jacques Paliard, in a meditation[15] of capital importance, emphasizes the intellectual rather than the religious aspect of the Anselmian experience. The "experience of reflexion" and the struggle to extend thought beyond the limits of the concept (*dépassement*) is at once an experience of our own limits and an intuition of Being that has no limits and cannot be transcended (*l'indépassable*). In full consciousness of its own limitations, the mind transcends itself to "touch" that which has no limits, and by that very act is aware of itself as existing only in and by the One than whom no greater can be conceived. In this act, too, Being itself, manifesting itself in my own conscience, at the same time affirms itself as a transcendent object of knowledge and encloses me empirically within the limits of my own self in that I-Thou relationship which is essential to religious *adoration*, but which in *contemplation*, tends once again to vanish with the disappearance of divisions and limitations.

---

15. Jacques Paliard, "Prière et Dialectique, Méditation sur le *Proslogion*," in *Dieu Vivant*, n. 6, pp. 53-70.

Professor Southern's examination of the *Cur Deus Homo*,[16] St. Anselm's "greatest intellectual achievement," is particularly interesting and complete. In discussing the question "Why God became man," St. Anselm first of all rejects the conservative Augustinian thesis that Adam's sin had somehow given the devil real *rights* over the human race, and that the "price of redemption" had consequently to be paid to the devil, in order that man might be ransomed. At the same time, St. Anselm did not go to the other extreme, reached by a more modern and liberal theology, of saying that there was in fact no atonement and no redemption at all, an answer which solves the problem by dismissing it altogether.

On the contrary, the relentless insistence on *ratio sola* in the first part of the *Cur Deus Homo* is by no means the complacent rationalist indifferentism which evades the problem of sin and redemption. Anselm strives quite successfully to show that once the Christian revelation on the nature of sin is accepted, reason can only lead one inexorably to the conclusion that the problem *has no human solution*. Yet, accepting also the revelation of the divine economy, and God's plan for the world, reason shows that God owes it to His own wisdom and justice to solve this problem which is otherwise completely insoluble.

Authority and Freedom

Hence the *Cur Deus Homo* is by no means an exercise in blind voluntarism – "Christ had to die on the Cross because it was His Father's inscrutable will." The emphasis is all on the freedom which alone could give Christ's death its redemptive power. The *Cur Deus Homo* is perhaps the greatest of all meditations on authority and freedom.

The problem of the need to satisfy the divine justice and re-establish order was made particularly acute for St. Anselm by the delicacy of his sense of monastic obedience and of feudal loyalty. It is in these terms that he works out his theory of re-

16. *Op. cit.*, pp. 77-121. We may mention here the new critical edition of the *Cur Deus Homo* in Latin and French by René Roques, *Sources Chrétiennes*, n. 91, Paris, 1963.

demption in which the justice and mercy of God are reconciled. Yet we must not imagine his solution is merely juridical and negative.[17] In being merciful to man, God is certainly paying no debt to the devil, and the redemptive death of Christ on the Cross is offered not to appease the forces of evil, but to do full honor to the infinite Life and Truth which are one with God Himself, and thus to overcome death. In the freely accepted redemptive death of the Man-God, justice and mercy become one, since God fully satisfies not a hypothetical appetite for revenge, but a real and concrete intention to bring His creature to perfection and to unite man with Himself in blessedness and light.

Yet St. Anselm never for a moment doubts the reality of the debt to be paid to God: a debt so great that man alone could never be capable of paying it. Southern explains this debt in terms of the feudal concept of *honor*, without falling into the excesses of those who explain Anselm's soteriology purely in terms of Lombardic law. We must not think of feudal honor merely in terms of self-esteem and wounded feelings, offended dignity, injured reputation, loss of face and so on. In the eleventh century, the honor of a feudal Lord was quite concrete and objective. It concerned his estate and the network of relationships and loyalties in which he functioned. The concept is much more in the spirit of those Classical Chinese social relationships expounded in the Confucian *Analects* or the *Hsiao Ching*.[XVII] For St. Anselm, also, the loyalties of man to man in the social hierarchy tend to reflect something of the order built into the universe by its Creator. The universe is bound to God by ingrained loyalties in a relationship of service (and the Greek Fathers explored the liturgical implications of this concept). Angels and men are appointed to praise Him in their proper hierarchical orders. A refusal on the part of one or the other immediately puts the disloyal offender outside the beauty and order of the universe. Not only is he punished by his exile from the harmony and order of love by which God rules His creation, but creation itself is marred: God is dishonored because the place that should have been occupied by one of His chosen creatures is left conspicuously empty. (Note that in threatening to "return his ticket" to heaven, Ivan Karamazov

---

17. See E. Fairweather, "'*Iustitia Dei*' as the '*Ratio*' of the Incarnation" in *Spicilegium Beccense*, pp. 327-335.

was implicitly admitting this concept of the cosmos, which is in its way very Russian.) The problem of restoring God's honor is then twofold: that of getting man back into his proper place, and that of finding means capable of achieving this, since the work has to be done by man himself. The answer was the Incarnation and the death of Christ on the Cross, both of which have made it possible for any man, indeed for all men to recover their freedom and to return in willing submission to God's loving plan for His universe.

Eadmer's New Type of Biography

In 1093 St. Anselm became Archbishop of Canterbury[XVIII] – a post for which he had no taste and not much natural aptitude. He became, at the same time Abbot of the Cathedral monastery, a community made up of English monks who were embittered by the Conquest, and Norman-French monks who did not know English and were not congenial to their English brethren. It does not seem that Anselm himself was received with undue coldness, and Eadmer, a monk who had grown up from childhood in the cloister at Canterbury and who sadly remembered the pre-conquest monastery, became Anselm's personal sacristan, his companion in exile and his closest friend. It was Eadmer who wrote both the public life of Anselm in the *Historia Novorum* and his more intimate and spiritual biography in the *Vita Anselmi.*[18] The *Vita Anselmi* stands out among medieval hagiographies as a remarkable and original work of art, a new type of biography that is more interested in the person and character of the saint than in his miracles. The portrayal of character demanded "mastery of the difficult art of recording the spoken word in a vivid and natural way." Against all the conventions of his time, Eadmer reported the words of Anselm simply and naturally just as they were actually spoken and, as Southern says, "This was more than a technique of writing. It was the stirring of a new vision."[19]

For most of his years as Archbishop, Anselm had to be absent from Canterbury and from England, in exile, and while he

18. See note #2.
19. Southern, *op. cit.*, p. 333.

guided the affairs of the community from afar by letter, he left his various English Priors to run it, in agreement with the monks themselves. Thus it was that under Anselm the community began to revert to the English customs that had been abolished by Lanfranc, and busied itself with the erection of a new Cathedral which Anselm had decided to build after he had seen the recently dedicated basilica of Cluny (the largest Church in Christendom until the present St. Peter's).

Intellectual Awakening at Canterbury

Busy with this task, and growing in material prosperity, the divided community became united and settled down to a respectable and peaceful existence. The splendid Cathedral, with altars of the Anglo-Saxon bishops and saints, Dunstan and Elphege flanking the High Altar, "had never so eloquently expressed the union of the community with its earthly past and its heavenly future," as Southern remarks (p. 267). Under the inspiration of Anselm there was an intellectual awakening, which was expressed in the writings of Eadmer on the Immaculate Conception, the Letters and sermons of the Prior Elmer, recently discovered and edited by Dom Leclercq,[20] and the works of other Cantuarians and disciples of Anselm such as Gilbert Crispin and Ralph, Abbot of Battle, author of several of the meditations and prayers formerly ascribed to St. Anselm himself.

Prior Ernulf, another author and disciple of Anselm, also installed five enormous bells in the cathedral tower. This was a sure sign of the revival of the old English spirit, as the English had always been notorious for their attachment to bell-ringing. Lest it be thought that five bells in a Cathedral hardly indicate an obsession, we might add that it took sixty-three men to ring them.

However, at this moment of prosperity and solemn splendor, Canterbury suffered a humiliating reverse in the controversy with York over the "primacy" of England. The monks took this very seriously, and attributed their failure to a lack of zeal and ability on the part of their Primate, Anselm. They never entirely

20. "Ecrits Spirituels d'Elmer de Cantorbéry," *Analecta Monastica* II., *Studia Anselmiana* Fasc. XXXI. Rome, 1953.

forgave him. They always compared him unfavorably with Lanfranc, who was a more capable administrator, though Anselm was certainly not lacking in a sense of responsibility to his See, even in the most temporal of rights and dignities. Yet because of his relative lack of success in the controversy with York, the Canterbury community seems to have questioned the sanctity of Anselm, and this is reflected, as Southern has shown, in the various reactions of Eadmer's *Vita Anselmi* which, in any case, was more widely copied and disseminated in Flanders and Burgundy than in England.

Anselm was never fully at home at Canterbury as he was at Bec, and we may regret that Southern's book does not treat the peaceful and productive years at Bec as fully as he does the more restless background of Canterbury. However, this is a more important and controversial period and it must be said that Southern's chapters on Eadmer and on the Canterbury community are among the most valuable and original in his book. He concludes with this apt remark on the spirit of the Canterbury community at the turn of the twelfth century:

> In the history of English monasticism as a whole, it was an ominous sign that a great community should have been so easily dispirited by a political reverse, and so easily satisfied by such a catalogue of bells, carpets and costly vestments as that with which Conrad (one of Anselm's priors) was credited.[21]

St. Thomas a Becket

The Canterbury community was more interested in the external celebration of its own collective importance than in the holiness of the great exile, though he was accepted gradually, and cooly, as a "beatus." But it was St. Thomas a Becket who did most for Anselm – and Anselm did more than anyone for him. By mod-

---

21. *Op. cit.*, p. 271. A letter of Prior Elmer of Canterbury discussing the virtues of the monastic life compares them to priestly vestments and ornaments, while the virtuous monk is elaborately compared to a curtain! Epistola V., n. 9-14, *Studia Anselmiana*, pp. 78-82.

elling himself on his holy predecessor, Becket initiated that conversion of life which prepared him for his struggle and his martyrdom. It was Becket who got a liturgical feast for St. Anselm. Paradoxically, the martyrdom of St. Thomas led to an eclipse of St. Anselm's popularity at Canterbury.

Professor Southern's really remarkable biography and study of Anselm's monastic background is one of the finest works of medieval scholarship in a period that has been extremely productive of good books. It shows us the real greatness of a man who is far more than one of the Makers of the Middle Ages, and of Christian civilization.

St. Anselm, Doctor of the Church, is also one of the great thinkers of all time, certainly equal to St. Bernard, St. Bonaventure, and St. Thomas, in the Middle Ages. Indeed, as an influential force in medieval thought he is probably second only to St. Thomas himself, when we consider that Duns Scotus is in many ways a disciple and interpreter of Anselm.

Monk and Philosopher

But we must realize that the thought of St. Anselm was the thought of a monk. The "Argument" of the *Proslogion* came to him at Matins after he had struggled with the problem night after night in choir (and certainly St. Bernard and William of St. Thierry must have regarded this with disapproval if they knew of it!). But thinking about philosophical problems in choir does not make a philosopher monastic, or a monk a philosopher. It was the profundity and fervor of Anselm's monastic contemplation that opened his mind to the light of the "argument," which fits in perfectly with his whole outlook on the monastic life.

Prior Elmer quoted Anselm as giving the following definition of a monk: "The very being of a monk (*monachi esse*) is to rejoice in being not his own, for the sake of God." The use of *esse* instead of *essentia* or *existentia* twice in this short sentence ought to make us think twice before classifying Anselm as an incorrigible Platonic realist, though his thought is certainly Platonic and Augustinian. It also shows us, more pertinently, that the anachronistic term "ontological argument" might acquire a deeper meaning in Anselm's case if it were stripped of its Kantian presuppositions. Anselm's contemplation and his dialectic were both rooted in the sense of *being*, in his appreciation of the different degrees of being, and in his realization that the monk's greatest glory was to "be" only for Him who truly *Is*.

In conclusion, we might quote a few well-known lines of Pascal's *Pensées* which explain the Anselmian experience quite perfectly:

> The heart has reasons which the reason does not know at all; that is evident in a thousand things. I say that the heart loves universal being naturally and itself naturally in the measure that it surrenders itself to it; and it hardens itself against one or the other as it chooses.... It is the heart that senses God and not the reason.[22]

Did not Anselm know this as well, or better, than Pascal? Yet instead of setting heart and reason in opposition, he united them in his *ratio fidei*, surrendering both to God in an act of understanding in which the "reasons of the heart" become lucid and beautiful witnesses that convince the mind of God's infinite being.

But the "*insipiens*" is one who has hardened his heart against universal being, and he consequently knows no "reasons" beyond dialectical and verbal propositions without meaning or message for the whole man.

The Anselmian experience is a profoundly monastic and contemplative realization of Christian understanding as both reflexion and event, speculation and "sacrament," philosophy and epiphany. Here we see the monk as the "true philosopher" in every sense of the term.

I. Text reads: "*De Grammario*".

II. Text reads: "… Benedictine Centuries ever saw."

III. David Knowles, *The Monastic Order in England: A History of its Development from the Times of St Dunstan to the Fourth Lateran Council*

---

22. *Pensées*, IV.

– *940-1216* (Cambridge: Cambridge University Press, 1940; 2nd ed. 1963) 92 (text reads: "96").

IV. According to Southern, "Anselm, at his first appearance as a writer, was and claimed to be an *Augustinus minor*" (*St. Anselm and His Biographer* 33).

V. *Proslogion*, cc. 2, 15 (J. P. Migne, ed., *Patrologiae Cursus Completus, Series Latina* [*PL*], 221 vols. [Paris: Garnier, 1844-1865] vol. 158, cols. 228A, 235C) (text reads: "*maior*") ("That than which no greater can be conceived").

VI. "*fides quaerens intellectum*" (*Proslogion*, *Prooemium* [col. 225A]).

VII. *Vita Herluini*, quoted in Knowles, *Monastic Order* 97, which reads: "he speaks of the school of Bec, which made of all its monks philosophers."

VIII. See André Wilmart, OSB, *Auteurs Spirituels et Textes Dévots du Moyen Âge Latin: Études d'Histoire Littéraire* (Paris: Bloud et Gay, 1932) c. 10: "Une prière au saint patron attribuée à saint Anselme" (147-61); c. 11: "Le recueil de prières addressé par saint Anselme à la comtesse Mathilde" (162-72); c. 12: "Les meditations réunies sous le nom de saint Anselme" (173-201); c. 13: "Prières à sainte Anne, à saint Michel, à saint Martin, censées de saint Anselme" (202-16).

IX. *Proslogion*, *Prooemium* (col. 223B).

X. I.e. the date of the death of St. Bernard.

XI. "It can be said that, practically, Saint Anselm's confidence in reason's power of interpretation is unlimited" (Étienne Gilson, *History of Christian Philosophy in the Middle Ages* [New York: Random House, 1955] 129).

XII. *PL* 158, col. 145A.

XIII. Anselme de Cantorbéry, *Pourquoi Dieu s'est Fait Homme*, ed. and trans. by René Roques, Sources Chrétiennes 91 (Paris: Éditions du Cerf, 1963); *S. Anselmi Cantuariensis Archiepiscopi Opera Omnia*, ed. F. S. Schmitt, OSB, 6 vols. (Edinburgh: Thomas Nelson, 1946-1961) ("Not so that you may confirm me in the truth, but so that you may make me, already confirmed in truth, joyful in the understanding of it").

XIV. Evdokimov was in fact a layperson, not a priest: see "Bread in the Wilderness: The Monastic Ideal in Thomas Merton and Paul Evdokimov" in Rowan Williams, *A Silent Action: Engagements with Thomas Merton* (Louisville, KY: Fons Vitae, 2011) 23.

XV. Text reads: "greatest than can be conceived"; this phrase is not actually found in the *Monologion*, but it is evidently the interpretation that Gaunilo made of the argument there and in the *Proslogion*; see *Liber pro Insipiente* 1: "*Et ideo necesse est ut maius omnibus, quod iam probatum est esse in intellectu, non in solo intellectu, sed et in re sit;*

quoniam aliter maius omnibus esse non poterit" (*PL* 158, col. 243A) ("And therefore [according to Anselm's argument] it is necessary that what is greater than all things, which has been proved to be in the mind, is not only in the mind but also in reality, because otherwise it could not be greater than all things"). In his reply, Anselm objects that to say "that than which no greater can be thought" is not equivalent to Gaunilo's "that which is greater than all others," since the latter does not necessarily entail existence in reality: "*Nusquam in omnibus dictis meis invenitur talis probatio. Non enim idem valet, quod dicitur; maius omnibus, et, quo maius cogitari nequit, ad probandum quia est in re quod dicitur*" (*Contra Gaunilonem*, c. 5 [*PL* 158, col. 254B]) ("Such a proof is never found in all my writings. For to say 'greater than all things' and 'that than which no greater can be conceived' are not of equal value in proving that what is spoken of exists in reality"). See Barth's discussion of this question (*Fides Quaerens Intellectum* 84-85): "Gaunilo persistently so understood Anselm's formula and in numerous passages so quoted it as if Anselm had actually written in the *Proslogion* which he was criticizing: *Aliquid, quod est maius omnibus*. We may well wonder at the gentleness with which Anselm protested at this substitution and at the fact that even despite this negligence on the part of his opponent, so confusing for all concerned, he did not hesitate to acknowledge at the end of his reply Gaunilo's good-will. By this negligence Gaunilo failed most seriously to appreciate that the formula which Anselm used in the *Proslogion* did not simply have a more particular content but a different content altogether from the definitions which he utilized in the *Monologion* in connection with Augustine" (citing Augustine's statement in *De Doctrina Christiana* 1.7 that God is the greatest that can be imagined – the closest equivalent to Merton's formulation here).

XVI. John 1:9.

XVII. For Merton's comments on the *Analects* see *Life of the Vows* 46-47; on the *Hsiao Ching* see *Mystics and Zen Masters* 78-80.

XVIII. Text reads: "1190".

Reflections on Some Recent Studies of St. Anselm

On January 1, 1964, Merton wrote to the Jewish Medievalist R. J. Zwi Werblowsky (who had sent Merton an article he had written about Anselm's disciple Gilbert Crispin): "I have done two articles on Anselm, in which I agree with Barth that to call him an 'apologist' is really absurd. I cannot imagine why Schmitt, the editor of Anselm's works, is so silly as to insist that Anselm is writing apologetics" (*Hidden Ground of Love* 586). Thus Merton's second Anselm article had also been written before the end of 1963. It largely concerns the treatise *Cur Deus Homo* (*Why God Became Man*), which had been recently been published in a new Latin/French edition. On September 23 Merton records in his journal that he had been reading "some of the fabulous chapters" of the work while in the hospital and that his love for "such theological harmonies" represents "what seems to me to fit best the patterns of my life" (*Dancing in the Water of Life* 19). He returned to the work with an even deeper appreciation a month later, writing in the journal that he has now "suddenly grasped the magnificent Chapter I.9," which he had "read in the hospital and marked some of the right lines, but they had not struck deep." His insight here is that Anselm is not arguing that the Son is forced to undergo the suffering of the cross to satisfy the infinite affront of sin to the divine majesty by a concomitant sacrifice that can only be accomplished by a being Himself divine, but that this act of total self-surrender on the part of Christ is actually the acceptance of an unjust condemnation as "the way of total renunciation of power" in reconciling God and humanity. "The Father willed the salvation of man but left Jesus entirely free to specify the means .... Hence the Father's will is not that the Son suffer, but that He use His freedom as He pleases in order to save man.... And Christ, as man, elects to save man by the renunciation of power, by total poverty, annihilation and death since in this glory of the Father is manifest .... It is anything but blind and desperate subjection to an irreversible decree of death" (*Dancing in the Water of Life* 28). As Merton develops this insight in the revised version of this passage, the light in which Anselm sees the meaning of the Redemption "is the intuition of *rectitudo* as authentic freedom, and not simply the accomplishment of duty. The *rectitudo* of Christ in the Redemption does not consist for

Anselm primarily in the acceptance of a condemnation to death imposed by the Father" even though numerous "interpreters of Anselm see it that way," but in a complete, completely free identification in love and compassion with broken, sinful humanity: "He was most completely identified with man, and also most freely witnessed to the nature of love as supreme freedom – a freedom that is not limited or stayed even by death" (*Conjectures of a Guilty Bystander* 312). Merton's second article, in which this perspective is set out at length, must have been largely written at this time. Its appearance in print, though not without its own substantial delay, preceded that of its companion piece by almost a full year: "Reflections on Some Recent Studies of St. Anselm," *Monastic Studies* 3 (July 1965) 221-34. The title of the article suggests, somewhat misleadingly, a certain casual, unsystematic approach to the material, and does allow not only for a discussion of the *Cur Deus Homo* but for appreciative consideration of Southern's biography of Anselm and his edition of Eadmer's *Life* (which Merton was likewise reading in the autumn of 1963, and which he praises in a journal entry written on November 5, about a week after his extensive comments on Anselm's soteriology, for its "wonderful therapeutic atmosphere" that highlights "the healing, tender, 'motherly' quality of Anselm's concern" [*Dancing in the Water of Life* 31; in revised form in *Conjectures of a Guilty Bystander* 313-14]). This allows Merton to emphasize the intrinsically monastic quality of Anselm's life and thought, and to note, as he had in his second conference to the novices (evidently based on Southern's treatment of Eadmer's *Life* in his own biography), the radical difference between the traditional hagiographic approach that focuses on the marvelous and miraculous and the "quite original and new attempt to evaluate the character and personality of a saint" provided by Eadmer. But the major focus of the article, in which discussion of Southern's work constitutes a kind of appendix, is on the *Cur Deus Homo*, and Merton is anything but casual in his challenge to the conventional understanding of Anselm's theology of redemption, and indeed of his Christology, "inseparably connected with his doctrine of *rectitudo* that is to say his doctrine on the freedom and dignity of the human person created in the image and likeness of God and redeemed by that passionate love of justice and of the divine glory which brought the Word made flesh to His death on the Cross." Once again he cites Barth and Evdokimov in their refusal "to reduce his contemplative theology to the level of banal argumentation, on which faith, reason, myth, science and whatever else you like meet together as equals in a hugger-mugger of confused debate. Anselm's *ratio* always begins and ends with a religious experience of the truth of faith concerning which his reason meditates and inquires." Once again he cites the contributions of scholars in the *Spicilegium Beccense* and elsewhere, who show that properly understood, Anselm's concept of satisfaction "is not a question of God's honor being repaired by the punishment of sin in Christ's death, though that death is indeed a perfect satisfaction for all the sins of the world. But here we see that God's honor demands, above all, man's salvation and restoration – a fact which is overlooked by those who see only the 'juridical' aspect of Anselm's doctrine.... Hence the honor of God that is wounded by sin and demands satisfaction is seen to be nothing other than His infinite goodness and loving concern for man His creature." Merton even goes so far as to compare Anselm's vision of redemption to that of Julian of Norwich, "whose optimistic theology in many respects resembles his," and to find in "Anselm's concept of *iustitia* which is perhaps more ontological than juridical," and even in that of Augustine his great model and predecessor, who likewise emphasizes that Christ overcomes Satan "by justice and not by force," an anticipation of and "a striking theological justification for that non-violence which Gandhi appealed to as the pure force of truth (*ahimsa*)" – a far cry from the portrait of a vengeful God demanding satisfaction of His outraged honor by the "immolation of an innocent Victim of infinite worth" that dominated traditional interpretations of Anselm's soteriology.

Karl Barth, the most distinguished Protestant theologian of our time, has said: "Tell me how it stands with your Christology and I shall tell you who you are."[I] What does he mean by this? That the knowledge of Jesus Christ is central to all Christian knowledge whatever, whether theological or otherwise: a thesis typical of the fervor and intransigence of the eminent Doctor of Basel who has made so deep an impression on such Catholic admirers as Hans Küng and Hans Urs von Balthasar. Nor is it inappropriate to quote Barth here, since he is not only a diligent student of St. Anselm, but has done perhaps more than any other one man to stimulate study and discussion of Anselm in the twentieth century. His famous essay on the so called "ontological argument" has recently been published in English.[1]

Barth's aphorism on Christology is certainly true of Anselm. Nowhere are the thought of the Benedictine doctor, his character and his outlook, with their power and their possible deficiencies, more apparent than in the *Cur Deus Homo*. Second in importance among his works to the *Proslogion*, this treatise on the Incarnation and Redemption is the fruit of his full maturity, his greatness and his exile.

Cur Deus Homo

The most recent scholarly edition of the *Cur Deus Homo* is the Latin-French text edited, translated and introduced by René Roques in *Sources Chrétiennes*.[2] Meticulously annotated and indexed, each page of the Latin text is marked to show the corresponding columns in Migne's *P. L.* 158,[II] and Dom F. S. Schmitt's definitive edition of St. Anselm.[3] René Roques has written an in-

1. K. Barth, *Fides Quaerens Intellectum* (Richmond, Va.: John Knox Press, 1960). Cf. H. Bouillard, "La preuve de Dieu dans le *Proslogion* et son interpretation par K. Barth," *Spicilegium Beccense* (Paris: Vrin, 1959) pp. 191 ff.
2. Anselme de Cantorbéry, *Pourquoi Dieu s'est fait homme* (*Sources Chrétiennes*, 91), texte latin, bibliographie, introduction, traduction et notes de René Roques (Paris: Éditions du Cerf, 1963) 525 pp. (*Cur Deus Homo*, together with the *Monologion* and *Proslogion*, has recently been reprinted in the English translation of S. N. Deane [Lasalle, Illinois: Open Court Publishing Co., 1951]).
3. *S. Anselmi Cantuariensis Archiepicopi Opera Omnia*, F. S. Schmitt, ed.

troductory study on Anselm and his soteriology which is a book in itself. One can certainly not complain that this edition is lacking in important information or in scholarly detail. In his difficult task of summing up Anselm's soteriology Roques follows the Swedish theologian, G. Aulèn,[4] who is perhaps too inclined to overemphasize the juridical character of his doctrine. However, Roques admits that a true perspective of Anselm's thought can be had by comparing the *Cur Deus Homo* with his meditations.[5]

The Christology of Anselm is in fact completely central to all his thought on man, on the world, on moral life and of course on the monastic life itself, because his Christology is inseparably connected with his doctrine of *rectitudo*[6] that is to say his doctrine on the freedom and dignity of the human person created in the image and likeness of God and redeemed by that passionate love of justice and of the divine glory which brought the Word made flesh to His death on the Cross.

The thirtieth chapter of Eadmer's *Vita Anselmi*[7] describes

---

(Sekau and Edinburgh: Thomas Nelson and Sons, 1938-1961), 6 vols.

4. G. Aulèn, *Christus Victor* (London, 1931).
5. *Op. cit.*, p. 185.
6. In an unpublished thesis, "The Idea of Rectitude in St. Anselm" (Toronto: Pontifical Institute of Medieval Studies, 1932), Robert Pollock says: "Things disclose their inner being only when the soul of man is really there to confront them. When he is all that he ought to be, his discourse will not fail to accomplish its role" (p. 95). "Discourse in rectitude, as an expression of man on his proper level, brings about the possibility of man's redeeming the universe through love" (p. 96). "Freedom of choice … possesses the power of conserving the rectitude of the will for the sake of that rectitude, never for the sake of something else" (p. 104). "The will conforms to its rule when it is so wedded to the will of God that there are no longer two wills but one" (p. 111). "Only in prolonging God's power is there truth and rectitude in man's actions" (p. 120). "The rectitude that constitutes the truth of things must be preserved by men" (p. 123). "The very flower of Anselm's *fides quaerens intellectum* is his doctrine of rectitude … out of it flows all the rich variety of his thought" (pp. 160, 161).
7. The *Vita Anselmi* has recently been edited in a critical edition by R. W. Southern (see note 20) and will be discussed later in this article. In it we read: "Thus we took up our abode on the mountain top as far removed from the thronging crowd, as it were in a desert. When Anselm saw this, his spirits rose with the hope of future quiet, and he said: 'This is my resting place, here shall I live.' He ordered his life therefore on the lines of his early routine before he became abbot, which he deplored more than

how Anselm, in exile in Italy, in 1098, withdrew into solitude to complete the *Cur Deus Homo* on which he had been working intermittently since 1094, that is to say since the year after he became Archbishop of Canterbury.

A few pages later (chapter 33), a very interesting passage of the *Vita Anselmi* shows that at this time Anselm also had contact with the Moslem soldiers in the army of Roger of Sicily, and that he made a deep spiritual impression on them. This is an important fact because it explains who precisely were the "gentiles" that Anselm had in mind in marshalling his arguments from reason to prove the necessity of the Incarnation and Redemption in the *Cur Deus Homo*. His disciple, Gilbert Crispin, wrote a dialogue against the Jews which he and Anselm discussed together. The arguments of Jews and Moslems against the Christian faith have always been very much the same, and in the *Cur Deus Homo* Anselm confronts the Moslem viewpoint, not without a very earnest sympathy, or perhaps better, empathy. It must be understood from the first that Anselm is never the aggressive apologete who stands in a position of invincible authority from which he delivers hammer blows to crush all arguments, irrespective of their worth. Such apologetics tend to assume from the start that the opponent is absolutely wrong no matter what he may say, and that therefore there is not much point in trying to understand his argument except in so far as may be necessary for an expeditious refutation.

Here in the *Cur Deus Homo* the speakers, Anselm and his disciple Boson, instead of belaboring an imaginary Moslem, in effect place themselves in the Moslem's position in order to inquire whether they can, by reason alone, discover a clue to the mystery of man's eternal salvation apart from Jesus Christ. This is another indication of what we would now call an "ecumenical" spirit in St. Anselm. This ecumenical outlook in Anselm has al-

---

ever having had to give up since he became archbishop: day and night his mind was occupied with acts of holiness, with divine contemplation, and with the unravelling of sacred mysteries. Being then moved by his love of the Christian faith, he put out a remarkable book which he entitled *Cur Deus Homo*. He had begun this work, as he explains in the prologue to it, in England; but he finished it while living in this place, in the province, that is, of Capua" (p 107).

ready been sympathetically noted by an Orthodox theologian, P. Evdokimov, in connection with the *Proslogion*.[8]

This raises the question whether Anselm in the *Cur Deus Homo* is writing as an apologist at all. Here is a tract on the mystery of the Redemption, and though it explicitly procedes by "reason alone" (*ratione sola*), it is certainly not an attempt to establish a proof of the central mystery of Christianity that would enable us to get along without faith. Anselm is sometimes referred to as a "Christian rationalist" but the expression is absurd unless the word "rationalist" is used in a very specialized and qualified sense which it lost in the eighteenth-century "enlightenment."

Yet no one is more categorical in affirming that Anselm is a "rationalist" and "apologist" that Dom F. S. Schmitt, the learned editor of his complete works. Schmitt has not the slightest hesitation in interpreting the "purely rational method" of Anselm as the expression of "a basic apologetic tendency." Anselm is, for Schmitt, a pure apologist and this is proved, he thinks, by a simple reminder that "where we join *ratio* with belief, we have apologetics."[9] At this rate, all theological science is nothing more than apologetics. One feels that the definition is a little too sweeping.

Schmitt concedes that Anselm is not a rationalist in the pejorative sense, but insists that his method is "rationalistic," and indeed asserts that it was Anselm's "tragedy" (*sic*) to have attempt-

---

8. In a very remarkable article, "L'aspcct apophatique de l'argument de S. Anselme," *Spicilegium Beccense*, pp. 233 ff., P. Evdokimov concludes that in the thought of Anselm as represented by the "ontological argument" East and West fully met for the last time, at the moment of the great schism. "Peut-être pour le dernière fois l'orient et l'occident se sont rencontrés avec une telle evidence dans le miracle que constitue l'argument de S. Anselme" p. 257.[III] Anselm participated in the Council of Bari 1098 and argued against the Orientals on the *Filioque*; see *Vita Anselmi* c. 34 and his book *De Processione Spiritus Sancti* (finished 1102).

9. F. S. Schmitt, "Die wissenschaftliche Methode in Anselms *Cur Deus Homo*," *Spicilegium Beccense*, pp. 349 ff. He speaks of "die rein rationelle Methode Anselms" (p. 366) and Anselm's "apologetische Grundtendenz" (p. 365). "Wo wir die ratio mit dem Glauben verknüpfen, haben wir schon Apologetik" (p. 367). "Die Zuversicht mit der *ratio* das Dogma beweisen zu können, und so den Ungläubigen zu überführen, den Gläubigen zu rechtfertigen und zu erfreuen, war ein Irrtum. Darin liegt die Tragik Anselms" (p. 370).[IV]

ed to "prove" the truths of faith by reason. Having concluded his edition of all Anselm's works, Fr. Schmitt dismisses him with a sigh: *Amicus Anselmus, magis amica veritas*![V] One feels that such prolonged intimacy with the thought of the greatest Benedictine theologian might have resulted in a better understanding on the part of so learned an editor.

The "tragic" failure of Anselm is, however, perhaps neither tragic nor a failure, if only we cease to use terms like "rationalism" and "apologetics" in a completely anachronistic sense when speaking about the Anselmian *ratio fidei*. Barth and Evdokimov, among others, have been much more sensitive to the deeply religious quality of Anselm's thought. They have both refused to reduce his contemplative theology to the level of banal argumentation, on which faith, reason, myth, science and whatever else you like meet together as equals in a hugger-mugger of confused debate.

Anselm's *ratio* always begins and ends with a religious experience of the truth of faith concerning which his reason meditates and inquires. He seeks indeed to "convince," perhaps better to "satisfy," the unbeliever, but he does so in two ways. First of all, by implicitly declaring the intense fervor of his own faith, and then by showing that this faith is in no way irrational but is, on the contrary, perfectly consonant with reason, and more, that it fulfils all the inmost aspirations of reason itself. This means that the *Cur Deus Homo* is something much more subtle than an attempt to convert the unbeliever *sine die*, bludgeoning his intellect with "invincible" arguments. Without abandoning the level of faith, and yet without demanding that the unbeliever place himself on the level of faith, Anselm institutes an intelligent, sympathetic dialogue in which the truth of faith makes itself accessible and highly attractive on the level of reason. Here is the genuine essence of ecumenical dialogue in which, without one interlocutor trying to establish that he alone is "right" on all points, both strive to share as much as they can of a truth they possess to some extent in common.[10]

---

10. The *ratio fidei* must be carefully examined in all Anselm's works, for it is always the basis on which his meditation rests, and it is always the same *ratio*. The question under discussion in *De Casu Diaboli* is not whether there is a devil, or whether he sinned, but how he sinned: *Peccasse illum*

But Anselm's dialogue is actually for Boson and himself even more than it is for the hypothetical Moslem. His purpose is to increase, by reason, their Christian joy in revealed truth. Intelligible joy is regarded by Anselm as one of the characteristic fruits of monastic study and prayer. The understanding which faith attains by meditation, study, prayer and intuition stands half-way between the obscure assent of faith and the pure light of the beatific vision.

Anselm's Soteriology

The *Cur Deus Homo* is often treated as a purely juridical soteriology. This approach ends only in a caricature which reduces Anselm's thought on the relation of man to God to that of the feudal serf to his lord, or worse still, a possession to its owner, and then procedes ambiguously to treat the disorder of sin as though it were a violation of commutative[VII] justice. This view contains internal contradictions which finally make it unintelligible, and modern scholarship has happily and clearly established that Anselm's idea of justice is by no means a mere extrapolation of tenth-century Lombardic law.[11]

Far from regarding sin purely and simply as an infinite offence against an infinite will, and reducing the problem of redemption to the question of placating an infinite rage by the immolation of an innocent Victim of infinite worth, Anselm

---

non dubitas quoniam a iusto Deo non potuit iniuste damnari; sed quaeris quomodo peccavit (c. 4).[VI] Obviously this has nothing whatever to do with apologetics in the modern sense of the word. It is a theological meditation on the nature of liberty, grace and sin, not an attempt to convince someone who doubts the existence of the devil or of sin. Paradoxically, Anselm's non-apologetic *ratio* is much more relevant to modern thought than a conventional apologetic approach might be! See the discussion of *De Casu* by D. P. Henry, "Remarks on St. Anselm's Treatment of Possibility," *Spicilegium Beccense*, pp. 19 ff.

11. Cf. E. Fairweather, "'*Iustitia Dei*' as '*Ratio*' of the Incarnation," *Spicilegium Beccense*, pp. 326 ff. He says: "A conventional interpretation of the *Cur Deus Homo* along merely juridical lines would seriously misrepresent Anselm's argument" (p. 330), and "We are a long way from a duty made in the image of an 'ancient Lombardic King' self-assertively and anxiously jealous for his honour and prestige" (p. 334).

develops a soteriology that implies and suggests a profoundly contemplative view of God's plan for man and for the cosmos. He takes with the greatest seriousness the evil of sin as an injury and dishonor to God's love for us, as our Creator and Father; but we must ascertain precisely what Anselm means by God's honor.

The traditionally accepted language of sin as an "outrage" and "insult" to God must not be interpreted too exclusively in an anthropomorphic sense. Anselm stresses the concept of God's honor because it emphasizes that sin is an offence against His *Person* even more than His nature.[12] But at the same time he does not make any undue use of images that suggest wounded or outraged "feelings" on God's part, as if God were an extremely sensitive and vulnerable human. The injury done by sin strikes at God not in His being[13] but in the order and harmony of His creation, and the reparation of this injury must consist first of all in a restoration of the violated order willed by God in His wisdom and love.[14]

---

12. Cf. M. Nédoncelle, "La notion de personne dans l'oeuvre de S. Anselme," *Spicilegium Beccense*, pp. 31 ff.
13. Anselm says: *Deum impossibile est honorem suum perdere* (*Cur Deus Homo* I, 14, Roques, p 276)[VIII] and *palam igitur est quia Deum, quantum in ipso est, nullus potest honorare vel exhonorare; sed quantum in se est hoc aliquis facere videtur, cum voluntatem suam voluntati ejus subjicit aut subtrahit* (*ibid.* p. 280).[IX]
14. See E. Fairweather's contribution to the First International Conference of Medieval Philosophy, held in 1958, "Truth, Justice and Moral Responsibility in the Thought of St. Anselm," published *in L'homme et son destin d'après les penseurs du moyen âge* (Louvain, 1960). After stressing the crucial importance of Anselm's dialogue *De Veritate* for all his thought, Fairweather rightly highlights Anselm's doctrine of *rectitudo*, or the *veritas* which the creature possesses in itself in so far as it is conformed to the being of its divine Creator. Perception of this *veritas* as a result of perfect union of minds and wills with Him is the perfect *intellectus* which ought to be the fruit of *ratio fidei*. But the creature must make this understanding itself fruitful by acceptance of the responsibilities and obligations which it manifests to him. In other words, the will must will rectitude for its own sake, and this constitutes its freedom and likeness to God. Hence the rectitude of the creature is not mere submission to an arbitrary will of a despotic Creator, but free and loving acceptance of the wisdom of the Creator as manifested in the order He has established. Fairweather concludes; "Anselm's soteriology, then, like his doctrine of grace and sin on the one hand and his picture of the structure of reality on

Here St. Anselm's meditation on Redemption (*Meditatio Redemptionis Humanae*[x]) provides a perfect commentary on the important chapters which open the second book of the *Cur Deus Homo*. The *Meditatio* is perfectly clear that the death of Christ on the Cross was not intended to assuage a supposed divine thirst for vengeance, nor was it simply an expression of the infinite power of God venting itself on the evil of sin in the form of an infinitely virulent punishment. The mystery of the Cross is something far deeper than this: it is a mystery of love in which justice and love are seen to be not opposed but one in the infinite holiness of God. And this, indeed, is the divine honor in its highest sense: for an honor that would be fully restored by a mere exercise of force would not be worthy of an infinitely wise and loving God. His transcendent honor is satisfied not by punishment alone but by reconciliation. The love and rectitude which repair the violation of divine truth and goodness as reflected in the order of creation, restore man to the friendship of God, and reestablish him at the same time in that truth and rectitude which give him a central place in God's wise plan.

The *Meditatio* says:

> The divine nature could not labor or be humiliated, and it did not need to be. But it was needful that these things be done by a human nature, *in order that humanity be restored to that dignity for which it had been made*. Yet neither human nature itself, nor anything else that was not God, could suffice for such a task. For man cannot be restored to that for which he was made (*homo ad quod institutus erat non restituitur*) unless he is promoted to a likeness of those angels in which there is no sin [hence the need for a perfect satisfaction for sin] … IN ALL THIS, THE DIVINE NATURE WAS NOT HUMBLED BUT HUMAN NATURE WAS EXALTED. NOR WAS THE DIVINE NATURE CHANGED, BUT HUMAN NATURE WAS MERCIFULLY AIDED. (*In omnibus his non est divina natura humiliata sed humana*

---

the other, is indissolubly linked with the all-pervasive idea of *man's moral responsibility for the maintenance of justice and truth*" (p. 391).

> *est exaltata. Nec illa est immutata, sed ista est misericorditer adjuta.*)[XI]

Here of course we are at the very heart of Anselm's Christology, and therefore at the heart of all his thinking, whether theological, monastic, ascetic, or what you will. This concept, that emphasizes above all the liberty of Christ, His spontaneity in sacrificing His life to the Father, thereby to restore the violated order to the universe by *putting man back in his original place* among the angels, is far from the quasi-materialistic view that considers the destruction of the humanity of the Son both necessary and sufficient to appease the Father! What a notion of that Fatherhood from which all paternity in heaven and on earth takes its name! Anselm exclaims: "It was not that the Father compelled this Man [Christ] to die by His command, but that the Son spontaneously did that which He understood was pleasing to the Father and profitable to man."[XII]

Here every word is important, including the word 'understood" (*intellexit*), for the sacrifice of the Son was not a blind submission to an arbitrary and incomprehensible will, having infinite power over Him. It was perfectly free, clear-sighted, spontaneous choice, and what was pleasing to the Father in this sacrifice was not so much the shedding of physical (albeit infinitely precious) Blood, as the supreme generosity of the love which such obedience implied. Anselm emphasizes that this sacrifice was not something that the Father could justly demand of His Son (*non enim eum ad hoc Pater potuit cogere quod ab eo exigere non debuit …*[XIII]). This again is crucial to Anselm's concept of the divine honor: the "honor" of God does not reside in His infinite power to exact every form of blind submission to an arbitrary will, but in the perfect concord of transcendent justice and love, expressed in the joyous liberty of the sacrifice accepted by the Son for the glory of the Father's love and for the salvation and happiness of men.

Boson shrewdly remarks[15] that we would owe no thanks to God if the sacrifice of the Cross had been solely a reparation of His own honor, as if He had to save man or lose His honor. Here we already find ourselves in a totally new perspective. It is not a question of God's honor being repaired by the punishment of

---

15. *Quomodo ergo negari poterit plus hoc propter se facere quam propter nos?*

sin in Christ's death, though that death is indeed a perfect satisfaction for all the sins of the world. But here we see that God's honor demands, above all, man's salvation and restoration – a fact which is overlooked by those who see only the "juridical" aspect of Anselm's doctrine.

Anselm makes it quite clear that the satisfaction given to God for man's sin was not something that God required for Himself alone but rather for mankind and for the beauty of His cosmos: *hoc propter nos, non propter se, nullius egens suscepit.*[XVII] Indeed, in creating man, God, so to speak, obligated Himself beforehand to "perfect the good He had begun" even though He foresaw man's defection: *tamen bonitate sua illum creando sponte se ut perficeret inceptum bonum quasi obligavit.*[XVIII] Hence the honor of God that is wounded by sin and demands satisfaction is seen to be nothing other than His infinite goodness and loving concern for man His creature. Anselm brings us close to the superb mystical vision of the cosmos and of Redemption which we find in Dame Julian of Norwich,[XIX] whose optimistic theology in many respects resembles his.

Both Roques and Fairweather make this clear. The rational creature honors God by understanding and accepting the created order, in which His uncreated perfections are reflected and made manifest, and by freely taking his proper place in that order. Where sin dishonors God, is then, in refusing to recognize and accept His will in the order of creation and in the truth where He has made us stand.[16]

Aut si ita est: quam gratiam illi debemus pro eo quod facit propter se? Quomodo etiam imputabimus nostram salutem ejus gratiae, si nos salvat necessitate? (*Cur Deus Homo*, II, Roques p. 358).[XIV] Here as usual the emphasis is on the divine liberty, manifested in the redemption as primarily a work of love and justice, and not merely of "necessity" by which God would be, so to speak, compelled to seek His own "satisfaction." Anselm shows that in being committed to justice and love, God freely follows a higher necessity. *Cum vero ipse sponte se necessitate benefaciendi subdit nec invitus eam sustinet, tunc utique majorem beneficii gratiam meretur.*[XV] The context is important for Anselm's monastic doctrine, as he draws an analogy between this spontaneous *necessitas* in God and the obligation of a monastic vow. *Tale est cum quis sanctae conversationis sponte vovet propositum ... non minus sed magis gratus est Deo, nec sancte vivere dicendus est necessitate, sed eadem qua vovit libertate* (*ibid.* pp. 358-360).[XVI]

16. "L'honneur de Dieu veut que soient respectés l'ordre et la beauté de sa

Anselm himself sums this up in a magnificent passage, which recalls the cosmology of the twelfth-century school of Chartres:

> When any creature observes the order which is its own and which is, so to speak, prescribed for it, whether by nature or by reason, it is said to obey God and to honor Him. THIS IS ESPECIALLY SO OF RATIONAL NATURE FOR IT HAS RECEIVED THE GIFT TO UNDERSTAND WHAT IT OUGHT TO DO (*cui datum est intelligere quid debeat*). Therefore when [a rational being] wills what it ought [or what it owes, *quod debet*] it honors God, not in the sense that it confers some benefit upon Him, but because it freely submits to His will and His disposition. In so doing it preserves, in so far as it can, His order in the cosmos and the beauty of the cosmos itself.[17]

These intuitions of Anselm's soteriology are supported and clarified by comparison with St. Augustine. It is true that St. Anselm is quite free of every trace of that primitive doctrine of the "rights of the devil,"[18] traces of which are still found in Augustine. But

---

création" (Roques, p.126).[XX] Fairweather points out that God's *iustitia* in creation is His own *rectitudo*, the right ordering of all things patterned on the hidden beauty and truth of His own nature. The *iustitia* that is violated by sin and must be repaired is then not an abstract juridical norm, but the reflection of the divine love, wisdom and goodness in the order established by Him for His creation. "The reality of things is their *rectitudo*, and expresses the *justitia Dei*.... Anselm sees in creaturely being a reflection of creative *justitia*.... Man's *nuditas justitiae* violates the intrinsic order of reality, the *rectitudo* whose ultimate principle is God's own being."[XXI] We know God by a right use of our freedom fully and spontaneously according to His truth, in a way that upholds the order which expresses His nature in creation. See Fairweather, "'*Iustitia Dei*' as '*Ratio*' of the Incarnation," *Spicilegium Beccense*, pp. 332, 334.

17. *Cur Deus Homo*, I, 15; Roques, p. 228. Hence we see the full justice of Roques' penetrating summation: "What strikes us in this theology, which is in so many respects characterized by the primacy of God's honor, is the primacy of man and of his salvation." For "it is essential to the honor of God that humanity, destined by Him for blessedness, should not perish" (p. 66).
18. This is the old idea that by original sin the devil had acquired a strict right over fallen man and that the price of man's Redemption therefore had to be paid to the devil. In other words the death of Christ is thus regarded not

already in Augustine we see the beginnings of Anselm's concept of *iustitia* which is perhaps more ontological than juridical.

Already in Augustine there is a contrast between power and justice. The devil is the one who strives to exercise power, and the sacrifice of Christ, far from being a submission to the power of death wielded by the devil, and thus in some sense an acknowledgement of a diabolical triumph in sin, is a conquest of diabolical power by pure justice that totally relinquishes power. The devil is a lover of power (*amator potentiae*) and for the sake of power he abandons justice along with everything else. "It was therefore pleasing to God," says Augustine, "that in order to wrest man from the devil's power, the devil should be overcome by justice and not by force, and that thus men, in imitation of Christ, should seek to overcome the devil by justice and not by force."[19] Here we have a striking theological justification for that non-violence which Gandhi appealed to as the pure force of truth (*ahimsa*).[XXII]

Two Biographical Works

The thirty-seven pages of detailed bibliography in Roques' edition of *Cur Deus Homo* were printed too soon to include the latest and most excellent biographical works on St. Anselm, both by Professor R. W. Southern of Oxford. One of these is his new critical edition of the *Vita Anselmi* by Anselm's disciple Eadmer,[20]

---

only as a satisfaction owed to divine justice but also in some way owed to diabolical power!

19. *De Trinitate*, XIII, 13 (*P.L.*, 42, 1026-1027); see J. Plagnieux, "Le binome *Justitia-Potentia* dans la sotériologie augustinienne et anselmienne," *Spicilegium Beccense*, pp. 141 ff. Plagnieux shows on this basis that in the soteriology of Anselm "it is far less a question of law than of evangelical spirituality." The Redemption is not the issue of a struggle within God between His infinite justice and His absolute power, but rather "the option of the Savior determined to fulfill all justice without recourse to the facilities of a simple trial of strength." Hence the opposition is not between "the power of law and the law of power, but between love of justice and the will to power" (see p. 143).
20. *The Life of St. Anselm Archbishop of Canterbury by Eadmer*, edited with introduction, notes and translation by R. W. Southern (Edinburgh: Thomas Nelson and Sons, 1962). Eadmer actually wrote two biographical accounts of his master, one dealing more with his public life, the *Historia Novorum*

the other is Southern's own historical study of *St. Anselm and His Biographer*.[21]

Roques, in a passing reference to Eadmer's *Vita Anselmi* treats it as a conventional medieval hagiography in which, he says, "the writer is entirely conquered by his subject and is naturally inclined to emphasize all the marvelous events that would confer upon him a greater glory" (p. 11). Is this a fair evaluation of the *Vita*? Southern, on the contrary, treats Eadmer's life as a quite original and new attempt to evaluate the character and personality of a saint, while discussing his miracles with objectivity and caution.[22] Southern does not hesitate to characterize Eadmer's *Vita* as "the first intimate portrait of a saint in our history by an observant pupil and ardent disciple." His chapter on Eadmer's life of Anselm in *St. Anselm and His Biographer* is particularly helpful in its evaluation of the three kinds of traditional hagiography in the middle ages, and in the evidence it gives that Eadmer's *Vita* fell outside these categories.

The special value of Southern's works for us is that they are filled with important monastic material. He has studied in great detail the monastic background in England after the Norman Conquest, and particularly the Cathedral monastery at Canterbury in Anselm's time. He has given us a survey of the spiritual writings produced at Canterbury and elsewhere by Anselm's disciples, and this can be completed by those texts of the Anselmian school recently published by Dom Leclercq.[23] Above all, Southern shows

---

(*P. L.*, 159, 347 ff.) and the *Vita* which is more personal, and so to speak a character-study of the saint.

21. R. W. Southern, *St. Anselm and His Biographer: A Study of Monastic Life and Thought, 1059–c. 1130* (New York: Cambridge University Press, 1963). Southern points out that just as Eadmer wanted his two biographies to complete each other, so, Southern's edition of the *Vita* and his own book are also complementary: "The two books are quite distinct, but Eadmer's own words in describing his two attempts to portray his master may (I should like to think) be applied to them."[XXIII]

22. See *St. Anselm and His Biographer*, p. 317. Also, "Eadmer would have been glad to see miracles but he somehow failed to see anything very conclusive. Why was this? Probably because he was a rather exact observer" (p. 331). Southern stresses Eadmer's fidelity to what he actually saw, in contrast to some other companions of Anselm who were much more readily able to see what they wanted to see.

23. See *Studia Anselmiana*, 31 (1953): texts of Elmer of Canterbury, Gilbert

us how Anselm's theological thought was preeminently the thought of a monk, and arose out of an authentically monastic experience. The *Proslogion* itself, though its celebrated "ontological argument" has been so frequently and hotly discussed, was in no way a controversial work but the result of reflection in monastic peace, and of an illumination received at Vigils. "All his writings of this period [at Bec] are the witness of this peace [of thirty years in the quiet of his monastery]: his intimate correspondence with friends at Canterbury and elsewhere, his prayers and meditations, his *Proslogion* and *Monologion* – themselves meditations on the nature of God – and his philosophical dialogues, which were the product of his teaching in the cloister."[24]

The main purpose of Eadmer's *Vita Anselmi* is to portray Anselm not as a miracle worker and a charismatic figure, but rather as a perfect monk, a father and friend to his monks, a man of profound humility, full of love for his vocation and his brethren, totally absorbed in that charity of Christ which was constantly pressing him to struggle for the truth and rectitude which formed the heart of his teaching.

The study of St. Anselm is essential for a complete view of monastic theology. One wonders how it happens that St. Anselm was omitted from the thick volume recently devoted to essays on this subject,[25] especially since it is now well known that the English monks who were his disciples formed their own school of monastic spirituality. To conclude in words of Dom A. Wilmart: "St. Anselm, a man of mildness already honored by his contemporaries, is an admirable genius whom one reads with great pleasure; his imitators and followers, though less gifted, are not company to be despised."[26] Wilmart adds that Anselm is not to be

---

Crispin and Odo of Canterbury; see also: "Une doctrine de la vie monastiquc dans l'école du Bec," *Spicilegium Beccense*, pp. 477 ff.

24. *St. Anselm and His Biographer*, pp. 47-48. For further studies on Anselm's monastic ideas see the following essays in *Spicilegium Beccense*: Dom P. Consir: "Les relations de S. Anselme avec Cluny," pp. 439 ff.; Dom J. Laporte, "S. Anselme et l'ordre monastique," pp. 455 ff.; Dom J.-M. Ponchet: "La componction de l'humilité et de la piété chez S. Anselme," pp. 489 ff.; Dom P. Salmon: "L'ascèse monastique dans les lettres de S. Anselme," pp. 509 ff.

25. *Théologie de la vie monastique* (Paris: Aubier, 1961).

26. "La tradition des prières de saint Anselme," *Revue Bénédictine*, 36 (1926), pp. 70-71.

accounted for by any contemporary influence: "He is explained only by his personality; after Augustine it would be vain to seek greater gifts in the West, and the like will not be seen again until St. Thomas."[27]

Professor Southern has earned the gratitude of monks by his biography of Anselm above all by making known to us the monastic milieu at Canterbury in the early twelfth century.

I. Karl Barth, *Dogmatics in Outline* (New York: Harper, 1959) 66.

II. J. P. Migne, ed., *Patrologiae Cursus Completus*, *Series Latina* [*PL*], 221 vols. (Paris: Garnier, 1844-1865) vol. 158, cols. 259C-432B.

III "Perhaps for the last time, East and West met with such evidence in the miracle that St. Anselm's argument embodies."

IV. "the purely rational method of Anselm … a basic apologetic tendency.… where we join *ratio* with belief, we have apologetics.… The confidence to prove to know dogma through reason, and so to convict disbelief and to vindicate and celebrate belief, was an error. Therein lies the tragedy of Anselm."

V. "Anselm – a friend, but truth a greater friend" (Schmitt, *Spicilegium Beccense* 370).

VI. "You do not doubt that he had sinned, because he would not have been unjustly damned by a just God; but you seek how he sinned."

VII. Text reads: "communative".

VIII. "It is impossible for God to lose His honor" (text reads: "p. 376").

IX. "Therefore it is clear that no one can honor or dishonor God as He is in Himself, but someone seems to do this in himself, to the extent possible, when he subjects or withdraws his will for God's will" (1.15).

X. *PL* 158, cols. 762C-769B.

XI. Col. 765B (emphasis added).

XII. "*Non enim illi homini Pater ut moreretur cogendo praecepit; sed ille quod Patri placiturum et hominibus profuturum intellexit, hoc sponte fecit*" (*PL* 158, col. 766B).

XIII. *PL* 158, col. 766B ("For the Father could not compel Him to this which He ought not demand of Him").

---

27. "Un traité attribué à saint Bernard," *Auteurs spirituels et textes dévots du moyen âge* (Paris, 1932), p. 88.

XIV. "How then can it be denied that He does this more for His own sake than for ours? But if it is so, what thanks do we owe Him for what He does for His own sake? How will we attribute our salvation to His grace, if He saves us out of necessity?"

XV. "Truly when He Himself submits voluntarily to the necessity of doing good, and does not put up with it unwillingly, then certainly He deserves greater thanks for His good work."

XVI. "Such is the case when someone freely vows commitment to a holy way of life … he is not less but more pleasing to God, and should not be said to live in a holy way out of necessity, but out of the same liberty with which he made the vow."

XVII. "In need of nothing, He undertook this on our behalf, not His own" (2.5).

XVIII. "Nevertheless by creating him by His goodness, He freely committed Himself, in a sense, to complete the good work He had begun" (2.5).

XIX. For Merton's reflections on Julian of Norwich, see *Conjectures of a Guilty Bystander* 191-92 and *Mystics and Zen Masters* 140-44.

XX. "The honor of God desires that the order and beauty of His creation be respected."

XXI. See *De Conceptu Virginali et Originali Peccato*, c. 24; "*Haec nuditas iustitiae descendit ad omnes ab Adam, in quo humana natura se spoliavit eadem iustitia*" (*PL* 158, col. 457B) ("This nakedness of justice descended to all from Adam, in whom human nature stripped itself of this justice").

XXII. Though Merton uses the Sanscrit word for non-violence here, his reference to "the pure force of truth" is the equivalent of the term Gandhi himself created for his non-violent resistance: *satyagraha*.

XXIII. Eadmer, *Life of Anselm* vii.

Guigo the Carthusian
(c. 1083–1137)

The Solitary Life – A Letter of Guigo

On February 5, 1963, Merton wrote in his journal, "Today (a good warm day, almost spring like after all the cold) I translated this beautiful letter of Guigo [misread as "Guido"] on solitude" (*Turning Toward the World* 296). The reference was to the letter headed "*De Vita Solitaria ad Ignotum Amicum*" by Guigo, fifth prior of the Carthusian Order, that Merton had found in the bilingual Latin/French edition published the year before in the Sources Chrétiennes series. On February 23, Merton sent a copy of this translation to Dame Marcella Van Bruyn, OSB of Stanbrook Abbey in Worcester, UK, in response to her inquiry, prompted by their mutual friend Jacques Maritain, about the possibility of the abbey press printing a limited edition of some work by Merton (see *School of Charity* 160-61). A month later he wrote to the abbey printer, Dame Hildelith Cumming, OSB, saying: "I assure you that I am brimming over with confidence in you, and delighted that you will print the Guigo Letter. Your plans sound excellent" (*School of Charity* 161). Correspondence with Dame Hildelith about fonts and other details of printing continued over the coming months (see *School of Charity* 168, 171, 175, 203). On September 23, 1963, while he was in the hospital, Merton wrote in his journal: "Proofs of Guigo's *Letter on the Solitary* Life reached me here from Stanbrook and they are handsome" (*Dancing in the Water of Life* 20). The final result was a small (6.5' x 3.75') eleven-page booklet, issued in December 1963, entitled *The Solitary Life* (a somewhat unfortunate title as it had previously been used for another limited-edition publication, an original essay by Merton printed by his friend Victor Hammer on his hand-press in 1960), and subtitled "A Letter of Guigo," consisting of a four-page introduction by Merton and five pages of the translated letter. On July 22, 1964 Merton wrote to Dame Hildelith, "Everyone likes *The Solitary Life* immensely and all are struck by the beauty of the printing" (*School of Charity* 223). The book was dedicated, quasi-anonymously (initials only), to Merton's friend and correspondent Dom J.-B. Porion, Carthusian Procurator General (see *School of Charity* 162, 210-11), to whom Merton had first mentioned Guigo in a letter of February 9, 1952. Merton's initial encounter with Guigo, in his book of *Meditations*, had been less than enthusiastic: in a September 7, 1947 journal entry, he wrote, "I don't think as much of Guigo I's *Meditations* as I once thought I might. Very lapidary, but not on an interesting enough level. Why was he apparently writing for seculars? Or was he? I'd better read them some more before I can say" (*Entering the Silence* 105). He evidently did not pursue the study of Guigo to any great extent at this time, writing to Jean Leclercq on October 9, 1950 that "we would like to get Wilmart's *Pensées du B. Guigue*, if this is Guigo the Carthusian. I have never yet gone into him. His lapidary style fascinates me. He is better than Pascal. Yet I love Pascal" (*School of Charity* 25). By the time he writes to Dom Porion, he has found a kind of model in Guigo, noting that his own current writing is mainly in the form of maxims and adding, "sometimes they seem to be a little like Guigo. I think he is very fine. I like his lapidary quality"; he goes on to say that he sometimes uses Guigo's meditations in spiritual direction and imagines assembling of book of these laconic sayings with his own brief reflections on them (*School of Charity* 33-34). Merton's rekindling of interest in Guigo in the early 1960s is most evident in the extensive discussion of the *Meditations* in the novitiate conferences on St. Bernard, being presented at the very time when he translated the letter on solitude (see *Cistercian Fathers and Their Monastic Theology* lxxxvii-lxxxix, 81-101). He notes that Guigo's gift of a copy of the *Meditations* to St. Bernard prompted the letter on love of the abbot of Clairvaux to Guigo and his monks that was appended to his treatise *De Diligendo Deo* (*On Loving God*), and was a principal source for Bernard's own doctrine of love. In fact Merton spends considerably more time in these conferences discussing Guigo's maxims than he does on the (much better known) letter they inspired. He quotes dozens of the aphoristic reflections of Guigo on truth, on self-love and attachments, on true and false charity, on the power of good to overcome evil. Though largely a tissue of quotations, most still in the original Latin, Merton's discussion of Guigo's collection of aphorisms exhibits an enthusiasm that clearly carried over to the letter on solitude that he introduced and translated. In his Introduction, Merton calls Guigo "one of those extraordinary figures in literature and in spirituality who, unknown and perhaps in some sense inaccessible to the many, have been accorded the most unqualified admiration by the discerning few," and in reference to the *Meditations* he adds, "Some of the most fundamental ideas in Bernard's own doctrine of love were inspired by his Carthusian friend." He calls the letter itself, thought to have been written toward the end of Guigo's life, "a masterpiece of its kind," filled with many of the traditional "classical tropes on the solitary life" that date back to the patristic era, an invitation not only to its unknown recipient but to the wider audience of its subsequent readers to "struggle with the falsity and delusion in ourselves" in order to "break through the deceptive veil" by which "the world" estranges its followers from truth, from reality. He concludes: "There is an inimitable naked power in the austere style of Guigo the Carthusian from which every suggestion of ornament, indeed every useless word is ruthlessly excluded. The extraordinary compression of this thought and language convey something of the fervor, the passionate seriousness of this saint and genius, a pure exemplar of the Carthusian spirit and certainly the greatest Carthusian writer."

Guigo is one of those extraordinary figures in literature and in spirituality who, unknown and perhaps in some sense inaccessible to the many, have been accorded the most unqualified admiration by the discerning few. Thirty years ago Dom Wilmart, editing Guigo's *Meditations*, did not hesitate to say that he considered this little book "the most original work that has come down to us from the truly creative period of the middle ages."[I] No small praise when we reflect who Guigo's contemporaries were! Dom Wilmart names a few: not only Hildebert, William of Conches, Bernard of Chartres, Honorius "of Autun," Gilbert de la Porrée, but even Abelard, Hugh of St. Victor and St. Bernard himself. The opinion is neither rash nor even new. The very ones Wilmart names were among the first to praise Guigo without reservations. Peter the Venerable called him "the fairest flower of our religion."[II] We know what effect the *Meditations* of Guigo had on Bernard of Clairvaux (see St. Bernard, *Letter xi*[III]). Some of the most fundamental ideas in Bernard's own doctrine of love were inspired by his Carthusian friend. Wilmart compares Guigo, without exaggeration, to Pascal. We find in the *Meditations* the same psychological finesse as in the *Pensées*, the same metaphysical solidity, the same religious depth. But we also find in the twelfth-century Carthusian a rocklike wholeness and coherence, untroubled by the anxieties and ambivalences that stirred the solitary of Port Royal. The difference is doubtless to be sought not only in the characters of the two and in their lives, but also in their times.

Fifth Prior of the Grande Chartreuse, Guigo was born in 1083 in Dauphiné. He entered the Chartreuse at the age of twenty-three, and three years later was elected Prior. We cannot suppose that the Carthusians were given to impetuous or ill-considered action. The choice is significant. In fact, Guigo held this post for thirty of the most crucial years in the early history of the Carthusians. He made the first foundations and wrote the *Consuetudines* (Customs).[IV] He edited the letters of St. Jerome (and the edition has recently been found). He wrote his *Meditations*, as well as a life of St. Hugh, Bishop of Grenoble.[V] In 1132 he rebuilt the Grande Chartreuse which had been destroyed by an avalanche.

The present letter[VI] is supposed to have been written after this event, toward the end of Guigo's life. (He died 27 July, 1136.) We do not know to whom it was addressed, nor do we know how he responded to the invitation.

The letter itself is a masterpiece of its kind, surely worthy of an assiduous reader of Jerome. It contains some of the classical tropes on the solitary life: the *otium negotiosum*, or the contemplative leisure which is more productive than any activity; the *militia Christi*, in which the monk, soldier of Christ, fights not against others but against his own passions, overcoming the world in himself, offering his bodily life in sacrifice to Christ. The hermit, sitting alone in silence and poverty, is the "true philosopher" because, as Guigo says in another place, he seeks the truth in its nakedness, stripped and nailed to the Cross. *Sine aspectu et decore, crucique affixa, adoranda est veritas!*[VII]

It is this utter devotion to truth that has led Guigo himself, we feel, into solitude. To love solitude is to love truth, for in solitude one is compelled to grapple with illusion. The solitary life is a battle with subjectivity in which victory is to be gained not by the subject, but by Truth. Unless we struggle with the falsity and delusion in ourselves, we can never break through the deceptive veil of rationalizations with which "the world" adorns and conceals its empty wisdom.

There is an inimitable naked power in the austere style of Guigo the Carthusian from which every suggestion of ornament, indeed every useless word is ruthlessly excluded. The extraordinary compression of this thought and language convey something of the fervor, the passionate seriousness of this saint and genius, a pure exemplar of the Carthusian spirit and certainly the greatest Carthusian writer.

Abbey of Gethsemani
Lent, 1963.

* * * * * * *

TO AN
UNKNOWN FRIEND
Written at the
Grand Chartreuse
in the last days of his Priorate
about 1135

TO
THE REVEREND N
GUIGO
LEAST OF THOSE SERVANTS
OF THE CROSS
WHO ARE IN THE CHARTERHOUSE
TO LIVE AND TO DIE
FOR CHRIST

One man will think another happy. I esteem him happy above all who does not strive to be lifted up with great honors in a palace, but who elects, humble, to live like a poor country man in a hermitage; who with thoughtful application loves to meditate in peace; who seeks to sit by himself in silence.

For to shine with honors, to be lifted up with dignities, is in my judgement a way of little peace, subject to perils, burdened with cares, treacherous to many, and to none secure. Happy in the beginning, perplexed in its development, wretched in its end. Flattering to the unworthy, disgraceful to the good, generally deceptive to both. While it makes many wretched, it satisfies none, makes no one happy.

But the poor and lonely life, hard in its beginning, easy in its progress, becomes, in its end, heavenly. It is constant in adversity, trusty in hours of doubt, modest in those of good fortune. Sober fare, simple garments, laconic speech, chaste manners. The highest ambition, because without ambition. Often wounded with sorrow at the thought of past wrong done, it avoids present, is wary of future evil. Resting on the hope of mercy, without trust in its own merit, it thirsts after heaven, is sick of earth, earnestly strives for right conduct, which it retains in constancy and holds firmly for ever. It fasts with determined constancy in love of the cross, yet consents to eat for the body's need. In both it observes the greatest moderation, for when it dines it restrains greed and when it fasts, vanity. It is devoted to reading, but mostly in the Scripture canon and in holy books, where it is more intent upon the inner marrow of meaning than on the spume of words. But you may praise or wonder more at this: that such a life is continually idle yet never lazy. For it finds many things indeed to do, so that time is more often lacking to it than this or that occupation. It more often laments that its time has slipped away than that its business is tedious.

What else? A happy subject, to advise leisure, but such an exhortation seeks out a mind that is its own master, concerned with its own business, disdaining to be caught up in the affairs of others, or of society. Who so fights as a soldier of Christ in peace as to refuse double service as a soldier of God and a hireling of the world. Who knows for sure it cannot here be glad with this world and then in the next reign with God.

Small matters are these, and their like, if you recall what drink He took at the gibbet, who calls you to kingship. Like it or not, you must follow the example of Christ poor if you would have fellowship with Christ in His riches. If we suffer with Him, says the Apostle, we will reign with Him.[VIII] If we die with Him, then we shall live together with Him.[IX] The Mediator Himself replied to the two disciples who asked Him if one of them might sit at His right hand and the other at His left: 'can you drink the chalice which I am about to drink?'[X] Here he made clear that it is by cups of earthly bitterness that we come to the banquet of the Patriarchs and to the nectar of heavenly celebrations.

Since friendship strengthens confidence I charge, advise and beg you, my best beloved in Christ, dear to me since the day I knew you, that as you are farseeing, careful, learned and most acute, take care to save the little bit of life that remains still unconsumed, snatch it from the world, light under it the fire of love to burn it up as an evening sacrifice to God. Delay not, but be like Christ both priest and victim, in an odor of sweetness to God and to men.

Now, that you may fully understand the drift of all my argument, I appeal to your wise judgement in few words with what is at once the counsel and desire of my soul. Undertake our observance as a man of great heart and noble deeds, for the sake of your eternal salvation. Become a recruit of Christ and stand guard in the camp of the heavenly army watchful with your sword on your thigh against the terrors of the night.

Here, then, I urge you to an enterprise that is good to undertake, easy to carry out and happy in its consummation. Let Prayers be said, I beg you, that in carrying out so worthy a business you may exert yourself in proportion to the grace that will smile on you in God's favor. As to where or when you must do this thing, I leave it to the choice of your own prudence. But to delay, or to hesitate will not, as I believe, serve your turn.

I will procede no further with this, for fear that rough and uncouth lines might offend you, a man of palaces and courts.

An end and a measure then to this letter, but never an end to my affection of love for you.

I. *Meditationes Guigonis Prioris Cartusiae: Le Recueil des Pensées du B. Guigue*, ed. and trans. André Wilmart (Paris: J. Vrin, 1936) 9; actually Wilmart is slightly less apodictic – he writes: "Voici, peut-être, l'ouvrage le plus original que nous ait laissé la période vraiment créatrice du moyen âge" ("Here, perhaps, is the most original work that the truly creative period of the Middle Ages has left us").

II. See *Epistola* 3 (to St. Bernard): "*singularis suo tempore, et praeclarissimus religionis flos, domnus Guido prior Carthusiensis*" (J. P. Migne, ed., *Patrologiae Cursus Completus, Series Latina* [*PL*], 221 vols. [Paris: Garnier, 1844-1865] vol. 189, col 402A) ("the outstanding man of his time and the fairest flower of religion, Master Guigo, Prior of the Carthusians").

III. For Merton's discussion of this letter, written in response to the gift of Guigo's *Meditations* and appended to Bernard's treatise *On Loving God* (*De Diligendo Deo*), see *Cistercian Fathers and Their Monastic Theology* 72, 81, 89, 96-107.

IV. *PL* 153, cols. 636-757.

V. *PL* 153, cols. 761B-784D.

VI. *Lettres des Premiers Chartreux*, trans. par un Chartreux, Sources Chrétiennes 88 (Paris: Éditions du Cerf, 1962) 135-49.

VII. "Without an appearance of beauty, nailed to the cross, Truth must be adored" (*Meditationes* 70 [#5]).

VIII. 2 Timothy 2:12.

IX. 2 Timothy 2:11.

X. Matthew 20:22; Mark 10:38.

Blessed Guerric of Igny
(d. 1157)

The Christmas Sermons of Blessed Guerric

In his October 24, 1955 letter to artist and printer Victor Hammer, the first extent item of correspondence in what would soon become a close friendship, Thomas Merton writes: "This is to let you know that work is fast progressing on the translation of the Guerric Christmas sermon. I have enlisted the aid of a nun at Seton Hill College, a good Latinist, who has attacked the job with enthusiasm" (*Letters of Thomas Merton and Victor and Carolyn Hammer* 19). The reference is to a projected volume of translations of the five Christmas Sermons of Blessed Guerric of Igny (d. 1157), considered one of the four Cistercian "evangelists," a monk of Clairvaux whom St. Bernard had appointed abbot of the daughter house of Igny in the Marne valley. The English versions were to be provided by Sr. Rose of Lima, accompanied by an introduction by Merton himself. On November 26, Merton sent Hammer a copy of the completed translations, noting however that in the unlikely event that any "erudite Jews" came across the material they might well "not understand the references to the rejected synagogue as if all this had something to do with anti-Semitism. This might be another obstacle to printing the book. I had not thought of it, of course, when preparing the material" (*Letters* 23-24). Though Merton rather cavalierly dismisses this interpretation, the traditional contrast of Church and Synagogue in these sermons does indeed have an anti-Jewish tone to which Merton would become more sensitive in coming years. Though in his introduction he presents the allegory in these sermons without comment, he will later write, at the conclusion of a longer analysis of the growth of medieval anti-Semitism: "In the theology of the time, the transition from Old to New Testament was more and more the esoteric privilege of those who, understanding the 'mystical sense' of the Old Testament types, were able to see the Charity and the Spirit of Christ in the 'carnal figures' of the Old Testament. But since the mystical understanding implied, in fact, not only a very special culture, but also a highly developed spirituality, it was not the affair of many. The fact that in monasteries there were many monks who could not transcend in this way the Old Testament symbolism and ritual of the monasteries constituted something of a problem. Blessed Guerric of Igny, the Cistercian, in his Christmas sermons (which like all his sermons are very

Pauline) upbraids these severe and rather pessimistic monks and calls them 'the Jews.' Thus again there was a renewal of a very bad conscience among those who were thought and supposed to be the best of Christians. If many of these were still 'no better than Jews,' what about the Jews themselves, down at the bottom of the social scale?" (*Conjectures of a Guilty Bystander* 120). In the event, Hammer and his wife Carolyn decided not to print the sermons volume on one of their hand presses, and it was eventually issued by the Abbey of Gethsemani itself in late 1959. In sending a copy to the Hammers on December 12, 1959, Merton makes disparaging comments on the quality of the printing, "neat and tidy" but otherwise undistinguished, even "silly"; "I tried a new type face," he adds; "well, the less said about it the better" (*Letters* 83-84). The volume opens with the lengthy introductory essay by Merton included below (*Christmas Sermons of Blessed Guerric of Igny* 1-25), highlighting four key themes of the sermons: Christ's birth as God's supreme gift for us and to us; the necessity of accepting that gift personally and communally in a spirit of joy for the gift to be efficacious; the role of "motherhood" of the infant Christ that belongs to the Church, to the monastic community and to each individual member of both; and the importance of receiving Christ the Incarnate Word in the same humility and silence revealed by the Infant in the crib.

The Cistercian Fathers of the 12th century reveal themselves most fully to us when they are contemplating the mercy of God in the mystery of the Incarnation. It is in the sermons for Advent, Christmas, the Epiphany, the Purification, the Circumcision that we are able to find at the same time the great themes common to St. Bernard and his chief disciples, and the particular traits which characterize the individual teaching of each writer. Bl. Guerric[1] is no exception. In order then to get a good introduction to his personality, his spirit and his style, let us consider the five sermons in which he announces the mystery of Christmas.[II]

In these five sermons, Bl. Guerric shows that he has most perfectly absorbed the doctrine of St. Paul and made it entirely his own, in such a way that his perspectives are often purely

---

1. *Blessed Guerric and the Abbey of Igny*. Four great spiritual writers of the school of St. Bernard have been called the "four Cistercian evangelists." Of these the greatest was Bernard himself, Abbot of Clairvaux and Doctor of the Church. The other three were his friends and disciples, William of St. Thierry, Bl. Ailred, abbot of Rievaulx in Yorkshire, and Bl. Guerric of Igny. Of these four, only Bernard is really well known. Ailred and William are beginning to be read in English translations. As far as we know this is the first time anything by or about Guerric has been presented in book form to the English reader. Bl. Guerric, who died in 1157, was second abbot of Igny, a Cistercian monastery founded by Bernard in the Marne valley. Of this celebrated abbey a historian of the Cistercian Order has written: "No house ever had holier abbots and none was more dear to the heart of St. Bernard." Guerric had been recruited in Belgium, where he was a cleric and schoolmaster at the Cathedral of Tournai, by Bernard on one of his preaching tours. Drawn to Clairvaux by the primitive humility of the Grey Monks, living there as "poor brothers of Christ," he spent sixteen years in the obscurity, poverty and peace of the common life before being elevated to the abbotship of Igny. There he became the spiritual father of three hundred monks for whom he had to provide spiritual nourishment in the daily Latin chapter sermons. Some of these were set down in writing, and Guerric asked that they be destroyed when he was about to die. Fortunately a copy survived, and we possess them today in all their original freshness and beauty. They have the clarity, simplicity and joy of the austere Cistercian architecture of the time: a true witness to the authentic spirit of Cîteaux, a radiant joy flowing from perfect abnegation and trust in the mercy of God. For men like Guerric, Christmas was more than a social celebration: it was the mystery of God present among us in the Infant Christ. Suppressed in the French revolution, Igny was restored by Trappists in 1876 and became the scene of the famous conversion-retreat of J. K. Huysmans.[I] Destroyed in World War I it rose again from its ruins in 1925 to become a convent of Cistercian nuns.

Pauline. We find in him the mystery of our new life in Christ, the birth of Christ in the soul which is to be divinized by Him, the pre-eminence of faith, hope and charity over exterior works and practices, the contrast between the faith of the Church and the blindness of the synagogue, the idea of the Pleroma or the Church as the "filling out" of Christ, which brings humanity to its maturity in Him, and gives meaning to the otherwise inexplicable course of human history.

We find above all a spirituality in which joy and gratitude are of obligation, and his sermons have a pronounced "Eucharistic" flavor. The strongest argument he uses to enkindle in our souls a burning charity is that Jesus has come to make our salvation and sanctification easy and joyful, and that if we will only look at Him, and see the greatness of God's mercy radiating from the gift of the Incarnate Word, we will be unable to resist His love, unable to remain cold, despondent and sad. We will respond to His gift of Himself with the spontaneous gift of our own selves in trust, a gift without which the monastic life will always be little more than a sad formality.

1 – *Born for us ... Given to us.*

Three times out of five, Guerric's sermons begin with the text of Isaias, *Puer natus est nobis* (A child is born to us). Each time he emphasizes the fact that the divine child is *born for us*, and *given to us*. In the other two sermons, the same idea dominates. In the fourth he celebrates the fact that the Incarnation has brought about the "fulness of time" because it makes accessible to us the fulness of grace. Finally in the fifth sermon, he invites us to pass over with the shepherds to Bethlehem and "see this word … which God has shown to us" (Luke 2:15). And again it is the same theme, for in "showing us" His Word made flesh, God has revealed all His wisdom to us, and has indeed given Himself as a little one to the little ones: "He is born a Child that He may be given to children" (Serm 5:3. col. 45).

Bl. Guerric, then, sees deep into the implications of the dative – *nobis*. He insists on the fact that the Incarnation is the supreme gift of God's infinite generosity. And therefore the Christmas mystery is one of the most beautiful and complete revelations of the whole mystery of God. The Lord of heaven had nothing to gain from the Incarnation, and yet He gave Himself entirely to us. What is this but a proof of His need to give Himself – a proof that God is *charity*. And so, all has been given us in Jesus.

Not only has God given us all creation, He has given us Himself. The gift could not be more perfect or more complete. The *sublimity* of the gift will be more evident in the Epiphany sermons: but here, on the feast of Christmas, Guerric considers above all the special *delicacy* with which God made Himself a little one in order to become most easily accessible to us. He has not only given Himself, but given Himself in such a way that it is almost impossible for us to fail to receive the gift. And yet we shall see Bl. Guerric lamenting the folly of those who, through their pride and selfishness, refuse so wonderful a favor. "Every best gift and every perfect gift is given to us in Him" (Serm 2:3). All the treasures of God are given to us in Christ, with all the riches of heaven. Of these, most are still hidden in Him. We receive them, but do not see them or enjoy them fully until we have reached heaven. Others are made available to us now, to help us reach heaven.

Among the gifts we can appreciate and use even in this life, we find all the virtues and graces necessary for salvation, in Christ: *subsidia sacramentorum, fercula scripturarum, gradus et ordines ministrorum* (Serm 2:3).[III] But also the Church has been enriched with "the palms of the martyrs, the glory of the confessors, the crowns of the virgins" (id.).

These riches come to us by virtue of the marriage of Christ to His Church in the Incarnation. Refused and rejected by the synagogue, He has brought us the two Testaments, all the Sacraments, His Kingship and Priesthood, the true worship of the true God, all that was contained in figure in the Old Testament is given to us in Christ in Whom all is fulfilled.

> Christ the Lord is the plenitude of all good. In Him the whole treasury of wisdom and knowledge is stored up. He is full of every grace. In Christ the whole plenitude of Deity is embodied, and dwells in Him. (Serm 4:1)

And Guerric goes on to show how we now live truly in the "fulness of time." Receiving from Him grace, virtue and salvation, we also receive His very divinity by being born again in Him.

> He who was born God for Himself is born man for us. Leaving His Godhead and passing over the angels He came down even to us and became one of us. He Who was born eternally for Himself and is the angels' beatitude is born temporally for us and is our redemption. (Serm 3:1)

The doctrine of our redemption through the mysteries of Christ comes out very clearly in Guerric's consideration of Christmas. By virtue of Christ's temporal birth, we are mystically reborn to God. His nativity has "healed" and "purified" our human birth and enabled us to be reborn on a spiritual level as sons of God.

> How blessed, Child Jesus, how amiable is Your nativity that rectifies our birth, betters our condition … and if anyone is ashamed of having been born reprobate let him remember that he can be reborn most blessed. (Serm 3:1)

The last two words, *felicissime renasci* effectively sum up the spirit of Bl. Guerric's Christmas sermons. We are to be happy, not with a mediocre happiness but with a superabundant supernatural joy in God. Happy not only at *considering* this mystery, or imitating the virtues of the infant Christ from afar, but in a new life which we receive as a grace of the feast, by the hidden spiritual power of the Mystery of Christ's birth into the world and time. The whole purpose of the celebration of Christmas is not the commemoration of Christ's birth but the *renewal of this grace of rebirth and spiritual infancy* in the hearts of the faithful. This consists first of all in a new realization that our Christ-life is a gift of the infinite mercy of God. It means also a renewal of gratitude for His generosity. It means new joy in His love. These are the particular means by which the grace of Christmas energizes our spirit and enables us to receive a fresh increase of charity and supernatural life.

The theological root of this grace, imparted to souls in time, is the eternal birth of the Word in the bosom of the Father. Of this eternal birth, His temporal nativity at Bethlehem and His rebirth by grace in our souls are only outward manifestations. The very first sentences of the first sermon strike this keynote, as Guerric wonders at this child who is at the same time the "Ancient of days." *Puer antiquus dierum* (Serm 1:1).

> A Child in the exterior likeness of body and age; the Ancient of days in the eternity of the incomprehensible Word. And yet in the very ancientness of His days, although not a child, He is nevertheless ever new. And not so much new as newness itself which remains in Him ever renewing all things. Whatever recedes from Him grows old and whatever draws near is renewed. (id.)

This generation of the Word is the expression of the infinite life of God, and of His inexhaustible fecundity. It is through the Word, ever springing up from the abyss of the Father's infinite riches, that all life and all reality are communicated to the created world. The mystery of the temporal nativity of the Word Incarnate makes a special, spiritual communication of life possible, a union with God in which, by His "birth" or mission in our souls the Word invisibly unites us to Himself in His divine sonship. *Puer natus est nobis innovandis*.[IV]

Hence the full meaning of *Puer natus est nobis* is now clear. Not only is Jesus born in Bethlehem to save us from sin. Not only do we celebrate Christmas to recall to mind the consoling fact that He is our Redeemer. Not only does He come bringing us graces and gifts. Not only is He born to give Himself in some manner to us. There is much more: He is born in Bethlehem in order that He may be born in us. He gives Himself to us as a child in order to share with us not only His infant smiles and caresses, but above all His very birth and infancy. He is born Son of Man in order that we may be born sons of God, our souls being Bethlehems in which He is born "for us." In this last sense of the word, we see a new nuance of the dative "*nobis*." Just as strictly as He died "for us" – He accomplishes in us a mystical birth that we could never experience without Him. When we are born to eternal life, and when we receive a new increase of eternal life, He accomplishes within us and "for us" our own spiritual birth and growth.

2 – *Born in vain unless also given.*

Now Guerric turns from the objective character of the grace of Christmas, to the importance of its subjective reception by the Church and by the individual Christian. The objective grace of

Christmas would be of no use unless Christ were to be effectively received and "born" in the Church. And this reception of Christ depends not only on the infinite generosity of God, Who gives Himself in His Son, but also on the faith and love of men. This free gift of Love must be received with free and grateful love. Otherwise it cannot be received at all. Bl. Guerric therefore emphasizes the spontaneity and gladness of heart which are the sign of a true Christian spirit: a spirit of joy based on total and trusting acceptance of God's will.

He contrasts the Church and the Synagogue. Israel was "ungrateful, incredulous and impious" (Serm 2:1), and therefore the Word was taken away and given to the Gentiles. And then we see the two figures, Church and Synagogue, depicted in terms that evidently inspired the sculptors of the Medieval cathedrals (for instance, Strasbourg).

> The Church rejoicing this day in thanksgiving for the Son given to her fills the heavens with the voice of praise, but the Synagogue sits mute in the darkness or wearies the lower world with her lamentations. Miserable and blind, why does she not notice how manifestly her God has passed to us, how plainly she is repudiated? (Serm 2:2)

He goes on to show that the Synagogue sits alone, clinging to the Law which merely proves her an adulteress, while the Church has all the adornments of the true Bride. Bl. Guerric considers this mystery thoughtfully. The coming of Christ which brought light to the whole world, brought darkness to the souls of those who ought to have been most enlightened. For the Gentiles He was salvation, and for the Jews a scandal. Why? Because the Church received Him and the Synagogue received Him not. The Church obeyed the message of faith, the Synagogue, attached to the ritual and moral prescriptions of the Law, rejected the word of faith, the *verbum abreviatum*,[v] not precisely because it was too hard but because it was too easy, too simple, not sufficiently complicated and formalistic. The Incarnation was a "sacrament." In taking flesh, Jesus was as it were mingling His divinity with the "slime of the earth" and making mud to anoint the eyes of men that they might understand Him. The Synagogue despised this "sacrament" for its plainness, its commonness. It was too simple to appeal to any but the little ones.

> But it scandalizes you, O Jews, that God is hidden and appears as man to our eyes, as mud made from spittle, to give sight to the blind that they might see Him. (Serm 3:3)

As a matter of fact, the "fulness of time" which is effected by the Incarnation brings to maturity not only the goodness of God's plan for the world, but also the evil of His adversaries. Hence we are confronted not only with a fulness of joy in those who receive Him, but a fulness of sorrow in those who reject Him.

This concept is extremely important. It is not only a matter of the Church being saved and the Synagogue being lost. After all, the Jews have yet to be saved at the end of time. The battle between light and darkness, joy and sorrow, still continues. To be more exact, this fight is the great contest of love and hatred, gratitude and ingratitude. Locked in mortal combat, they are battling for victory in the arena. The Word, Divine Wisdom, descended into the arena for this struggle: the struggle of "Wisdom" against "malice." His aim is to overcome evil with good. Jesus Himself, Divine Wisdom, has already won the victory for His Church. But the struggle goes on still in the rest of mankind. It goes on, above all, in our own hearts. Our interior resentments, anxieties and temptations to discouragement are not merely subjective moods but incidents in a cosmic struggle between good and evil. This is the chief reason why we must resist our passions and not be dominated by them.

> Grace contends as though on a race-course. Wisdom once fought against malice and now descends again into the arena of this world. Wisdom fights not wishing to be overcome by evil but striving to overcome evil by good. (Serm 4:3)

Let us insist on the close connection between wisdom, joy and gratitude on the one hand, and malice, sorrow and ingratitude on the other. It is very important. So important that it is in a sense the key to the spirituality of Christmas in Bl. Guerric and indeed in all the Cistercian Fathers.

Bl. Guerric even goes so far as to say that if Christmas brings us no joy we are among the impious. If the mystery does not edify us, we are among the reprobate. A hard saying: but here are his own words: "If I do not rejoice that the Word of God appears today in the substance of my flesh I am among the impious and if I am not edified, among the reprobate" (Serm 5:1).

These words need to be explained.

First of all, Guerric does not deny that monks may be sad on hearing a "Christmas sermon." "And, brothers, I have sometimes seen the word that is from God listened to with tediousness but the Word that is God should never be seen without joyousness" (id.). Evidently, one may go through the exterior motions of celebrating Christmas without any particular joy. What Guerric means is that one can hardly come to real contact with God, through a realization of the meaning of the Incarnation, without feeling deep joy and peace. Why? Because true faith works through charity, and true charity liberates the inner sources of vital spiritual activity which are also the fountainhead of joy. This is true even on a natural plane, and much more so where there is question of supernatural love, an immanent activity which leads to the realization not only of our own inner potentialities but of the presence and action of God within our souls.

Whatever we may think of the strong terms he uses, it is unquestionable that Bl. Guerric could not understand how a Cistercian monk could be really sad in the depths of his soul. If we are true monks, we have found Jesus. If we have found Him, how can we turn our eyes away from Him? But if our eyes are fixed on Him, and if we constantly remember what the Incarnation means, what is given to us in Him, we can never be truly depressed or discouraged, except of course in a superficial and sensible way that does not enter into the depths of the will. We may *feel* sadness but we will never fully *give in* to it. We cannot take sadness really seriously.

What Guerric is criticizing – and he criticizes it with vehemence and power – is a certain spirit of pessimism and self-pity which sometimes creeps into pious people and infects their souls with resentment and gloom. It is the spirit which expresses itself in murmuring and complaints, a spirit that is dissatisfied with everything, both God and man. This spirit cannot find rest, and constantly seeks to satisfy its restlessness by lamenting and attacking the evil that it sees all around it, even in the monastery. But this says Guerric is the spirit of ingratitude. Those who suffer by it, suffer through their own fault. Guerric applies to the sad monk this text of Ecciesiasticus (14:10): “An evil eye is towards evil things, and he shall not have his fill of bread, but he shall be needy and pensive at his own table.” And again (id. 8) “The eye of the envious is wicked, and he turneth away his face and despiseth his own soul.”

This sadness, proceeding from what today we might call neurosis, deprives the Christian of the daily bread of his soul, makes him a “miserable, brutish and stupid and envious animal, who cheats himself of the enjoyment of this ‘good day’ [the fullness of time – the Incarnation] … He passes through this day which is all feasting and joy, with a sad and fasting heart, as though the Bread of Heaven had not filled the mangers of the simple and humble” (Serm 4:5). The root of this sin is the implicit conviction that God has not been good to us – that there is nothing to be grateful for – that we have a *right* to be dejected. Sadness, fully consented to, is a denial of God’s mercy – it leads to infidelity and despair. He adds the reason (which refers back to the text of Ecclesiasticus):

> His soul is not filled with good things, because his eye is upon evil, nor is his eye turned back that it might look upon the good, that it might consider with faith and love those things prepared for him on the rich man’s great table. (id.)

The ungrateful man hardens his heart and refuses to see the goodness and mercy of God. He does not want to see them!

Clearly then the cure for this sadness is for us to consider closely, with faith and love, the meaning of the Incarnation, in such a way as to be nourished interiorly by the true Bread of life which contains in itself all delights. Now for Guerric, this means most of all becoming aware of the mercy of God as it is displayed in the greatness and completeness of His gift of salvation in Christ. Here is precisely the gratitude and “*pietas*” in the sense of filial love, are most of all necessary.

If the gift of God is to be seen as it really is, we must realize that He has made salvation easy for us. But the sad ones, whom Bl. Guerric rebukes so roundly, are always precisely complaining of the hardness of their lot, of the sufferings and crosses and labors which they have to undergo, as if God had not done everything to make life sweet and easy for them. They refuse to turn their eyes to the merciful love which lightens all our burdens. They refuse to realize that heaven can be purchased with a cup of cold water.

> How great is this fulness of time which Christ brought with Him from heaven! Precious and costly as it is, Christ set it at a very low price. In two minutes, whether with a cup of cold water or with the mere intention, one may buy the Kingdom of heaven. But now Christ can find few buyers among a whole multitude of rich people. (Serm 4:2)

And yet, says Guerric, we draw back from this bargain, and lament and complain as if we were being cheated, as if the little that is asked of us were altogether too much. We refuse to look at the infinite worth of the treasure we are purchasing with a little labor on this earth, and we cry out that our lot is insupportable. "This is a bad bargain, that is a bad bargain: this is heavy, that is insupportable; who can bear such evils?" (Serm 4:2).

Penetrating deep into the psychology of this melancholy attitude, Bl. Guerric shows us the connection between our ungenerous sadness and the legalism of the Synagogue. It is only another aspect of the same spiritual illness that made the Jews reject their Saviour. Instead of looking at Him and His love, we are too preoccupied with ourselves and with our own actions and reactions. We cannot believe in anyone but ourselves, and in our vain attempt to believe in ourselves we are overwhelmed with doubts which we direct against the whole world and even against God Himself. Infected with a self-love that is really self-hatred, miserably preoccupied with what we see and find in ourselves, we make our hearts narrow and distrustful, incapable of trusting anyone, even God. We simply do not believe.

There was one man at least under the Old Law who was not thus infected. It was David. He, says Guerric, was a simple man without recrimination, who had nothing to do with this trickery, this inertia and infidelity of the business mind. He said: "Because I have not known learning, O Lord, I will be mindful of Thy justice alone" (Ps. 70:15, 16). Not involved in bargaining and haggling, not narrowed and frozen with a selfish spirit of contract-making, he considered not his own justice but only the justice of God. Consequently he did not exaggerate his sufferings or aggrandize his own merits.

Guerric has clearly seen the root of all the trouble. It is selfishness and pride. It is the instinct to magnify the self, in order to bargain with God and force Him to give us a reward on our own terms. In other words, it is simply an attitude that is basically irreligious because it makes God subservient to man. "I will not be mindful of my justice," concludes the Abbot of Igny, "to exaggerate my labors and magnify my merits. Rather will I remember Your justice alone, for You have pledged Yourself my security" (Serm 4:2). All the emphasis is placed therefore on the hope in the goodness and mercy and power of God.

This forgetfulness of ourselves and of our own merits is, says Guerric, true prudence. It enables us to make good use of our weaknesses and limitations, even of our faults. But above all, it is *true*. This concern is one which Guerric shares with all the Cistercian Fathers. He cannot bear falsity. He loves what is really genuine. His whole monastic life is a search for the authentic. When he has found it, he gives all his substance in order to possess it.

> So he buys prudently since he refuses to resort to deceit and avarice in his dealings. He has found a pearl of great price and in his desire for it he sells not only all his possessions but even himself. (Serm 4:2)

3 – *Watch, O Holy Mother.*

These ideas that we have been considering are not only important in themselves, but also in a special way significant to us in our study of Guerric, since they form the immediate matrix in which is embedded his doctrine of the formation of Christ in us. It is well known that Bl. Guerric lays a characteristic emphasis on what he calls our "motherhood" of Christ. This metaphor describes, for him, the life of grace by which the soul receives Christ into itself and cherishes His growth with tender faith and solicitude. In the third Christmas sermon, his exposition of the doctrine follows immediately from the contrast he makes between the Church and the Synagogue. Christ, born for all, is not given to all because the synagogue refuses to receive Him. She clings to her heavy burden of laws and precepts, and will not relinquish it to take the divine Infant into her arms. But the Church has received Him into her bosom as a bundle of myrrh, and henceforth she never lets Him go. Truly, then He is given to the Church. "Though born of the Jews, He is born for us; because taken away from them He is given to us" (Serm 3:4).

In his application of this truth, Guerric brings out all that we have been saying about the spirit of sadness and ingratitude, of contention, hard-heartedness, and resistance to love. These are the elements which prevent us from receiving the Incarnate Word as God's supreme gift to us. Therefore they are the chief obstacles to the "motherhood" of Christ in the faithful soul.

The spirit of ingratitude and coldness is also a spirit of envy. Unable to see the goodness and mercy of God in His gift to us, it not only refuses the gift but tries to prevent others from receiving it. The jealous and selfish synagogue, blinded by its own jealousy, desires that the divine Infant may perish so as not to be received by anyone.

> The veil is there because jealousy keeps it there: whence they do not even see the veil, but are jealous that "a child is born to us, a Son is given to us." They are jealous not because they wish to have Him for themselves but because they want Him to perish for themselves and for us. (Serm 3:4)

Here we come upon the application Guerric makes of the story of the two harlots and the dead child – a story which, with a simplicity which perhaps astonishes the modern mind, becomes for him one of the clearest explanations of his doctrine of the faithful as "mother" of Christ. How, he says do we discover the soul that is truly a "mother" of the Lord? By the "sword of Solomon." *Gladius Salomonis matrem invenit.*[VI]

Fr. Deodat de Wilde,[VII] in his thesis on Bl. Guerric (p. 39), rightly points out that Guerric's doctrine of the "spiritual motherhood" applies not only to the Church but to the individual soul.

The title of the chapter in which he discusses this theme – *De Anima "matre Christi"* might seem to imply that Guerric's emphasis was always on the individual soul as mother of Christ. This however is not the case in the Christmas sermons. The Church and the individual soul are both considered as "mothers" who receive the living Infant. But the emphasis remains rather on the motherhood of the community rather than that of the individual, although the "motherhood" of the individual is certainly very important, since the community is a "mother" by reason of the individuals which compose it.

The judgment of the true Solomon results in the child being taken from the synagogue and given to the Church. *Date Ecclesiae infantem vivum, haec est enim mater ejus* (Serm 3:4).[VIII] Immediately, Guerric himself replies: "Lord, you call me mother; I profess to be the handmaid. I am the handmaid of the Lord; be it done unto me according to Thy word. Indeed I will try to be a mother by loving solicitude, but my lowly condition proclaims me only a handmaid" (id.).

Why does Bl. Guerric use the first person here? Is he speaking in his own name, or in that of the Church? The answer is: both together. As a prelate, charged with the formation of Christ in his own Church, he speaks in his own name and in that of the Church of Igny. Then he turns to his monks and reminds them: *O fratres, hoc nomen matris non est singulare praelatis*.[IX] The other monks too are mothers of Christ. But how? In the same way as the Abbot: they too share his responsibility for the formation of Christ in their Church, their community. "Although maternal care and kindness belong especially to prelates: it is also shared by you who do the will of God" (Serm 3:5).

Bl. Guerric then goes on to speak in terms that show how the care of the brethren for the formation of Christ in the community is in fact identical with their care for His formation in their own souls. Both are a matter of union with the will of God. Guerric would never by any means *oppose* these two motherhoods. He simply shows that they are but two aspects of the same motherhood of Christ. And, in fact, as he develops the allegory, we see that Guerric is thinking especially of those trials and contentions which form an obstacle to the growth of Christ *in the community* first of all, and then, as a result, in the individual soul.

"Watch, therefore, O holy mother, over the care of this infant new-born" (id.) The "holy mother" whom Guerric addresses here is at the same time the individual monk and the whole Church of Igny: but it is primarily the Church of Igny, embodied in the individuals who compose it.

After a detailed comparison between the two "mothers" which we will discuss presently, Guerric concludes his third Christmas sermon by urging all the brethren to keep carefully the faith, implanted in them by the Holy Spirit, which is the Christ-life in them. The words in which he does so makes it clear that the grace of being a "mother" of Christ belongs at once to the community and to the monks that are in it.

> And so, brothers, faith working in you through charity, has been born of the Holy Spirit. Guard it, nurture it tenderly, as the Infant Christ, until the Child Who was born for you may be formed in you. (Serm 3:5)

BI. Guerric is keenly aware of the delicate frailty of this spiritual life, so vulnerable especially in its beginnings. It must be fostered with a tender and loving care, with fidelity and deep respect. But it also must be nurtured with zeal. The "rival," the "false mother" who exists at once in each individual and in the community, is a fleshly spirit, insensitive to true spiritual values. Let us consider, for a moment, the characteristics of this dangerous force which extinguishes the true Spirit, given to us from God.

First of all, as we have seen, it is *carnal*. It is *neglectful* and *inert*,[2] that is to say spiritually *lazy*. But its spiritual laziness is not without a great deal of harmful and turbulent activity: for it is also a spirit of *contention*. Conscious of its own deficiencies, this spirit substitutes wrangling for true fervor. It does not live the spiritual life, but argues about the spiritual life. Hence it is also a spirit of *falsity* and the reason for this is that it is basically a spirit of *pride*. And now we can fully appreciate the fact that this is the same spirit of ingratitude and hardness of heart which Guerric has already ascribed to the synagogue. The comparison of the

---

2. Spiritual *inertia* is the vice of *acedia* a special form of laziness which refuses the effort to rise above subjection to the immediate demands of impulse. *Acedia* is then a complex combination of sadness, guilt, resentment, inertia

two "mothers" – the true and false spirit in the monastic life – is simply a prolongation and a special application of the allegory of the Church and the Synagogue.

How does he describe the contest between them? Like the two harlots in the book of Kings,[3] the two "mothers," or the two contesting spirits in the monastic life, both claim to possess the truth. Each claims to be the genuine monastic and Christian spirit. Each claims to have received the living Child Who is "born unto us." But the spiritual Christ is born, in reality, only to the spiritual souls in the community, who form really healthy members of His Mystical Body. The others, who do not possess Him, envy that life which they see in the "spiritual" brethren, and they envy also the authority which the presence of true spiritual life creates in them: *aemulantur sibi religionis auctoritatem, cujus spirituales habent veritatem* (Serm 3:5).[XI]

This passage is not absolutely clear. Guerric has just spoken of the fact that the "carnal" element shows its contentiousness "*etiam in capitulis ubi verus Salomon invisibiliter judex praesidet*" (ibid.).[XII] It is implied that they resist the hierarchical authority of the Abbot.[4] But at the same time Bl. Guerric also indicates that he is considering a broader, more charismatic "authority" which resides, with the Spirit Himself, in the spiritual men who, according to Paul, must "judge all things" (I Cor. 6:2). These two are resisted by the carnal and envious. Why? Principally because they want the "glory" of being spiritual without making the sacrifices necessary to become so. Then also because they wish to have a spiritual authority of their own so that they can live according to their own will.

---

and confusion. The inertia involved is not necessarily incompatible with a great deal of exterior activity, but the activity is useless and trivial because it is nothing but an escape from boredom and interior discontent. The cure is in that "faith which worketh through charity,"[X] and which opens our hearts to receive the mercy of God with gratitude.

3. See *III Kings* 3:16-28. This is a characteristic example of the freedom with which the Cistercian Fathers made use of the Scriptures as an inexhaustible mine of allegories.

4. According to the Rule of St. Benedict, the Abbot is the visible representative of the invisible Christ, the true Abbot. In the monastic chapter room, the Abbot teaches as an instrument or mouthpiece of Christ. Hence the chapter is the *Schola Christi*, or the "school of Christ."

> If this authority is taken away (from the spiritual), then the carnal souls think they are free to follow the pleasures of sense ... So the carnal monk desires to retain the honor of holiness and leave the labor of mortification to others. (ibid.)

How is the judgment to be made between these two? By the sword of Solomon. Consistent with the whole allegory, Guerric points out that the judgment does not depend on the intrinsic qualities of each mother, but on each one's attitude toward the infant-life about which they are at odds. And hence, the true Solomon (Who is God Himself) reveals the truth beyond all doubt.

The true mother wishes the infant to remain alive, and be given to the rival. That is to say, the truly spiritual man is perfectly willing to lose the "authority," that is to say the prestige, that comes to him from being spiritual. He is also, by implication, willing to be thought un-spiritual, willing to be thought a bad monk, rather than endanger the life of the divine Infant Who has been given to us by God – that is to say, the unity of faith and of charity. Finally, the spiritual man is even willing to renounce his own ways, his own manner of acting, which is in itself more spiritual, and accommodate himself to the "false mother" for the sake of peace. In a word, the spiritual man is quite ready to be thought "wrong" and "un-spiritual" provided that he can keep alive the *reality* of the Spirit – which lives in us by charity.

> But the true mother not envious of her glory as long as she has virtue, wishes the infant to be given alive and whole to the jealous one ... The sword of Solomon finds the mother to whom he gives the child undivided. Her charity and fervor in good works win for her authority and prestige. (ibid.)

The false mother wants only the reputation or appearance of sanctity. She wishes to justify herself, rather than be justified by a gift of God. She is satisfied to be thought holy, and she will sacrifice charity and unity in the community, in order to win an argument that will make her seem "right" and a "spiritual authority." But Solomon finds the true mother by her undivided charity. Her efforts to preserve charity even at the cost of sacrifice of her own reputation, proves her to be fervent in good works, and truly spiritual. Hence he awards her also the "power" and "authority" which she herself does not seek for herself. It belongs to her not for her own sake, but by virtue of her charity, by virtue of the fact that the Spirit Himself is present in her.

4 – *The silent Word of God in the midst of men.*

Bl. Guerric is not one who diagnoses sicknesses without attempting to suggest a cure. And here again we return to all the virtues made manifest by the Divine Infancy, and demanded of us by the Infant Savior Himself. The Holy Babe is the *Verbum breviatum*, the short and simple word in which God has resumed all His wisdom, all His will for us, all that we need to know to come to Him. If the synagogue cannot receive this "short word" precisely because it is too short and simple, the cure of all her ills is nevertheless clear: simple and humble faith. This faith, this humble charity which puts aside the complexities of the carnal spirit and forgets the wrangling of human tongues, prefers to contemplate in silence the Word Who is spoken in the infinite silence of God.

Bl. Guerric's fifth Christmas sermon takes us into this mystery of silence, in which all the virtues of the divine infancy are nurtured and brought to their maturity in the faithful soul.

Even the preaching of the word of God is sometimes ineffective, and it takes more than a Christmas sermon to arouse true fervor in the hearts of men, as Bl. Guerric admits (Serm 5:1). One must not only listen, one must see. And in the Infant Christ, God has made Himself visible to us. The true grace of Christmas is to be found not in listening to a message of words about the Word, but in silent contemplation of the Word made Flesh Himself (Serm 5:2).

How do we see Him? By the eyes of the soul, in meditation, illuminated by the grace of piety. *Si tantum pietas oculum illuminet intuentis* (Serm 5:2).[XIII] If piety gives eyes with which to "see" Him upon Whom the angels desire to look, then our silent contemplation of His beauty will effortlessly produce in us the greatest of virtues. It will bring us hope and charity, it will build up our whole spiritual life, bringing us at the same time all health and delight of soul.

Therefore, in the last analysis, the best Christmas sermon is preached by the silence of the Divine Infant in the crib.[5] Those who have ears to hear must listen to what the "loving and mystical silence of the eternal Word says to us" (ibid.). By the effect of this upon their souls, the saints who contemplate Him are reduced to deep and reverent silence, and in this silence they hear the message which His silence speaks to them: it is the message of *peace*.

The silence of the Word made Flesh, lying in the crib of Bethlehem, "with great weight and great authority commends the practice of silence, and with great fear silences the restless wickedness of tongues and storms of words." "What commends the practice of silence with greater weight and authority than the silence of the Word Incarnate? What checks the noise of tongues and blatant voices so effectively as the silent Word of God in the midst of men?" (ibid.). What madness it would be to want to speak and make oneself great with one's words, when the Word of God is silently submissive to a human Mother? In this allusion to the authority of the divine silence, we can better understand what was said above about the "authority" of the "spiritual" men who prefer silently relinquishing their prestige without argument, in order to preserve the life of charity in the community. Their spiritual strength is derived from their simplicity and humility, which comes to them with the life of the divine Infant diffusing itself spiritually in their souls.

If we would find divine Wisdom, and if we would have the divine life grow in our souls, there is no other way than the constant meditation of the humility and silence of the Word made Flesh. We must become conformed to Him as little ones, in humility and simplicity, for the Wisdom of God to be made known to us – "Only with children is He at home and only with the quiet and lowly is He at rest" (Serm 5:3).

---

5. The pious custom of building Christmas cribs and laying an image of the Holy Child in the manger did not exist in the 12th century. It owes its origin to an inspiration of St. Francis of Assisi in the 13th. Guerric is not referring to this venerable custom here. However it is to be noted that he does speak of the silence of the Divine Child "born" on the altar in the Blessed Eucharist – *positum in praesepio altaris* (Serm. 5:5).[XIV]

> If we wish to become such let us again and again make our way to Bethlehem and gaze upon this Word made Flesh by Almighty God Who has become a little one. In this visible Word cut short we may learn the wisdom of God which has become humility. (Serm 5:4)

Bl. Guerric concludes like a true Benedictine. All wisdom is contained in humility. All our life is there in the Divine Infant. All God's Wisdom is made accessible to us in Him. He lives in us by conforming us to Himself in His mysteries – "He, not only by being born but by living and dying, has handed over to us the pattern which we must follow" (Serm 3:5).

It only remains to point out that the humility of the Incarnation is the sacred humanity, the *caro Christi*,[XV] in which He was clothed and enveloped by a poor and humble Mother, just as the poverty of Mary wrapped Him in swaddling bands. Whenever we mention the wisdom and the humility of the Incarnation, we mention implicitly the Blessed Mother of God, the Seat of Wisdom and the Mother of Humility.

Such, then, is the spirit of these typically Cistercian chapter-sermons of the school of Clairvaux. Here is the Gospel message in all its original simplicity, undyingly new: the message that man is really loved by God, that sins are really forgiven, and that the mercy of God, beyond all our comprehension, has come to drive out forever the bitterness of selfish hearts and fill us instead with the sweetness of His presence forever.

I. Joris-Karl Huysmans (1848-1907), French novelist best known for his early association with naturalism and the decadent movement and for later works that fictionalized his return to the Catholicism of his childhood after his 1895 retreat at Igny.

II. *Sermones de Nativitate Domini* 1 (J. P. Migne, ed., *Patrologiae Cursus Completus, Series Latina* [*PL*], 221 vols. [Paris: Garnier, 1844-1865] vol. 185, cols. 29B-32C); 2 (cols. 32C-34D); 3 (cols. 35A-38D); 4 (cols. 38D-41A); 5 (cols. 41A-44D).

III. "the helps of the sacraments, the food of the scriptures, the ranks and orders of ministers" (*Christmas Sermons* 36) (2.3 [col. 34B]).

IV. "A Child is born for us to be renewed" (1.1 [col. 29C]).

V. “the Word in brief” (5.3 [col. 44D, which reads: “*verbum ... breviatum ... verbum ... abbrevians*”]).

VI. “The sword of Solomon finds the mother” (*Christmas Sermons* 45) (3.5 [col. 38C]).

VII. Deodat de Wilde, OCSO, *De Beato Guerrico, Abbate Igniacensi eiusque Doctrina de Formatione Christi in Nobis* (Westmalle: Typis Abbatiae, 1935).

VIII. “Give to the Church, he says, the living infant. She is his mother” (*Christmas Sermons* 44) (col. 37D).

IX. “O brothers, the name of mother does not belong to prelates alone” (see *Christmas Sermons* 44) (3.5 [col. 38A]).

X. Galatians 5:6.

XI. “They are jealous of the authority which the genuine spirit creates in the spiritual souls” (*Christmas Sermons* 45) (col. 38C).

XII. “even in chapter where the true Solomon invisibly presides as judge” (*Christmas Sermons* 45) (col. 38B).

XIII. “If the eyes of your soul are illuminated with filial piety” (*Christmas Sermons* 57) (col. 44A).

XIV. “laid on the manger of the altar” (*Christmas Sermons* 60) (col. 46B).

XV. “the flesh of Christ.”

Guerric of Igny's Easter Sermons – Conferences

In an April 15, 1959 letter to a fellow novice master, Mark Weidner, OCSO of Our Lady of Guadalupe Abbey in Oregon, Merton responds to a request for advice on background reading in preparation for presenting conferences to novices. After mentioning various contemporary authors as well as early monastic writers such as John Cassian, Merton goes on to stress the importance of introducing their charges to classic writings of the early Cistercians: "of course top priority belongs to our own Fathers. Guerric is one of the easiest to break into in Latin. And perhaps the most representative" (*School of Charity* 119). Following his own advice in this letter, Merton presented conferences on Guerric's liturgical sermons at various points in his decade-long tenure as novice master. An undated set of notes on the theme of spiritual rest, presumably given as a conference at some point before Merton's classes began to be recorded in late April 1962, is included as an appendix to his lengthy set of conferences on the Cistercian Fathers, principally St. Bernard (*Cistercian Fathers and Their Monastic Theology* 313-20). Here Merton discusses Guerric's Third Sermon for the Assumption (along with Baldwin of Ford's treatise *De Requie Caelesti*), which takes as its text a verse from Ecclesiasticus [Sirach] 24:11: "In all these I sought rest." Preached during harvest season, as the monks pause in their work to celebrate the Marian feast, the sermon emphasizes that "spiritual rest for the Cistercian Fathers does not mean avoiding labor, but the grace to work with such peace and faith and hope that in our labors we already rest in the foretaste of heaven." Guerric finds in Mary the model of one who not only rests in God but welcomes the Wisdom of God to rest in one's own heart and life. "Unless Wisdom can find rest in our hearts," he says, "we will never find rest in heaven," and Wisdom, Christ the Word, is at rest when He is recognized and cared for in the poor, when work is done not in restless anxiety but in quiet liberty of spirit. Wisdom is at rest in the "generosity and self-forgetfulness that enables us to find rest in all things, because we are ready for everything .... upset by nothing" and "do all things willingly, in order to rest in Christ." On April 7, 1963, Palm Sunday, Merton makes a brief notation in his journal: "I like Guerric's Easter Sermons" (*Turning Toward the World* 311). The comment was prompted by the fact that on that day and the preceding one he presented a pair of conferences on these sermons in preparation for Easter (Gethsemani recordings 48.4, 51.2). Transcribed and published in rearranged and compressed form after Merton's death (Thomas Merton, "Guerric of Igny's Easter Sermons," *Cistercian Studies* 7 [1972] 85-95), they are presented here *in toto*. While he provides some comments on the Third Sermon in the latter part of his second conference, the bulk of the discussion focuses on the First Sermon. Merton had earlier included a rather extensive consideration of this same sermon in his novitiate conferences from 1956-1957 on the Book of Genesis (currently being prepared for publication), in which he sees Guerric's allegorical interpretation of Genesis 45:26-28 as a summons to wake up to the central message of new life in the Spirit, received through union with Christ in the paschal mystery: "the Apostles came to know the risen Jesus by the fact that He gave them the Holy Spirit – they knew Him, in other words, by the effects of the Resurrection in their own souls, that is, *in their own spiritual resurrection*. This applies to all of us: it is the Holy Spirit within us Who testifies to the truth of the resurrection, and without Him we cannot know the Risen Christ. The grace of Easter is then the gift of the Holy Spirit … leading up to the fullness of His coming at Pentecost. Hence the Paschal season is a season of new life in the Spirit of the Risen Jesus." In this gift enabling the disciples to "truly live in Him and no longer need to live in and for ourselves," Merton finds "the true consummation of the monastic life, the real summit of Cistercian prayer and spirituality." The first conference begins with an overview of Holy Week and its ceremonies, with particular attention to the Palm Sunday procession that many in his audience will be experiencing, and participating in as the angelic choir, for the first time at the abbey. This gives Merton the opportunity to consider the element of time in the liturgy, in which past and future are made present: "when you are participating in this procession the whole of human history is taking place and the Passion is taking place and the glorification of Christ is taking place and the Last Judgment is taking place." Turning to Guerric, he emphasizes his immersion in the liturgical milieu as well as the byplay with his audience (not unlike that of Merton himself with his novices) as he anticipates their puzzlement at being "fed" on an Old Testament text for the climactic event of the New Testament redemption story – at hearing of the dreamer (*somniator*) rather than the Savior

(*Salvator*) – only to recognize the figure of the risen Christ hidden in that of Joseph encountered among the living: the nourishment concealed within the egg, to be appreciated all the more when it is discovered. Merton points out that here Guerric uses the Genesis story of his brothers' encounter with Joseph and Jacob's reaction – the revival of his spirit – as a foreshadowing of the resurrection and the gift of the Spirit to the disciples on Easter night, an experience made available to his – and Merton's – listeners as well. The "modernity" of Guerric, or rather the perennial relevance of his message even if expressed in typically medieval fashion, is highlighted at the opening of the second conference, at the expense of the ostensibly more "literal-minded" Garnier of Langres, whose outlandish explanation of the source of the wood of the cross is ready-made for Merton's patented humor. Guerric in contrast is able to develop his allegorical treatment of the good news of Joseph's renewed presence and salvific rescue of his family, fanciful on one level, but applicable on a deeper level to the lives of the monks, who are called to say with Jacob that if their brother and redeemer is alive nothing else matters, an articulation of the doctrine of pure love purged of all self-interest, so characteristic of St. Bernard and the early Cistercians generally. But as Merton, following Guerric, goes on to note: "This whole business of pure love is fine, but it is equally good if a person purely and simply wakes up and with a very realistic sense of where he actually is, says to himself, 'I am now going to start moving in this direction.' That's all that's necessary, because this anybody can do. This is a much better kind of awakening. The practical awakening for every one of us is that he wakes up where he actually is and starts moving from where he actually is. It's of absolutely no use whatever to wake up where you aren't and start going from there." The heights of mystical self-donation are only approached along a very simple, humble route that takes into account more ordinary and accessible encounters with Christ in prayer, in the scriptures, in work, as Merton illustrates by reference to Guerric's Third Sermon, to various delightfully naïve stories of early Cistercians included in the *Exordium Magnum*, and to the favorite Cistercian Easter text of the disciples on the road to Emmaus, whose hearts burn within them as they hear and make their own the word of salvation.

1.

Well, tomorrow's Palm Sunday. Some of you have seen it before and others of you haven't. This Holy Week now, each day has its own particular character. There's a great deal in all this, and of course the chief thing tomorrow, I would say, the big thing tomorrow is the procession. The procession isn't secondary on Palm Sunday. It's really one of the most important things in Palm Sunday. It's the real grand entrance into Holy Week. It's the solemn opening of Holy Week, and it has an eschatological character. What's eschatological mean? It refers to the last things. The Palm Sunday procession is a preview of the whole week; it sums up the whole week. The meaning of the whole week is all packed into that procession. In the old days they used to have a responsory that had to do with the Passion,[I] which they threw out because it was too hard to sing. It's still there but they use this hymn instead. This responsory about the Passion was a very complicated fourth tone job – you can't sing fourth tone in procession. It's too mystical for procession. But anyway, this profound thing is a meditation on the Passion, and of course the hymn is that way too. It's an adoration of Christ as a victorious king, so from the idea of the Passion you've got the idea of the victory of Christ, Christ having overcome death, having overcome sin; and then what's the *Gloria Laus*[II] all about? You fellows are singing it – incidentally, you don't sing behind the doors any more. You're out in the cloister, aren't you? In the old days it used to be behind the doors. You're inside the church, but the door is closed. I don't know why they took you out of there. It's a fine place to be, because nobody sees you, and you hear these sort of timid angelic voices coming out from inside the church. You should be inside the church. Well, of course there are only supposed to be two – the *duo fratres*[III] are supposed to do this, and here it's always a mob scene. Well it's alright, but the idea is, you come to the end of the procession after this adoration of Christ as King, and then you hear these voices singing "Glory and Praise to God" and so forth from inside the church, and we respond outside the church. Then the doors of the church open, and we all enter into the church. Now what does that suggest to you? What do you suppose is the meaning of that? entering into heaven! Now there's where the eschatological business comes in. It's a preview of the last day.

Now when you say you have something eschatological in the liturgy, it's not just the idea, it's the action. It's a sacramental action. When you participate in a sacramental action in the liturgy, what happens? There's a telescoping of time: the past and the present and the future are all telescoped. What takes place in the liturgy is always outside of time. There's a special liturgical time. When you're in the liturgy, it isn't any more just 9:30 in the morning. You're *in illo tempore* when you're in the liturgy. You're "in that time," the sacred time. You are at once in the time in which Christ entered into Jerusalem and the time when we will all enter into Jerusalem, into the heavenly Jerusalem – everything telescoped together in one, and by faith we enter into this mystery. This is what liturgy does. The characteristic example of that is the Mass! The Mass is outside of time. It isn't just the 9:30 Mass or the 11 o'clock Mass, and you've got to get out of the 11 o'clock Mass fast so that the 12 o'clock Mass guys can get their cars in the place. We're obsessed with that aspect of time. The Mass is timeless. You're outside of time. At the Mass you are simultaneously at Calvary and in the Cenacle and in heaven – the beginning and the end, the alpha and the omega come together in the Mass, and in all liturgical functions it's the same way. The liturgy is outside of time, so that when you are participating in this procession the whole of human history is taking place and the Passion is taking place and the glorification of Christ is taking place and the Last Judgment is taking place. It's all in one. It's all there, and each one has his little part to play in and when they want angels to sing the "*Gloria Laus*," where do they come? (the wrong place!) the novitiate. They get novices and put them in there to sing the "*Gloria Laus*" because they're angelic! Anyway, *duo fratres*. The idea is that we go into the church and are heading into the heavenly Jerusalem. This is an act of faith at the beginning of Holy Week, saying that the whole of Holy Week is the same kind of eschatological thing, that through Holy Week it's going to be a whole renewal of life, a whole renewal of everything, and we're going to come out of the other end of Holy Week, we'll have gone through everything: death, resurrection and everything. We're new men on Easter Monday, Easter Sunday, Easter night or whenever. (Of course you go to communion

Easter night, don't you? That's nice.) So you have to see these dimensions, otherwise you just get a ceremony here and another ceremony here and you've got these ceremonies that don't.

A lot of Holy Week of course is purely and simply communal meditation on scriptural texts – not the kind of communal meditation where somebody sits in the back of the chapel and says "point one" – that sort of thing. It's the Church meditating on readings. Good Friday is nothing but a long liturgical meditation with readings and prayers, and then the ceremony of the adoration of the holy cross. The thing that throws people off on Good Friday is, there isn't any Mass. Well what are we doing? Well what are we doing, we have an office. It's an office in which there's reading and the whole thing is the reading – that's all. You just have to know what they're reading and the best thing to do is bring a book and follow the reading. Of course most of the reading are these tracts that you sing, these long tracts – really psalms. Holy Saturday is an empty day. It's a non-liturgical day. It's supposed to be. There isn't supposed to be anything on Holy Saturday except the office, a real simple office. There's no Mass on Holy Saturday – it's all at night, so then Holy Saturday, don't be disconcerted. There isn't anything going on. There isn't supposed to be anything going on. It's empty, and so what happens? There's actually a lot of time for work on Holy Saturday, and then Good Friday is as I say. Of course the morning the psalter is meditated, practically speaking. It's the choir just reciting psalms, and we used to have to go through the whole thing – four-and-a-half hours, 150 psalms. You just started and went on to the end. It wasn't bad. It was nice. It's a pretty good system. After you go through that, you're really ready for anything. If you want some good reading for all this – of course you don't need to add a lot of reading on top of everything else in Holy Week, but if you want some good reading for the Easter mystery, read something like *The Victory of Christ* by Vonier.[IV] It's a fine book, a good theology of Easter, and of course this book *The Resurrection* by Durrwell[V] is absolutely tops; it's one that you should all read somewhere along the line before they plant you back there. It's a fine book; it's a really good theology of the resurrection, and the theology of the resurrection is just theology. Our whole theology is built around the resurrection. Our whole monastic life is built around the resurrection.

So what I want to do today for the Cistercian part of this, and maybe I'll carry it on tomorrow – we'll have a conference tomorrow evening, Palm Sunday – maybe I'll just carry this on tomorrow. I'll take Blessed Guerric's Easter homilies[VI] because they're very fine and it fits in too with what we've been saying about pure love,[VII] because his first Easter homily is really in part a homily on pure love, and if we get to that, which we probably won't get to today, the second part of the homily, you'll see how it fits in with all this business on pure love that we've been talking about. It becomes strictly a homily on pure love. Blessed Guerric is one of the best theologians in the Cistercian Fathers, and the thing that outstanding with him – and really he's the best Cistercian Father to read from a certain point of view. Of course he's in Latin (I think there's an English translation here) but he's a good Father to read because of the fact that if you're going to read him in Latin, his Latin's easy, but also because of the fact that his theology is very clear. With some of the others it's not so clear. With St. Bernard – you know what St. Bernard does – he rambles along. He brings in a lot of beautiful poetry and so forth, but his theology, although it's there and is very strong, isn't nearly as clear as Guerric. Guerric is entirely scripture and liturgy. He sticks very close to the liturgy. He uses the liturgical texts and then he gets other texts which fit in with the texts of the liturgy. He's the best commentary on the liturgy that you can get in the Cistercian Fathers. He's really closest to the liturgy and most in the spirit of the liturgy and more solid. The thing that differentiates him from the other Fathers in his use of scripture – the Cistercian Fathers – is that they tend to use scripture as a springboard. They start out – they'll take a text – "Mary was weeping outside" or something, and then they'll say, "Oh yeah, 'outside.'" Then they'll go off into some long thing. It's very interesting, but it doesn't have anything to do with that particular text. Guerric tends to stick much closer to scripture. He comments on scripture in the best way, which is using other scriptural passages. You comment on scripture by scripture. You take a passage of scripture and you compare it with other passages that are related to it that throw light on it, or that can be thought to throw light on it. He isn't too extreme. I mean he usually sticks to things that really do throw light on each other.

However in this First Easter Sermon, he's a little bit excited. He's got to the end of Lent and he's in this state that we're talking about. He's sort of keyed up and he really wants to give them a good sermon. It's a very nice sermon, this First Easter Sermon but it's one where, as the Fathers sometimes do, he comes in with an unexpected text, a text that apparently has nothing to do with Easter, and then he goes into a tremendous effort to show how it really has all of Easter right there. It's all right in this text. What do you suppose it is? Has anybody read this sermon? Does anybody know what it is? There's no use trying to guess because you couldn't possibly guess it. What would be a normal text for an Easter sermon? Think of the gospels of Easter. Think of the gospels of Easter time: "I have risen and I am still with you."[VIII] When Mary Magdalene comes to the tomb and finds it empty: "*resurrexit sicut dixit*" – "He has risen as he said."[IX] You get a very fine sermon out of that. Good Shepherd – you get a fine Easter sermon out of that.[X] Just think of that: you've got a whole list of sermons all lined up in terms of this eschatology – get a fine patristic homily out of that: the Good Shepherd Who came from heaven down to earth and became man and dwelt among His own and then came to seek the lost sheep and bring him back to heaven and so forth. How does Gregory use it?[XI] What's the lost sheep? Man, and the other sheep are the angels; the lost sheep is the one of God's spiritual creation who got away from all the other spiritual creation – angels – and were brought back with the rest of the spiritual beings. "My flesh has burst back into flower again"[XII] – you get a fine sermon on that. Haven't hit the best one yet, the favorite Cistercian gospel for Easter, but the ideal one for Cistercians is this Easter Monday gospel: the disciples going to Emmaus.[XIII] They love that. They're crazy about it. There's a whole sermon about that in one of these: St. Bernard – it isn't by St. Bernard, it's by an unknown Cistercian,[XIV] and he just raves about this thing, because it's beautiful. Why do they stress this business of the road to Emmaus and Our Lord appearing with the disciples? What's the point of that, besides the fact that it's a beautiful story? Love and unity; experience – it's the experience of the risen Christ that's the thing that the Cistercians are most interested in. The beauty of this gospel of the disciples going to Emmaus is this experience of the risen Christ. They know that He's alive because He has appeared to them and He's given them the assurance that He lives.

Now that is the theme of Guerric's First Easter Sermon, and see how beautifully he does it. You've got to get yourself in this real wacky Cistercian mood now. What's his text? His text is from Genesis. That's going pretty far back: forty-fifth chapter of Genesis. It's the end of the Joseph story, towards the end of the Joseph story. Joseph has sent all his brothers – he's now revealed himself to his brothers in Egypt. They know who he is and they've gone back to get Jacob, and he sends them back with a whole train of wagons, back to Palestine, and says, "Now get the old man and bring him down here, because there's going to be a famine and we're going to feed you down here"; and they go. So here's what happens: "So they went up out of Egypt, and came to the land of Canaan to their father Jacob. And they told him, 'Joseph is still alive, and he is ruler over all the land of Egypt.' And his heart fainted, for he did not believe them." (Now this is the wrong translation[XV] for the Cistercians – I should've got another one – because it said "he was like awakening from sleep";[XVI] it isn't that "his heart fainted" but "as though awakening from a deep sleep.") Jacob said he did not believe them. He thought it was a dream, but when they told him all the words of Joseph, which he had said to them, and when he saw the wagons which Joseph has sent to carry him, "the spirit of their father Jacob revived, and Israel said, 'It is enough. Joseph my son is still alive. I will go and see him before I die.'" That's a very beautiful text. If you suddenly see that the way this man handles it – it all of a sudden becomes the resurrection, and the theme is: "Joseph my son is still alive – that is enough for me."[XVII]

The theme of the sermon, which we won't get to now, is the idea that Jesus is alive – that's enough for us. What more do we want? The fact that he is alive is sufficient. This is our whole life. Nothing else matters. Nothing that happens to us is of any consequence. The fact that He has risen and is alive is the whole story. This is everything to us. Then he takes that and shows how this is a sign. This is an expression of pure love – that all we care about is that Jesus is risen, and we don't care about anything else, and that that alone is sufficient. We don't need anything else.

How does he approach this subject? Some of these Cistercian sermons are very nice because there's a lot of by-play between the abbot and the community. Of course there isn't a dialogue, but you can see him answering objections that he anticipates from the community, and making remarks about how they probably feel, and how they look at the end of Lent and all that sort of thing. Now there's a lot here about just being hungry. I mean I'm not the only one! Blessed Guerric is also. He says, "It's the end of Lent. You're famished, and you're famished for what? You're famished for the New Testament and for Jesus, and here I am giving you the Old Testament. You're going to be mad at me." Then he has a lot of by-play about how he wants to satisfy their hunger with the Paschal Lamb who is Jesus, and yet here he comes with this Joseph. Then he says, "You will say to me: '*salvatorem volumus non somniatorem*.'"[XVIII] What was that: "*salvatorem volumus non somniatorem*"? "Give us the Savior not the dreamer." Then he goes down a whole list of things. "What do we want with Joseph? Give us Jesus." That's the whole point, and here is this Easter sermon. "You're giving us Lenten fare still." What does that indicate? That means that for the Cistercians, they believe that Lent was a time for meditating on the Old Testament: Old Testament readings – that's for Lent; New Testament readings – that's for the paschal time. You've got a whole new life is started. You don't want the Old Testament in paschal time. I think you find that in fact there aren't very many Old Testament texts in paschal time. There are one or two, but they are always texts that refer to what? Two great sacraments – baptism for example, confirmation later on. There's an Old Testament text of course on Pentecost, about the Spirit reviving these dead bones and so on.[XIX] But see Naaman for example: there's the gospel of Naaman in the Jordan. I think that's in Easter week – no, it's not a gospel, it's a lesson, of course – about how he goes and bathes seven times in the Jordan.[XX] That refers to baptism. You might have some that refer to the Eucharist that could be used, but normally they're not Old Testament readings.

Then he says, "Well, now look." He said there's this: "*volumus non enim qui pavit ventres, sed qui pascit mentes, sed esurientes*."[XXI] Now what does that mean? What's he doing there, just from the sound? What's going on? He's rhyming. He's got interior rhyme: "*non qui pavit* VENTRES, *sed qui pascit* MENTES, *sed* ESURIENTES": *-entes -entes -entes*. But he's being also quite coy here: "not him who fed the stomach, but he who feeds the mind – but hungry." But the hungry minds – this is sort of a curious construction, which is very modern as a matter of fact. There's a modern way of talking where you say: "but such and such." So Guerric is right up to date. He says, "All right, you're hungry.

Well this text is an egg. Now what you've got to do is, if you look at it on the outside, it's not going to do you any good. You've got to break it and get the egg out from inside and eat the egg." Notice he's referring to an egg – maybe they got eggs for relief on Easter or something! He says, "Inside this text, inside the shell of this egg, you will find the Paschal Lamb." Of course it's an Easter egg! I didn't think of that! He says, "Now the reason for presenting texts like this, in which it is hidden" – now this is a standard – I mean the Fathers all say this: "It tastes all the more sweet because you have to work to get it." So that's a standard patristic approach; that is a standard Cistercian approach, and it's just natural, really. You have to get through the surface and get down to something below the surface, and you discover something. Then there's much more joy to it. It may be something perfectly familiar by the time you've got it, but the mere fact of doing that work – why is that true? It's just an ordinary human fact: we like to use our faculties. We've been given these faculties by God. It's a joy to work with them. Then he leads us on that way and then the joy of discovery. That's one of the real satisfactions that a man can have, finding out something new. Usually we keep it on too low a level. Who's working over there now? Who got fired? That's finding out something new, but it's not on a very interesting level. It should be on a spiritual level: discovering Christ. That's what we're here for. We're seeking God, and the joy of our life comes in discovering Jesus in different things, where we didn't think He was, all of a sudden finding Him when He wasn't there, or we thought He wasn't there, we thought He couldn't possibly be there, and all of a sudden, there He is.

He says, for this it is necessary to have Jesus Himself as your teacher, Jesus Who rises today and Who reveals to His brethren on the road the letter which kills and opens the scriptures. Of course this is a reference to the Emmaus gospel. Right away they're always alluding to this gospel, and it's the idea that Our Lord himself is going to be present with us in the Easter mystery. He's present with us in the liturgy and when the gospels are read in the church and sung in the church and these texts are sung in the church, the Spirit of Christ present in us opens the meaning of the texts to us if we're paying attention, so this is standard. This is the regular Cistercian approach. This is the way he looks at these things, and there's a great deal to this. This is the basis for contemplation in the liturgy, which shows that if you pay attention to the texts, and your heart is open, and you have the right disposition, faith and love and so forth, that light comes to you through these texts and leads you on to a personal encounter with Our Lord. That's what we're here for. We come here to seek Him and to find Him, and there are all sorts of ways and places in which we come face-to-face with Our Lord, and we find "Him Whom our soul loveth."[XXII] That's what we're here for. That's the joy of our life. That's all we want. These Cistercian Fathers talk about it in their sermons, and you see what it meant to them and it can mean the same thing to us.

2.

I thought today I'd talk about some of the Cistercian Fathers as I already talked about yesterday to the juniors and novices[XXIII] – some of the Cistercian Fathers' Easter homilies. We were talking about Guerric, and I think I'll continue to talk about Guerric because he's very good. But before that I'd like to mention another Cistercian Father. It's interesting to compare him with Guerric because he's not so good at all! This is a very obscure bird by the name of Garnier of Langres – in Latin it's *Guarnerius Lingonensis*. He was a stuffed shirt, an abbot of Clairvaux who became a bishop. What has Langres got to do with Clairvaux? Does anybody know? Clairvaux was in the Diocese of Langres. He became Bishop of Langres. His stuff is in *PL* 205;[XXIV] it's not in English at all, and if it never gets translated into English it won't be too soon. It's good to contrast these two people: you've got Guerric, who's real deep and very spiritual and very mystical, and this other fellow who's not deep and not spiritual and not mystical. He's sort of a literal-minded person; he's got a lot of learning; he's quite well up in a lot of things. As a matter of fact he's quite interesting from many points of view. From the point of view of liturgy, he has a lot of little statements about what they did at the time, and what they thought they were doing. He explains why they do certain things and why they don't do certain things. It's very interesting from that point of view, but these are just sort of facts, little statements of fact, historical fact. Today he would be a scientific-minded critic. A scientific-minded critic in the Middle Ages is just about zero, because he's got nothing to work on.

He'll come up with things like this: in one of his Easter sermons,[XXV] he gets halfway through and he starts talking about the Cross and the wood of the Cross. Of course you know where the wood of the Cross came from, he says. This is supposed to be a matter of fact. This isn't spiritual interpretation. There's nothing mystical about this. This is supposed to be history. Where the wood of the Cross came from, he says, is the Queen of Sheba brought this great big piece of wood from Africa to King Solomon, and then King Solomon put it under the Pool of Siloe, and this was what the angel used to stir the pool with to heal those guys! On the day when the crucifixion was supposed to take place this wood was allowed by divine dispensation to float to the surface, and the people walking around said, "Hey, here's a good piece of wood!" That's the kind of stuff that you've got to look for from a literal-minded man in the Middle Ages.

I think it's a really interesting point to see how, of these two people in the Middle Ages, you'd be inclined to say that a literal-minded man would be closer to us, because we're literal-minded. But as a matter of fact the person who's more modern is Guerric. This other fellow is completely isolated in the Middle Ages and there's no contact with him anymore. He's finished; he's gone; he's way back; he's twelfth-century and that's all there is to it. He's no more modern than a twelfth-century concept of the universe! He simply is dated, he's finished, whereas Guerric is still modern, is still new. I think that's a very good point, because it gives you a lot of insight into the reality of this spiritual view of things that the Cistercian Fathers take. As a matter of fact, the reason why Guerric is very new and close to us is not only that he is mystical but also that he has this emphasis on experience, and therefore he speaks more or less as a kind of existentialist. He talks about actual concrete experience of the person, rather than just general abstract principles. That's what existentialist means – in the nice sense of the word. (If you want to use it as a bad word, it means something other than that, or it means that, but in a narrow sense.) In a broad sense of the word, an existentialist is a thinker who is interested in the validity of personal experience as a starting point for everything – personal spiritual experience as a kind of point of reference by which you judge everything – not just individual, but in any case personal, rather than purely abstract things which may not fit everybody. These personal things don't necessarily fit everybody either, but they at least fit somebody. It's possible to have abstract principles that get so far out that they cease fitting anything anymore. They're just purely figments of the imagination, so with an existentialist you're at least dealing with something that fits somebody. At least it's real in one case.

We were talking about Guerric's First Easter Sermon. The beauty of Guerric, as I said yesterday to the group, is that he's such a good commentator on the liturgy because he keeps so close to the liturgy and so close to scripture. He's very theological in his dealing with scripture. He has a very fine theological grasp of scripture. He's not just poetic and fanciful in his use of scripture. He really uses scripture theologically. What were we saying about the First Easter Sermon of Guerric yesterday? It's not just playing with texts. It has its validity. He picks as a text for his Easter sermon the end of Genesis 45. I'll read you the end of Genesis 45 and we'll go on and see how he uses it: "And they went up out of Egypt and came into the land of Canaan to their father Jacob. And they told him saying: Joseph thy son is living and he is ruler in all the land of Egypt. Which when Jacob heard he awaked as it were out of a deep sleep, yet did not believe them. They on the other hand told the whole order of the thing. And when he saw the wagons and all that Joseph had sent his spirit revived. And he said: It is enough for me if Joseph my son be yet living, I will go and see him before I die." This is his Easter sermon. It's based on this. You can see how he's going to use this. What he's talking about is a very beautiful way of approaching things. He's talking about the fact of the love of Christ in the Christian heart and the experience of the grace of Easter. When the Cistercian Fathers preach, they don't preach about an idea. They preach about a grace. If a Cistercian Father preaches an Easter sermon, he's preaching about the grace of Easter. You may say he's preaching about the mystery of Easter, but the mystery of Easter contains the grace. Now Garnier of Langres – he'll bring in all kinds of information, but a Cistercian Father is going to talk about how on a feast the soul of the individual monk, or the soul of monks as a genus, enter into contact with Christ in this mystery – how Christ is experienced in the mystery of Easter, how Christ reveals Himself in the mystery of Easter to our soul. That's what he's interested in.

What does this text say about that? How does he develop this text? He's got two points: the experience of this old man – they come back from Egypt and they find this old man in a stupor. He's real old and he's finished and he's done and he's got nothing to live for and he's just blah. He's extinct. They come in and say, "Hey, Joseph is alive!" He doesn't come out of it immediately. There are two steps here. First he just shakes his head and begins to come back, and then they say, "He's alive, and he sent all these wagons and we all are going to go to Egypt and we're all going to be with Joseph." Then the old man – he's fully back to himself, and he says, "It is enough to me that Joseph is alive." This is a tremendous thing. This is a fundamental experience because this is the resurrection of the monk at Easter. He works on this all through his Easter sermons. He keeps coming back to this basic kind of experience. He says in various places in these three sermons that by the end of Lent, and having gone through Good Friday, how do we feel? If you live through Good Friday just from morning to night, blow by blow until you come to the evening, you are in a stupor; you're beat; you're physically beat and you're mentally beat. There's something gone out, Good Friday is arranged in that way; the last three days of Holy Week are made in that way. They're supposed to have this effect. Of course communion comes in and modifies that now; with communion there is a little bit of a lift but without communion there was no lift at all, so that when you used to get to the end of Good Friday in the old days, you were just simply hollowed out. Everything was gone. You were just shot. There wasn't anything you could do. You couldn't go to make a visit to the Blessed Sacrament. There wasn't any Blessed Sacrament. You didn't feel like reading. If anybody gave you a book you'd throw it at him. (You wouldn't have the strength!) You didn't feel like anything and you hadn't had anything to eat, but you didn't feel hungry. You were just blah. About the only thing you were ready for is to go to bed – just ready to sleep. This is the condition that we're in. He develops this idea that we're even in this condition from contemplating the Passion of Christ. This in a certain sense comes from the way we liturgically die with Christ in our liturgy. You just go through this long, long thing and in the end, you're finished. Then of course Holy Saturday comes in as a completely empty day, when you remain that way – sort of bewildered. You don't know where you are! This is supposed to be. You're supposed to be completely empty.

Of course now we've got it a little better than the Cistercian Fathers because we actually go right from sleep down to this new fire thing. You get down there; you're in a daze; you don't know whether you're coming or going; besides it's dark and everybody's falling all over everybody. All of a sudden somebody starts singing "Alleluia" and you suddenly realize that all this stuff is real, that you are really entering into the resurrection of Christ spiritually. This is not only *a* reality – it is *the* reality. It's the only reality. The Church has this way of bringing it home to you. There isn't anything else. Having emptied you out completely, there's no room for anything else to register. This simply hits you right between the eyes. This is the thing that he's talking about. He stresses two words in the Genesis narrative: *revixit spiritus* – "his spirit came back to life."[XXVI] The grace of Easter is a spiritual coming back to life in us on a new level. Easter is not a repetition of last Easter. In the Christian liturgical life, in the Christian mysteries, nothing repeats anything. Easter is not a repetition of any Easter. It's a totally new Easter. There's only one Easter, but it's the same Easter totally new. It's old and it's new. It's a brand new thing. We're not made over, we're made new. We're not remade men; we're not fixed-up men. We're new men. The grace of Easter, the resurrection of Christ, is a newness of life, a newness of life in Christ. What this comes from is a gift of the Holy Spirit.

Developing this idea, the key chapter in this First Sermon is the fourth section. What are we doing when we're celebrating Easter? We're celebrating the truth of the resurrection, which is *the* truth. This is the great revelation of God to the world. We aren't commemorating it. It is not like the Fourth of July. We're celebrating. We're proclaiming it to the world, and this truth is not something we have heard about. It isn't that somebody came to me and said, "Now look. What you're going to do, you're going to go through all these ceremonies and this is going to mean to some people up in the gallery that Christ is risen. It's like acting out a play. You're going to play your part and you're going to sing your bit good, and then if you do well they'll see that you're telling them that Christ is risen." You're passing on a message that we got out of this book here. It isn't that at all! What we are doing at Easter is that Christ living in us speaks through us, sings through us, so that as a group and as individuals, we testify to the world that Christ is risen. What we do testifies that Christ is risen because He lives in us, is risen and lives in us and speaks through us. Of course this isn't only Easter. This is all the time. He says therefore that what's important is not seeing the risen Christ but receiving the Spirit of the risen Christ. None of us see the risen Christ but we all receive the Spirit of the risen Christ. The grace of Easter is a giving of the Spirit already, before Pentecost. Remember that on Easter Sunday the Holy Spirit is given in a sort of a private, unofficial kind of way; Pentecost, the Holy Spirit is publicly poured out over the whole Church, but the Holy Spirit is already given at Easter in a sort of a modified, secret kind of way, and it built up to the big giving at Pentecost. This gift of the Spirit is terribly important in the whole Easter mystery. The Easter mystery isn't just the resurrection of Christ. The resurrection of Christ without the giving of the Spirit isn't the whole thing.

This is where Guerric is a real theologian. It's because the Spirit is given to us to live in us and to speak in us and to awaken in us that we bear witness to the resurrection. What he says here is that it's this gift of the Spirit which is an indubitable witness and argument of the resurrection and the life. This is his basic theme that he's got in all his Easter sermons. The Spirit is given and therefore the resurrection is true. It isn't the other way around – the resurrection is true and therefore the Spirit is given. This is what I mean by an existential approach. This is an existential statement: the Spirit is given; therefore we know that the resurrection is true, because we've got the Spirit. We receive the Holy Spirit; therefore we know the resurrection is true and that Christ is the resurrection and the life. He says the Spirit is He who bears witness in the hearts of the saints and through their lips that Christ is the truth, that He is the true resurrection, and that He is the life. That's the grace of Easter – that the Spirit in our hearts bears witness that Christ is the truth, the resurrection and the life. He said that it was not enough for the apostles to see the risen Christ. They had to have the "*gustum spiritus vivificantis*"[XXVII] – "a taste of the life-giving Spirit." You see how he works these ideas. Then he says, "*plus est corde Iesum concipere, quam oculis videre, vel auribus de ipso audire*"[XXVIII] – "It is better to conceive Jesus in the heart than to see Him with the eyes or to hear about Him with the ears." This is a tremendously important statement. If somebody ever asks you: "Give me fifteen statements that summarize Cistercian spirituality," this is one of them. This is a contemplative spirituality.

This is what the contemplative life means for us: to conceive Jesus in the heart. This is typically Guerric. This is the great doctrine of Guerric: that we are all mothers of Christ. This gets into his Marian spirituality, which isn't in the Easter sermons. It's the idea that each Cistercian monk imitates Mary to the extent of conceiving Christ in his heart. Jesus is born in us through the mediation of Our Lady. This has a tremendous influence on Louis de Montfort. Louis de Montfort quotes Guerric several times.[XXIX] I don't know where he ever got to him, but he quotes him.[XXX] The idea of Mary, Mediatrix of all graces is very strong in this. This is part of his theology.

The operation of the Spirit is all the more strong, is much more strong with the senses of the inner man than the operation of bodily things is with the senses of the external man. This is another strong statement. We've got exterior senses and we've got interior senses – mystical senses, spiritual senses, and the interior senses are more powerful than the exterior senses and more reliable. These people have great faith in the power of the interior senses. Remember what these interior senses are.[XXXI] Remember that these people use a different kind of terminology, and when they say interior senses, today we would say faith or the gift of understanding or something like that. We've got a different terminology for it. Remember, we have got other interior senses. What's the problem that arises? What are these other interior senses? It isn't a mystical sense; it isn't an exterior sense: imagination. He's not talking about the imagination. Imagination is a powerful interior sense, but it's not a mystical sense, so therefore this creates a problem. You have to look out. A person could suddenly imagine that there's all sorts of stuff operating inside. If you get too sold on that it isn't the real thing. It's just too bad, that's all. There has to be a distinction made, and there again, you get back to the inevitable solution. You've got to take it back to somebody else. Somebody's got to help you judge. Then he says, "What is the root of this interior certainty?" This is strong stuff again. He says, "Why is it that our interior senses operating in mystical experience are absolutely indubitable?" They're absolutely certain. Like I say, you've got to watch it. He says there's no room left for doubt. "There can't be any doubt when He who gives the witness and he to whom the witness is given are one Spirit."[XXXII] This is fine, provided they are one spirit. What this presupposes is that there is the Spirit of God and our spirit, and that the two are united, and that what the Spirit of God says is perceived within this unity. But if we've just got our own spirit and we're not united to anything, we can get a certain kind of a definite feeling of certitude by just telling ourselves something real strong, and nobody else ever gets in there. But that isn't it. This is all very nice if it's the real thing. It's got to be the real thing. This raises all kinds of problems.

Let's develop this a little more here. He goes into this idea of pure love. This is his next step. Now he gets into the realm of talking about how this is guaranteed. What's this based on? How can you judge the reality of this experience? What is the great Cistercian criterion for any mystical experience? Pure love. This is the central thing: absolute purity of love. What's pure love for Cistercian Fathers? What's it mean? What's purity of love? Love for love's sake, without any self-seeking whatever, and actually without any self to seek. Love is pure when there's no self in it, when self is so far gone that self is no longer experienced in any way, so that from the moment there is a self which is experiencing all this stuff, the love isn't that pure. This may sound mysterious, and I'm not going to try to explain it because it remains mysterious. But this is what the idea of pure love is. Sometimes you get the expression outside the Cistercian field, the annihilation of self[XXXIII] – total forgetfulness of self, as if self isn't there. Self is there ontologically. The person is not ontologically destroyed. The person is still there, and ontologically distinct from God, and yet mystically one with God in such a way that there's nothing left of self.

This is where he brings in this idea of Jacob saying, "It is enough to me that Joseph is alive." He says this is like pure love. "It is sufficient to me that Jesus is alive." We wake from the torpor at the touch of the Spirit of Easter, the Easter grace. He says, "In this you will know that your spirit has fully come to life in Christ – if it can say sincerely, 'It is enough to me that Jesus lives.'"[XXXIV] There you've got the doctrine of pure love packed into a very short phrase. That means, literally, the person who loves Jesus is content that Jesus is risen. It doesn't matter what happens to us. It doesn't matter if we get anything out of it. We'll see how he develops this. He says this is the word which is truly worthy of friends of Jesus. You know the fortune of the phrase "the friends of God."[XXXV] This runs all down through the Rhineland mystics. A friend of God is one who is united to God in a completely disinterested relationship. He's not seeking anything out of it for himself. All he wants is to love God, to please God. Basically, to put it in practical terms, it's the person who cares nothing about anything except pleasing God. "If God is pleased, I'm pleased." That is to be a friend of God. Of course it has a Gospel basis. What's the Gospel basis for this idea of friends of God? Where do you get that in the Gospel? "I have called you friends." This is John's Gospel.[XXXVI] "You are no longer servants. Everything which the Father has revealed to me I have revealed to you. I have called you my friend." This is what He says to those to whom He has given His Spirit. When Christ gives all that He has to His friend, that is, the Spirit, then all that the friend has belongs to Him. All that He has belongs to the friend. This is perfect friendship. This is what it means to be a friend of God.

Then he goes into this "*O castissimum affectum*."[XXXVII] This is purely and simply an echo of St. Bernard: "O most chaste love." If you read Gilson,[XXXVIII] there's a whole raft of quotations – "*O amor castus et purus*"[XXXIX] and so forth. This is standard. This is straight St. Bernard in here. Then he says, "If Christ lives, then I live, because my soul depends entirely on Him, and indeed He is my life. In that case, if He lives, then nothing is lacking to me. But this is only true if I live entirely in Him. If I live for myself, it doesn't matter whether He lives or not. My life is in me. But if my life is entirely in Him, then if He lives, I live, and if He doesn't, then I don't." It says, "Even if Jesus Himself is absent from me, provided that He lives, that's all I care about." The Latin says: "*dummodo ipse vivat vel sibi*."[XL] This is a particular kind of Latin syntax. How would you translate that? "If only He lives, at least to himself." It's almost colloquial. He's got plenty of ways of using little phrases that are quite colloquial. "Providing He's living, anyway for Himself"; "Let Him live, anyway for Himself." "For me, I don't care." This is tremendous. Then he says, "Pure love is a love which has absorbed all the affections of a man."[XLI] That's again St. Bernard: that's Sermon 83 on the Canticle of Canticles.[XLII] St. Bernard defines pure love: it's pure when there are no other affections left in the soul but love. What does he mean by that? He means that love has swallowed up fear. This is standard Cistercian. There's no more distinction between fear and love: that now you fear, now you love. There's no distinction. You just love. There's no longer any desire for gain. Christ Himself is my gain: "*mihi vivere Christus est*."[XLIII] Death is gain, he says: "For me to live is Christ and death is gain." There is no sadness. There is no grief. There is no special joy outside of love. Love has absorbed all the affections. This is a standard Cistercian approach. He says finally, "The soul is completely neglectful of itself, forgetful of itself, thinks only of Jesus and seeks only those things that are pleasing to Him, and therefore I will say that in such a soul charity has become perfect."[XLIV] So here you've got this whole lineup, based on this Genesis text. He takes this Genesis text and pulls all this out of it.

But now the problem is: where does that leave us? What's the problem with this kind of thing? Does this pose any kind of a difficulty to anybody? (If you direct people it does!) Does this require any kind of qualification? He's saying, this is the grace of Easter. The grace of Easter is this pure love. You forget yourself. You're carried away with love. What kind of a problem is that going to present to about 95% of us next week? We're not necessarily going to be carried away with love next week! None of us probably will! This is all very nice; this is beautiful. But once in a blue moon, occasionally, somebody gets this. Maybe he doesn't get it on Easter. Maybe he gets it the second Monday after the first Tuesday of something totally un-liturgical. So then, where do we stand? Right away he qualifies this. What he is saying here is this is the central ideal of the thing. This is the way it is when it's perfect. This is the model experience. It's not so unrealistic to present the model experience, and then go from that to imperfect and rather less developed experiences of this. So he says, "Alright, so you don't feel this." He gets further on in the sermon: "Well, now what you have to do is at least seek Him, anyway."

What matters is that you be like Jacob, and you take a look, and you say, "Hey, there are all the wagons. Let's get in the wagons and let's go!" This is very practical, because for him, the wagons are the sacraments.[XLV] (Alright, don't throw anything. This is a Cistercian of the twelfth century!) This whole business of pure love is fine, but it is equally good if a person purely and simply wakes up and with a very realistic sense of where he actually is, says to himself, "I am now going to start moving in this direction." That's all that's necessary, because this anybody can do. This is a much better kind of awakening. The practical awakening for every one of us is that he wakes up where he actually is and starts moving from where he actually is. It's of absolutely no use whatever to wake up where you aren't and start going from there. There's sort of a Zen saying: "Where do you go from the top of a twenty-foot pole?"[XLVI] If you're not even on the top of a twenty-foot pole and you think you are, where do you go from there? That's a great problem, but if you once realize where you are and you see the wagons all lined up and you get in the wagons and you're ready to go, this is fine. So he has all kinds of practical conclusions that he draws from this.

In another sermon, in the Third Sermon, he comes down to earth and puts it in terms that are very useful for everybody. He says: "Fervor in prayer and work are signs that we love God."[XLVII] Now we're happy. We can do this! He says the first sign of life returning to a man is if he is zealous for action, and then his perfect resurrection is when he is zealous in contemplation. Now he's being real nice and giving us all happy categories that we're aware of. This is good. But what does he do then? He throws in another scripture text. Here's the one he throws in. This Third Easter Sermon is a very beautiful one. It's about the sunrise. We were talking about Easter texts that you could use for a sermon. We missed one big one yesterday. Has anybody thought of any special texts? We really missed a lulu: it's the versicle of every hour of the office on Easter Sunday and Easter Week: "This is the day the Lord has made." – "*Haec dies quam fecit dominus*."[XLVIII] On this text he talks about sunrise and the blazing sunrise of the risen Christ and the day that the Lord has made and all kinds of days and all kinds of dawns and all kinds of waiting for the dawn and all this sort of stuff – about fifteen thousand texts that he lines up and they're beautiful. It's tremendous! He mixes up

Mary Magdalene at the tomb with the man knocking at the door of Wisdom.[XLIX] This is great. This is good stuff. This is Cistercian contemplation. What you're going to do is, you're going to get to like this stuff, so that you can kind of swim in it. It's very pleasing. It's very delightful to fool with this kind of thing. It's like sparring with about ten people, a great big boxing round. You get hit from all angles. You don't know where it's coming from. He runs all these texts together. He does a very good job.

We may not get to that, but in this one where he's talking about the Easter grace and this resurrection in us – this isn't going to please you too much! This is the one that we had just the other day, about Eliseus raising the dead child.[L] What does he do? What's the story about Eliseus raising the dead child? He lies down on the child and his mouth on his mouth, his eyes on his eyes, and all this sort of stuff. Incidentally this is a very nice thing for one of the sacraments. Which one? Extreme unction. I don't know if the Fathers have ever used it this way – obvious one to use for extreme unction because in extreme unction all our senses are signed with the grace of the corresponding sense in Christ. When your eyes are anointed, your eyes become the eyes of Christ. When your lips are anointed, your lips become the lips of Christ in the eyes of the Heavenly Father. They have all the merits of all the works of Christ, so that as you go into death you are changed into Christ. You're completely made over into Christ by the sacrament. This is what gives you the strength of the sacrament. But anyway, "Eliseus therefore went into the house and behold, the child lay dead, and going in he shut the door upon him and upon the child and prayed to the Lord and he lay upon the child, put his mouth upon his mouth, his eyes upon his eyes, his hands upon his hands and he bowed himself upon him and the child's flesh grew warm."[LI] First thing. Then he returned and he walked around the house and so forth and he goes back and this time, what did the child do? He yawned. How many times – it's very important: seven times.[LII] Why? What does Guerric do with this?[LIII] He gets the spiritual life out of this. This is the grace of Easter again. The first thing is when his flesh gets warm, this is the grace of getting into the active life. It's the purgative way, if you like. You get busy. You start moving and start doing something. This is not to be neglected. There's no harm in getting down to business. It's all very nice to be thinking about pure love and chaste love but maybe there's just some ordinary stuff that we need to be doing. Maybe there's something we just have to get down to and get busy and do it, and maybe that's the beginning. The second thing he says: this yawning. What does he apply this to? What's the point of this yawning here, in the story? He just doesn't yawn. What's it for? He's starting to breathe again. This yawning is actually an opening up of the man's heart so that he can draw breath again. The child is stretching and opening up his muscles so that his lungs can start working again, so I think it's a very good image of prayer, because prayer is purely and simply nothing other than breathing. "*Os meum aperui, et attraxi spiritum.*"[LIV] "I open my mouth and draw in the Spirit." (Now don't do this literally. A lot of wide open mouths – the next thing will be a snore or something!) That's what prayer is: you open up your heart to draw in the Spirit, so the grace of our life and the sacraments and of Easter is that it opens up this life of prayer so that we start to breathe. We start to function and we start to operate. Then finally – I don't know where he gets this – he's got to get the contemplative life out of it somewhere. So finally he says the perfection of this grace is when the intellect is illuminated for contemplation. They've got a beautiful line-up on the Eucharist – we'll have to skip that – and he's got all this terrific line-up of texts, which I'll skip also.

The last thing that he says, and this kind of ties in with what we've just been talking about – after talking about prayer all through this Third Sermon and talking about watching in the early dawn for the coming of the Lord and using every possible kind of scripture text to give you the idea of what it's all about to awaken our hearts to this, he finally says, "Watch, my brethren, so that the morning light, Christ, may rise for you, and that He may reveal to you once again the mystery of His early morning resurrection, the new sun emerging from the netherworld wounds the eyes and yet it opens the day of eternity to those that are watching for Him."[LV] This is a very beautiful thing. This is all right. Supposing that you don't find Christ in prayer. There again he gives the average monk a break. You don't find Him in prayer, then what? He says, "Then maybe you'll find Him in work,"[LVI] and this is true. This is the Cistercian way. After saying all these wonderful things about the contemplative life and about prayer and so forth, he says, "Okay, so you don't find Him in prayer, then what? Well, find Him in work," and he says, "How do you do this?" This I think is very useful. "The experience of many of you," he says, "proves that very often while they have sought Jesus, so to speak, at the tomb" – he says *ad memorias altarium*[LVII] – what does that mean? I don't know! He's got all sorts of funny phrases – you have sought Jesus "at the memories of the altars." Who's an old-timer here? Who can remember what that probably is? What was one of the devotions – Dom Vital[LVIII] was all the time going around all the altars? Maybe that's what this is. That's a very old Cistercian thing, a very old Cistercian devotion. You get it in the *Spiritual Directory*.[LIX] Not everything in the *Spiritual Directory* is a very old Cistercian devotion, but this is. It's an old Cistercian devotion that Dom Vital always used to recommend in the novitiate and nobody else ever did. You'd see his novices going around; you'd see a regular procession around the back of the church. You had to go to every altar in the church – of course there's more now. "Now do this. This is an old Cistercian devotion." I'll get fired and can live in the woods! You'd pray at each altar. You'd pray to the saint. In those days they had little statues so you'd know which altar it was. Now it's pretty hard to tell who's what. It's just an altar. It could be that. He says, "You've been looking for Jesus and you haven't found Him. You haven't found Him going around the altars and you haven't found Him in your prayer." Then what happens? "Unexpectedly He meets you in the ways of your work."[LX]

This should be a standard Cistercian approach. How does he say that one should be disposed for this? You've got some beautiful stories in the *Exordium Magnum*[LXI] about work. There are some very fine stories which give you the spirituality of the early Cistercians with regard to work. One of them is the brother who used to plow with his pair of oxen, and Our Lord used to come and help him.[LXII] He'd be going along and he used to plow and Our Lord would walk along with him, and they'd talk: "Pretty hot, isn't it?" "Yeah." "Okay, I'll take over. You go rest." This is a very standard thing in early Cistercians. There was a cook – this was Blessed Albert who later became a hermit. He was cooking and he used to take off from the kitchen and disappear someplace and an angel would cook the dinner.[LXIII] This is sort of a standard early Cistercian thing. They'd be working and then they'd be going along with some saint or some angel or Our Blessed Mother would appear. They'd all be harvesting wheat or something. The Blessed Mother and St. Anne and St. Mary Magdalene would come down and give them all a drink.[LXIV] This is all right. I'm all for reviving this. We could use a little more of this. There was one monk at Clairvaux who had his own little patch in the cloister garden. He had a little patch of herbs and he was growing all these herbs for making medicine. He had all these medicines that he was taking all the time, and one morning he comes down to church and the Blessed Virgin is standing at the door of the church with a bottle and a spoon, and everybody that comes in, she's giving them this wonderful stuff out of this bottle. They're all really radiant when they get it; and he comes up with, "My turn. Can I have some?" "No, I don't give you any. You've got your own medicine!"[LXV] So read the *Exordium Magnum* because it has all this kind of stuff.

But anyway, Guerric ends up with this idea of talking to Our Lord while we work and being with Him while we work, working with Him and what does he use, what text does he use in describing this – the obvious one from the Gospel about the disciples of Emmaus! The Cistercian monk at work is like the disciple going to Emmaus with Our Lord appearing unexpectedly by his side and doing what? Opening to him the scriptures, so that his heart is burning. The essential element is that what the monk is doing is, at his work he's remembering the scriptures that he's read or that he's had in the office, so that what it really amounts to, to be practical, is that he's ruminating in his heart the words of the scriptures while he's working. So that's the early formula. Happy Easter.

I. "*Circumdederunt me viri mendaces, sine causa flagellis ceciderunt me, sed tu, Domine defensor, vindica me*" ("Lying men surrounded me; without cause they struck me with their whips. But you, Lord my Defender, protect me").

II. The traditional hymn for the Palm Sunday procession, beginning "*Gloria, laus et honor tibi sit Rex Christe Redemptor, / Cui puerile decas prompsit Hosanna pium*" ("Glory, praise and honor be to You, Christ, Redeemer King, / To Whom the loveliness of children brought forth reverent hosannas").

III. "two brothers".

IV. Anscar Vonier, OSB, *The Victory of Christ* (London: Burns, Oates & Washbourne, 1934); see Merton's reference to this work in *Life of the Vows* 70-71.

V. F. X. Durrwell, *The Resurrection: A Biblical Study*, trans. Rosemary Sheed (New York: Sheed and Ward, 1960); see Merton's comments on this book in his journal entry for April 16, 1961 (*Turning Toward the World* 101).

VI. *Sermones de Resurrectione Domini* 1 (J. P. Migne, ed., *Patrologiae Cursus Completus, Series Latina* [*PL*], 221 vols. [Paris: Garnier, 1844-1865] vol. 185, cols. 141B-144D); 2 (cols. 144D-148B); 3 (cols. 148B-152B).

VII. In his conferences on the Cistercian Fathers, Merton had been discussing the doctrine of pure love in Guigo (March 9, 23, 30 [Gethsemani recordings 47.3, 50.1, 50.3]) and would continue to do so after Easter on St. Bernard (April 20, 27, May 4, 11 [Gethsemani recordings 52.2, 53.2, 53.4, 54.3]); see *Cistercian Fathers and Their Monastic Theology* lix-lx, 88-96, 115-23.

VIII. Introit for the Mass of Easter ("*Resurrexi, et adhuc tecum sum*") (Ps. 138[139]:18).

IX. Matthew 28:6.

X. The gospel for the Second Sunday after Easter (Jn. 10:11-16).

XI. St. Gregory the Great, *Homiliae in Evangelia* 24 (*PL* 76, cols. 1246A-1259A).

XII. Psalm 27[28]:7.

XIII. Luke 24:13-35.

XIV. "*In Feria II Paschatis*" (*PL* 184, cols. 965B-972B).

XV. Revised Standard Version (Gen. 45:25-26).

XVI. "He awaked as it were out of a deep sleep" (Douay-Rheims) ("*quasi de gravi somno evigilans*").

XVII. "*Sufficit mihi, si Ioseph filius meus vivit*" (1.1, 3, 4 [cols. 141B, 143A, 143C]).

XVIII. Col. 141C, which reads: "*esurimus; salvatorem non somniatorem.*"

XIX. Ezekiel 37:1-28.

XX. 4[2] Kings 5:1-19.

XXI. 1.1 (col. 141C) ("we desire not the one who fed stomachs, but who feeds minds, hungry ones").

XXII. Song of Songs 3:4.

XXIII. Merton's Sunday afternoon conferences were open to the entire community, so that some of his audience would not have been at the previous day's conference.

XXIV. *PL* 205, cols. 559C-828B.

XXV. *Sermo* 17 *in Die Sancto Paschae* (col. 682CD).

XXVI. Cols. 141B, 143A, 143C, 143D.

XXVII. 1.4 (col. 143B).

XXVIII. 1.4 (col. 143C).

XXIX. "Let us not think that there was more glory and happiness in dwelling in Abraham's bosom – which is another name for Paradise – than in dwelling in the bosom of Mary where God has set up his throne. (Abbot Guerric)" (*Secret of Mary* 53); "Abbot Guerric says, 'Do not imagine there is more joy in dwelling in Abraham's bosom than in Mary's, for it is in her that our Lord placed his throne'" (*True Devotion to the Blessed Virgin* 199) (*God Alone: The Collected Writings of St. Louis Mary de Montfort* [Bay Shore, NY: Montfort Publications, 1988] 276, 352).

XXX. According to the note for the quotation from *True Devotion*, drawn from Guerric's Fourth Sermon on the Assumption, "Montfort borrowed this text from Poiré, *Crown of goodness*, 8th star" (*God Alone* 390) (i.e. François Poiré, SJ [1584-1637]).

XXXI. On the interior or spiritual senses, see *Introduction to Christian Mysticism* 82-96.

XXXII. "*Quis enim dubietati relinquatur locus, ubi qui testificatur, et cui testificatur, unus fuerit Spiritus?*" (col. 143C).

XXXIII. On the use of this terminology see *Introduction to Christian Mysticism* 174, 195, 304, 325.

XXXIV. "*In hoc sane noveris quod spiritus tuus plene in Christo revixerit, si quod sequitur ex sententia dixerit: Sufficit mihi, si Iesus vivit*" (1.5 [col. 144A]).

XXXV. On the Friends of God, see *Introduction to Christian Mysticism* 196-98.

XXVI. John 15:15.

XXXVII. "O most pure affection" (1.5 [col. 144A]).

XXXVIII. See the discussion of pure love in St. Bernard in Étienne Gilson, *The Mystical Theology of St. Bernard*, trans. A. H. C. Downes (New York: Sheed & Ward, 1940) 140-49.

XXXIX. "O chaste and pure love"; see St. Bernard, *De Diligendo Deo* c. 10.28: "*O amor sanctus et castus! o dulcis et suavis affectio! o pura et defaecata intentio voluntatis!*" (*PL* 182, col. 991A) ("O holy and chaste love! O sweet and pleasant affection! O pure and clear intention of the will!").

XL. 1.5 (col. 144A).

XLI. "*amor Christi* [the love of Christ] *totum absorbuerit affectum hominis*" (1.5 [col. 144B]).

XLII. *PL* 183, cols. 1181C-1184D; Gilson's discussion of pure love is based principally on this sermon, which he translates in his text (133-40).

XLIII. "For me to live is Christ" (Phil. 1:21).

XLIV. "*negligens et immemor sui nonnisi Iesum Christum et ea quae sunt Iesu Christi sentiat, tunc demum, ut arbitror, perfecta est in eo charitas*" (1.5 [col. 144B]).

XLV. Actually the body of Christ is likened to the provisions on the wagons and the Spirit to the wagons themselves: "*Caro Christi est viaticum, spiritus vehiculum. Ipse est cibus, ipse currus Israel et auriga eius*" (1.6 [col. 144C]) ("The flesh of Christ is food for the journey, the Spirit the vehicle. He Himself is the food; He Himself is the chariot of Israel and its charioteer").

XLVI. Merton quotes this saying (though with "a thirty-foot pole") in his final talk in Thailand on the day of his death (*Asian Journal* 338-39).

XLVII. See 3.5 (col. 151A): "*Resurgat itaque ac reviviscat spiritus omnium nostrum, sive ad vigilantiam orandi, sive ad instantiam operandi, ut quadam rediviva ac vivida alacritate probet se de novo portionem accepisse in resurrectione Christi*" ("Therefore may the spirit of each of us arise and revive, whether to watchfulness in praying or to perseverance in working, so that with a certain reanimated and lively eagerness each may show himself anew to have received his share in the resurrection of Christ").

XLVIII. 3.2 (col. 149A) (Ps. 117[118]:24).

XLIX. 3.2 (col. 149BD) (Mt. 27:61; Lk. 24:1-8; Wis. 6:13-15).

L. 4[2] Kings 4:18-37.

LI. 4[2] Kings 4:32-34.

LII. 4[2] Kings 4:35.

LIII. 3.5 (cols. 151B-152B).

LIV. Col. 151B (Ps. 118[119]:131).

LV. "*Vigilate, inquam, ut oriatur vobis matutina lux, Christus scilicet, cuius quasi diluculum praeparatus est egressus, paratus utique vigilantibus ad se, mysterium suae matutinae resurrectionis saepius innovare*" (3. 3 [col. 149D]).

LVI. "*non solum inhaerentes studio contemplationis, sed etiam ambulantes iuste ac pie vias actionis, Iesus dignatur et occursu et manifestatione sui*" (col. 150C) ("Jesus deems not only those committed to the discipline of contemplation but also those walking justly and reverently in the ways of action worthy of His encounter and manifestation").

LVII. 3.4 (col. 150C).

LVIII. Dom Vital Klinski, retired abbot of Achel in Belgium, lived at Gethsemani from 1927 until his death on June 3, 1966, serving for much of that time as Master of the Brother Novices, whom he would have trained in the devotional practice mentioned here; he served as Merton's confessor for much of his time in simple vows in the mid-1940s. For Merton's tribute to him after his death, see Thomas Merton, "Dom Vital at Gethsemani – August 1966," *The Merton Seasonal* 41.2 (Summer 1916) 5-9.

LIX. [Vital Lehodey, OCSO,] *A Spiritual Directory for Religious* Translated from the Original French Text "*Directoire Spirituel à l'Usage des Cisterciens de la Stricte Observance*" by a Priest of New Melleray Abbey, Peosta, Iowa (Trappist, KY: Abbey of Our Lady of Gethsemani, 1946).

LX. "*saepe Iesus quem quaesierunt velut ad monumentum, ad memorias altarium, nec invenerunt, insperatus occurrit eis in viis laborum*" (col. 150C).

LXI. *Exordium Magnum Cisterciense sive Narratio de Initio Cisterciensis Ordinis*, ed. Bruno Griesser, *Corpus Christianorum Continuatio Medievalis*, vol. 138 (Turnhout, Belgium: Brepols, 1961); English translation: *The Great Beginning of Cîteaux – A Narrative of the Beginning of the Cistercian Order: The Exordium Magnum of Conrad of Eberbach*, trans. Benedicta Ward, SLG and Paul Savage, ed. E. Rozanne Elder, Cistercian Fathers vol. 42 (Collegeville, MN: Cistercian Publications, 2012).

LXII. *Exordium Magnum* 4.18: "About a Lay Brother, a Cowherd, Who in a Vision Saw the Lord Jesus Helping Him Herd His Cows" (*Great Beginning* 353-54).

LXIII. This story is not found in the *Exordium Magnum* but is told by Merton in his biographical sketch of "Saint Albert, Lay-brother and Hermit at Saint Andrew of Sestri, near Genoa, Italy" (*Valley of Wormwood* 256-61), in which the "mystical cook" prolonged his post-communion thanksgiving when he was supposed to be preparing dinner; his fellow monks complained to the abbot, who summoned him to the kitchen, where they arrived "in time to see an angel standing over the uncooked food make a sign of the Cross, by which everything was instantly and completely cooked and made ready to be served up to the brethren" (259).

LXIV. *Exordium Magnum* 3.13: "How the Monk Rainald, of Blessed Memory, Saw Mary Visiting the Monks Who Were Reaping" (*Great Beginning* 252-57) – the third figure with the Blessed Mother and Mary Magdalene was St. Elizabeth rather than St. Anne.

LXV. *Exordium Magnum* 3.21: "About a Brother to Whom the Blessed Virgin Mary Gave Heavenly Food in a Vision" (*Great Beginning* 285-87).

Guerric of Igny's Advent Sermons – Conferences

Merton returns to Guerric the following year at another high point of the liturgical cycle, its beginning. On December 7, 1964, he writes in his journal of "Guerric's beautiful Fourth Advent sermon on the consecration of the desert, and the grace placed in it by Christ, 'preparing a new place for the new life' and overcoming evil not for Himself 'but for those who were to be future dwellers in the wilderness.' Not just evil, the Evil One! The desert is given us to get the evil unnested from the crannies of our own hearts. Perhaps again my tendency to find this in solitude rather than community is simply subjective. After twenty-three years all the nests are well established. But in solitude and open air they are revealed and the wind blows on them and I know they must go!" (*Dancing in the Water of Life* 177). On this day Merton presented the second of three Monday conferences (November 30, December 7 and 14) on Guerric's Advent sermons (Gethsemani recordings 134.1, 134.4, 135.4). Though he would not discuss this Fourth Advent Sermon for another week, the resonance of its theme for his own life had already made a deep impression. In these conferences, transcribed here for the first time, Merton once again praises Guerric for his scriptural focus, and for his ability to apply unconventional texts to the mysteries of the liturgical cycle and so stimulate interest and reflection on the part of his audience. After a bit of humorous byplay about the ready availability of the 1959 volume of the *Christmas Sermons*, free for the taking, Merton turns to the whole question of the meaning of salvation as presented in the Advent liturgy, which speaks to something fundamental in the human psyche, the desire for the fulfillment of being, the fullness of being: "there's no point in continuing to be if our being is not complete. So therefore there's this aspiration to eternity, and to completeness, and we know very well that there's no natural answer to this completeness in eternity. We don't have it in ourselves; we don't have it in the world; and no matter what you do in the world, you can't find this. Yet there must be an answer, and what is the answer? Well naturally, people don't know, and you get certain religions – they sort of aspire to this answer, and this is part of the Advent. From the very moment that this is built into man, man is an Advent being. Man is looking for a solution to this need for wholeness and completeness." Merton finds Guerric speaking to this need in his Second Advent Sermon (he never discusses the First), with its text from Proverbs: "A good messenger from a distant land is like a cup of cold water to a thirsting soul" – or alternatively: "Like cold water to a thirsty soul, so is good news from a far country." The thirst is for this fullness of life, and the good news is three-fold: "the coming of a Savior; the reconciliation of the world; and the good things of the world to come." After considering the irrelevance of most of the traditional images, positive and negative, of the world to come, Merton goes on to point out that for Guerric the good messengers are not only the prophets and apostles but even the world's seekers, those "who precisely because they were human and because they realized the state of man and so forth, realized their need for a savior yet couldn't express it clearly." Finally the response to the good news, according to Guerric, should be that leap of faith exemplified by the unborn John in his mother's womb at the arrival of Mary and her own unborn child. Rather than taking the message of salvation for granted, something that is no longer news, "our spirit should leap up with lively joy .... should raise itself above itself and seek how to run out to meet Christ who comes. It's this idea of this shock of recognition, that the Savior comes on this completely spiritual level and that we're lifted above ourselves by this realization of the truth of salvation. This is the meaning of Advent." The following Monday's conference again begins with a look at the liturgy, with a lively discussion of the inadequacy of "behold" as a translation of the "*ecce*" of the Advent antiphons, in contrast with the vitality of the Italian "*ecco*" signaling the arrival of a transformative event. It is this aspect of transformation, Merton proposes, that Guerric and the Cistercian Fathers generally emphasize in their teaching on the three advents – the first advent of Christ's incarnation, the final advent of Christ's return in glory, but above all the present advent of his "coming in grace, now, in our own hearts.... so that for the Cistercian Fathers, the middle advent is actually the present advent of our life, is contemplation and mystical union, and so they develop this doctrine of mystical union." In Guerric's words, "when He is present He is a light to the soul and to the mind, and by this light the invisible is seen and the unthinkable is thought." This should lead, according to Guerric, to a kind of "stupor," a wonderment that breaks through the usual inattentive drifting of the human mind and heart, an experiential recognition of the nothingness of one's own being and the infinite fullness of the divine reality. Such an awareness, Merton concludes, is potentially available to everyone, but only if one truly surrenders all pretensions to an autonomous selfhood, all illusions of spiritual fulfillment as a possession to be obtained or an accomplishment to be attained: "if the person has reached the center of his nothingness and is completely abandoning himself totally to God and not acquiring anything for himself, and not wanting anything for himself, and desiring only the glory of God and not seeking this or that experience, and not emphasizing a self that can have this or that experience, then he's on the right track. But then it doesn't matter whether he gets anything or doesn't get anything. This is for God to decide, and you leave this to God. So the great thing therefore, the central thing, is this idea of humility." In the third and final conference, Merton first considers Guerric's Third Sermon, based on a text from Amos chapter 4, in which encountering God may be a moment of judgment in which one's true motives and attitudes are revealed, but may also be a time of boldly making claims on God like the neighbor demanding bread for his newly arrived guest, or the Syrophoenician woman refusing to take no for an answer to her request for her child's healing. To prepare to meet your God, as Guerric, drawing on a passage from Isaiah 64, concludes, is also to become ready to experience the final advent of the Lord as a time of eschatological vindication, of the ultimate victory of justice and love. While Merton's final evaluation of this Third Sermon is that it basically takes a "simple ascetic approach: the Last Judgment is coming; prepare and meet it," he finds the fourth and final Advent Sermon, on which he had commented in his journal the week before, to be "a really monastic sermon, profoundly monastic, and also deeply contemplative," focused on "the grace of the desert and the blessedness of the wilderness," particularly as it is experienced in Cistercian life. The desert for Guerric and the early Cistercians generally has an almost sacramental dimension, an outward sign of the inner solitude and peace that is to be found in monastic life: "with a certain amount of austerity and discipline, then the monastery is a place of peace and we hear the Holy Spirit." While such a "desert" is not for Cistercians the literal geographical place of solitude it was for the early Egyptian monks and for some of the more eremitical Western expressions of monasticism, in Guerric's use of the term, Merton says, "we have a sort of early witness of the fact that the Cistercian life *does* have this desert quality, but it is a desert quality that is combined with community, the combination of solitude and community." Yet, Merton concludes, there may be room in Cistercian life, as there is for the Carmelites, for a more intense form of solitary monastic experience, at least on a temporary basis – though he adds, to laughter: "Some of course would be there permanently!" In these final comments in this final conference on a key witness to the early Cistercian spirit, one may hear Merton's own conviction that a more solitary life, such as the one he will begin to live on a full-time basis some eight months later, is not only compatible with Cistercian monastic life but an authentic exemplification of its intrinsic "desert" character.

1.

I'm going to talk about Blessed Guerric's Advent sermons,[I] and this is good because you're getting into a twelfth-century Cistercian and his approach, and how he uses scripture above all. One good way to read these twelfth-century Cistercians is to try to follow up some of the scripture that they bring in and see how they're using it, and Guerric is especially good. Blessed Guerric is, I would say, really the Cistercian Father that I think most people can get most out of, because it's really good theology, and it's Pauline theology, and it's fairly easy to read. It's not as flowery as St. Bernard. It's not as technical as William of St. Thierry; and on the whole it's very good. However, is it in English? Well, we've got a mimeograph; we've got a typed one in English here, I think. They published the *Christmas Sermons*[II] – of course read those – and read the commentary too! Incidentally, if you want a volume of those Christmas Sermons to send home to your Aunt Lizzy or something – why you can have them! We've got lots of them! Br. Ralph and Co. would be glad to get rid of them! So anyone who wants a volume – that includes professed and so forth – send them around! Somebody you don't like – send them one!

So what is Advent all about? Today in the epistle we have this statement which is so important: "Everyone that calls upon His name shall be saved."[III] So we've got to get down to the basic thing: Advent is centered on the mystery of salvation, and salvation is not necessarily what everybody thinks about most today, even in religion. So what is meant by salvation? What do you mean – salvation? Advent is the preparation for the coming of salvation. Well, you ask that question – you have a tendency to answer it with other phrases. Salvation means going to heaven and that sort of thing; but what does it really mean? I think we should stop and think a little bit. What does it mean that a Savior comes? That's what these Advent sermons are all about. These Cistercian Advent sermons are full of this awareness that salvation has come from God, and this is what Advent is about. It's not just a preparation for the Feast of Christmas, but it is the recognition of the coming of salvation – that it wasn't there, and it came. There was a time when the world was not saved, and now it is saved, and during all the time that the world was not saved, there were people expecting it to be saved, looking forward to it being saved. So what do you mean – salvation? What does it mean to anybody? If you're drowning, and you're saved, it means you're pulled out of the water. Salvation – you have to think of it. You're healed instead of dying of a disease – put it that way. We take it for granted – well, we're saved, so we don't fuss about salvation. We're thinking about something else, more important, like what are they going to do about the liturgy? How are they going to change the rules – something like that. What are we really expecting, what are we really looking forward to? Well, we're looking forward to – maybe next year I won't have this job anymore! I'll be living in a cave in Edelin's Valley over there! (This is one of the rumors that's going around, so I'm looking forward to that. I'm *not* looking forward to living in any cave, I tell you – anybody wants to live in a cave in this weather, they can. I'll take a house! A house – alright; a house – that's another matter! They can't build a house that fast; and anyway I got a house!) So what are we looking forward to? We've lost this sense. If a man is going down for the third time in the water, and he sees somebody heading for him with a lifeboat and throwing a life preserver, well, his expectations are at their height. He is really reaching for something. Now this is what it means to be saved.

Salvation means being made whole. You stop and think: it's actually the way we're made. There is something in our being – cats and dogs, as far as I know, don't worry about whether they're saved or not, and cows and horses don't particularly care whether they're saved or not. It doesn't occur to them. The problem doesn't arise. For man, the problem arises. It arises out of the way he's made. There's something in the very nature of man that tells him that his life is, so to speak, in the balance, and that he can come out well or not. Other beings apparently don't have this. We have it, and from the moment that a man stops and thinks a little bit, he realizes that he is a being whose being is in question, and it can come out good or it can come out bad. The reason for this is that there is in our being an aspiration, something that's built into us – an aspiration to live and to be; and what it gets down to is, fundamentally, there is in every man – and this is just the basic thing: people deny it and so forth, but you can't get away from the fact – there is in every man a fundamental desire, just from that fact that he *is*, to go on being. Man does not want to stop being. Animals – they try to save their lives and so forth, but there is something in us that's conscious of the fact that we should not stop being, that once we have begun to be, we should continue to be. It should not stop.

But there's no point in continuing to be if our being is not complete. So therefore there's this aspiration to eternity, and to completeness, and we know very well that there's no natural answer to this completeness in eternity. We don't have it in ourselves; we don't have it in the world; and no matter what you do in the world, you can't find this. Yet there must be an answer, and what is the answer? Well naturally, people don't know, and you get certain religions – they sort of aspire to this answer, and this is part of the Advent. From the very moment that this is built into man, man is an Advent being. Man is looking for a solution to this need for wholeness and completeness and continuing and going on and so forth. All your different religions, all the higher religions, have something to do with this Advent, this preparing for the answer which is the complete answer, which is given in Christ. The Hindu religion looks for a solution to this wholeness of being and it says that man finds his wholeness in simply getting into, falling back into, the totality of Being – that he can't be really separated from the totality of Being anyway. So this is a metaphysical answer, but it's not a salvation; later on they bring in the idea of salvation a little bit, and they develop it; and Buddhism, the same sort of answer. But in Christianity, you've got this idea that here is man, left in his helplessness, and he is lost unless he's saved, and this is clear. It isn't just a question of missing the boat. You see for the pagans the answer – it wasn't too much of an issue either/or. If you missed the boat, maybe you get another chance, or maybe it doesn't matter so much, or maybe there's some way it's taken care of. It's not this clear business; see, the pagans have ideas of hell, but it's more or less just an underworld where everybody goes – they're all there; they go down and cross the River Styx and there they are, all crowded around.

But with Christianity there comes this realization: that until man realized he was saved, he didn't realize that he was lost, to a great extent. You see in the Old Testament, it's not too clear – this business of being saved or lost. In the Old Testament you don't find it too clearly. You find being punished and not being punished, and the people being unfaithful to God and therefore being taken in exile, and then being brought back from exile, but you don't find much said about if you do such and such you're saved, and if you don't, you're not saved, and so forth; you've got the promise to Abraham. So now here's the situation, and the people who were very conscious of this, of this fact that man was lost and God came and saved him: "I came to seek and to save that which was lost."[IV] This is one of the fundamental ideas behind Advent. If you don't have this, Advent is meaningless.

So here's where Guerric comes in now, and here's Guerric's Second Advent Sermon. Of course the thing that these fellows do, they don't just take an obvious Advent text. It's very interesting how they choose their texts for the sermons and so forth. Now that the liturgy talks about homilies and so forth, one of the marks of a man who has a good flair for homilies is that he picks original texts, texts that you wouldn't think, and brings them in and ties it in to something and comes out with the Advent message. The text of Guerric's Second Advent Sermon is this: "A good messenger from a distant land is like a cup of cold water to a thirsting soul."[V] You've heard that before, in another form. Who says this all the time? Where do you get this text? Reverend Father's always saying it when he goes to the General Chapter! He puts it, "A letter from a friend is like a cup of cold water in the desert" or something like that. This is a way of saying, "Write me a letter when I'm at the General Chapter." Well, here's this text and Guerric uses it for an Advent sermon. It's from Proverbs 25:25. Let's see what it says. It might be totally different in here, but nevertheless it doesn't make too much difference. It's probably just about the same: "Like cold water to a thirsty soul, so is good news from a far country."[VI] So it's "good news from a far country." What he does, then, he takes this idea of good news from a far country, and what is the good news from a far country? It's the message of salvation, and the good news is three-fold: it's the coming of a Savior; the reconciliation of the world; and the good things of the world to come.

So this is our Advent. This is what Advent is centered on. It's not just a question of four weeks of special liturgy ending in the Feast of Christmas. It is a remembering of the fact that there has been announced to the world the coming of a Savior and the reconciliation of the world and then a new world, a world to come which is full of good things, in which all the evil and all the trouble and all the tears and sorrow of the present world are taken away. These are things that we have to believe in, and Advent is a season in which we make our act of faith. We renew our faith in these truths, and this is when Advent makes sense, when we renew our faith and our hope in the reality. These are the basic realities, and then the reconciliation of the world – a very important idea there – the reconciliation of the world with God, the reconciliation of all the parts of the world with one another. You look out at the world today – it's not a reconciled world. It's not reconciled with itself, and the world needs a Savior! The world never needed salvation more than it does now. Salvation has come, and yet the world needs it. The world doesn't have it. The world isn't in contact with it. Just think how many religious people outside or even in the monastery – I mean, we don't care about future life; we don't care that much. We believe it, sure – you know, future life – "I believe in the life of the world to come"; but we don't really care. We're not concerned about future life, are we? We're not concerned about that. It's one of the fantastic things: for some reason or other, psychologically, people are not geared to be concerned about that. They're worried. They don't want to be punished, that's true. They don't want to be wrong – put it that way. They don't want to have the feeling that they've messed up their life. I think people are more concerned, really, when they get to the end of their life, if they're good people, they want to feel that they made a good job out of it, that it was a fairly decent, a fairly successful thing.

I don't think people have any capacity for imagining a future life, and the reason, of course, is that we can't imagine it either! No, you can't imagine a future life, and the images of the future life are so inadequate! We just don't have adequate images, either of the good one or the bad one. The images of hell, to begin with – most of them aren't terribly Christian anyhow. All this business of devils with pitchforks and so forth is basically pagan. You find this in Etruscan tombs and so forth. All this imaginative was built up by the Middle Ages and so forth, but people don't care that much. Devils with pitchforks leave them cold! The average person nowadays if he gets in a real temptation he just thinks about devils with pitchforks – it doesn't help him a bit! They give a hoot about devils with pitchforks? For some reason, in the Middle Ages it bothered them a bit. And also for sitting on a cloud playing a harp! This doesn't attract – and what was read in the refectory the other day? What was that wonderful thing – "Who could stand alleluia and amen forever?" and I heard a big laugh from the refectory. It really went over very good! We don't want to sing "Alleluia! Amen!" all the time. So let's face it: we have to get a deeper view of the good things of the world to come and realize that they are very real but it's a much greater reality than anything that we can imagine based on the goods of this life. In the old days, when people had it tough, all they had to do was just to imagine things a little less tough and they could think of heaven. They had to work hard, so they would think, "Gee, resting is nice." They could think about resting and it felt good to them because they were tired. We're not tired. We don't work hard. We don't need to rest. We don't care about resting. We rest all the time! All we ever do is rest – rest from morning to night! The stuff we think is hard in choir – one of the hardest things in the Usages, that's so hard that they've abolished it, was the Good Friday Psalter, and that was proposed in the Constitutions as something easy! All the people from the infirmary had to go to it. It was easy because you were just sitting down! It was an easy observance. You just sat there for four hours. What's easier than that? The people used to get exhausted saying that Psalter! One of the first things that they all wanted to abolish was the four-hour Psalter, because it was so exhausting! You're just sitting there, but the way we're built, for some reason or other you sit there for four hours saying a Psalter – it puts us under a nervous strain, and we get exhausted and so forth. So now we can't think of heaven as being restful because we got all the rest we need; we got more rest than we need, and if we start thinking of heaven as things the people of the world really want, it's going to be a Moslem heaven rather than Christian, so that's kind of ruled out too. You can't think of a heaven of pleasures and that sort of thing; we can't think of that, so we've got nothing that we can think about, but nevertheless … !

Then Guerric comes in with this idea: who is this good messenger that brings the good news? He says there have been many messengers. There's one news but there have been many messengers all through time. This is a very impressive idea, too. It's this idea that after the coming of Christ you look back through time and you realize that there were not only all the prophets and all the patriarchs and all these people in the Old Testament, but even among these pagans, pointing to the coming of Christ, pointing to the coming of a Savior. It's true that for thousands and thousands of years, there were people, who precisely because they were human and because they realized the state of man and so forth, realized their need for a savior yet couldn't express it clearly. You get it in ancient literature when you start talking about Greek tragedy. You can see it reflected in Greek tragedy: a statement of the human condition shows that man needs a savior, that the problem of suffering calls for a solution that man doesn't have. So all these people have been pointing to this, and now comes the message of salvation. He says it comes from a far country, and he says: what is this far country? Of course this is typical homily stuff. This isn't scientific criticism at all. Modern criticism would say this is all arbitrary and so forth, because the man in Proverbs doesn't mean this. He doesn't mean this is the far country but Guerric says the far country is the land of the living, which is very far away from this land of dying beings which is us, and the message brings with it the water of saving wisdom. Then we have to receive this message and so now he gets into something very interesting about this reception of the message. Here without realizing it what Guerric does is very simple. He doesn't talk high-flowing mystical stuff, but before you turn around, you find that he is right in the middle of a mystical statement about this whole business of receiving the message of salvation, because for the Cistercians this whole idea of Advent and receiving the message of salvation is all a unity. They did not divide up the ascetic life and the mystical life the way a lot of modern theologians do – the ascetic life is for everybody and the mystic life is for a few people. For the early Cistercians the whole thing is a unity, and the deeper you go into it the more you experience this unity.

So now you find that he's talking about this drink of cold water. What happens when you hear this message of salvation? How do you respond to this message of salvation? He says, it's like Elizabeth and Mary.[VII] When Our Lady comes to Elizabeth, what happens? She gives her this salutation, and what happened to Elizabeth then? The child leapt in her womb. So therefore, he says, this is the way our spirit reacts to the message of salvation:

as though it were a child within us, leaping in the womb. What he's saying is that there's a sort of a leap that takes place inside in our heart, in the depths of our spirit, and most of this sermon goes on talking about this mysterious inner reaction of the spirit, which is the response of the soul to the message of salvation; and so therefore he's talking about the life of prayer. This is standard thing, and this is something, actually, that you can say that is part of the Cistercian life of prayer.

In our life of prayer, what have we got? We're reliving this mystery of Advent, and in this mystery of Advent the message of salvation is announced to us and in some way or other we respond. The Cistercian sermons always sort of bring us back and put us in the position of someone like John the Baptist and Elizabeth and the prophets and so forth, and we experience with them the joy of the hope that they felt when they realized that a Savior is coming into the world, so therefore he says this. This is a theme he sketches out very simply, but it's something that you find developed in some of the mystics like Ruysbroeck for example. Ruysbroeck, in the beginning of this thing on *The Spiritual Betrothal* we've got out here,[VIII] talks about – for pages he goes on about – this idea: "Behold, the Bridegroom cometh; go forth to meet Him."[IX] What does it mean: "Go forth to meet Him"? Well what does it mean to go forth to meet the Bridegroom? It can mean all sorts of things. He takes it on all kinds of levels. It means responding to the word of salvation. So how? Take it on the ascetic level for instance: by good works, something like that – I hear the message of salvation and then I make a resolution. I'm going to fast because it's Advent, so this is one way, real simple way. Something happens in us and redirects our life in a new direction as a result of having heard this word of salvation, but Ruysbroeck takes it deeper and deeper and deeper and goes down into this kind of an interior transformation that takes place in our heart at the recognition. I think that the real thing, what I would say is – somebody has used the phrase somewhere, "the shock of recognition." Let's remember this as something quite useful in this context: the shock of recognition. I would say that what happens in our heart at this coming of the message of salvation, which you could call a basically Advent experience, is a renewal in us of this shock of recognition that all these prophets and all these wise men and so forth all felt, or that St. John the Baptist above all felt in himself, and the click that takes place when our human heart, which thirsts for salvation, realizes that salvation has been given. I would say that this is one of the fundamental religious experiences of man. This is something that we have to cultivate and it's something that the liturgy gives us to cultivate. It's a reawakening to the fact that this is for real. This is not fantasy. The world is full of words and ceremonies and rites, and things are happening and people are doing this and they're going this way and that way and they're making statements, and people are lining up and so forth, and then through all this, right through everything, cuts the word of God, the truth of God. You get it in so many of these Advent antiphons. Your *Benedictus* and *Magnificat* antiphons every day are kind of little bombs that come through, a little bit of an explosion of this message to awaken in our hearts again the shock of recognition of the fact that the Savior has come and He's seeking us. Supposing some important person comes to the monastery, and he's looking all through the crowd of all the monks, and he's got a personal message for some one person, and then he realizes it's for you. He's looking for me! Or somebody comes in the refectory with a telegram and then he goes down the table looking around and all of a sudden it's for me – a telegram: "Pope: you've just been made cardinal." Drop dead! You think that's funny, but this is a much greater message than that. If somebody came and said you've been made cardinal, you'd be all a-dither. Somebody comes along and says you're saved – Ah, thanks. Let's go on to something else. Read any good novels lately? This is something of tremendous importance! It breaks through everything, cuts through everything, and comes through with this eternal truth.

So he says what happens is that – what should happen is that – our spirit should leap up with lively joy and run out to meet the Savior. Then he talks about how our spirit should raise itself above itself and seek how to run out to meet Christ who comes.[X] It's this idea of this shock of recognition, that the Savior comes on this completely spiritual level and that we're lifted above ourselves by this realization of the truth of salvation. This is the meaning of Advent for these people. Then he says this: just as our bodies will spring to life and movement at the Second Coming, so our souls must spring to life and movement in this Advent. (I've got a good poem about the Second Coming in the rising of the dead – maybe I'll bring it in on Saturday and tie it in with this.[XI]) But it's this idea of this springing to life on a whole new level – all our life we're living on a lower level, and in us there's something that asks for life on a higher level, and we can't do anything to get it. Then all of a sudden, one day, something comes along that says: it's yours – here.

2.

Now about Advent: the pattern of Advent is the pattern of movement. You go from here to here, and the liturgy makes it move. It's designed in such a way that you get this idea of movement, of moving from place to place. He's coming towards us and we're going towards Him, and this idea of movement – you get it very clearly. The liturgy brings it out if you pay attention. How does the liturgy bring this out? It's very obvious if you pay attention to what the different antiphons are saying. How does the liturgy do this? Just taking it in time, you've got how many days of Advent? 25 days of Advent, let's say, more or less. It builds up: it starts out the First Sunday of Advent. You've got these different kind of antiphons. He is coming and it's all in the distance, and it's sort of with clouds, and He's coming sometime. He's going to come sometime. Already this week they're already more precise: He's coming soon; and then you get the O antiphons[XII] – this is sort of a buildup of the last eight days, and they're preparing. Once again with the O antiphons, you know that you're getting close. Then in the middle, on December 21, for some unknown reason, they have the *Benedictus* antiphon: "and on the fifth day the Lord will come";[XIII] and then on the Fourth Sunday, He's real close. He's just about to come; and then the day before Christmas Eve: "Behold, all things are fulfilled that the angel said to the Virgin Mary"[XIV] and so forth; and then tomorrow on Christmas Eve: "Today you will see, and tomorrow He will come."[XV] It's a real buildup there. Now to get this, let's look at a couple of these antiphons before we go into Blessed Guerric.

One of the things that you have to understand, one reason why these antiphons don't get through to us, is that there's a little word in there in the Latin – I don't know how it comes out in the brothers' office, but there's probably not much you can do with it except make it come out "behold." Well "behold" is just about nothing to us. Nobody ever says "behold." You're going around, you don't say "behold." You're looking for the spinach in the kitchen or something: "behold the spinach" – you don't say that! "Behold" is no word. It doesn't exist in the English language any more. If you want to get the real meaning of "*ecce*" – you want to understand what "*ecce*" is all about – anybody who's had any kind of contact with Italian families, anybody's got an Italian grandpa or something, what's the Italian equivalent of "*ecce*," and how does it operate? "*Ecco*!" Now "*ecco*" is something quite different from "behold." It has all kinds of meaning – we're going to go into this a little bit. It has a whole gamut of developments that go into this "*ecco*" that you don't get in just "behold." "Behold" sort of is just nothing – but "*ecco*"! Now one of the things of "*ecco*": you're standing on the street and all of a sudden Uncle Joe appears round the corner: "*Ecco*, *ecco* Uncle Giuseppe!" It's not only that he's appeared but here a whole flowering of things come up; or you're trying to find something or you're working on a problem – you're working on a jigsaw puzzle together. Where is it? "*Ecco*, *ecco*!" You find it! The way the Italians give it out, it's one of the central words in the language. If you just know that one word you can already get someplace in Italy! It means, now we have found the solution, so that which we are waiting for has appeared! That which we've been wanting all this time has suddenly been found! It's sort of the lost groat type of discovery[XVI] that you get in the Gospel. It isn't just "behold." To get the feeling of it: you're standing on the street again and you're waiting for a bus and you gotta get someplace, and time is running out, and you don't know when the bus is coming along, and you're looking down the street, and the bus appears, and already there's a change. You're not absolutely sure it's the bus you're waiting for, but it's a bus and it comes and "*Ecco*! *Ecco*!" It's twenty-one – it's the one we're looking for. From that moment, from the moment that this has met your gaze, and you've seen this, you're a different person. Something's happened to you. You have changed. Something irrevocable has taken place. It's never going to be the same again.

What has happened is that the possibility has become an actuality, and this is what happens in life. The whole of life is made up of possibilities and actualities. There's nothing else but that; and when a possibility becomes actual, something has happened. That is an event. This is what life is made up of. Something that was possible now becomes actual. Tomorrow is possible. When tomorrow arrives there will have been an event. It will be actual; it's no longer possible. Today is no longer possible – today is actual; it's realized. Therefore it's unrealizable. It's got to be the way it is. It can't be any different from what it is. Ten minutes from now is still realizable, still possible. So now here's this thing, this "*ecce*" which is in all the antiphons. That which was a big possibility is all of a sudden coming to be realized. It's on the way to being realized. So what's going on in us is on the way to being realized. Our whole life consists in the realization of this great possibility. It's possible that we can be saved, and what we're looking for is that this possibility becomes actual. Now this is what this Advent is saying. It's saying that this possibility can be actualized, and in fact it's going to be actualized. Now just take the difference between two terce antiphons: the terce antiphon of last Sunday: "*ecce, Dominus veniet*" – "Behold, the Lord shall come" – "*et omnes sancti ejus cum eo: et erit in die illa lux magna*"[XVII] – all the saints. This is the big general picture that you get on the First Sunday: "Behold, he's going to come" and all the saints are going to come, and on that day there's going to be a big light. So when you see that light, remember – all together: "*ecco*!" This will be about a few thousand years from now on the last day, but you guys remember that. When we arrive on the last day, we gotta all yell "*ecco*!" Here it is! It's arrived. Now this Sunday is already a little bit different: "*Ecce apparebit Dominus*" – "Behold the Lord will appear and He will not lie; and if he delays wait for Him because He is certainly coming and He isn't going to be long, alleluia."[XVIII] What this keeps emphasizing is the fact that He has said it and He's going to do it, so what this whole Advent thing emphasizes is that we are looking for the Lord. We are looking to see the Lord and He has promised that we shall see Him and He's going to fulfill His promise and it isn't going to be long. It's just as literal as that. We hesitate to get into the reality of this thing. We sort of put it off. "I believe in the beatific vision." It's just an article of faith: in heaven the saints have the beatific vision. But no – it is the thing that I am going to see God. I am on my way to seeing Him, and it is close. It is going to be soon. Then of course think of the effects that this has. If a person once becomes convinced of this, what effect does this have in his life? There's a nice little Advent prayer that I've got in another book, that I haven't got here, but it's a prayer: "Lord, develop in us the faith that we are going to see You, and then we won't be fooling around with any kind of trivialities." Once that this becomes sure, then we don't fool with trivialities anymore – nothing secondary. Everything else doesn't matter; and once a person is convinced of this, the ascetic life and everything like that goes right along with it. This takes care of that. Once this is predominant, then a person isn't going to have to go into a great routine about denying himself this and denying himself this. He's not interested. All he seeks is God.

So now, getting back to Blessed Guerric, the thing that he says is that in Advent God is producing this event. He is working in our hearts to bring about this event, this encounter with Him and He's working in us. During Advent we are undergoing a spiritual transformation which is preparing us to see the Lord, and the spiritual transformation is part of this whole long process, and then another part of the process is the final transformation is going to be a bodily transformation, but the spiritual transformation is taking place now. When the Cistercian Fathers want to talk about this spiritual transformation that goes on in us – you get this all the time: I think Fr. Regis brought it up in his Advent sermon; you get it in all the Cistercians' doctrine on Advent as they emphasize these three advents. So what are the three advents?[XIX] (You've got it in the *St. Andrew's Missal*,[XX] if it comes to that.) It's a standard Cistercian doctrine. What are the three advents: past, present and future. The past one is which? the coming of Christ, the Incarnation. The future one is the Last Judgment. The present one is which? the coming in grace, now, in our own hearts. They emphasize this dynamism of these three advents – the past, the present and the future, and the present advent is the important one. It's the one on which everything else depends. He came in the humility of the flesh; He is going to come in the glory of the judgment; and in the middle He comes in a very special way in the present. This special way is secret, and so the present advent is in the secrecy and the silence of grace, the silence of the heart and so forth. Now when you really develop this idea of the middle advent, what does it amount to? It amounts to a doctrine on contemplation and on mystical union, so that for the Cistercian Fathers, the middle advent is actually the present advent of our life, is contemplation and mystical union, and so they develop this doctrine of mystical union.

Now here's the way Guerric talks about it: "He is not seen as He comes and He is not understood as He goes, but when He is present He is a light to the soul and to the mind, and by this light the invisible is seen and the unthinkable is thought."[XXI] This is standard. There is nothing new about this. This is the kind of stuff that the Cistercians of the twelfth century were thinking about all the time. In terms of Advent, that's what they were thinking about, so that the Advent of our life is a life of contemplative prayer in which we're transformed by Christ. The purpose of the monastic life is that we go through it in this light of faith, this Advent of faith in which we are constantly transformed and prepared for the big event of meeting God face to face and the ultimate event of the total transformation of our whole being, body and soul, at the Last Judgment. This is the serious thing in life. Everything is centered on this, so this does not become secondary. This remains the primary thing, and everything else is secondary. We need to get this perspective back a little bit. "Sure, it's nice; prayer, it's a very nice thing; transforming union is great. We read St. Teresa – it's there" and so forth. Meanwhile, however, I've got something else I have to do.

This is the central thing and here's another, and of course one of these usual deals with the Cistercian Fathers – you have to take their stuff and weigh the words and see what they're saying. So now here's how he describes this, and every word is important. He's talking about contemplative prayer, and he calls it a stupor! It isn't quite the same in Latin as in English, but it's a stupor. Now what does he mean, a stupor? In what sense is it a stupor? It's more the idea of wonder. We're going to come across one of these in one of these poems that I'm going to analyze if we live that long and get that far. The words for amazement and for wonder and so forth, many words of that type, have come to mean now being in a state of coma! I can't think of the ones at the moment but they have been, through constant misuse they've finally reached the point, instead of meaning the person is fully awake and fully functioning, it means he's out. He's had it! He's no longer functioning, and you've got many words like this. Sometimes it works the other way: the word "amazing" – that's one that I'm thinking of – a person who is amazed, the original meaning of the word "amazed" means he's completely shot – he's blinded by the vision of something. Now you're amazed, you're somewhat surprised! You're amazed – that means you're paying attention; you've noticed it. I'm amazed, I have to take account that you just did this. This is a stupor – what this implies is that the whole man is involved in gazing upon God and it's "*suavis et felix*"[XXII] – it's sweet and happy – a sweet and happy stupor. So just think a little bit about a sweet and happy stupor. It helps you to get into one if you think about it a little bit. We should think of this a little more. It's good to realize these things exist. In this sweet and happy stupor of contemplative prayer, what happens? Two things: the soul is suspended and then, he says, expended. Of course they like to run words together, that they kind of make them rhyme a little bit, and I don't know what he means by expended, because I didn't look it up, but it may be somewhat related to our word "expendable," but anyway it's suspended and expended.[XXIII] Well you can get the general drift. What's he talking about when he says it's suspended and expended? What do you suppose he's driving at? What it means in ordinary parlance is just simply that one is on a level that is different from that of a whole lot of ordinary acts. To be in suspense in this sense of the word is to be not concerned with the usual routine of one thing that leads to another. It's just to be drawn out of this kind of mechanical thing where one thought leads to another thought. I mean the routine of mechanical associations.

One of the things of contemplative prayer is that it breaks this routine of associations, although these may be going on in the imagination and so forth, but they don't preoccupy the mind at all. The way that we ordinarily go, just one thing leads to another by association, and again, you go all over the lot, as you know. You start with the bell ringing and that leads to one thing and another thing and another thing, and you just drift. This suspends this drifting, or it suspends all the kind of the planning and stuff that we do. Just think the figuring that we do, and the analyzing that we do – sort of half-logical and half-mechanical – just think what your mind does all day long. Stop and realize how useless a lot of it is, but there's not much you can do about it. You just can't force it to stop, because if you force it then it does even worse things; but the only thing is to get yourself suspended. Then when you're suspended, all this doesn't affect you so much.

Then he says, what happens? I think this is a very good definition of contemplation, of the real meaning of contemplation. All the bones of the interior man – now what are the bones of the interior man? The interior man hasn't got any bones, but he doesn't worry about that. Why does he use this term "all the bones of the interior man"? because he's going to use the term "the bones are crying out" and this comes from scripture somewhere.[XXIV] The bones of the interior man are crying out. What does he mean, "the bones of the interior man are crying out"? Does this mean you've got a kind of a spiritual arthritis or something? What does he mean, "the bones of the interior man are crying out"? This is one of the biblical expressions for saying that which is most interior to a man. When they say "bones" they mean the marrow of his bones, and from a certain point of view, that's as far inside as you can get. If you get into the marrow of his bones, that's the end of the line as far getting inside, penetrating the inmost being of a person, and it does represent a kind of a feeling of joy that we do have. When a person is really joyful it's as though joy is sort of sprouting out from his inmost being. It's as though the marrow of his bones were turned into a source of joy, and out of all this you become a very completely joyful being. What is this joy? This is the important thing too; this again is an important note about contemplation. He says that the bones of the interior man are crying out, shouting or exclaiming, "Lord, who is like unto Thee?" Now this is very important. This is the essence of contemplative prayer. It's the essence of all really deep prayer, and it has its implications. When these Fathers talk in terms of saying: "Lord, who is like unto Thee?" what's the first implication that this has? That this nothing is including me: I'm not. The first thing that this implies is the annihilation, the reduction to nothing, of the self, so that there is, so to speak, no self left in the presence of God.

This is simply a way of expressing, in the most concrete possible terms, the reality of adoration. Adoration: we say the Blessed Sacrament's up here and there's a prie-dieu and you go kneel on the prie-dieu – that's adoration. You kneel there for a half an hour – that's adoration. Well that's true, that's correct. If you were there, you made your half-hour adoration. But this is the most superficial sense of the word adoration, and the deepest sense of adoration – why do you kneel at all in the first place? You kneel because that's the way Sister told us we had to do! Why do you kneel? What's the idea of kneeling? You're lowering yourself. All these expressions of reverence – remember where they come from. They come from inter-human relations, interpersonal relations. People do these things to express before God the thing that they express before a powerful man. Supposing two men meet and they've both got swords. If one of them puts his sword aside and kneels down in front of the other one, he's putting himself in a position of total vulnerability. He's saying, "Okay, you're the boss." He's putting himself in a position where he can't fight back. When you're on your knees, you don't fight, normally – although we can do it if we try hard enough! So normally speaking, when a person is on his knees, he is before God saying, "You are everything and I am nothing, and I am at your disposal." If a person kneels before a powerful man, on his knees, he means to say the powerful man can tie him up and drag him away and so forth. "There I am. I'm helpless." But there's a deeper expression of adoration. What's the deepest external expression of adoration? full prostration. What does that add to the concept of kneeling? What more is there? Your head's on the floor! He can step on it without even having to lift his foot up! He could kick you in the head while you're kneeling if he wants to, but it's going to take effort, whereas if your head is on the floor, he can just use you as a doormat! But the person simply spreads himself out completely and says, "I am nothing. You are everything."

This is all very nice, this bodily expression of this, but what's important is the spiritual expression of it, the spiritual experience of it, and the Cistercians pick up this expression: "Lord, who is like unto Thee," which is a biblical expression, and it's the expression of the totality of being in God and the nothingness of ourselves as creatures; and that is reality. That is the experience of reality as it really is. Simply to experience oneself as more real, if it doesn't imply this, it's not an experience of reality. It's an experience of unreality. If it implies this, then it is an experience of reality, so therefore that the highest reality is to experience that God alone is fully real and that everything else is nothing. They bring this in very well. Then Guerric goes on and develops this idea.[XXV] This is really profound stuff, but it's just an ordinary little Advent sermon that he preached to these monks. It wasn't even a high-class monastery, just a little secondary monastery called Igny. (It's now a monastery of nuns.) This is beautifully done and it's got all the traditional doctrine packed into that.

What's the big question that arises out of this? If he's preaching this to the monks, what question arises? Well, people say, "What about it? Is this for everybody or isn't it?" What would you say? Supposing your little nephew comes and visits you: "Father, can I attain to mystical prayer?" What do you say to your little nephew? Do you refer him back to Sister? What are you going to say to your little nephew if he comes and asks you that? What would you say to a novice if he asks you that? In this particular sense: "yes – if…" "Should I desire this?" "Yes – if …" What's the "if"? The big "if" is, if you understand what it's about and if you understand that it means this total annihilation of yourself before God. If on the other hand – see the great dangerous thing that comes in here, that the Cistercians keep making very clear, is if it is a question of curiosity, then it can't possibly work, because it's a contradiction in terms. You know what the meaning of curiosity is for the Cistercians of the twelfth century.[XXVI] It's a special thing. It means to say that I am here. Here I am with all my I-ness, and I am going to have this experience, and I'm going to add to all my other achievements this experience: I am a mystic. Well this is baloney! This doesn't work, so that if a person is going to be there in his selfhood, and is going to maintain all his selfhood in its particularity and so forth, and he's going to acquire the experience of mystical prayer on top of all this selfhood, then he is going to bust his head. They bring in always this idea that what happens to somebody who goes into it in this selfish way and as an achievement for himself and so forth, is that he is oppressed by glory. He runs into more than he can handle. He runs into what squashes it. But if it is on the other hand a question of total humility, if the person has reached the center of his nothingness and is completely abandoning himself totally to God and not acquiring anything for himself, and not wanting anything for himself, and desiring only the glory of God and not seeking this or that experience, and not emphasizing a self that can have this or that experience, then he's on the right track. But then it doesn't matter whether he gets anything or doesn't get anything. This is for God to decide, and you leave this to God. So the great thing therefore, the central thing, is this idea of humility. This is the key, and this is the answer, and if we fully understand the real nature of humility and descend completely into the real depths of humility, then there are no further questions and problems.

3.

Well let's move along with Guerric. You guys don't seem to like Guerric! I notice that a large number of people have ceased to come very fast! What's the matter with Guerric? What about him? What's the trouble with Guerric? You guys that are still here – you're still holding on – what's your comment on him? There's not much around to read. How does he strike you? Does he sound very different from St. Bernard or anything like him? He's pretty much the same as St. Bernard. I suppose the same criticism would apply to him as to St. Bernard. Of course the thing about him actually is there's some very good mystical doctrine in there, if you can sort of squeeze it out. It's not too difficult.

Anyway, in this Third Advent Sermon, he takes a text from Amos, and that fits in pretty well with what I was saying yesterday.[XXVII] This is a good chapter – Amos – chapter four of Amos, fits in very well with this whole business of Advent from yesterday's point of view. It's a long chapter, one of these chapters in which you've got a repeated message over and over again, with a kind of a refrain that goes with it: the Lord says, "I did this and did this and did this, and yet you did not return to Me, says the Lord," and it goes on like this. Let me read you a little bit of it. He just took part of this as his text. It goes like this: "'I smote you with blight and mildew; I laid waste your gardens and your vineyards; Your fig trees and your olive trees the locusts devoured; yet you did not return to me,' says the Lord. 'I sent among you a pestilence after the manner of Egypt; I slew your young men with the sword; I carried away your horses; and I made the stench of your camp go up into your nostrils; yet you did not return to Me,' says the Lord. 'I overthrew some of you, as when God overthrew Sodom and Gomorrah, and you were as a brand plucked out of the burning; yet you did not return to Me,' says the Lord. 'Therefore thus will I do to you O Israel; because I will do this to you, prepare to meet your God, O Israel!'"[XXVIII] It's a good strong thing. That's what he takes as his text: "Prepare to meet your God, O Israel" as one of his Advent sermons. The chapter ends: "For lo, he who forms the mountains and creates the wind, and declares to man what is his thought, who makes the morning darkness, and treads on the heights of the earth – the Lord, the God of hosts is his name."[XXIX] What's the idea of that ending? The idea of the ending is that all these things are leading up to the fact that God is God and nobody's going to change it. His action in the world is all tied up with the fact that He is God and He is going to manifest Himself. If people don't pay attention, He's going to manifest Himself anyway!

So now this Third Sermon – there's not much to it. The Third Sermon is just an ordinary simple sermon: "Prepare to meet your God." Well, he says, prepare to meet your God. It deals especially with the particular judgment, so I'm not going to go into great detail about that. You've heard sermons on the particular judgment. We'll have a retreat and there will be a sermon on the particular judgment. The only thing that's interesting is, how does he approach it? He says familiar things. All you've got here are the very familiar truths that anybody would use if he had to preach an ordinary sermon on the particular judgment. What are the ordinary familiar truths that anybody would preach? Supposing the brothers had to start preaching, and you're informed that within ten minutes you'd got to get up and address the brethren on the particular judgment. What would you tell them: "get ready!"

Of course the great thing is that it's not certain. The judgment is certain, but heaven and hell is uncertain. It's in the balance. Nobody knows! There isn't a single one of us here that knows whether we're going to heaven or going to hell. We believe, we hope, but we don't know. It's not certain. Knowledge means certainty, so we don't have the certainty. So anybody who's going to preach on the particular judgment, if the particular judgment is a foregone conclusion, preach it to somebody else. This isn't to do with me. He brings out this fact – this is certain: that it's going to come. It's not certain when it's going to come and it's not certain what the outcome is. Therefore the obvious thing for us is not to be secure. The only security, he says, is never to be secure.

This is a standard sort of approach in a sermon, but still it's true. What's the point of this? The idea is to wake people up. Advent is the season where you're supposed to wake up, supposed to get on the ball and so forth. We need this, because we're up and we're down and so forth. But this is not something that we necessarily have to emphasize all the time. We heard this before. We hear it frequently.

This is the way he approaches it. It's interesting to see, and then of course, what does he do? He talks about death. He talks about some of the saints who have died a good death, who died a holy death. He mentions a few examples and so forth. What do you want to know after that, though? It's going to come and you're going to die. He just doesn't leave you there. What else would you add? What are you going to do? Well what *are* you going to do? What would you tell people to do if you're preaching the sermon? Actually you can tell them anything good: pray – that's one of his points. You set the thing up: you've got people in a position where they're going to be judged, and then you have to sort of leave them. They've got to go out with something positive. Don't just say, you're going to be judged, and then shut up shop and walk away and leave them – although that wouldn't do any harm either; let them figure it out for themselves! Prayer, obviously – the thing that's interesting about this sermon is: how does he handle the subject of prayer? He just doesn't say, "Now pray, brethren." No, he takes a Gospel text on prayer. Which one would you take on prayer? He backs all this up with stuff from the scriptures. Somebody give me a Gospel text on prayer now – a story would be better. You're dealing with all these people. What would be a good parable on prayer?

There are one or two parables in the Gospel I don't think we think of enough. One's a parable, another one's an actual event in Our Lord's life, that really push very far the idea that prayer should do "violence" to God, that prayer should make Him change His mind: the judge and the widow – she just bothers him.[XXX] There was something she wanted and he didn't want to give her and she just bothered him until he gave it to her; or the one where the fellow comes in the middle of the night[XXXI] – you get this on rogation days.[XXXII] He comes in the middle of the night and he starts banging on the door of his friend. It's a beautiful picture of this guy shouting from the inside, "Leave me alone!

I'm in bed, and all the kids are in bed too." They're all in one bed. He can't get out without waking up the whole family. He's got to climb over them all to get out on the floor! "Go away! We're all asleep! Don't bother us!" and so forth. But the fellow keeps on knocking, and so finally the man gets up and gets him a loaf of bread and says: "Scram! Get out of here! Leave us alone!"

Well, there's that, and then there's the story of the Syrophoenician woman,[XXXIII] which is the one that Guerric uses. This isn't a parable; this is an event. What's the story of the Syrophoenician woman? She's a pagan. She's a Phoenician pagan woman. Jesus is going through this area that's outside of the Jewish area. It's in the territory of Tyre and Sidon, and this pagan woman comes up and asks Him to cure her daughter, and He says, "No! Leave me alone. I'm only preaching to the children of Israel, and it's not right to take the bread of the children and give it to the dogs." The disciples say, "Go on, scram! You heard the master. Beat it," and she says, "No!" Dom Robert[XXXIV] in the novitiate really used to push this one! He was great on this one: "Even the little puppies under the table," he said, "get the crumbs." Then Our Lord says, "O woman, great is thy faith. Be it done." But it's true. That's the way it's supposed to be. Our Lord wants us to bother Him if there's something important in life – not just for trivialities, or get a new shirt or something like that (you just write a note – you get it). But for things that are important, and especially for our salvation, He wants us to really batter on the door! So alright, Guerric brings that in, and then he brings in other ideas, the idea of charity – that if we're living in charity, we're doing good to others and so forth. This is a preparation. Prayer is a preparation – it's insistent prayer. Psalmody is a preparation: he talks about psalmody, how psalmody purifies the heart. He says that an essential part of Advent is this *psallite sapienter*[XXXV] – this idea of singing wisely, that is, with knowledge, with understanding. To sing the psalms with knowledge and understanding prepares a way for the Lord, and when He comes, then He comes and illuminates.[XXXVI] We experience this. We know this. If you're in your office, or you're just saying your psalms privately or something like that, to pay attention to the psalms brings light. It opens the way to the coming of the Lord, and this is all clear.

Then he's got another chapter, from Isaias. He brings in this toward the end of his sermon. He doesn't use the whole chapter,[XXXVII] but again this is a very good Advent chapter. It backs up what I was saying yesterday, so I'll read little bits of it. This is Isaias 64, and it's one of the big chapters. Some of this comes into if not our Advent liturgy – well it does, too – but it comes into something we sing very frequently at benediction too. It starts out: "O that Thou wouldst rend the heavens and come down, that the mountains might quake at Thy presence – as when fire kindles brushwood and the fire causes water to boil – to make Thy name known to Thy adversaries, and that the nations might tremble at Thy presence."[XXXVIII] There are two aspects of judgment: God comes in judgment simply to judge. We think of ourselves being judged, but He also comes in judgment to judge the persecutors, and so therefore in the connection of yesterday is the idea of God coming to reestablish what is right. The right and the truth have been systematically flouted and so forth. He's going to come and He's going to reestablish it. He's going to make things right. He's left people the job of taking care of the truth and of justice, and they haven't done it, so He will come Himself and do it. Then it goes on like this: "Behold, Thou wast angry, and we sinned; in our sins we have been a long time, and shall we be saved? We have all become like one who is unclean, and our righteous deeds are like a polluted garment. We all fade like a leaf, and our iniquities, like the wind, take us away. There is no one that calls upon Thy name, that bestirs himself to take hold of Thee; for Thou hast hid Thy face from us, and hast delivered us into the hands of our iniquities."[XXXIX] This is, again, this idea that I was trying to bring out yesterday – that where there is a presence of evil it is a sign that God has, in a certain sense, turned away His face. If people are left to their sins, it's because God wills that they should be left to their sins. He turns away His face. They're left to their sins so they should realize where they are – without Him. This is a deep truth there. The idea of Advent comes out very clearly in this, and so when you're reading your Isaias, you have to see this.

Of course the trouble is with this biblical language. This translation is alright in many ways – this is the Revised Standard – but it's not powerful enough. It seems to me that the old translations are much more powerful, some chapters of Isaias. Actually one of the best is the Douay version, and King James is good. It's real strong stuff – really pile it on, with a few funny words here and there and so forth. This is just half and half. The New English one is absolutely the worst. It is the most colorless and anywhere that had any kind of life in it, they've just squeezed all the life out of it, and you get just sort of a colorless statement. In all the other translations they've left some life, but the English translation's got it all gone. It's finished! Pretty soon we're going to get it like this: the angel comes to Mary and says: "Hello, Mary. You are a good girl." That's the way it sounds, most of the stuff. I'm going to produce an English version to end all versions: "Hello, Mary. You are a good girl. The Lord is here someplace" – no: "the Boss"! Pardon me – this gets bad! I'm sorry – shouldn't be like that.

Let's get back to the next Advent sermon of Guerric, and this is a good one. This is fine. This is a very deep one. This other one was just simple ascetic approach: the Last Judgment is coming; prepare and meet it. But this is deeper. This is a really monastic sermon, profoundly monastic, and also deeply contemplative. This is a much better sermon. Of course it's one that I like very much – it's about solitary life. It's about the desert. The text for this one is the voice crying in the desert – "I'm a voice crying in the desert."[XL] So he starts out with this idea of the desert. The first section of the sermon is all packed with traditional stuff about the desert.[XLI] The monastic life basically, essentially, is a desert life. This is one of the themes of the monastic life. Even though we're in community, and so forth, it's a desert life. It's a life of solitude – solitude in community or solitude out of community, but either way it's a life of solitude. If the monastic life ceases to be a life of solitude, it's no longer a monastic life. There has to be some form of solitude, and obviously there are various ways in which the monastic life is a life of solitude.

We've got two big ways in which our life is a life of solitude – what are they? How do we guarantee solitude in our life: silence in community; enclosure. It's an obligation in our Order to be as far away from cities and towns as one can reasonably get and still remain somewhat useful. It's basic that you never build a monastery in a town or in a village. The first law of the Order, the first thing in the whole legislation of our Order,[XLII] is that all monasteries are built in remote locations, and if the town catches up with you, you've got to do anything you can to move, and that's what they always do – maybe some faster than others. You've got one monastery – actually it's on the edge of a town and runs the local power station! It's Port du Salut. They're right on the edge of town and one of the things they do is they've got the river and they've got a dam, so they just generate power for the town. The monks are running the power station – and making cheese!

He starts out this sermon with the idea of the grace of the desert and the blessedness of the wilderness. This is kind of the preface to his sermon. This is an Advent sermon. Advent is a desert season too, going out into the desert. "First of all, I believe that we should consider the grace of the desert, the blessedness of the wilderness, which deserve to be consecrated from the first moment of grace [that is, the first moment of God's giving of the New Testament] to the *quies sanctorum* – to the rest of the saints."[XLIII] This word *quies*, or rest – all these are consecrated themes. Dom Leclercq has just written a great big book all about this,[XLIV] how these themes are used in the Fathers of the Church and especially in the early monks. The desert is a grace. Solitude is a grace. Solitude is a gift and there's a blessedness in it. The thing about the desert, the thing about solitude and so forth, is that to the average person it does not appeal, except for once in a while, occasionally. But the idea here is that there is a special grace hidden in solitude and a special blessedness hidden in solitude. The blessedness is this blessedness of a silence and an interior peace which enables one to hear the voice of the Lord and not only enables one to hear the voice of God but to hear it better than anywhere else. This is the purpose of solitude. The purpose of solitude is to get away from noise and the racket and distraction of the world so as to hear God more perfectly and respond to Him more perfectly, so he brings this out and he says it very well. He makes this clear.

He's considering the desert almost as what? not just a geographical place or not just even an empty place. When he talks about grace of the desert and it's consecrated and all this sort of thing, he's considering it almost as what? on the analogy of a certain kind of gift, with the sacraments. He considers the desert almost as a sacrament. What's a sacrament? A gift of God containing a hidden grace, something in the material order which God has endowed with the capacity to communicate grace, and to communicate the grace which it symbolizes. That's a very strong statement. It's something that monks should respond to, that monks should be interested in – this idea that the desert is endowed by God with a kind of a sacramental grace, analogously – as a sacramental type of grace, something that has hidden in it a special happiness, a special grace, a special consecration.

Then he ties up the idea of the desert with John the Baptist and his baptism.[XLV] He baptizes in the Jordan – and incidentally there's all these fathers tend to take the same line. There's a Syrian one that I've been reading that has this same kind of idea, that Our Lord was baptized in the Jordan and the first place He went after that was the desert.[XLVI] St. Paul was converted in Damascus, and the first place he goes is the Arabian desert. There's a connection between baptism and the desert, because what does he say here? When Christ went into the desert, when Jesus went to the desert, before he went to preach to sinners, to preach to penitents, He prepared a place for penitents by going into the desert. Our Lord was in the desert and the fact that Our Lord went out into the desert has consecrated the desert. He makes this clear and He prepared a place for penitents. The desert is the place for penitents. People want to do penance, they go out into the desert, the most appropriate place for penance for all sorts of reasons. Then he talks about how the prophets went into the desert. He says, always to the prophets the desert was a friendly place because it was an *auditorium spiritus*, a place where you go to hear the Spirit.[XLVII]

Of course that term as a place for hearing the Holy Spirit you find very frequently in Cistercian Fathers, applying to the Cistercian monastery.[XLVIII] The Cistercian monastery is an *auditorium spiritus*. It is a place where you listen to the Holy Spirit and therefore it follows from that that the obligation is to keep the monastery as a place where the Holy Spirit can be heard, which means to say primarily a place of peace. Of course this goes with austerity. In the monastic life peace and asceticism go together. Without austerity you don't have peace, because if there's no austerity there's no peace, because the passions are running around wildly, and everybody who feels like throwing things throws them, and anybody wants to make a noise makes a noise, and things are a general racket. But with a certain amount of austerity and discipline, then the monastery is a place of peace and we hear the Holy Spirit. After having laid down this general principle – the monastic life is the life of the desert – he's preaching to Cistercians, so obviously his next step is all cut out for him. What's it going to be? He's going to say: how does this apply to Cistercians? He's saying, it's the life of the desert, but we're not in the desert; we're not absolutely alone in the desert. We're in a community. We've got fields and so forth. Here we have a sort of early witness of the fact that the Cistercian life *does* have this desert quality, but it is a desert quality that is combined with community, the combination of solitude and community. So he uses the phrase "in our deserts …"[XLIX] This is a standard term for a monastery. You call a monastery a desert. It's a traditional expression for a monastery.

Now there are certain monastic communities that are called deserts. What are they? Who's ever heard of a place called a desert – a special type of monastic community? There are places that are technically called deserts: the Carmelites have had this; the Franciscans have had this. Maybe someday the Cistercians will have it. It's a good idea. It's the idea of a special community for the Carmelite friars. They have them in Spain. They still have them: they've got one in Spain; they've got one in France; they've got one in Belgium. It is a special community with special rules, and there are five or six people living there all the time, and then others, a sort of a floating community that comes and goes for a year or so. If priests have been on the missions and so forth are sent for a year to the desert. Let's say at the beginning of 1964, you've got your desert community of the one superior, who lives there all the time, two or three fellows who live there all the time – a couple of friars and a couple of brothers – and then six people who have been appointed there for this year, a year on retreat. There's no active work whatever. There's no contact with the outside. It's a small community. Most of the time it's in total silence, and each one is in his room or something like that. They have these simple offices and so forth. Attached to this are hermitages, where if a person wants even more then he can go out to the hermitage for six months or something like that. Now this is a standard procedure and they're getting back to this in the Carmelites.

It's something we could very easily have here; and it's on paper – this is where all these rumors are coming from. But this is on paper for us. I don't know whether it would ever work out like this, but it's something to pray for. We could have something like this, where people could go just for a week. (Some of course would be there permanently!) People could go for a week, or just for the day – on the property. You'd have to have it in such a way that they would keep some pretty strict rules, and if they didn't keep the rules they wouldn't come back. Of course there would be separation anyway. They wouldn't be mixing up. They wouldn't be talking. The person who went there for a week would have to just shut up and keep to himself. Put him in a room and let him be quiet, and anybody who went to a thing like this and didn't keep the rules and started messing around with the other people – he just wouldn't come back, that's all. It'd be his last trip. But anybody who wanted to go to a place like that could make good use of it. This is something that I think could be done. Of course the objection is – if it becomes a desert community, a little desert community, it's going to meet objections from the higher-ups because it's a special kind of Cistercian community: "What's this? You're breaking up the unity of the Order in this new kind of institution." So the thing to do is just keep the thing totally simple so that there's the least possible amount of institutionalism, because a big Cistercian monastery cannot perfectly keep this sort of silence, and a small Cistercian monastery has all kinds of particular headaches of its own. So here's a third solution – hanging onto a big Cistercian monastery, you have a little outfit that does not have to make its own living and does not have to have a whole lot of business and does not have to train novices and that sort of thing and is just a place where people can go, supported by the big community. This is something that could very easily work very well if it's done properly. That's something to think about.

I. *Sermones de Adventu Domini* 1 (J. P. Migne, ed., *Patrologiae Cursus Completus, Series Latina* [*PL*], 221 vols. [Paris: Garnier, 1844-1865] vol. 185, cols. 11A-14C); 2 (cols 14C-17D); 3 (cols. 18A-21D); 4 (cols. 21D-25D); 5 (cols. 26A-30A).

II. *The Christmas Sermons of Bl. Guerric of Igny*, trans. Sr. Rose of Lima, Introduction by Thomas Merton (Trappist, KY: Abbey of Gethsemani, 1959); see above, pages 164-85.

III. Joel 2:32; Acts 2:21; Romans 10:13; the epistle for the Feast of St. Andrew (November 30) is Romans 10:10-18.

IV. Luke 19:10.

V. "*Aqua frigida animae sitienti, et nuntius bonus de terra longinqua*" (Prov. 25:25) (col. 14C).

VI. Revised Standard Version.

VII. 2.1 (*PL* 185, col. 15A) (Lk. 1:39-45).

VIII. Jan van Ruusbroec, *The Spiritual Espousals*, trans. Eric Colledge (London: Faber and Faber, 1952).

IX. Matthew 25:6; the entire three-part text, on the active, interior and contemplative lives, is built around this text.

X. 2.2 (col. 15BD).

XI. Merton did read and briefly discuss John Donne's sonnet "At the round earth's imagined corners" in his conference on poetry on Saturday, December 5, though he did not refer back to the present conference in doing so.

XII. A series of seven invocations used in the Advent liturgy from December 17 through December 23, each highlighting a specific aspect of the coming Christ (see *Breviarium Cisterciense, Pars Hiemalis* [Westmalle, Belgium: Typis Cisterciensibus, 1935] 228). In his novitiate conferences on the Liturgical Year (now being prepared for publication), Merton calls them "seven great and solemn invocations, the cry of the Church bringing down the Savior from heaven. The Church, the Bride, lifts her voice in the darkness of the world, and her voice, filled with the power of the Holy Spirit and with the longing of all mankind, resounds sweetly and irresistibly in heaven. All the supernatural longing of the inspired prophets and patriarchs is concentrated here. In these great cries of love, adoration and supplication, we are intimately united with Abraham and Isaias, and the saints of the Old Law. We are intimately united with the prayers and longings of Our Lady. We are united with the whole Church, all the blessed and all the saved on earth and in the bosom of Christ, who cry out for the second coming. And we are at the same time united with the inarticulate longings of all the peoples who, though they do not know the name of Jesus our Redeemer, yet seek God in ways that are hard to identify and recognize. Finally, and above all, we are giving voice to the cry of the oppressed, the poor, the downtrodden, the persecuted, all those whom Christ seeks out with preference. All this is in our hearts when we sing the O antiphons. They contain the very essence of Advent prayer. They resume the longing of the Old Testament for the Messias by repeating the sevenfold call with seven different names of the Holy One."

XIII. "*Nolite timere, quinta enim die veniet ad vos Dominus noster*" (*Breviarium Cisterciense, Pars Hiemalis* 228).

XIV. "*Ecce completa sunt omnia quae dicta sunt per Angelum de Virgine Maria*" (*Breviarium Cisterciense*, *Pars Hiemalis* 228).

XV. "*Hodie scietis quia veniet Dominus; Et mane videbitis gloriam ejus*" ("Today you will know that the Lord will come; And tomorrow you will see His glory"). (*Breviarium Cisterciense*, *Pars Hiemalis* 229).

XVI. Luke 15:8-10.

XVII. "Behold, the Lord will come, and all His saints with Him; and there will be a great light on that day" (*Breviarium Cisterciense*, *Pars Hiemalis* 185).

XVIII. "*Ecce apparebit Dominus, et non mentietur; si moram fecerit, expecta eum, quia veniet et non tardabit. Alleluia*" (*Breviarium Cisterciense*, *Pars Hiemalis* 197).

XIX. On this motif see Thomas Merton, "The Sacrament of Advent in the Spirituality of St Bernard" (*Seasons of Celebration* 75-79).

XX. Gaspar Lefebvre, OSB and monks of St. André Abbey, *Saint Andrew Daily Missal*, 4 vols. (Saint Paul, MN: E. M. Lohmann Co., 1947); rev. ed. (Bruges: Biblica, 1960).

XXI. "*Nec veniens quippe videtur, nec recedens intelligitur, qui solummodo, dum praesens est, lumen est animae et intellectus, quo invisibilis videtur, et incogitabilis intelligitur*" (2.4 [col. 17A]).

XXII. 2. 4 (col. 17B, which reads: "*suavi et felici stupore*").

XXIII. "*suspendat et expendat animam contemplantis*" (2.4 [col. 17B]) ("He suspends and examines the soul of the contemplative").

XXIV. "*omnia ossa interioris hominis acclament ei, Domine, quis similis tui*" (2.4 [col. 17B]) (Ps. 34[35]:10: "All my bones shall say: Lord, who is like to thee?").

XXV. 2.4 (col. 17BD).

XXVI. Curiosity is presented as the first degree of pride in St. Bernard's *De Gradibus Humilitatis* (*PL* 183, col. 957B-963A). In *Spirit of Simplicity*, Merton writes: "*Curiositas* is that vain and illusory knowledge which is really ignorance, because it is the exercise of the intellect not in search of truth but merely to flatter our own self-satisfaction and pride" (105); see also Étienne Gilson, *The Mystical Theology of Saint Bernard*, trans. A. H. C. Downes (New York: Sheed & Ward, 1940) Appendix I: "*Curiositas*" (155-57).

XXVII. On the previous day, December 13, Merton had discussed the racial problems in Mississippi (Gethsemani recording 135.3).

XXVIII. Amos 4:9-12 [Revised Standard Version].

XXIX. Amos 4:13 [RSV].

XXX. Luke 18:1-8.

XXXI. Luke 11:5-8.

XXXII. In his conferences on "Liturgical Feasts and Seasons" (currently being prepared for publication), Merton explains the origin of these traditional days of prayer and fasting (April 25 – major; three days preceding the Feast of the Ascension – minor): "The rogation days, instituted by St. Mamertus, Bishop of Vienne, in time of earthquakes, are a kind of supplement to the ember days (processions are made barefoot, with ashes on heads). The rogation processions are a sacramental by which the Church strives to sanctify our daily life."

XXXIII. Mark 7:24-30; Matthew 15:22-28 (2.4 [col. 20D]).

XXXIV. Robert McGann, OCSO (1886-1957), Merton's novice master, who became abbot of the Monastery of the Holy Spirit in Conyers, GA in 1948 and remained in that position until his death.

XXXV. "sing wisely" (Ps. 46[47]:8).

XXXVI. "*Si enim psallas sapienter, in via immaculata veniet; veniet qui et illuminabit abscondita tua, ut quae nescis intelligas mysteria Scripturarum, eritque ut dicas: Psallam et intelligam in via immaculata, quando veniet ad me*" (col. 21D) ("For if you sing wisely on the unspotted way He will come; He will come Who will illuminate your darkness, so that you may understand the mysteries of the Scriptures of which you are ignorant; and it will be as you say: 'I shall sing and I shall understand on the unspotted way when He comes to me'") (Ps. 100[101]:2) .

XXXVII. "*Occurristi, inquit Isaias, laetanti et facienti iustitiam: in viis tuis recordabuntur* tui" (col. 21D) (Is. 64:5) ("Thou hast met him that rejoiceth, and doth justice: in thy ways they shall remember thee").

XXXVIII. Isaiah 64:1-2 [RSV].

XXXIX. Isaiah 64:5-7 [RSV].

XL. Isaiah 40:3; Mark 1:3.

XLI. *PL* 185, col. 22AC.

XLII. *Instituta Capituli Generalis* [1134], c. 1: "*Quo in Loco Sint Construenda Coenobia*" ("In What Place Monasteries Are to Be Built"): "*In civitatibus, castellis, villis, nulla nostra construenda sunt coenobia, sed in locis a conversatione hominum semotis*" (J.-M. Canivez, ed., *Statuta Capitulorum Generalium Ordinis Cisterciensis ab Anno 1116 ad Annum 1786*, 8 vols. [Louvain: Bureaux de la Revue d'Histoire Ecclésiastique, 1933-1941] 1:13) ("Our monasteries are not to be built in cities, towns or villages, but in places removed from human activity").

XLIII. "*Primo omnium considerandam arbitror gratiam deserti, beatitudinem eremi; quae ab initio gratiae, quieti sanctorum meruit consecrari*" (col. 22A).

XLIV. Jean Leclercq, OSB, *Otia Monastica: Études sur le Vocabulaire de la Contemplation au Moyen Âge* (Rome: Herder, 1963).

XLV. Col. 22A.

XLVI. Merton is referring to Homily 9 of Philoxenos of Mabbug, whom he was reading in preparation for his pre-Benedictine monasticism conferences on this Syrian hermit and bishop, whom he will discuss in classes between March 21 and August 15, 1965, his final conference in this series before retiring as novice master, in which this homily is the main focus. See *Pre-Benedictine Monasticism* 298-309 for an extended analysis of Homily 9, which Merton also discusses in his essay "Rain and the Rhinoceros" (*Raids on the Unspeakable* 9-23).

XLVII. Col. 22A.

XLVIIII. See St. Bernard, *In Nativitate S. Joannis Baptistae* 1 (*PL* 183, col. 397D, which reads: "*auditorio spirituali*"); Adam of Perseigne, *Epistola* 11 (*PL* 211, col. 616C).

XLIX. "*in his desertis nostris quietem habeamus solitudinis*" (4.2 [col. 22C]) ("In these deserts of ours may we have the quiet of solitude").

St. Aelred of Rievaulx
(1210–1267)

St. Ailred of Rievaulx

Merton first encountered Aelred of Rievaulx and his work during his novitiate years, as he notes "with nostalgia" in an August 31, 1947 journal entry, recalling "the old days when I got so much consolation out of the Cistercian Fathers … the bright fall days four years ago when I opened Migne and found St. Ailred" (*Entering the Silence* 104). Included in an extensive list of proposed works that Merton submitted to the Cistercian General Chapter in 1946 is a biography of Aelred. (Chrysogonus Waddell, OCSO provides a translation and extensive discussion of this document in his article "Merton and the Tiger Lily," *The Merton Annual* 2 [1989] 59-84.) The project is subsequently described in a September 9, 1949 letter to Merton's editor Robert Giroux as a combined "biography, study of his doctrine and selected texts from his writings" (*Giroux-Merton Letters* 49). It is mentioned repeatedly in Merton's correspondence with Giroux through the rest of 1949, and the following year it was one of four books Merton contracted to write; in a January 11, 1950 letter Giroux tells Merton: "I hope we may expect the St. Aelred manuscript soon.… It ought to be in proof before Easter" (*Giroux-Merton Letters* 58). Merton replies five days later that he would prefer to wait for the impending publication of Aelred's newly discovered treatise *De Anima* (*On the Soul*), as "it will naturally affect many of my statements about other parts of his work" (*Giroux-Merton Letters* 61) and is reassured by Giroux on February 13 that "there is no rush about it" (*Giroux-Merton Letters* 62). There is no further mention of the book for more than four years, but in a June 5, 1954 letter Merton tells Giroux, "I also want to finish that St. Aelred job" (*Giroux-Merton Letters* 180). The book, however, never appeared. But between 1985 and 1989 the surviving material was edited by Merton's former secretary Patrick Hart, OCSO and published in *Cistercian Studies* in five segments as "St Aelred of Rievaulx and the Cistercians" (20.3 [1985] 212-23; 21.1 [1986] 30-42; 22.1 [1987] 55-75; 23.1 [1988] 45-62; 24.1 [1989] 50-68). It is evident that the text as extant is incomplete, either never finished or with significant material subsequently lost. Merton writes, "We shall consider Ailred's *Rule* for his sister on a later page," which does not happen, and earlier had referred in a footnote to meditations from the same text as being "among the excerpts printed below," likewise missing. The final pages of the published essay veer off into a discussion of the antagonism between Archbishop Thomas Becket and Gilbert Foliot, the Bishop of London, to whom Aelred had dedicated a set of sermons, without returning to Aelred himself. There is no discussion of his final days and death. Still the material that is available and is reedited here from the original typescript is the most extensive single text on any of the Cistercian Fathers apart from St. Bernard. It is clearly intended for a broad, non-monastic audience, explaining basic terms and customs and written in a popular, even devotional tone characteristic of Merton's style in the late 1940s (though with occasional anomalous inclusions of untranslated Latin excerpts from Aelred's works). The first four of the eight (misnumbered nine) numbered sections provide an overview of the founding of the Order, the major Cistercian authors of the twelfth century, the "Cistercian school" of spirituality, and the early period of the Cistercian foundations in England – again a clear indication that the work is primarily intended for an audience largely unfamiliar not only with Aelred himself but with his Cistercian background. Turning to his principal subject, Merton provides a thorough discussion of most of the major events of Aelred's life and a detailed description of his singularly attractive character, highlighting his skills as a spiritual director, his genius for friendship both within and beyond the monastic walls, his unusual yet successful approach as an administrator, his role in the wider English Church of his time, and of course his talents as an author, touching on some but by no means all of his works. Along the way he provides numerous anecdotes illustrating Aelred's relationships with his monks, drawn largely from his biographer Walter Daniel, who is himself given significant attention as his abbot's disciple and friend. Like Walter's, Merton's portrait of Aelred is above all that of a saint, one that he proposes as still serving as a fitting model for contemporary readers.

1. *The Cistercians.*[I]

When St. Robert of Molesme[II] left his Benedictine Abbey with twenty companions, in March, 1098, to settle in the marshy solitude called Cîteaux, he hardly could have dreamed of what a tree would spring from the small seed planted in that wilderness. The old abbot – a man whom we like to picture as being gnarled as the roots of trees, according to St. Theresa's description of St. Peter of Alcantara,[III] seems to have had no idea whatever that he was founding a new Order. Cîteaux was apparently nothing but one of the hundred new communities that had sprung up in forests and out-of-the-way places all over France and Italy in the eleventh century, which had been an age of monastic reforms. Dissatisfied with the conventional pattern of monasticism, which had become so closely integrated into feudal society that the monk could not always be sure that he had really renounced the world and all that it stood for, there had been restless movements of men into the wilderness, seeking sainthood in solitude and penance and poverty. The life of St. Robert of Molesme himself had been little more than a long succession of attempts to escape the world and to work out a solution for the problems presented by the big rich monasteries whose endowments brought with them such embarrassing social obligations, so many cares, so much business, so many distractions. All these attempts had failed. Paradoxically, the reason why they failed was that Robert himself was so much of a success. When the hermits of Colan succeeded, by appealing to the Holy See, in obtaining him from the Benedictine monks of St. Michel de Tonnerre, as their own Superior, the reputation of the new community attracted so many postulants and so many benefactions that the hermitage of Colan soon turned into the Abbey of Molesme – and Molesme, although a fervent and respectable community[1] was once more

1. Some historians, in order to explain the Cistercian reform, have treated Molesme as if the house had gone into a complete and sudden decadence, within twenty years of its foundation. Molesme was not decadent. It was a perfectly regular Benedictine monastery, on the pattern of Cluny: but its wealth and the conventional mentality of most of its monks made a *literal* interpretation of the *Rule* of St. Benedict unfeasible. In order to make a real return to sources, a complete break with the existing monastic order was necessary.

nothing but a small replica of Cluny, and that was precisely what St. Robert was trying to escape.

At first sight, there was not much to distinguish Cîteaux from Colan, or from the scores of ascetic communities that could be found in the central mountains of France or in the rolling woodlands north of the Loire and on the confines of Brittany and Normandy.[2]

However, there was a difference. Among the Cistercians were two monks who were not only ascetics and saints but also men of far-seeing religious wisdom and genius for organization. St. Alberic,[IV] the second abbot of Cîteaux, and St. Stephen Harding,[V] the third, had acquired such clear insight into the essence of the *Rule* of St. Benedict, and were able to formulate their notions in such clear and simple and practical terms, that Cîteaux became not only the center of a spiritual revival, but the seat of one of the most significant monastic reforms in the history of the Church. More, it became the cornerstone of the first monastic Order, in the western Church, with a centralized organization that really deserved the name of an *Order*. Cluny had been a huge monastic kingdom in which hundreds of abbeys and priories depended immediately on the huge Abbey in Burgundy, whose Basilica was bigger than St. Peter's in Rome. They were simple tributaries of the one Abbey. The General Chapters, meeting each year at Cîteaux, according to the prescriptions of St. Stephen's *Carta Caritatis*[VI] were to unite hundreds of autonomous monasteries in a democratic union which enabled them to work out their problems by discussion and the framing of true laws. The Holy See, granting the Cistercians every possible exemption from outside control, set the new Order free to function as a vital legal and spiritual unit.

At once, Cîteaux began to make foundations all over Europe. The extraordinarily rapid diffusion of the new Order was due above all to the influence of its greatest Saint, Bernard of Clairvaux, whose arrival at Citeaux with thirty companions in 1110 assured the success of the new foundation. St. Bernard was never

2. For instance, St. Vital's foundation at Savigny (Normandy), St. Stephen's at Grandmont (Limousin), another St. Stephen's at Obazine (Aquitaine), St. Robert of Arbrissel in Normandy.

the head of the Cistercian Order, still less its founder. And yet he played such a tremendously important part in the growth of the Order and the formation of its spirit that writers unfamiliar with Cistercian history have sometimes spoken of Cîteaux as the "Order of St Bernard."

The tremendous influence which St. Bernard exercised in twelfth-century Europe was certainly providential. This ardent contemplative, who was so often drawn out of the cloister and into the affairs of the world against all the desires of his monastic heart, impressed something of his own character upon the whole age in which he lived, and not only upon his religious Order. The twelfth century was the "age of St. Bernard" and it was largely Cistercian in its character, just as the thirteenth century breathed the spirit of the Mendicant Orders.

What was this Cistercian spirit? What was the character which the monasteries of Cîteaux communicated to the world of their time?

This Cistercian spirit is something which does not altogether belong to the past. Since the Cistercian Abbeys of our own day still do what they can to preserve the purity and simplicity of monastic life as it was conceived by the reformers at Cîteaux, those who are interested in the Cistercian spirit can form at least a vague notion of it by visiting a Trappist monastery, breathing the silence of the cloister, walking in the fields tilled by the hands of the monks, or listening to their chant in the monastic choir.

The Cistercian spirit is a beautiful combination of ardor, simplicity and strength. At the roots of the Cistercian reform was a hatred of artificiality and an intense impatience with the illogical compromises into which monks are led when they yield to the obscure enticements of the world, the flesh and the devil, and live like worldlings under a religious disguise. St. Stephen Harding and his monks were consumed with a passionate desire for truth. They wanted to find out the real essence of St. Benedict, and live the *Rule* as it was meant to be lived. Since the monk's chief obligation is liturgical praise, the Cistercians ruthlessly eliminated from the choir and from the sanctuary everything that seemed to them to be secondary or non-essential in order that their worship of God might be utterly untrammeled and pure. Obsessed with the need for truth in everything, St. Stephen Harding made his own Latin revision of the Scriptures, consulting Rabbinical scholars in order to solve difficulties in the text. He wanted to make sure that his monks were singing what had actually been revealed by God. Haunted by the same desire for the authentic, St. Stephen sent some of his monks on foot to Metz, others across the Alps to Milan, to copy what he thought would be the original texts of the Gregorian antiphonal and the Ambrosian Hymnal.

The real explanation for the austerity of the first Cistercians is to be found not so much in a mere desire to punish the flesh as in this same ardent passion for the truth. They wanted to be poor and live by the labor of their hands because that was the way a genuine monk was supposed to live. *Tunc vere monachi sunt si labore manuum suarum vivunt, sicut et patres nostri et Apostoli.*[3] What is more, as St. Bernard himself pointed out with characteristically Cistercian logic, since Christ, the Incarnate Word, came to this earth to express the Truth in all things by His life and passion and death and Resurrection, and so to bring us to the perfect possession of the Truth in heaven, the surest way to this possession is to live as Christ lived on earth. But Christ's life was poor and obscure, a life of suffering and labor and hardship, embraced, of course, not out of sheer economic necessity, but freely, for the love of God. The Cistercian, then, would possess Christ's Truth by truly living as He, the embodiment of Truth, had lived on this earth.[4] And that was St. Bernard's version of the ideal so concisely formulated by St. Stephen Harding in his *Exordium Parvum*[5] when he summed up the Cistercian ascesis in the phrase *pauperes* [*vivere*] *cum paupere Christo*.[VIII]

The first work that came to light from the genius of St. Bernard was a tract that contained all that was most typical in the teaching of the great Cistercian mystic: the little book on the

---

3. *Rule* of St. Benedict c. 48.[VII]

4. *Sermo* 3 *in Nativitate Domini* 2 (J. P. Migne, ed., *Patrologiae Cursus Completus*, *Series Latina* [*PL*], 221 vols. [Paris: Garnier, 1844-1865] vol. 183, cols. 123C-124B) and *De Gradibus Humilitatis* 1.1 (*PL* 182, cols. 941C-942B).

5. The Official account of the foundation of Cîteaux and the legislation of the first Cistercians (see *Nomasticon Cisterciense, seu Antiquiores Ordinis Cisterciensis Constitutiones A.R.P.D. Juliano Paris* … Editio Nova, ed. Hugo Séjalon [Solesmes: E Typographeo Sancti Petri, 1892] 53-65; and *PL* 166, cols. 1501B-1510B).

Degrees of Humility and Pride. The theme of this work is an outline of the whole spiritual life, which is described as an ascent to perfect union with God's truth by three degrees of truth, beginning with that humility which is the basis of all spirituality and which he defines as "a virtue which gives a man *so perfectly true a knowledge of himself* that he becomes cheap in his own sight." *Humilitas est virtus qua homo verissima sui agnitione, ipse sibi vilescit.*[6] From the very beginning, St. Bernard wants his monk to strip himself of all illusion about himself, and this is the most radical beginning of all, for as long as we deceive ourselves about ourselves, it will do us little good to penetrate the illusions of others. So, too, the virtue of discretion, which literally means the power to sift out true from false and good from bad in the motions and impulsions of the interior life, takes on a place of primary importance in the Cistercian ascesis. Indeed, St. Bernard even calls it the "mother of virtues and the consummation of perfection"[7] and, once again, it is because it teaches us to do precisely what is God's will for us without being deceived by any inordinate and subtle appetite of our own, under the guise of good, or by any devil masking as an angel of light.

Finally, it is sufficient to remember that the proximate reason which the founders of Cîteaux were forced to admit that they could no longer in conscience remain at Molesme was the fact that the *Rule* of St. Benedict, as it was read each day in Chapter, seemed to have so little relation to the life to which they were actually vowed as Benedictine monks.[8] The fundamental reason for the foundation of Cîteaux was that the founders wanted to be true to their vocation. Devotion to the truth, devotion without compromise and without reserve, was the very heart of the Cistercian reform.

---

6. *De Gradibus Humilitatis* 1.2 (*PL* 182, col. 942B).

7. *Sermo* 3 *in Circumcisione* 11: "*mater virtutum et consummatio perfectionis*" (*PL* 183, col. 142A). The reason why discretion is the consummation of perfection is that it arms those who are nearly perfect, against the subtle temptations which afflict the saints.

8. "*Saepius inter se Dei gratia aspirati, de transgressione Regulae beati Benedicti patris monachorum loquebantur, conquerebantur, contristabantur, videntes se caeterosque monachos hanc Regulam solemni professione servaturos promisisse, eamque minime custodisse*" (*Exordium Parvum* 3 [*Nomasticon* 55]).[IX]

It is from this that all the other characteristics of the Cistercian spirit were to flow. This devotion to truth accounted for the extreme simplicity of the Cistercians which, in its ultimate and most perfect expression, rejoins the mystical simplicity of that union with God which was so tirelessly preached by St. Bernard. "*Qui adhaeret Domino, unus spiritus est.*"[9] Cistercian simplicity is most perfectly expressed and fulfilled in a pure love for God which excludes every other love or which, rather, absorbs every other affection into itself[10] and thereby reduces everything in the soul of the monk to unity and peace in the tranquility of contemplation in which the infinitely simple Truth of God steeps our hearts in silence and joy and mystical repose: *tranquillus Deus tranquillat omnia.*[11] This is the deep meaning which the earliest Cistercians could find in the phrase in which St. Benedict summed up the monastic vocation: *si vere Deum quaerit*: "if the monk truly seeks God."[12]

The monastic life could not, then, be anything else but supremely simple, both in its exterior, and in the interior of the monk's own soul. The infinite simplicity of God's own Truth demanded this simplification in the soul of the contemplative who desired to possess him. *Simplex natura*, says St. Bernard,[13] *simplicitatem cordis exquirit.*[XII]

This intense desire for Truth explains the Cistercian emphasis on obedience, not only because obedience is the very heart of the *Rule* of St. Benedict, but because by obedience we give up that

9. 1 Corinthians 6:17: "He who is joined to the Lord is one spirit [with Him]."
10. "*Amor sibi abundat, amor ubi venerit caeteros in se omnes traducit et captivat affectus*" (*In Cantica* 83.3 [*PL* 183, col. 1182D).[X]
11. "The tranquil God tranquillizes everything in us" (*In Cantica* 23.16 [*PL* 183, col. 893B]).
12. *Rule* of St. Benedict, c. 58 (McCann 130/131).
13. *De Diversis* 33.9 (*PL* 183, col. 643C). In the context we find St. Bernard again explaining that the ascent to union with God means an uncompromising devotion to His Truth and His will: "*Veritas est Deus, et tales quaesitores requirit qui quaerant eum in spiritu et veritate*" (col. 643D).[XI] He has previously explained that those who thus truly seek God already, in some measure, possess Him, because they could not seek Him unless He had already given Himself to them by grace (nn. 4-5 [cols. 641A-642A]).

source of blindness and error which is our own judgment.[14] We have already remarked that it was the root of Cistercian teaching on religious poverty.

The practical result of this doctrine, leavening the souls of contemplatives under the powerful and secret action of the Holy Spirit, was to release spiritual energies that performed most wonderful and irresistible works in the Church of God. There was hardly a function of monastic living that was not developed, by the Cistercians, to the height of fruitful activity. Cistercian architecture was the purest and most chaste and most powerful of all Gothic. Indeed the genius and versatility of the Master Builders who were Cistercian laybrothers, in their attempt to solve the problem of simplicity and poverty in monastic architecture, led to a revolution in medieval construction. In the same way, the energy of the Cistercians and their engineering skill opened up tracts of marsh, mountain and forest and turned the waste wilderness into rich pastures and smiling fields of grain – and, incidentally, modified the whole economic system of the feudal age. Everything the Cistercians touched turned, spiritually, not to gold but to energy. The vitality that surged in the souls of these men who had been liberated for the highest spiritual action by the way of Cistercian ascesis, poured itself out over the whole world of their time and would not brook resistance. Cîteaux changed the course of medieval history and affected the whole social life of the twelfth century in all its departments: architecture, politics, agriculture, engineering, economics, monastic and clerical reform, dogmatic theology and Church discipline, mysticism above all.

It was, therefore, to be expected that one of the important fruits of the Cistercian reform would be yet another expression of this marvelous vitality in a new movement in literature.

2. *The Cistercian Writers of the Twelfth Century.*

The austerity of the first Cistercians banned painting and sculpture from their monastic Churches, and there was even a cer-

---

14. See St. Bernard, *Sermo* 3 *in Tempore Resurrectionis* 3 (*PL* 183, cols. 289D-290C), and *The Spirit of Simplicity* (Gethsemani, 1948) 114 ff.

tain amount of legislation to limit the production of books,[15] but this legislation could hardly have a very serious effect when the greatest Cistercian saint was himself a prolific writer and speaker and perhaps the greatest literary and theological genius of his time. Étienne Gilson has shrewdly remarked that although the Cistercians were very austere in their architecture, they were far from being restrained in their literary style.[XIII] The beauty of Cistercian churches and cloisters was arrived at indirectly and, we may say, by accident, because what the architects had primarily in mind was a purely functional simplicity that harmonized with their poverty, both as an ideal and as a cold, economic fact. But the rich and elegant vitality of Cistercian prose – most of which is sheer poetry – betrays an overflow of literary productivity which did not even need to strive for its effects: it achieved them, as it were, spontaneously. It seemed to be second nature to St. Bernard, William of St. Thierry,[XIV] Adam of Perseigne, Guerric of Igny, to write with consummate beauty prose full of sound and color and charm.

There were two natural explanations for this. The first is that the prolific Cistercian writers of the Golden Age were men who had already been thoroughly steeped in the secular literary movements of the time before they entered the cloister. All of them had rich experience of the current of humanism that flowed through the twelfth-century renaissance. Not that many of them were what we would call professional writers or poets. The converted poets who had really been *troubadours* in the world came later. Bl. Helinand of Froidmont,[XV] and Bl. Foulques of Marseille[XVI] both belong to the thirteenth century, and they had been poets of some reputation in courtly circles of northern and southern France. But the writers of the twelfth century had been brought up as clerics, and had been exposed to classical humanism rather as a philosophic than as literary movement. Indeed, what brought them to the cloister was in many cases an explicit reaction against the secular current that was flowing through the

---

15. *Instituta Capituli Generalis* [1134], c. 20: "*De Sculpturis et Picturis, et Cruce Lignea*" ("Concerning Sculptures and Pictures, and the Wooden Cross") (*Nomasticon* 217); c. 58: "*Si Liceat Alicui Novos Libros Dictare*" ("Whether It Is Permitted to Anyone to Dictate New Books") (*Nomasticon* 225).

cathedral schools of the twelfth century, where the clerks were all too familiar with Ovid and Terence and Juvenal and Persius, not to mention Livy and Cicero.[16]

In any case all the Cistercian writers of the Golden Age were formed outside the cloister. We know of no Cistercian theologian of any importance, in the twelfth century, who was entirely educated in his monastery. The rather intense intellectual life that is presupposed by the contemplation that flourished at Clairvaux, Rievaulx, Igny, Signy, l'Étoile, Perseigne and so on, was not entirely nourished in the monasteries themselves. This intellectuality is something that the monks had brought in with them. And that is a fact that needs to be remembered. After all, the Cistercians of the twelfth century sometimes seem to take a definitely anti-intellectual stand. Some of St. Bernard's remarks about learned men are easily misinterpreted, and need to be properly understood.[17]

The monks knew well that the highest knowledge of God is the knowledge that is directly communicated to the soul in mystical experience and that such knowledge cannot possibly be arrived at by human efforts. Indeed, as St. John of the Cross says, "Any soul that makes account of all its knowledge and ability in order to come to union with God is supremely ignorant in the eyes of God, and far removed from that wisdom."[18] We come to this perfect knowledge of God rather by "unknowing" than by knowing, and study is of little immediate use. But that does not alter the fact that a deep intellectual appreciation of dogma, and the understanding of theology that is arrived at by the intellect that is submissive to the guidance of faith and grace, is of immense importance in the remote formation of contemplatives, so much so that in monasteries where theological study is neglected,

---

16. Even the monks of Cluny got Livy and Cicero for their Lenten Books (see André Wilmart, OSB, "Le Convent et la Bibliothèque de Cluny vers le Milieu du XIe Siècle," *Revue Mabillon* 11 [1921] 113-15).[XVII]

17. V.g. St. Bernard, *Sermo* 3 *in Festo Pentecostes* 4 (*PL* 183, cols. 331D-332A); see also *Sermones* 35-36 *in Cantica* (*PL* 183, cols. 962A-971A) and *Spirit of Simplicity* 92 ff.

18. *Ascent of Mount Carmel* 1.4.4 (*The Complete Works of Saint John of the Cross*, ed. and trans. E. Allison Peers, 3 vols. [Westminster, MD: Newman Press, 1949] 1.26).

contemplation is also generally at a rather low ebb. It is a fatal mistake to suppose that a contemplative monk can discard books altogether and let his mind lie fallow all his life, with no other nourishment than a few pious legends and one or two elementary slogans about the holy will of God. In the ordinary course of things, a solid contemplative life requires a real basis of theological study. In a later age, when certain Trappist monasteries went to an extreme in their contempt for learning, sometimes the monks rapidly degenerated into pious but sadly materialistic farmers or brewers or chocolate manufacturers, who often had very little real interior life. The problem is one that needs to be pondered.

The real answer to the supposed anti-intellectualism of writers like St. Bernard who were among the greatest intellectuals of their time is to be sought in the fact that they were contrasting the "science" of the theologian with the "wisdom" of the mystic, and like a great Catholic philosopher of our own day[19] they were acutely, I might say painfully aware of the inadequacy of "science" to fully satisfy a soul that has begun to taste the perfect knowledge of God that can only be had by experience, that is, infused contemplation, mystical wisdom.

There is a second explanation for the rich exuberance of theological prose in the twelfth-century monasteries of Cîteaux. If contact with classical humanism had stimulated a certain intellectual vitality in these clerics, it also generated a conflict in their souls. The refined natural excitements produced by philosophical speculation, by art, poetry, music, by the companionship of restless, sensitive and intellectual friends merely unsettled their souls. Far from finding peace and satisfaction in all these things, they found war. The only answer to the problem was to make a clean break with everything that stimulated this spiritual uneasiness, to withdraw from the centers in which it was fomented, and get away somewhere, discover some point of vantage from which they could see the whole difficulty in its proper perspective. This vantage point, of course, was not only the cloister, since Ovid and Tully had already become firmly established there, but the

---

19. Jacques Maritain, *The Degrees of Knowledge* (London: Centenary Press, 1937); see Preface, the "Grandeur and Misery of Metaphysics."

desert – the *terra invia et inaquosa*[XVIII] in which the Cistercian labored and suffered and prayed.

The energy of Cistercian thought and writing often clearly betrays, by its dialectic between the two schools of love, the source of its vitality. William of St. Thierry, for instance, begins his treatise on the *Nature and Dignity of* (*Divine*) *Love* in formal defiance of the humanists who have chosen Ovid for their master and who are studying the ways of another love, the end whereof is destruction.[20] St. Bernard of Clairvaux never ceases to remind his monks that they have left the schools of the world where the subtleties of Plato and Aristotle are in honor, and are living in the School of the Holy Spirit, Who teaches them not by words but by grace how to become the true children of God.[21]

The tension generated by the conflict between secular humanism and the Christian humanism, which seeks the fulfillment of human nature through ascetic renunciation and mystical union with God, was one of the proximate causes of the powerful mystical writing of the Cistercians.

However, once these two natural factors have been considered, we must recognize other and far more decisive influences belonging to a higher order. When these clerics and intellectuals gave themselves entirely to the service of God in that *schola divini servitii*[XX] which is the *Rule* of St. Benedict, lived in all its austere purity, they discovered that they soon began to run "with indescribable delight in the way of God's commandments."[22] The tension and effort which marked their first steps in the monastic way, dominated by what is technically known as "fear," soon

---

20. *De Natura et Dignitate Amoris* 1.2 (*PL* 184, cols. 381A-382A). William of St. Thierry states his main theme: love is natural to man and God Himself is the only true teacher of the highest love. He it is Who guides and shapes man by grace, drawing him on to the perfect union of wills with Himself, which is the supreme fulfillment of love. Disordered and sinful love, *cupiditas*, centered in selfishness, is a perversion of the love for which man was created.

21. "*Gaudeo vos esse de hac schola, de schola videlicet Spiritus, ubi bonitatem et disciplinam et scientiam discatis*" (*Sermo* 3 *in Festo Pentecostes* 5 [*PL* 183, col. 332A]).[XIX]

22. "*Processu vero conversationis et fidei, dilatato corde, inenarrabili dilectionis dulcedine curritur via mandatorum Dei*" (*Rule* of St. Benedict, Prologue).[XXI]

gave way to a breathless expansion of interior liberty in which everything that had before seemed hard became easy and delightful because all that they did was now elevated and transfigured by an unction which surpassed their understanding and which was infused into their souls by the Holy Spirit as a free gift of His mercy even more than as a reward for their efforts. This was what St. Benedict had promised his faithful disciples. If they were generous in God's service, "fear" would give place to that charity "which casteth out fear,"[23] and which fills the soul with supreme delight. The Cistercian writers of the twelfth century, dazzled with the joy of their discovery, could only interpret St. Benedict's words to mean one thing: the path of Benedictine asceticism led not merely to a reward in heaven. It envisaged a consummation that began even on earth. It was designed to prepare the monk for the joys of mystical contemplation and that "marriage" of the soul with God which theologians call transforming union.

It is the relish and savor that only experience can give, that communicates to the writings of the twelfth-century Cistercians all the vitality and vividness and impassioned sincerity which are peculiarly their own. Their freshness and originality certainly do not spring from a new subject matter or from any consciously new direction in the treatment of traditional themes, for the Cistercians wrote about the same mysteries of the same faith that had preoccupied the Fathers and saints of the Church for centuries. They searched the Scriptures for light on the great doctrines of the Incarnation and Redemption which lie at the very heart of revelation and which are the key to all the vital problems of human and moral existence. They commented on the sacred text, and indeed they had made Scripture so much their own that half of what they wrote was quoted from the Bible and applied to their own context. The Cistercians, like all other monks of the early days, had absorbed Scripture to the point where they actually did their thinking in the very terms of the Prophets and

23. "*Monachus mox ad caritatem Dei perveniet illam, quae perfecta foris mittit timorem (cf I. Joan.): per quam universa quae prius non sine formidine observabat, absque ullo labore velut naturaliter ex consuetudine incipiat custodire, non jam timore gehennae, sed amore Christi et consuetudine ipsa bona et delectatio virtutum: quae Dominus jam in suo operario mundo a vitiis et peccatis, Spiritu Sancto dignabitur demonstrare*" (*Rule* of St. Benedict c. 7).[XXII]

Evangelists. What distinguishes the writing of the twelfth-century Cistercians from the earlier Benedictines is that the White Monks speak with accents of a more personal and more lyrical conviction that everywhere betrays the influence of an intimate and mystical experience. Not that the Black Monks were not mystics too: St. Gregory the Great and St. Anselm were among the greatest contemplatives. But on the whole a St. Bernard or a William of St. Thierry (who left the Benedictines and became a White Monk precisely in order to find liberty and contemplation) reveal to us more explicitly the secrets of their own inner life than St. Gregory or St. Bede.

It is the personal, experiential character of Cistercian mysticism that gives the prose of the White Monks its vivid freshness. Cîteaux did not produce speculative Scripture scholars – and certainly the allegories which the Cistercians were able to discover in the Old Testament would be well calculated to try the patience of a modern and scientific exegete. But whether or not you would be prepared to agree with everything St. Bernard has to say about the symbolism of the *Canticle*, it is clear that his exposition is never dusty and technical and that, for all his liberties, he generally manages to communicate far more of the spirit and life of the Scriptures than the scientific commentators for whom the Old Testament is little more than a Jewish history.

No, for the Cistercians Scripture was definitely something more than a mine of subtle exegetical problems. The revealed word of God had an almost sacramental character for St. Bernard and his disciples. Hidden under the outward appearances of the "letter" was the deep, vivifying grace which was the "spirit" or the life implanted in the text by God Himself. St. Bernard says, of the figures of Scripture, that they "insinuate" into the believing soul the very reality of God Who is hidden in their "mystery." It is almost as if he applied to Scripture the axiom by which theologians explain the effects of the Sacraments: "they effect what they signify."[24]

24. St. Bernard's words are these: "[*Scriptura*] *nostris verbis sapientiam in mysterio absconditam loquitur;* nostris affectibus Deum, dum figurat, insinuat*; notis rerum sensibilium similitudinis tamquam vilioris materiae poculis ea quae pretiosa sunt, ignota et invisibilia Dei mentibus propinat humanis*" (*Sermo in Cantica* 74.2 [*PL* 183, col. 1139C]).[XXIII] It is needless

Since the theology of the Cistercians was so intimately personal and experiential, their exposition of it was bound to take a psychological direction. All that they wrote was directed by their keen awareness of the presence and action of God in their souls. This was their all-absorbing interest. Consequently, there were three subjects which occupied almost all their attention. Starting from the lowest rung, the point nearest home, there was the nature of the soul itself. Hidden in the soul was the image of God, for God had made man in "his own image and likeness."[XXIV] This image implied a capacity for union with God. The soul could, in a manner of speaking, contain the infinite God in so far as it was a mirror capable of reflecting His triune life and participating fully in that life. But how was such a participation possible? By charity. *Deus caritas est.*[XXV] The soul that is possessed entirely by the pure love of God becomes, by analogy, what God Himself is. Hence the Cistercians wrote *ex professo* both on the nature of the soul and the nature and action and degrees of charity. These were two of their favorite and most characteristic subjects. The third was bound to be the God Himself Who had created the soul in His image, and had created it for union with Himself by charity, and Who, infusing charity into the soul, also gave Himself entirely to the soul as an uncreated Gift. Every line of investigation taken up by the White Monks led them without delay to the God they sought so ardently – the God of Love, the God Who had revealed Himself to mortal men in Jesus Christ, the God Who deigned to make Himself known in the depths of their souls by the "visits" of mystical grace.

Everything else that the Cistercians wrote about – whether the virtue of humility or the nature of faith or the union of Christ and His Church – all can be reduced to these three interests which, for that matter, can be summed up in one great theme: the union of the soul with God.

One remark must be added, before we go on to introduce some of these writers, so little known in our own time. It is this. The Cistercians are often said to have practically "discovered" the humanity of Jesus Christ. Not that Christ as Man had been

---

to point out the obvious allusion to Holy Communion in the language of St. Bernard here.

unknown to a St. Ambrose or a St. Augustine! But there was a new warmth, a new depth of understanding and sympathy and personal affection for Christ in the writings of St. Bernard and St. Ailred and Bl. Guerric of Igny which proved beyond doubt that these men were truly the friends of Jesus and truly knew Jesus. He had certainly revealed His soul, His Sacred Heart to them in a way that He had not done to anyone since the Apostles who had walked with Him along the shores of Galilee. It was because they were poets and psychologists that they were able to make Jesus and His Virgin Mother so real and so living to everyone else – for here too their psychological bent of mind manifested itself. They would enter into the souls of Christ and His Immaculate Mother and study the thoughts and the desires of these most spotless mirrors of the Godhead. But it was above all because they were mystics that they were able to find such material for their psychology. For it was in the fire of contemplation, and in the intimate union of Love that they had learned the secrets of the Heart of God.

3. *The Cistercian School in France.*

St. Bernard of Clairvaux (d. 1153) needs no introduction here. He is a Doctor of the Universal Church, and has been the object of ceaseless study since the twelfth century. His reputation as a mystical theologian was so astonishing, in the Middle Ages, that legend attributed to him the singular privilege of having seen God "face to face" even in this life, a grace which tradition seems to accord to only two others: Moses and St. Paul.[25] Dante, in the highest reaches of his Paradise,[26] could find no more competent guide than the Cistercian mystic. St. Bernard's commentary on the Canticle of Canticles, above all, exercised a lasting and formative influence over all subsequent Christian mysticism, at least until the seventeenth century. Ruysbroeck and Tauler, the Flemish and German schools of the thirteenth and fourteenth centuries, all stem from Bernard of Clairvaux. Spanish mysticism, for instance in Fray Francisco[XXVI] de Osuna, owes much to him. St. John of the Cross appeals to him[27] as a classical source

25. St. Thomas Aquinas, *Summa Theologica*, II-II, q. 175, a. 3.
26. Dante, *Divine Comedy* Cantica 3: *Paradiso*, cantos 31-33.
27. *Dark Night* 2.19-20 (Peers, *Complete Works of Saint John of the Cross*

without, however, having read him. In non-mystical spiritualities St. Bernard's influence was just as great, if not greater. St. Ignatius of Loyola evidently owes much to him. All the modern devotion to the Sacred Heart can be traced back to him. A whole trend of affective spirituality, expressed by rather complex and florid devotions, enthusiastically claimed St. Bernard as its progenitor in the spiritual decadence of the fourteenth and fifteenth centuries, with the result that the stream of Bernardine tradition became somewhat corrupted by an inflow of devotional treatises of inferior quality which crept in among the genuine works of the saint and hid themselves under his name.

Obviously, St. Bernard's influence in his own Order and in his own time, was tremendous. In the case of the Benedictine Abbot *William of St. Thierry* this matter of influence was not altogether a one-sided affair. William was already a profound and original theologian and a contemplative in his own right when he first visited Bernard at Clairvaux in 1118. It was about this time that William's own literary production was beginning with the *De Natura et Dignitate Amoris*[XXVII] and the *De Contemplando Deo*,[XXVIII] characteristic works on the nature of the soul and of love. William's admiration of St. Bernard was, needless to say, unbounded. He saw that the Abbot of Clairvaux was a saint, a mystic whom suffering and sacrifice had elevated to the very pinnacle of the spiritual life. But nevertheless the two were able to meet on equal terms, with that exchange of ideas and of inspirations, the giving and receiving of spiritual goods which makes for the friendships of saints as well as of intellectuals. In receiving light and stimulation from the mind and heart of Bernard, William was able, in his turn, to stir up the fire of mystical speculation in the mind of the Abbot of Clairvaux to an even more intense ardor, while at the same time he could contribute new ideas and, by virtue of his more technical training, aid St. Bernard in the construction of a solid dogmatic edifice to support his mysticism. William was the instigator of more than one tract that has come to us from the pen of the Abbot of Clairvaux. The most important of these were controversial, the *Apology* for Cistercian monachism,[XXIX] against the Cluniacs, and the *Dispute against PeterAbelard*[XXX] which led to the latter's condemnation at Sens.

1.463-70).

Meanwhile, William himself became a Cistercian at Signy, a small foundation in the Ardennes, where he produced his own most mature theological and mystical writings, the *Meditativae Orationes*,[XXXI] a profoundly interesting *Commentary on the Canticle of Canticles*,[28] treatises on the nature and the psychology of faith[29] and the more famous *Golden Epistle* to the Carthusians of Mont Dieu.[XXXII]

William of St. Thierry is one of the most profound psychologists and the loftiest contemplatives of the Cistercian school. Indeed, his commentary on the *Canticle* is a much more systematic and thorough treatment of the mystical life than is St. Bernard's more rambling discussion of the Sacred Text. There are more detailed and searching analyses of mystical union in William of St. Thierry than will be found anywhere in St. Bernard, and this makes it all the more strange that he has been practically forgotten. He is without doubt a great and original theologian, and Étienne Gilson has been one of the first in our time to estimate him at his true worth.[30]

Bl. Guerric of Igny, the third of the "four Evangelists of Cîteaux," was a Canon of Tournai who heard St. Bernard preach in Belgium in 1131 and followed him to Clairvaux. Thence he was sent to the abbey of Igny in the province of Champagne, where he became Abbot. His only important works are his *Sermons*, preached to the monks in Chapter, and which he himself did his best to destroy at the time of his death in 1157.[31]

Guerric of Igny stands out among the Cistercians of his time not only as a psychologist and mystic, but above all as a dogmatic theologian. His *Sermons* are a luminous commentary on

28. *Expositio Altera in Cantica* (*PL* 180, cols. 473C-546D). The reason why this is called "another" exposition is that William had made two previous commentaries which were, however, only anthologies of comments taken from St. Gregory and St. Ambrose.
29. *Speculum Fidei* (*PL* 180, cols. 365B-397A). An excellent modern edition of the Latin text and French translation has been made by Dom J.-M. Dechanet, OSB (*Le Miroir de la Foi* [Bruges: Beyaert, 1946]); *Aenigma Fidei* (*PL* 180, cols. 397B-440D).
30. Étienne Gilson, *The Mystical Theology of St. Bernard*, trans. A. H. C. Downes (New York: Sheed and Ward, 1940) 198-214.
31. See *Exordium Magnum Cistercii, Distinctio* 3.8 (*PL* 185, cols. 1059B-1060A).

the traditional Pauline doctrine of the life of grace, and in many ways he reminds us of another Benedictine theologian of our own times: Dom Columba Marmion.[XXXIII] His reflections on the mysteries of the liturgical year are simple and fresh, full of a naïve charm that does not prevent them from striking into the very depths of the spirit and of Christian dogma. They draw their life and energy from the writer's most intimate affection for Jesus and His Virgin Mother, and there is probably no one in the history of Christian spirituality who has written in such detail and with such insight of the formation of Christ in the soul by grace, and of Mary's part in that work. This was Guerric's specialty.[32]

The Virgin Mother of God was very close to the first Cistercians. The Order was the first to have been dedicated entirely to her and from its very beginnings she seems to have presided over its spirit and its formation with an especially tender interest which bore fruit in a rich love and understanding of her in the theology of the Order, not to mention its mysticism and its legends. The courtly instinct which dominated the secular literature of the twelfth century also found a necessary outlet in the Mariology of the White Monks who were themselves knights, many of them, and would not be denied a certain element of chivalric and courtly idealism even in the cloister. The Blessed Virgin became their "Lady" in the technical sense of courtly poetry, the one to whom their whole life and all their strength was dedicated without recall. They loved to call themselves, and to become in actual fact her slaves. In doing so, they entered into the secret of her amazing prerogatives as no one had done before them. Led by St. Bernard, the whole Cistercian Order became aware of the glories of this great Queen who, at the first moment of her existence, had already outstripped the merits and virtues and prerogatives of all the other saints and angels put together, and who, "full of grace" when the angel came to her with his message, continued nevertheless to grow in grace beyond all understanding and belief by virtue of her constant and even physical contact with Him Who is

32. Cf. M. Deodat de Wilde, OCSO, *De Beato Guerrico, Abbate Igniacensi eiusque Doctrina de Formatione Christi in Nobis* (Westmalle: Typis Abbatiae, 1935), and "La Formation du Christ en Nous d'après le B. Guerric d'Igny," *Collectanea Ordinis Cisterciensium Reformatorum* 1 (1934) 193-98, 2 (1935) 9-18.

the source of all holiness and truth. Through Him and with Him she became the Co-redeemer of the human race so that He gave into her hands the power to dispense all grace to men, not only as a mechanical consequence of her consent to the Incarnation but by the free and elicited and conscious action of her own will, drowned in the abyss of His divine mercy for men.

The writings of the twelfth-century Cistercians are never more beautiful than when Our Blessed Lady is their subject. The first fruits of Bernard's genius were dedicated to the Blessed Mother in those homilies on the Gospel *Missus est angelus Gabriel*[XXXIV] whose style and color and harmonies he perhaps never again equalled. It is the subject of the Virgin Mother that brings out the best in Guerric of Igny. Other Cistercians are remembered only as Mariologists. Their claim to the attention of later centuries is based entirely – yet most worthily – on half a dozen sermons about the Blessed Mother. *St. Amedeus of Lausanne*[XXXV] and *Adam of Perseigne* are two of these, although Adam has also left some very interesting letters on spiritual direction.[33]

Among the commentators of the *Canticle of Canticles* which was favorite Cistercian territory, besides St. Bernard and William of St. Thierry, there was *Thomas of Cîteaux*[XXXVI] whose lengthy exegesis does not come near the others in merit. *Alan of Lille*,[XXXVII] who is supposed to have died as a laybrother at Cîteaux, is scarcely a Cistercian in anything he wrote except his own short investigation into the passages of the *Cantica* which can be taken to refer to the Virgin Mother. Alan's career as a theologian had run its course before he entered the cloister. He was something of a popularizer, more versatile than original, a compiler of commonplaces which he listed in systematic form in order to provide a sort of handbook for preachers. He wrote some long didactic poems, influenced by the classical and humanist trend of the time, but they do not make good reading today.

Isaac de l'Étoile, however, is another Cistercian of considerable interest. English by birth, he became abbot of an obscure monastery on an island off the Atlantic coast of France, Our Lady of the Star (*Notre Dame de l'Étoile*).[XXXVIII] About the time of St. Bernard's death in 1153, Isaac was planning or composing his

33. *PL* 211, cols. 538B-694C.

treatise *De Anima*,[XXXIX] a typical Cistercian psychology. He also wrote on the Sacrifice of the Mass,[XL] and his numerous sermons are rather more philosophical and technical than the general run of Cistercian preaching. Another psychological treatise, the *De Spiritu et Anima*,[34] is attributed to the novice master of Clairvaux, a certain *Alcher*, who also lived and wrote in the lifetime of St. Bernard. *Henry de Marcy*, Abbot of Clairvaux, and later Cardinal archbishop of Albano, has left a rather interesting treatise on the Mystical Body of Christ, *De Peregrinante Civitate Dei*.[XLI] Other minor Cistercian writers, represented by a few letters or sermons, include *Garnier* of Rochefort,[XLII] *Pierre le Borgne*, *Philippe of l'Aumone*, *Hugh of Troisfontaines* and *Jean l'Hermite*. These were all monks or abbots of monasteries that stemmed from Clairvaux and therefore, coming more directly under the influence of St. Bernard, have been separated off into a little school of their own for which Dom Anselme le Bail coined the name of *les claravalliens*.[XLIII] They have yet to be investigated thoroughly, but a casual glance at their sermons proves them to be not without erudition and perhaps overfond of complicated allegories. Some of them, like *Pierre le Borgne*[XLIV] or Cardinal *Henry de Marcy*, have left a reputation for sanctity, and the life of the former by the Benedictine, Thomas of Reuil[35] bears this out.

Outside the immediate influence of Clairvaux was *Otho of Morimond*[XLV] whose interests tended to history and politics rather than to the spiritual life, at least as far as his writing is concerned, although he was a severe ascetic. Then, passing beyond the borders of France, we come upon the sermons of *Ogier*,[XLVI] the Abbot of Locedio in northern Italy, and those of *Elias of Coxyde* in Flanders. The limits of this study do not take us beyond the twelfth century. If they did, we would find rich material in the writings of *St. Gertrude*[XLVII] and *St. Mechtilde*,[XLVIII] who can be called Cistercian mystics although they lived the Cistercian *Rule* in a convent which the General Chapter refused, along with scores of others, to accept into the Order when the number of Cistercian nunneries became too great to be conveniently controlled.

---

34. *PL* 40, cols. 779-832, included in works attributed to St. Augustine; the attribution to Alcher is made in *PL* 194, col. 1895.
35. *Acta Sanctorum* (October 13.53).

It is, however, in England that the Cistercians achieved their greatest spiritual as well as temporal prosperity outside France and it is there that they also produced their richest crop of spiritual writers. The greatest of the English Cistercians, whether as abbot, or theologian or saint, was Ailred of Rievaulx who is the subject of our volume. Let us turn to him and to the Cistercian school in England.

4. *The Cistercians in England.*

It was not yet seventy-five years since William the Conqueror had landed with his Norman army on the Sussex coast and defeated the Saxon King Harold on the downs of Hastings. England was slow in settling down under the new Norman rule, and the fact that half the country was still the depopulated wilderness of ruined towns and monasteries that had been left by the Danish invasions, did not make it easier for peace to settle upon the troubled island.

The monks had civilized England after the barbarians had wiped out the culture of colonial Rome, and monks were going to play a very important part in bringing back peace and prosperity to the land that had been ravaged by the Danes. The great old English monasteries of Benedictines would come back to life. New foundations would be made in England from Cluny. Monastic Cathedral Chapters would appear in great centers like Canterbury and Durham. And then, most important of all, the new Orders would come from the continent.

It was in the north of England that the situation was most crucial. The wild moors of Yorkshire, the woods of Northumberland, the Border hill country and the mountains on the western shore were thinly populated by groups that were spiritually abandoned and forlorn and living on the edge of barbarism. The country that had seen the great Anglo-Saxon Abbeys, the land of St. Bede and St. Cuthbert was left almost without sacraments. The priests were very few. The churches and monasteries lay, for the greater part, in ruins. There were only five abbeys north of the Welland and a few smaller monasteries and all of these were only now coming to life with the help of monks from the south. Monks from Evesham had settled again in the ruins of Jarrow. There were once again abbeys at Tynemouth and Wearmouth. Whitby had even made a foundation of its own, at York, in 1089. It was just a few years since the foundation of Molesme in Burgundy: and St. Mary's, York, was to prove a kind of English Molesme when the Prior, Richard, and his dissatisfied companions left the Abbey for the wilderness of Skelldale as Robert and his companions had left for Cîteaux, for precisely the same reasons but with considerably more violence and trouble surrounding their departure.[36]

The Cluniacs had founded the Priory of St. John at Pontefract in 1090, and between 1120 and 1130 the Austin Canons had made more than one foundation, one of them under the auspices of a Yorkshire knight, Walter Espec, of whom we shall hear more. In 1124 the austere Savignian monks (whose whole congregation went over in a body to the Order of Cîteaux in 1147) sent a colony to Furness in the West Riding of Yorkshire. These foundations were both the evidence of a great spiritual revival in the North and the cause of its intensification. When the first Cistercians appeared in the lonely valleys of those moors, Yorkshire was well prepared to understand and welcome their austere and contemplative Rule. Within twenty years of the foundation of Rievaulx, in March 1132, after the spectacular secession of the monks of St. Mary's to Fountains, where they were accepted into the Cistercian Order, after the foundation of six new abbeys and the accession of the Savignian foundations to the Order, Yorkshire was to become a stronghold of Cistercian monasticism. The bare moors, divided by wooded valleys, were indeed savage enough to be typical Cistercian country. It was the kind of territory few would live in by choice except White Monks or Carthusians.

Yet the very first colony of Cistercians that came to England did not settle in Yorkshire. In an out-of-the-way corner of the North Downs near Farnham, south of London, you may still see the ruins of Waverley where monks from L'Aumone, in Normandy, established the first English monastery of White Monks in 1128. In spite of the fact that it was so near the capital, Waverley was still hidden, as St. Ailred himself pointed out, in such an out-of-the-way corner that it attracted little attention, until the wide

---

36. Hugh of Kirkstall, *Narratio Fundationis: De Fundatione Fontanis Monasterii*, *Memorials of Fountains Abbey*, ed. J. S. Walbran, Surtees Society vol. 42 (Durham: Andrews & Co., 1863) 1-129.

reputation of the Cistercians in the north reminded men that Waverley was also a house of White Monks, and the southern abbey began, in its turn, to make foundations.[37]

The founder of Rievaulx was Sir Walter Espec, a Yorkshireman and a Christian knight somewhat more hearty and less sophisticated than the Knight in the *Canterbury Tales*, and perhaps more simple in his piety, which was in any case deep and sincere. Having already endowed the Austin Canons of Kirkham with land for a foundation he now consulted Archbishop Thurstan of York and on his advice invited St. Bernard of Clairvaux to send men to start a monastery in the valley of the Rye, some thirty miles north of York, and not far from Sir Walter's own castle of Helmsley.

St. Bernard was quick to accept the invitation, and took care that his first English foundation should be a success. He picked out a talented Englishman from among his monks and sent him with twelve others to London, armed with a letter of introduction to King Henry I.[38] The leader of this colony was one of the many English intellectuals who had been attracted to Clairvaux in the time of St. Bernard, and was probably himself a Yorkshireman. Perhaps he had studied at York under Henry Murdac, who also received the white cowl from the hands of Bernard in the Chapter Room of Clairvaux and afterwards became Abbot of Fountains and Archbishop of York. William, the first Abbot of Rievaulx, is still recorded in the Order's unofficial list of "Blessed."[L] He had been St. Bernard's secretary, and was also an authority on Gregorian plain chant. His skill as a cantor had given him a prominent place in the revision of the Cistercian antiphoner which finally became necessary when the experts in the Order found the Metz manuscript, copied with such labor by St. Stephen, to be so defective that it was completely intolerable.[39] William, then, had formed part of a Commission on Chant that brought out a revised antiphoner which was beyond reproach. From the beginning this

---

37. "*Waverlenses quoque fratres qui hactenus quasi in angulo latuerant, cognito quod eiusdem essent ordinis, Cisterciensium monasteriorum numerum auxerunt*" (St. Ailred, *De Bello Standardii* [*PL* 195, col. 704C]).[XLIX]

38. St. Bernard, *Epistola* 92 (*PL* 182, cols. 224B-225A).

39. It is some consolation to monks of our own day to realize that even in the best days of the Order the chant was sometimes far from perfect, and that this fact was a source of suffering and concern to the great and impassive

Cistercian Abbot was to count as a man of considerable influence in northern England. In any case, he soon had his abbey on a firm footing, and the discipline of his monks was so perfect that all Yorkshire was electrified. It was the example of Rievaulx that led immediately to the secession of the more austere element in the Benedictine community of St. Mary's York.

The land which Walter Espec had given to the monks was probably not a very exciting prospect on the March day when they arrived there. Spring comes late to Yorkshire, and the moors are always bleak even at their best. The dale that had been selected for the new foundation was lost in a labyrinth of deep, wooded valleys, and if the weather was wet and cold it must have been a forbidding place at first. However, there were probably one or two wooden buildings set up in a clearing down by the stream that ran through those deep woods, for the legislation of the Order demanded that temporary buildings be set up before monks were sent out to occupy new land.[LII] In any case, the monks soon set to work on the permanent stone buildings of their Abbey, and they were probably laying the foundations of one of the largest churches in England when a young courtier called Ailred, the Seneschal of King David of Scotland, rode down through the woods to visit them one day in 1134, and was so attracted by the simplicity and peace of their rough life that he rode away only to return the next day and remain forever.

5. *St. Ailred – His Youth and Early Career.*

Ailred[40] of Rievaulx came of one of the few Saxon Christian families that still gave priests to the Church in Yorkshire in the darkest ages. In that outlying wilderness, Church discipline was

---

ascetics of the twelfth century! St. Bernard himself says, of the Metz antiphoner: "*Examinatum displicuit ita quod et cantu et littera inventum sit vitiosum et incompositum nimis et paene per omnia contemptibile.... Tandem aliquando non sustinentibus iam fratribus nostris Abbatibus Ordinis ... mutari et corrigi placuit*" etc. (*Tractatus de Cantu* [Preface to the New Antiphoner] Prol. [*PL* 182, col 1121AB]).[LI]

40. I use this spelling because it is adopted by the best historian of English monasticism in our day, Dom David Knowles; see *The Monastic Order in England: A History of its Development from the Times of St Dunstan to the Fourth Lateran Council – 940-1216* (Cambridge: Cambridge

not very strictly observed because it was mostly unknown, and Ailred's father Eilaf was a hereditary priest, the scion of a long line of priests who sound rather more like the Old Testament than the New. His benefice was the ruined abbey of Hexham. He lived in the gutted buildings, half of which were unroofed so that the rain was washing the old frescoes off the walls and grass had overgrown the shrines of the Saxon saints. Ailred was probably born at Hexham in 1110, and is supposed, in his childhood, to have manifested some of the precocious signs of future sanctity which abound in the medieval *Vitae Sanctorum*. Nevertheless he was not destined for the Church. Eilaf, it seems, had good connections at Durham and was, besides, a person of enough sophistication to desire something more for his son than a dubious hereditary benefice. In any case, he himself had now done what he could to reform and rebuild Hexham, establishing a Chapter of Canons there and reviving the worship of God in some of its ancient splendor. The days of the hereditary priests were done.

Ailred, therefore, went off to the Court of Prince David at Edinburgh when he was about fourteen. It was a good place for a young man of his talents to seek training and a career. Scotland, too, was at the peak of a social and religious revival which dated back to the previous generation. The Queen, St. Margaret, mother of Prince David the heir apparent and King Alexander I who now wore the crown of Scotland, had brought something like Christian civilization to this very barbarous land. She was the grand-niece of St. Edward the Confessor, whose biography Ailred later wrote, when he was in his prime as Abbot of Rievaulx. David himself came to the throne of Scotland about the time Ailred entered his household, and the young boy grew up with the King's son and his stepson, Waldef.[41] With the latter in particular he formed ties of the most intimate friendship.[LIII] They had something of the same character, brilliant and sensitive, attracted by the new books and humanistic ideas that were circulating in the intellec-

---

University Press, 1940). The spelling "Aelred" is also frequently found. Other variants, like Aethelred, are seldom found. The fact that Ailred is probably a contraction of Aethelred is the only justification for the use of that strange name.

41. Also spelled Waltheof. Another variant of the name sometimes found is Walthen. The biographer of St. Waldef, Jocelyn of Furness, calls him "*Walenus*" in Latin.

tual world, fond of philosophical and religious speculation, eager to penetrate the real meaning of existence, and to enjoy it as well. Waldef was more retiring than Ailred and was the first to leave for the cloister, when he travelled south and entered the monastery of Austin Canons at Nostell, Yorkshire, in 1130.

Ailred was twenty years old at the time, and he seems to have been concentrating with single-minded purpose on a court career so that when Waldef went off to the monastery it disturbed and upset his own soul and made him begin to wonder if he, too, belonged in the cloister. At the moment, however, everything pointed to a prominent position at the court. He was already Seneschal, which meant that he had a busy and important post as *major domo* in the King's palace. It was not necessarily a job that gave full scope to his intellectual talents, but nevertheless there was a strong active and practical side to his nature which found some satisfaction in managing the royal household. It meant that he had his fingers on the pulse of court life and perhaps also that he had something to do with the actual tempo of that life. Since he was an intensely sociable person, vivacious and friendly and steeped in the enthusiasm for that "courtly" living which marked the spirit of the time, he probably found no little satisfaction in his position as Seneschal. There was, in fact, no reason why he should not have been intensely happy – except that he was one of those fortunate people who are incapable of deluding themselves that they find happiness in the prosperity and pleasures of the world.

Four years were to pass before St. Ailred's vocation matured. They were years of an obscure but mounting crisis. Evidently no one suspected what was going on in the soul of this brilliant and successful young man of the world. They envied him, rather, *O quam bene est illi!*[42] But Aelred has left us an account of his inner conflict and of his sorrow.[43] It is a vivid description of the anguish that precedes conversion. Ailred closely follows the style and the thought of his model, St. Augustine, and the whole passage reads like an excerpt from the *Confessions*, which was one of St. Ailred's favorite books and one of the only books he

---

42. Ailred of Rievaulx, *Speculum Caritatis* 1.28 (*PL* 195, col. 532A).[LIV]
43. *Speculum Caritatis* 1.28 (cols. 531B-532D).

was still able to read with profit when his life drew to its close. The *Confessions* are even explicitly quoted once in the chapter in which Ailred describes his own struggle.[LV] It is the same story: that of a man torn apart by the two laws in him, two attractions, one drawing him to God and to freedom in the life of grace, the other holding him a prisoner of passion and habit and pleasure.

Although the anguish that the saint is describing was evidently something subjectively very real, there is still enough vagueness in the general terms he uses to permit us to wonder whether or not he was exaggerating his "life of sin." He does not say what his sins were. Indeed, instead of mentioning sins he lists one or two things which are not in themselves sinful at all: "natural affection" (*amor sanguinis mei*), the "pleasures of society" (*vincula socialis gratiae*) and "above all the knot of a certain friendship, sweeter to me than all the pleasures of this life."[LVI]

The suspicion that Ailred might be exaggerating is supported by a statement in the first draft of St. Ailred's biography, by his disciple, the monk of Rievaulx, Walter Daniel.[44] Here we read that Ailred lived "like a monk" at the King's court.[LVIII] However, that remark of Walter Daniel's was an exaggeration in the other direction. Contemporary readers objected to it, and the enthusiastic biographer was compelled to climb down and make certain reservations. He said he meant that Ailred while he was still in the world possessed the virtues of humility and meekness in such a heroic degree that you would have thought him a monk and not a courtier.[LIX] This was evidently quite true. Ailred's success had made him a few enemies at court and we are told that he was able to accept insult from them with the perfect forbearance and charity which Jesus preached to the multitudes who gathered to hear him on the mountain near Capharnaum, at the beginning of His public life. However, Walter Daniel admitted that he could not give his Abbot credit for having been perfect in all the virtues when he was in the world. The promptness with which this admiring disciple allows reservations in the matter of Ailred's chas-

---

44. This life is printed, in great part, as the appendix to the article "Ailred of Rievaulx and His Biographer Walter Daniel" by F. M. Powicke in the *Bulletin of the John Rylands Library* (Manchester, England: July 1921-Jan. 1922) 310-51, 452-521. The *Vita* is found in Ms. Q.B.7, Jesus College, Cambridge.[LVII]

tity, as a courtier, throws the weight rather heavily on the side of Ailred's own evidence against himself. In the light of what Walter Daniel says, the reader may, if he insists, take Ailred's own word concerning his grievous sins. He was a passionate man in whom the capacity for great sanctity and heroic love of God implied at the same time a dangerous inclination to recklessness in human love, and he was just as likely to go to one extreme as to the other.

However, it would certainly not be true to say that Ailred had led a life that was notoriously disorderly or that his errors were anything beyond those that are unfortunately the more or less common lot of men. And the fact remains that the "attachment" to his home and his friends and to the society of the court, which he laments, was "sinful" to him because of the peculiar circumstance of his own vocation: he was becoming more and more certain that God wanted him to leave the world, and therefore what was more or less good for another now became a definite evil for him; after all, he could have married his "friend" and settled down. But success, positions, honors, friendship, a home and a prosperous family: these things were all very well for other men, who could enjoy them without danger. For his own part, if he stayed in the world, he felt that he would certainly end up in hell. And yet he could not make up his mind to leave for a monastery.

Providence neatly solved the problem. King David sent his Seneschal south, to York, on a routine diplomatic mission. Archbishop Thurstan of York was claiming that the Scotch bishops were his suffragans, and Ailred was probably chosen to discuss the matter and come to a solution. It was then about 1134. Ailred probably called on his friend Waldef, who was now Prior of the Austin Friars at Kirkham, near York. Perhaps Waldef was the first to tell him about the Cistercians at Rievaulx and about the excitement, in York, over the riots at St. Mary's Abbey and the secession of a party of reformers to Skelldale, near Ripon, where they were trying to emulate the severe life of the White Monks – and doing it with a vengeance, for they were much poorer and had made their start in the depth of winter, without any buildings and with very little food. In any case, York was still in a ferment over the affair. After all, when the Prior of St. Mary's had decided to leave, with his party of dissidents, and lead a stricter life elsewhere, the monks had tried to lock them in the Abbey, and, at the same time, lock the Archbishop out. It was Thurstan himself who had taken the part of the reformers and who had not allowed himself, by any means, to be intimidated by the monks. He had promptly placed the Abbey under interdict and had given the dissidents shelter in his own palace until they could settle in Skelldale. That had all happened in the autumn and winter of 1133. When Ailred arrived in York, the smoke had barely cleared.

If Skelldale had not been somewhat out of his way, he would have visited Fountains. But after all, the little isolated community of truculent reformers, who were not yet affiliated to any definite Order, interested him less than the new monastic colony from France. He knew he would find a perfectly functioning unit of that new and powerful spiritual organism that was branching out, all over Europe, from Burgundy, under the influence of that saint and genius who was called Bernard of Fontaines, the Abbot of Clairvaux. Ailred would naturally be welcome at the manor of the new Abbey's founder. Perhaps he had already met Sir Walter Espec before, at court, in Scotland. In any case, on his way back to Edinburgh, his road took him through Helmsley and he turned his horse aside at the gate of Espec's castle.

The Knight was one of those giants who are all huge, every bone and muscle being built in proportion. Although he was getting old, his hair was still black and his beard was long and thick. His bright eyes looked at you out of an enormous face, and Ailred says his voice was "like a trumpet."[45]

Ailred was received with great courtesy, and entertained at the castle overnight. The following day he visited Rievaulx. There was nothing very impressive about the monastery buildings: they were nothing but wooden huts, in a clearing of the vale. The colony was still small, although, under Abbot William, the monastery soon began to attract vocations. Everything about the place breathed silence and simplicity and austerity. Ailred saw the monks working in the fields, or digging the foundations of what would be their permanent abbey. He heard them chant the psalms under the plain beams of their wooden chapel. Something of the mighty tide of fervor that was surging in the new

---

45. See the whole description of Sir Walter in *De Bello Standardii* (*PL* 195, cols. 703D-704D).[LX]

community got into his own heart. He was shattered with sorrow and joy: sorrow and confusion at the insufficiency of his own life, joy that there should exist a place where men could live and taste a happiness which everything inside him cried out could also belong to him if he would only make up his mind to pay the price for it.

That night he returned to Helmsley. The next morning he set out for Scotland.

His road took him along the wooded ridge that overhangs the valley of the Rye. He could look down into the misty valley and descry the wooden roofs of the monastery, where a little twisting column of smoke rose from the bake-house chimney. The bell for prime had rung some time since and the monks were probably in Chapter, and would soon go out to work in the fields for the rising sun was slanting rays of gold across the moor and would soon penetrate their glen with its light. Ailred could not resist the pressure that threatened to burst his heart. He turned to his travelling companions and exclaimed: "Come, let us go down to the monks once again"[LXI] and he swung his horse around and took the track that plunged down through the trees toward the monastery by the Rye.

6. *St. Ailred at Rievaulx and Revesby.*

What was the reason for this strong, almost irresistible attraction which compelled Ailred, at last, to make his final break with the world and ask the monks to accept him as a novice at Rievaulx? There was already a force working in his soul that told him obscurely that he would find, here, all the peace which we know, from his writings, that he found indeed. Some instinct assured him that here, at Rievaulx, his soul would find rest and happiness in the "Sabbath" of contemplation which he later described in the sure language of one who writes from experience. Yet, at the moment, he certainly had in his mind no such detailed theory of the Cistercian vocation as he was later to evolve. What he did have was the one, basic, essential concept from which everything else was to develop. Like so many other hundreds of men in every part of Europe in the twelfth century, what Ailred had realized, on his first visit to Rievaulx, was that he had providentially stumbled upon a group of men who were leading the ascetic life Christ preached in the Gospel and leading it in all its perfection. They were literally following the teaching of the Lord Who had said, "If thou wilt be perfect, go, sell what thou hast and give to the poor, and thou shalt have treasure in heaven, and come, follow me."[46] "If any man will come after me, let him deny himself and take up his cross daily and follow me: for whosoever will save his life shall lose it; for he that shall lose his life for my sake shall save it."[47] The labor, the poverty and fasting of the monks, their austere life of silence and prayer, their wretched clothing, just sufficient to protect them against the winter cold, their common life in which they shared all the goods of the monastery in a family which obliterated all worldly distinction between knight and serf, scholar and artisan and laborer – all this could not help but bring to mind the community of the first Apostles and of the early Christian disciples who had gathered about them in Solomon's Porch, having sold all their goods and divided the proceeds among the poor.[48] He saw that, as a fruit of their sacrifice and of their detachment, these men were able to live together in a harmony and peace and contentment that surpassed anything that could ever have been compassed by the plans and ideals of mere men: for it was the work of the Spirit of God, uniting them in that charity which is the bond of perfection, and binding them together in a mystical union of souls, in Christ, which made them all, as it were, one man in Him. Like the multitude of the early Christians, they seemed to have "but one heart and one soul."[49] They were all one in Christ, *omnes in Christo unum*.[LXII]

In a word, the thing that drew Ailred so irresistibly to Rievaulx was above all the sense that here was Christian asceticism in its most perfect form: here the renunciation demanded by Christ was taken seriously and literally, and accepted with the most generous and ardent love, and as a result the sign which Christ Himself had promised would be the proof of his true followers was verified here: "By this shall all men know that you

46. Matthew 19:21.
47. Luke 9:23-24.
48. Acts 4:32-37.
49. Acts 4:32.

are my disciples, if you have love one for another."[50]

Ailred entered Rievaulx because he was dazzled and overpowered by the conviction that here he had found "the real thing." The undivided and ardent love for the Truth of the Gospel, the Truth of St. Benedict's *Rule*, and the unadulterated Christian ideal in all its perfection which was the characteristic of the early Cistercians, and which is, in other forms, characteristic of every other movement of monastic reform, was found to have this effect upon men who were ravaged by an obscure hunger for a spiritual ideal which could not be satisfied in the outside world.

And yet there were other expressions of the monastic ideal, just as austere, just as uncompromising as Cîteaux, and they flourished side by side with the Cistercian monasteries of the twelfth century. There were the monks of Savigny – who eventually amalgamated with Cîteaux. There were other cenobitic congregations – Tiron, Vallombrosa. There were the semi-eremitical rules of Grandmont, Camaldoli and the Chartreuse. Most of these had not found their way to England. The first English Charterhouse was founded in Somerset long after Ailred had gone to heaven,[51] and the Carthusians did not come to Yorkshire until the fourteenth century. Mount Grace Priory was founded in 1397.[LXIII]

But let us suppose Rievaulx had been a Charterhouse: would Ailred have entered it so readily? The Carthusians were, if anything, more austere than the monks of Cîteaux. Their strict solitude was a great contrast to the familiar pattern of cenobitic living, common to the monasteries of the West for centuries past. Their ideal was and is really quite different from that of Cîteaux, and the study of St. Ailred's life and spirituality permit us to say that there was nothing of the Carthusian in him. He was, on the contrary, as typically and characteristically Cistercian as any saint of the Order. The spirituality of St. Ailred is the spirituality of a complete and uncompromising cenobite. It is social and communal down to its very roots. By his very nature, Ailred was predisposed to love people and to love company, and when God's grace began to work on him to turn him into a contemplative, it by no means made of him a solitary. That was not Ailred's voca-

50. John 13:35.
51. Witham Charterhouse was founded in 1181.

tion. When, in his later years, his illnesses forced him to retire, with a dispensation from the General Chapter, into a little cell or cottage of his own, we find him in it, very often, not only not alone but surrounded by anything from a dozen to thirty of his monks, eager to hear him talk to them of God and of charity and of the peace of contemplation.

Rievaulx appealed, then, to St. Ailred, not merely because of the happy chance that he passed that way one day, when he was feeling disgusted with the world. The Cistercian common life had in it everything that was calculated to stimulate and develop, with the aid of grace, all the deepest resources of his rich and active nature. For though the Cistercian life is essentially contemplative, nevertheless there is in it, by its very nature, a generous proportion of activity. Not that the monks are active in the technical sense that they go out and preach and take care of parishes, hospitals and schools. But in the plain, obvious meaning of the word, they are "active" from morning to night because they are always doing things, passing from one duty to another, so that the Cistercian community is a big, vital organism that is almost constantly in movement. There is nothing quite so busy or so lively as a large Cistercian monastery. If the house is well run and has a good spirit, this "activity" has nothing incongruous about it, and is always peaceful and harmonious and smooth. Only where the *Rule* is not well kept and where a certain secret materialism begins to dominate the spiritual side of the life, does the activity within a monastery become agitated and hectic and confused.

The Cistercian life appealed to all the innate energy and ardor of Ailred's temperament. There was movement, there was work, there was study, there was choral prayer, the liturgy, centered on the stark and simple drama of the ancient Cistercian Mass rite. Above all, there was the community: there were the stimulation and the example of saints living all around him. The thing that Ailred most valued in the Cistercian life, and appreciated as no one before him or since has been able to appreciate it, was the warm sense of supernatural companionship and solidarity, the feeling of strength and support in mutual affection which is the very life-blood of a fervent monastic community. This is, indeed, the greatest and most characteristic grace of the Cistercian life. It was something that a man like Ailred could scarcely do without.

And it was so rich and meaty an element in his spiritual diet that the common life, instead of disturbing his contemplation, nourished and entertained it and made it grow to its full maturity. The necessity of living in the constant company of other men, rather than in absolute solitude, was not an obstacle to deep interior life for men like Ailred of Rievaulx. On the contrary, the graces of the common life were the very life-blood on which their prayer and contemplation were nourished.

Even though there is necessarily an element of movement and activity in the purely cenobitic life of the Cistercians, nevertheless the supernatural vitality that flows through the little "mystical body" of the monastery amply makes up for any of the physical handicaps that come from lack of pure solitude. To live with other men, bearing all their little defects of character and overlooking their shortcomings in order to honor Christ in their person is a most perfect school of purity of heart. It may be true that certain extraordinary vocations can reach a higher degree of contemplation in absolute solitude, but the Cistercians claimed, from the first, that their life was for all men who desired to find God by the renunciation of their own will. The average person called to the contemplative life can perhaps best fulfill his vocation in the cenobitic atmosphere where sacrifice is tempered by the consolations of society, where generosity is sustained by the power of example and where fervor is nourished by encouragement and brotherly affection. And above all, the constant obedience, which binds the pure cenobite more strictly than any other, is at the same time the most powerful ascetic instrument ever devised and the quickest way to interior liberty. The purely common life delivers the individual from all the countless worries and responsibilities over the material details of life which no solitary can escape unless he is able to live on bread and water all the time – and even then, he has to take steps to ensure his supply of bread and water! In a *cenobium* it is the Abbot – or the Cellarer – who does the worrying.

The seeds of sanity and simplicity which were sown by the first Cistercian Fathers bore rich fruits in the writings of St. Ailred and St. Bernard and their contemporaries, and the way they travelled, although it took them to great heights of the interior life, was still so much the common way that their spirituality retains an appeal to many who would be frightened by the seemingly inaccessible remoteness and the apparently cruel austerity of St. John of the Cross. We may add, at once, that St. John of the Cross is really no more austere than the first Cistercians, and that they, in their turn, are no more humane than the sixteenth-century Carmelite, who is more often read than understood. But the fact remains that it is relatively easy to understand a way of purification which is eminently based on obedience and charity and humility and the virtues of communal living: and this was the way of the Cistercians.

Ailred's doctrine and spirituality are the flowering of his cenobitic vocation. They prove that the busy, communal atmosphere of a Cistercian cloister is not, in itself, an obstacle to mystical prayer. If St. Ailred does not take us quite so deep into the heart of the mystical life as St. Bernard or William of St. Thierry, and if he does not tell us as much as they do about transforming union or the higher reaches of infused prayer, he nevertheless clearly introduces us into a well-defined mystical contemplation. Supposing Ailred was less of a contemplative than St. Bernard. If so, is this to be blamed on a more active temperament, or a heart too inclined to rest in the love of his brethren, and not sufficiently isolated in God? The answer to both these speculative questions must be "No," when we reflect that St. Bernard's life was much more active than St. Ailred's and that St. Bernard's heart went out, just as readily, to his community and to other men.

The monastery that St. Ailred entered in 1134, even though it was only two years old, was not exactly what one would call a solitude. It was never to be so. In St. Ailred's own lifetime the community was to reach an enormous size – roughly six hundred and fifty monks and brothers made up his Cistercian family in 1165. But even in the very first days, when Ailred settled down to wait for the customary three or four days in the guest house, before he was taken into the novitiate, we find the guesthouse itself was "full of people." Walter Daniel admits that there were certain restrictions tending to guarantee the sanctity of the enclosure. Women, hunting falcons and dogs that were not *bona fide* watchdogs were not allowed on the monastery premises.[52] Reading between the lines of his *Vita Aelredi* we are sometimes tempt-

52. "*Januas monasterii sui mulieres non ingrediuntur, non accipitres, non*

ed to think that practically anything else could get in. In any case, even the short probation in the guesthouse was marked by some excitement.[LXV] It is in his description of this event – a fire, in the guests' refectory, which Ailred extinguished by a "miracle" – that Walter Daniel shows us an excited crowd of monks, laybrothers, guests and hired men running about throwing things aimlessly at the fire. Some, he says, were throwing water. Others were throwing wine. Others were throwing any other liquor that came to hand. According to Walter Daniel, the only one who kept cool was the future saint. Ailred stood up with the beautiful dignity of a hero in a romance, and, with a sweeping gesture, emptied the contents of his own drinking mug into the flames, which had now spread to the wooden rafters and the ceiling. The mug was filled with good English ale. And it was such good ale that the fire immediately went out. It is not necessary to remind the reader that some of the things Walter Daniel described as miracles did not elicit the unwavering belief of all men, even in the Middle Ages.

After four days in the hospice, St. Ailred was received into the novitiate. In the twelfth century there was no distinct novice's habit, and the novices spent their year of probation in secular clothing. They received the tunic and white (or grey) cowl of unbleached wool when they were tonsured, on the day of their solemn profession.[53] The novitiate at Rievaulx was probably already crowded. We know who two of the other novices were. One of them was a certain Hugh, who later became prior of Rievaulx, and another was a young man called Simon, apparently of noble birth, who had run away from home and endured hunger, poverty, exposure and many other hardships in order to enter Rievaulx, to which he made his way on foot across the moors, eating whatever he found growing in the woods or wastelands along his way. This Simon was already well on the way to a high degree of spiritual perfection. He seems, from Ailred's description, to have

---

canes nisi tales qui frequenti latratu fures ab aedibus abigere consuerunt" (*Vita* [Powicke, "Ailred of Rievaulx and His Biographer Walter Daniel" 496]).[LXIV]

53. The present Constitutions of the Cistercians of the Strict Observance prescribe an extra year of noviceship beyond the canonical year. This is followed by three years of simple vows, and solemn vows are only taken when this five-year probation is over.[LXVI]

been one of those amazing people one sometimes finds in monasteries, who appear to have no difficulty in keeping recollected, who are humble and quiet and meek and well-regulated in everything that they do, who never seem to get out of hand, or lose patience, or become excited over anything. They never have any trouble about keeping silence. They do not burst out laughing at things which are supposed to be deadly serious – for instance, the pious reading in the refectory.

Ailred was fascinated by this model of perfection whom he found, at the same time, to be a singularly attractive character, so we are entitled to believe that Simon, besides being a paragon of virtue, was also human. Ailred, we know, was intensely human. Although they could not talk to one another or manifest any special marks of affection, they struck up a warm and lasting friendship which included also the future Prior, Hugh.

Simon was not destined to have a long monastic career. Ailred, who was only twenty-four when he entered Rievaulx, spoke of Simon as being "my son in years, my father in sanctity and my friend in charity"[54] and Simon's death occurred when Ailred was composing the first book of his *Speculum Caritatis*, which closes with an eloquent lament for the death of the young Cistercian. The *Speculum* was written in 1141-42, when Ailred was novice master at Rievaulx. We can assume that Simon was perhaps not much more than twenty-three, when he died after eight years of illness.[55] In any case, Ailred's lament gives us a good picture of the young monk who had reached that perfect tranquillity and peace which are the sign of a pure and detached heart. He passed from life to death with the unruffled, joyous calm of those who are serenely established in the depths of union with God.[56] He remains to us, in the pages of the English saint, as a portrait of a typical contemplative, one of the thousands of

54. "*Filius aetate, pater sanctitate, amicus charitate*" (*Speculum Caritatis* 1.33 [*PL* 195, col. 541D]).[LXVII]

55. The Cistercians did not receive candidates into the novitiate until they had completed their fifteenth year; see *Instituta Capituli Generalis* 78 (*Nomasticon* 230).

56. "*Et ideo exterius nihil paene inveniens quo oblectaretur, in interiorem mentis suae mentis solitudinem sese recluserat, solus sedens et tacens, non tamen otio torpens. Scribebat enim vel legebat vel meditationi*

nameless and unrecognized souls who have spent their existence in a secret, tranquil sacrifice of prayer and suffering, in the cloisters and cells of every monastic Order, and who are called by God to win an incalculable increment of grace and sanctity for the whole Body of the Church by living out their silent lives for Him alone. In the Carmels, and Charterhouses and Trappist monasteries of the world there will always be far more who will be sanctified like Simon of Rievaulx than like Bernard of Clairvaux. But the Bernards and Ailreds are raised up by God to perform a special and more public mission, and they are the ones whose works and whose sanctity have managed, at least to some extent, to make them famous in the militant Church. That does not necessarily mean that it is they who are, in God's eyes, the greater saints.

Ailred's novice master was also called Simon. He was, of course, a veteran monk, certainly one of the colony that had originally come over from France. Soon after Ailred's profession, the busy and rapidly growing monastery began to think of new foundations. Two of them were made in 1136. In the spring of the year Abbot William sent off a colony of Cistercians to take over the ancient Benedictine Abbey of Melrose, across the Scottish border, in the lands of Ailred's friend, King David. In December of the same year Simon, the novice master, started south to make a foundation in Bedfordshire, at Wardon. He took with him another of Ailred's close friends, the monk Yvo or Ives, who figures as one of the interlocutors in Ailred's famous dialogue on friendship,[57] which we shall discuss in due course.

Scripturarum, quippe cui erat vigil sensus, secretius intendebat. Vix cum priore saltem de necessariis loquebatur. Incedebat tamquam surdus non audiens et sicut mutus non aperiens os suum ... Verum si quis eum accepta occasione quolibet conveniret affatu, tanta mox redolebat in ejus sermone suavitas, tanta in vultu sine omni dissolutione apparebat hilaritas, ut quam fuerit silentium ejus vacuum amaritudinis, plenum dulcedinis et modus loquendi et humilitas proderet audiendi.... Tibi soli [he is now addressing the dead Simon] *pietas divina prospexit, ut tranquillam ac pacificam illam animam in desideratam tibi patriam ab hujus vitae miseriis cum omni tranquillitate transferret, ac corporei habitaculi vinculum, te paene nesciente, tanta solveret facilitate ut nec modicus mortis timor dilectam sibi animam molestaret*" (*Speculum Caritatis* 1.24 [*PL* 195, col. 543BD]).[LXVIII]

57. *De Spirituali Amicitia* (*PL* 195, cols. 659A-702B); English trans. *Christian*

Meanwhile, Ailred was marked out by his qualities of mind and spirit to play an important part in the affairs, not only of Rievaulx but of the whole Church in England. Abbot William early chose him as one of his private counsellors and admitted him to the discussion of the monastery's most important affairs. Nor did the affairs of the monastery alone provide matter for Ailred's conferences with his Abbot. William of Rievaulx, we must remember, had been St. Bernard's private secretary. He had seen, at close range, all the activity and reforming zeal of God's providential instrument in the affairs of twelfth-century Europe. He was well aware that St. Bernard, although he severely maintained the integrity of the Cistercian contemplative ideal, nevertheless felt that Abbots ought to keep in touch with what was going on around them in the world and even play an active part in defending the rights of God and of His Church where these seemed to be neglected. William had seen St. Bernard exercise his influence at a disputed episcopal election at Langres, in which diocese Clairvaux was built. He knew St. Bernard approved of a decree of the Lateran Council of 1139 which stated that representatives of religious communities should assist diocesan chapters at the election of bishops. In due time, William and other Cistercians would intervene in a hotly disputed election in their own Archdiocese of York. In all these affairs, Ailred, as the Abbot's adviser, would play an increasingly important part.

And so, although the first Cistercians insisted that their life was something entirely apart from the world, and although they renounced all active share in the affairs of the Church and of Kingdoms, the Cistercians of St. Bernard's generation had become one of the most important influences in the active life of the Church and even in European politics of their time. This influence reached its peak when the papal election of 1145 placed Bl. Eugene III, an obscure disciple of St. Bernard, on the chair of Peter. From then until 1153, when both Bernard and Eugene died, it was said, perhaps not without reason, that the Church was ruled from Clairvaux, and that the real Pope was St. Bernard himself.

Friendship, by Hugh Talbot OCR (London: Catholic Book Club, 1942); *L'Amitié Spirituelle*, text and French trans. by J. Dubois (Bruges: Beyaert, 1948).

Consequently, we must not imagine that all the Cistercians lived hidden and obscure lives into which no noise of the world was ever permitted to filter. Most of them, it is true, were able to enjoy the retirement of their wild valleys and forests in comparative peace. But anyone who had any talent or, worse still, any powerful connections, was likely to find himself in danger of leading an increasingly active life. Many Cistercians were called from the cloister, often against their repeated protests, to occupy episcopal sees and reform dioceses. We often find the General Chapter ordering them to accept such appointments. St. Bernard only prevented himself from becoming an archbishop by the most stubborn and energetic refusals. This, as we know, did not keep him from being one of the most active men of his time. There were Cistercians who were fortunate enough to escape honors and high offices and keep themselves out of the limelight of public affairs. They generally had to work hard to do so. We shall soon meet one of them, the second Abbot, Maurice, of Rievaulx, who retired soon after his election and again refused another abbacy later on, in order to remain in the obscurity of his community and lead the life of a contemplative monk. Occasionally we find Cistercians like Abbot Adam of Dore, on the Welsh border, who ran away to join the Carthusians in order to find peace at last.

St. Ailred, then, did not enjoy the silence and the solitude which the average Cistercian monk, or even Abbot, can have in our time when the White Monks have ceased to carry any weight in the temporal affairs of the Church or of nations! A few years after his profession we find him travelling northward to the borders of Scotland with his Abbot, to arrange the surrender of a Castle, belonging to Sir Walter Espec, to King David of Scotland. This event took place on the eleventh of November, 1138. England and Scotland were at war. Rievaulx was in the center of the war-theater, and the decisive battle of the campaign, later described by Ailred himself, was fought within a few miles of the Abbey. This was the famous "Battle of the Standard." It was an event to which no one at Rievaulx, and Ailred least of all, could remain indifferent. Here at the very gate of their enclosure two armies had come together, and on both sides Ailred's best and dearest friends had taken up arms against one another. The Scottish army was commanded by his patron King David, and how many of his court associates were fighting under David's banner. Then, on the English side, were his newer friends, and not the least of them was the giant knight, Walter Espec, the founder and neighbor of Rievaulx. In the same year, 1138, Ailred was in Durham on family business of his own. His old father, Eilaf, the hereditary priest of Hexham, had retired to the Benedictine Abbey to die in the habit of a Black Monk, and Ailred witnessed the arrangement by which he finally ceded all his rights at Hexham to the Canons he himself had brought in to ensure the worthy service of God in that ancient Church.

In 1140, Archbishop Thurstan of York died. In the election that followed, Ailred's friend, Waldef, the prior of Kirkham, was considered a likely candidate, but he was vetoed by King Stephen of England because he was too closely related to the royal house of Scotland. Waldef was, in all probability, delighted. He was to be one of those Cistercians who made it his life work to get out of being a bishop, although he could not quite avoid becoming an Abbot. However, when there was still talk of Waldef being archbishop, the Earl of Yorkshire and leader of Stephen's party, who might well have swung the King over to Waldef, proposed a simoniacal "deal" with the Prior of Kirkham, offering him the archbishopric in exchange for some of the land that went with it.

As the election finally turned out, William Fitzherbert, the treasurer of York, was chosen. Immediately the minority appealed against him. The main charge was that money had changed hands somewhere in the proceedings. Also, the archbishop-elect was accused of not living in a manner befitting a cleric. Abbot Richard of Fountains who had known him well in the days before the founders of Fountains seceded from St. Mary's, York, supported these charges, and the affair was brought to Rome. Things did not move very quickly, but eventually the Papal Legate put William Fitzherbert in full possession of his see. The matter did not end there. St. Bernard himself took up this contest which had enlisted the action of the most influential Cistercians in Northern England, and in 1146 the newly elected Cistercian Pope, Eugene III, deposed William of York. Finally, to make the whole thing look like a Cistercian plot, the austere Henry Murdac, recently ordered from Clairvaux to Fountains, became Archbishop of York.

This is not the place to examine the merits of the case. But there is no use denying that the Cistercians definitely used their influence to get precisely what they wanted. One might argue that this was far from the simple, contemplative ideal of Robert and Alberic and Stephen. The spectacle of a contemplative Order functioning, at the same time, as a political machine capable of exercising tremendous power, is not exactly one that edifies us today, let us admit it. However, we must put ourselves in the position of St. Bernard, and when we look through his eyes, we may find ourselves closer to agreeing with him. The Cistercians sincerely thought of themselves as disinterested defenders of the rights of the Church in this case as in so many others. They knew they had influence and they felt themselves obliged to exercise it in order to remove an unworthy candidate and to safeguard the purity of the unstained Bride of Christ, to whom St. Bernard had such a consuming devotion.

The biggest difficulty about this case, however, lies in the judgment posterity passed upon the two candidates. Henry Murdac was detested by most Yorkshiremen, and, indeed, he found it wiser and safer to live at Ripon than at York. But William Fitzherbert, deposed as a simoniac, was venerated after his death as a saint, and is still to be found in the Church's calendar.

What concerns us here is not the case itself, but St. Ailred's connection with it. In 1140, when William of Rievaulx decided that he was not getting enough action out of the Roman Curia, Ailred was sent to Rome as the special representative of the Cistercians. This journey was actually the making of the young Cistercian.

In the first place, Ailred passed through Clairvaux, where he met St. Bernard and perhaps was urged by him to put his talent as a writer to work. In any case, the stimulation of contact with this tremendous community must have been no less great for Ailred than for hundreds of other men of that time. What was more important, he was well received by Pope Innocent II, and Walter Daniel leads us to believe that Ailred made a very favorable impression in Rome.[LXIX] From then on he was doomed to a career. It is hard to tell whether he really objected. St. Ailred complains far less than St. Bernard of the conflict between action and contemplation. He had, it is true, far less reason to complain. But his temperament was also more active than Bernard's, and contact with the great ones of the world, and immersion in its troubles and interests, seems to have disturbed him less.

In any case, upon his return to Rievaulx, Ailred was made novice master. This was no sinecure. In ten years, the population of Rievaulx had shot from twenty-five up to three hundred and it was still growing rapidly. Although most of the vocations were laybrothers, and Ailred had nothing to do with the formation of *conversi*, there was still plenty for him to do directing the choir novices.

The fact that he wrote his longest and, on the whole, his most profound book during the short period when he was novice master at Rievaulx does not mean that Ailred necessarily had much leisure. Whatever time he had for writing had to be treasured and set apart by generous and vigilant sacrifice, and the *Speculum Caritatis* is a memorial not only to Ailred's spiritual genius but also to his tireless energy. It is, of course, the fruit of the years of meditation and silent reflection he had been able to enjoy since his entrance into the monastery.

Those first six or seven years of silence were the only ones in Ailred's monastic career that he could really call his own. He had been left in peace, immersed in the tranquil stream of grace that flowed silently through the big community. He had gone through his studies for the priesthood, and had been ordained. During all that time a deep and penetrating theology of the contemplative life had been taking shape in his mind, under the influence of his favorite master, St. Augustine. One of the former monks of St. Mary's, York, a pioneer of Fountains, who had recently gone to found a new Cistercian monastery in Lincolnshire, had conversed with Ailred on the subject of the interior life and had discovered this rich synthesis on the nature and degrees of charity that was in course of formation in the mind of the young contemplative. He urged him to put it all down on paper and get a book out of it. Ailred at first refused on the grounds that he had come to the monastery from the kitchen – an allusion to his position as seneschal at the Scottish court – and had no talent for writing. But he was wrong. He not only had talent, but contact with his novices stirred up a ferment of ideas which simply had to be expressed, and so he went to work in the *Speculum*.

It is inevitable that we should compare Ailred, at every turn, to Saint Augustine, whom he so much resembles. His style is typical of the whole Augustinian school. Pages upon pages read like the *Confessions*. And Ailred is so temperamentally akin to another Augustinian, St. Anselm, that several passages of Ailred's own writings found their way into the later codices of Anselm's meditations.[58]

In nothing does Ailred resemble Augustine and Anselm so much as in the facility with which he reveals the intimate depths of his own soul. The *Speculum Caritatis* contains many vivid as well as charming passages in which we catch glimpses of twelfth-century Cistercian life, especially of the Cistercian mentality, that cannot be equalled anywhere. And it is in the *Speculum*, the fruit of his meditations as a young monk and of his experience as master of novices, that we see right into the heart of the novitiate of Rievaulx. We are shown not only the external details of the Cistercian life – the fasts, the chanting in choir, the hard labor in the fields, and the book over which the tired novice so often finds himself dozing[59] – we do not have to go far out of our way to find all this described in twelfth-century sources. But what is peculiar to St. Ailred is his penetrating psychological study of the Cistercian novice of his time, as well as an irreplaceable record of the novice master's method of handling spiritual problems.

Let us say, at once, that the first thing that strikes us in reading the long dialogue between the novice and the novice master in the second book of the *Speculum*[60] is that they are by no means mediocre people. They are not living on the surface of the spiritual life. They are not pious automatons, content with a series of set formulas and stiffening in the mould of a hide-bound ascetical routine. They are men of flesh and blood, but, more than that, they are endowed with rich gifts of nature and grace. They

58. See André Wilmart, OSB, *Auteurs Spirituels et Textes Dévots du Moyen Âge Latin: Études d'Histoire Littéraire* (Paris: Bloud et Gay, 1932) c. 12: "Les meditations réunies sous le nom de saint Anselme" (173-201). These passages of St. Ailred, attributed to St. Anselm, all come from the *De Institutione Inclusarum* and are among the excerpts printed below, chapters 47 to 88.[LXX]

59. "*Est quidem cibus parcior, vestis asperior; potus e fonte, somnus plerumque in codice*" (*Speculum* 2.17 [*PL* 195, col. 562D]).[LXXI]

60. *Speculum* 2.17-20 (*PL* 195, cols. 561D-570A).

are intelligent and sensitive beings. In fact, one might as well admit it, they are in some sense intellectuals. To be exact, they are men who have renounced an actual or at least potential intellectual career in the world in order to become contemplatives in the cloister. They have escaped the moral dangers that beset the professional intellectual but they have not, for all that, renounced the intellect as such. On the contrary, if they have left their bodies outside the gate of the monastery, they have not neglected to bring their minds inside with them. And, above all, they are not afraid to make use of their intelligence to settle the problems of the spiritual life.

It is really quite a refreshing experience to come upon St. Ailred's dialogue with his novice, after ploughing through some of the mediocre spiritual literature of a later date. The contrast is striking. How often spiritual direction and spiritual conferences have tended to become forbidding and unpalatable formalities! There are abstract categories of virtues to be practiced and vices to be avoided. There are "exercises" in which one is urged to disport oneself. There are "acts" to be made – and they are all formulated in the most deadly and inhuman rhetoric! Pious emotions are to be stirred up, almost arbitrarily, it seems, at certain times, on fixed occasions. In short, the spiritual life degenerates into a crushing routine in which the director or novice master takes his own favorite system – ready-made by some standard authority who is considered entirely safe for novices and nuns – and imposes it by main force on all those who have the misfortune to fall into his clutches. It is the kind of spirituality that is patterned on the bed of Procrustes of which we read in an ancient myth. Procrustes was a giant who captured people and threw them on a bed, to see if they fitted it exactly. If they were too short, he stretched them. If they were too long, he trimmed off what was excessive. By the time they fitted his bed the guests of this monster were no longer in any condition to sleep in it.

St. Ailred did not settle the difficulties of the spiritual life by formulas. Still less did he try to submerge the troubles of his subjects under a flood of emotion. Surely, there could scarcely be a worse way of settling problems than to stir up a tide of feelings that may, or may not, wash the sense of difficulty momentarily out of the way!

It must have been a relief for the novices of Rievaulx to find there a director who was not only capable of meeting them on their own ground and listening patiently to their problems, but who could also discuss them in the light of intelligence. Ailred's dialogue with his novice is a bright and animated conversation between two sensible and intelligent friends. The Master and the novice meet on equal terms because they are talking about something in which they both take a vital interest. It is anything but a matter of professional routine. Ailred's "method" is to let the novice, as far as possible, do his own thinking. Consequently he keeps stimulating him with questions whose answers will lead to the solution of his difficulty. But, in arriving at these answers by his own efforts, the novice discovers that he has acquired a whole arsenal of weapons for the spiritual combat. And Ailred knew that when the direction was over the novice would not immediately forget everything that had been said. The whole dialogue is full of friendliness and animation. You feel that the interlocutors do not merely confront one another, they actually *like* one another. They are not talking about the spiritual life simply because it is prescribed, or because spiritual direction is a process that belongs formally to the very essence of the religious life: they are talking about God because they love Him, and they are trying to find out ways of loving Him that are more genuine and sincere.

And here again we come upon that characteristic Cistercian passion for Truth. It is precisely this that gives such intense vitality to Ailred's spiritual direction: this ardent and consuming hunger to get at the heart of the matter, to find the "real thing" in the spiritual life, is what enlivens the interest of both the Master and the novice. Both are looking for the truth. When you talk about the love of God, what do you really mean? What are the signs of the genuine love of God? What is its essence? How do you arrive at it? And since, of course, the ultimate end of the Cistercian life, as of all religious life, is to arrive at perfection by loving God with your whole heart and your whole mind and all your strength, the question is anything but academic: it concerns the whole reason for their existence. Upon the answer to this question depends their religious vocation and their faith and their life itself. No wonder then that their conversation is animated!

A glance at this dialogue in the *Speculum* and at the characters in that longer dialogue on Spiritual Friendship shows us at once that it was not a simple matter to satisfy the restless and sometimes tortured thirst for truth that burned in the minds of these brilliant young men that came to the novitiate at Rievaulx. The passion for truth brings with it a correlative mistrust of falsity and Ailred's novices were apt to be haunted with suspicions and doubts and questions. They wanted to test everything, and pass all things through the sieve of their own keen judgment. But when they had been for a few months in the cloister, their tendency to question and analyze became for them a source of the most acute torture. God soon led them into the darkness of that night which is the threshold of contemplation, and in which the soul must learn to walk in the darkness of faith rather than by the light of reason. And so, when these bright young Cistercians turned inward and set about analyzing their interior lives and passing judgment on the things that were going on inside them, they found that their analysis did not seem to work and that their judgment did not give them any satisfactory answer to their questions. Troubled and haunted by their questions, they would go to their novice master, whose task it was to teach them to travel by paths unknown to them and judge, not by the flesh, for the prudence of the flesh is death, but by the higher standard of the spirit, for "the sensual man perceiveth not these things that are of the spirit of God, for it is foolishness to him and he cannot understand, because it is spiritually examined. But the spiritual man judgeth all things."[61]

Ailred of Rievaulx had a special gift for dealing with the fearsome difficulties of intellectuals in the cloister. And together with this gift, he had another, which was more important: he had an almost infinite patience with them, because he loved them and understood them and knew that all the doubts that seemed like useless subtleties to the mere athletes and efficiency experts of the cloister, were, as a matter of fact, matters of searching and secret pain. These gifts were shared by other Cistercian theologians of the time. In William of St. Thierry, too, we find this tenderness and this understanding for the special problems of young intellectuals in the contemplative life. He must have been a godsend to some of the novices of Signy who had been upset by some of the new trends of thought that had been started by

61. 1 Corinthians 2:14-15.

Peter Abelard. Abelard's heretical conception of faith as a matter of opinion rather than certitude destroyed the very foundations of the contemplative life.[LXXII] When some books by Abelard's disciple William of Conches found their way to Signy, and filled the young monks with doubts that were "more painful than they were dangerous"[62] William of St. Thierry set to work to discover the true nature of faith. What was really meant by faith? What sort of experience was true faith? What certitude did it give concerning the Truth of God? In other words, it was the same Cistercian passion to calm doubts by finding the "real thing."

However, if Ailred of Rievaulx was able to penetrate and solve the spiritual problems of intellectuals, it was not by his intellect and by learning that he did so. His success was not a matter of mere brilliance. He was not a professor. Walter Daniel, himself one of those who had come to Rievaulx from the schools to be formed by Ailred, has left us a penetrating analysis of the saint's mind, contrasting him with the mere scholastic.

Ailred had, indeed, natural gifts of a higher order, *animam ingeniosam acceperat et habebat*,[63] but his wisdom was something that went far beyond the erudition so laboriously acquired in the schools. He was acquainted, no doubt, with the secular and classical authors who were causing so much excitement in twelfth-century Europe, but he had never entered deeply into them. He had no need of the elaborate and rather unwieldy machinery that encumbered the schools of his day, still waiting to be delivered, by a St. Thomas, from the dead weight of cumulative classification that was content merely to sort out the pronouncements of the Fathers and philosophers and the allegories of Scripture and arrange them in categories, without putting them to work. For his own part, Ailred proceeded by a higher light and his wisdom pierced to the heart of things without difficulty because his judgments were regulated by something higher than reason. He had arrived at the personal and intimate contact with Truth Itself, with the Word of God, *ipsa veritas*. Without hav-

62. See the Preface to the *Epistola ad Fratres de Monte Dei* (*PL* 184, col. 308A).[LXXIII] William's books on faith are the *Speculum Fidei* and the *Aenigma Fidei*.
63. Walter Daniel, "*Vita Aelredi*" (Powicke, "Ailred of Rievaulx and His Biographer Walter Daniel" 500).[LXXIV]

ing to proceed by all the difficult and tortuous paths of human learning he had arrived, in contemplation, at the possession of Truth not merely as an intellectual certainty but in the wholeness of an experience that called into play all the deepest powers of his being. His whole soul was united with Christ, Who, as the Word of God, contains in Himself supereminently all the truths which are the objects of the various sciences.[64] One of the tests of a true contemplative is his simplicity. A contemplation that expresses itself in an elaborate and subtle and peculiar system of thought, involved and complex and laborious to unravel, is always suspect. The true mystics, although they may speak and think and live on levels that are beyond the reach of the average man's understanding, are always essentially simple. Their view of truth is never complex, always unified. They see things as a whole and they do not need any complicated apparatus to support them. Ailred too, says his biographer,[65] was not one to obscure the truth under a flood of useless words or subtle concepts. But at the same time, Ailred did not make an affectation of rusticity either. He was too simple for such folly.[66] He spoke eloquently and clearly. His style is fluid and impassioned and his words ring with conviction. Every line he writes is alive and supple. He never encumbers his thought with the useless trappings of pedantry. He is never self-conscious enough either to show off or to be artificially bashful. He is too absorbed in what he has to say. Walter Daniel can sum up Ailred's whole character as a writer and as a Cistercian in the telling phrase *approbans puram et meram veritatem.*[LXXVII] It is impossible to convey all the connotations of the Latin words in a translation, but the word *approbans* implies

---

64. "*Et isti aristotelicas figuras et pitagorici computacionis infinitos calculos doctore indicante vix capiunt, iste autem* [*Aelredus*] *omnem numerum transvolans velocitate ingenii sui et omnem composicionem figure ficte vel facte supergrediens, ipsum intellexit in scripturis et docuit, qui solus habet immortalitatem ubi non est numerus et lucem habitat inaccessibilem ubi non apparet figura sed ipsa veritas que finis recte intelligitur universe doctrine naturalis*" (Powicke, "Ailred of Rievaulx and His Biographer Walter Daniel" 500-501).[LXXV] This is the technical language of mystical theology, concerning the experimental knowledge of God Who cannot be known, as He is in Himself, through the medium of any concept.

65. Powicke, "Ailred of Rievaulx and His Biographer Walter Daniel" 501.[LXXVI]

66. The Latin of Ailred's Sermons, in the text we now possess, is certainly extremely "rustic" but they are probably nothing more than literal translations into Latin of sermons that were originally preached in English.

that Ailred had reached possession of Truth in its purity and simplicity in the savor of immediate experience, and that henceforth nothing else could divert him from the vision.

What was the formation Ailred gave his novices? We shall see all that in greater detail further on, in our analysis of his works and especially in the translated selections taken from them. Suffice it to say here that the second book of St. Ailred's *Speculum Caritatis* contains, in substance, the same teaching as St. John of the Cross's *Ascent of Mount Carmel*. It is summed up in St. Ailred's Chapter on the true love of God[67] which reproduces the basic thought of the asceticism of St. John of the Cross: "God only permits and wills that there should be one desire, where He is, which is to keep the law of God perfectly and bear upon oneself the Cross of Christ."[68] And the reason for this is that the perfection of the mystical life (and of the whole Christian life, by that very fact) is a perfect union of wills with God which excludes the smallest voluntary attachment to anything less than God. St. John of the Cross describes the union to which all his writings strive to lead souls: "The state of this divine union consists in the *soul's total transformation, according to the will, in the will of God, so that there may be naught in the soul that is contrary to the will of God, but that, in all and through all, its movement may be that of the will of God alone*. It is for this reason that we say of this state that it is the making of two wills into one – namely, into the will of God, which is likewise the will of the soul. For if this soul desired any imperfection that God wills not, there would not be made one will of God, since the soul would have a will for that which God had not."[69]

St. Ailred says the same thing in his own words. After chapters that describe the futility of attachment to the consolations of prayer in language that anticipates the *Ascent of Mount Carmel*, St. Ailred goes on to say that perfection is not to be found in states and experiences of soul but in the union of the will with God. "*Suam enim voluntatem Dei voluntati coniungere ut quaelibet voluntas divina praescribat, his humana voluntas consentiat,*

67. *Speculum Caritatis* 2.18: "*In quibus amorem Dei stare credendum sit*" (*PL* 195, cols. 566B-567C).[LXXVIII]

68. *Ascent* 1.5.7 (Peers, *Complete Works of Saint John of the Cross* 1.33).

69. *Ascent* 1.11.2-3(Peers, *Complete Works of Saint John of the Cross* 1.52).[LXXIX]

ut nulla sit alia causa cur hoc aut illud velit, nisi quia hoc Deum velle cognoscit: hoc utique Deum amare est."[70] And St. Ailred goes on to point out that he is not speaking of a mere moral union, but of a mystical transformation operated in the soul by the Holy Spirit. "*Quae tunc fit cum Spiritus Sanctus, qui utique Dei voluntas et amor est, et Deus est, humanae se voluntati ingerit et infundit, eamque ab inferioribus ad superiora sustollens, totam in sui modum qualitatemque transformat, ut ei indissolubili glutino unitatis cum eo adhaerens unus cum eo spiritus efficiatur.*"[71]

Ailred was not long novice master at Rievaulx. There were other and more important jobs for him to do.

In 1142, William de Roumare, Earl of Lincoln, applied to the Abbot of Rievaulx asking for a colony of Cistercian monks to be sent to Lincolnshire to found a new monastery. Ailred was chosen as its superior. But it must not be imagined that he and his twelve companions (it was always customary to send twelve men and a superior to new foundations) simply left Rievaulx and went to Lincolnshire to sleep under the stars. Perhaps one or two of their number were sent on ahead to supervise the construction of a temporary monastery by secular workmen. This would be a group of wooden buildings which had to contain the bare minimum of "regular places" required for the normal life of a Cistercian monastery. A Statute of the General Chapter[72] defined explicitly what these "regular places" were: a chapel, a refectory, a dormitory, a guest-house and a porter's lodge, besides the necessary farm buildings that would be needed if the monks were to make their living, according to the rule, by tilling the fields and raising livestock. The site chosen was about twenty miles from Lincoln, the seat of the diocese. There was already a church on the property, dedicated to St. Lawrence. This would no doubt serve as a temporary chapel and it gave its name to the abbey. All Cistercian monasteries were dedicated to the Blessed Virgin Mary. When a saint came in for a dedication, the monastery was dedicated first to Our Lady, then to the saint. This new foundation became Our Lady of St. Lawrence, and went more commonly by the local place-name which was Revesby.

---

70. *Speculum Caritatis* 2.18 (*PL* 195, col. 566B).[LXXX]

71. *Speculum Caritatis* 2.18 (*PL* 195, col. 566D).[LXXXI]

72. *Instituta Generalis Capituli* 12 (*Nomasticon* 215).

Ailred left for the low, flat country where his new monastery was situated, with a couple of wagons containing the necessary baggage. Perhaps they brought a few cows along with them. In any case, the General Chapter prescribed that they must also have the books without which the regular life was impossible: a Missal, the *Rule* of St. Benedict, the psalter, hymnal, collectaneum (containing collects and other prayers of the office), lectionary, antiphoner and gradual.[73]

We know the identity of many of Ailred's community of twelve disciples. Under the leadership of the thirty-two-year-old abbot was first of all a priest called Henry, then one whom Walter Daniel calls Lord Gospatrick, forgetting that such distinctions are dropped at the gate of the monastery.[LXXXII] There was another monk who is named occasionally in the *Vita* as a witness of Ailred's miracles: he is called Ralph, and since Ralph was a common name, his nickname is added: Ralph "the short." The sub-cellarer of the new monastery was a relative of Ailred. His name is not mentioned. Finally there was one of Ailred's precocious intellectuals, a young monk whom Walter calls a *clericus scolaris*.[LXXXIII] This man was something of a problem child, and he remains as a witness to Ailred's patience and tenderness of heart. He was not one of those with whom Ailred's direction was successful. Agitated by the torments that afflict those who think too much and too emotionally, this young monk managed, by dint of constant interior argument, to keep himself always in proximate danger of leaving the monastery. He was always wavering in his vocation, and only the patient babying of his Abbot kept him in the cloister at all. Most superiors, starting for a new foundation, would have hesitated at taking along such a liability with them. Not so Ailred. He had a special love for this restless and tormented being. Aelred was convinced that this particular novice could not be saved outside the cloister: and perhaps he was right. The novice's weak and unstable character would not have served to defend him against the dangers of life in the world outside. In order to make sure of him, Ailred had prayed long and

73. *Instituta Generalis Capituli* 12 (*Nomasticon* 215). There is no mention of breviaries. The monks knew the psalter by heart, but the novices would need one in which to learn the psalms. The other books might possibly suffice for a small community, until others could be copied.

earnestly to God to strengthen the novice's vocation. The reason why Walter Daniel tells us the story of this wavering cleric in such detail is in order to show how, after many vicissitudes, Ailred's prayer was answered at last.

Already at Rievaulx the problem child had run away. He had first gone to Ailred and confessed he had made up his mind to return to the world. Ailred, according to the story, is supposed to have told him that he should not try to leave, because it would not be any use. The novice decided to leave anyway. He started out of the monastery, got lost in the woods and wandered about all day until finally, at sunset, he found himself back at the Abbey.

Ailred, as we have said, persuaded him to come to Revesby with the founders of the new monastery. A new foundation was hardly the place for a monk tempted against his vocation: difficulties would be multiplied and there would be many more temptations to take to the road. Ailred was counting on his own personal influence and his prayers to hold the restless *clericus*. Soon enough the temptation returned in full force. The young man came to Ailred and declared that he simply could not stand the Cistercian life any longer. There was not a detail of it that did not grate on his nature. The long hours of manual labor were too much for him, the long night vigils and the prayers of the office were a torture, the rough clothing made him itch all over and finally he admitted that he was convinced that the comforts and pleasures and affections of life in the world were necessary for him. Ailred offered to compromise and give him more delicate food, softer clothing, and all the mitigations that were compatible with the monastic life. "I wouldn't stay here," replied the cleric,[LXXXIV] "if you gave me all the money in the monastery."[74] Convinced that the young man was running straight to his damnation, Ailred replied with a vehement impulse of charity, declaring that he, in his turn, would not take any food until the cleric returned to the monastery. The young monk was not especially moved by this plea. He got his things together and made ready to leave. Meanwhile, the subcellarer, Ailred's relative, began to upbraid the Abbot for his foolishness. "What are you doing!" he

74. These details, contained in Walter Daniel, are omitted in Powicke's excerpts from the text of the *Vita*, but are found summarized in the life of Ailred by John Capgrave, cc. 1-2 (*PL* 195, cols. 199C-200C).

exclaimed. "You are going to go blind with your praying and weeping for this worthless wretch, and now, on top of everything else, you have made a vow to starve yourself to death for him."

"What is that to you," said Ailred, telling him politely to mind his own business. "Do not add to my troubles and sufferings. I am tormented in this flame, and I will die unless somehow my son is quickly saved."[LXXXV]

The unstable cleric got to the front gate of the monastery but, in the Capgrave version of Walter Daniel's story, even though the gate was wide open, he felt he had run up against a wall of iron. He could proceed no further.

No doubt some curious kink in the psychology of the *clericus scolaris* can explain this wall of iron: but in any case, Ailred's prayer was once again answered. However, now that we have found our way into the heart of this particular story and raised the issue of this wavering vocation: Walter Daniel's language in a later chapter suggests that, after all, the tempted cleric did finally become separated from the monastery. We see him, it is true, travelling with Walter Daniel's father (who was also a monk of Rievaulx before Walter himself) to visit a new foundation at Swineshead, in Lincolnshire, probably in 1148 or 1149. Swineshead was a daughter house of Furness, which had been a member of the Savignian congregation, recently affiliated *en bloc* with the Order of Cîteaux. Ailred had, by this time, returned to Rievaulx as its abbot and we are told explicitly that the party of monks was sent by him from Rievaulx to Swineshead to instruct the community in the Customs and Usages of the Cistercians. So far so good. There is nothing in this to indicate that the unstable cleric had lost his vocation, but quite the contrary. However, there are many suspicious phrases in Walter Daniel's account. First of all he begins the chapter by introducing the cleric as "the brother I spoke of above whose return to the world Ailred *delayed* [*retardavit*] by his prayer."[LXXXVI] If his return to the world was only delayed, then it afterward became an accomplished fact. The rest of the passage bears this out. Ailred has a dream. A "man of venerable visage" appears to him and tells him that "his monk"[LXXXVII] is going to show up at the monastery (with the party returning from Swineshead) at prime the following day. Ailred must see to it that the young man is brought into the enclosure and stays there, because in a few days this cleric is going to die unexpectedly, of a grave illness. This, of course, will be the final answer to Ailred's prayer. The wavering cleric will, at long last, end his career safe in the cloister. He will be saved.

The next day, at Prime, the *clericus* puts in an appearance at the gate of Rievaulx and asks for the Abbot to come out and speak to him. Ailred hastens to the gate, and begins to urge the new arrival to come in to the cloister, and join the community. But the *clericus*, with a smile, replies somewhat flippantly that he has no desire for anything so dull. He says he is going to visit his family and have a little fun at home for a while. Later he will return to Rievaulx. Ailred however persuades him to come in. After five or six days the "guest" falls ill. Powicke thinks that the word guest, "*hospes*," is not here being used in its precise sense.[LXXXVIII] The context makes this assumption seem very unlikely. If the *clericus* were really a member of the community, a monk in good standing, the word would never have entered Walter Daniel's head. Also, a monk in good standing would not call the abbot to the gate and interview him there. This is suspiciously like the modern procedure prescribed in the *Usages* for the reception of apostates or fugitives or those who do not have the proper monastic credentials.[75] On the contrary, however, a fugitive would be excluded from the community and received only in the guest house, unless the abbot wanted to take him back. Perhaps Ailred, in his anxiety to keep the monk at all costs, had given him as much rope as he could without losing him altogether and had allowed him to wander around outside the monastery without entirely severing his connections with it – a thing which is, needless to say, not encouraged by the General Chapter or the Holy See! But whatever the story may have been, it ended happily. The cleric fell ill, began having hemorrhages which would not be checked, and eventually died in the arms of his Abbot surrounded with all the consolations of religion.

The story is above all interesting to us for the light it throws on the gentleness and forbearance of Ailred's character. The man was so kind, so tender-hearted that many would have regarded him as perilously indulgent. We shall see later to what lengths he would go. There was no one wild enough, wicked enough,

---

75. *Constitutions* 42 (#185);[LXXXIX] cf. *Instituta* [1152] c. 16 (*Nomasticon* 216).

violent enough, ungrateful enough to be beyond the range of Ailred's forgiveness and forbearance and tender mercy.

Meanwhile, Ailred's foundation at Revesby was a great success. It attracted many vocations and grew rapidly. Ailred was increasingly busy, and developed multiple contacts with important people from the king of England on down. Already, too, men were beginning to speak of the Abbot of Revesby as a saint. Miracles were attributed to him and one of his monks, a simple and hard-working man, claimed that his paralyzed arm had been completely cured when he had made the sign of the cross over it and touched it with the pastoral staff of Abbot Ailred one day, taking it from the place where it was kept, just inside the door of the Abbey church.[XC]

7. *Abbot of Rievaulx.*[XCI]

Three years after the foundation of Revesby, Abbot William of Rievaulx died on the second of August, 1145. An aura of sanctity surrounded his memory with one or two beautiful legends and he is numbered among the Cistercian "saints." His successor was a quiet, mature contemplative, a man of learning and piety, deeply in love with the silence and humility of the hidden life, who accepted his election against the protest of all his own interior aspirations for solitude. This second abbot of Rievaulx was called Maurice, and he had come to the White Monks from Durham, where he had grown up from childhood in the sanctuary of St. Cuthbert, educated by the Benedictines whom he later joined as a monk.

Walter Daniel calls Abbot Maurice a man of great sanctity and wisdom. His profound learning and spirituality had earned him the reputation of being a "second Bede"[XCII] – which was high praise in the Yorkshire where the memory of the charming and erudite old Anglo-Saxon saint was still held in as high a veneration as St. Thomas Aquinas was to enjoy, in later days, in the whole Church of God. This Abbot was not a voluminous writer and of the little he wrote the greater part has perished. Perhaps his most important work was a treatise on the virtues of the monastic life, *Speculum Monasticae Religionis*. He wrote a poem on the interior life and a treatise on the same: the *Itinerarium Pacis*.[XCIII]

He also left some sermons and finally a few letters. One of these has been unearthed and reprinted in our own day, as a historical curiosity.[76] It is addressed to the future martyr, St. Thomas à Becket, the Archbishop of Canterbury. Becket had heard of Abbot Maurice's high reputation for sanctity, and, entering upon his perilous career, had gone to some trouble to get in touch with the Cistercian and ask a few words of advice and direction. Maurice, after the usual humble preamble, enters upon a sober moral exhortation in which he promises Becket the grace of a happy death if he will shun the vice of ingratitude. However, there is more to the letter than this platitude which history was soon to invest with such strange irony. Warning the new archbishop against the abuses in the political and ecclesiastical life of the time, Maurice of Rievaulx sensed that there was perhaps something providential in this election. And he wrote the following very impressive sentence: "Whatever may have been the intentions of men in thy promotion, who knows but that God hath granted thee the primacy of this Island in order that thy zeal for the house of Israel may now appear, and that thy industry remain not hidden."[XCIV] The Abbot had seen something deeper than had appeared to many men of the world, in the elevation of this court favorite to the primacy.

Maurice did not settle down comfortably in the Abbot's cell. He longed for the peace and retirement of the common life, the humble round of prayer, penance, labor and study, and so he resigned his office after two years in order to return to the community; *in claustro maluit consedere*.[77]

So, St. Ailred was elected Abbot of Rievaulx in 1147. He was thirty-seven years old.

Rievaulx was now one of the most important religious houses in England, and at this precise moment of its history, the Abbot of such a monastery was very likely to become a figure of some

---

76. F. M. Powicke, "Maurice of Rievaulx," *English Historical Review* 36 (January 1921) 26-29.

77. Walter Daniel, *Vita* in Powicke, "Ailred of Rievaulx and His Biographer Walter Daniel" 504. The words chosen by Ailred's biographer are significant. "He preferred to sit together with the brethren in the cloister."[XCV] The monastic community is the center and symbol of contemplation in a cenobitic Order.

prominence in the affairs of the realm. No doubt that was one of the chief reasons why the modest and contemplative Abbot Maurice had felt bound to retire. Rievaulx was certainly the leading Cistercian monastery in the country. Its position was strategic: it lay only a few miles from the Great North Road, the main artery of political and commercial life between England and Scotland, while at the same time it commanded the road to Carlisle and Galloway in the west. Furthermore, the Cistercian Henry Murdac was now archbishop of York, and had been put in that position by the Cistercian Pope, Eugene III.

A brilliant and capable young Abbot, with all the gifts of grace and nature that Ailred possessed, with all his connections, his favor with the Kings of both England and Scotland, and with the highest powers in his Order, and with the Pope himself, was doomed to greatness. Ailred accepted his fate without too much difficulty, not because he was essentially ambitious but because he was simple enough to take up, without complaint, a position for which everyone knew he was providentially fitted. That did not deliver him from ordinary trials that success automatically brings with it. Envious men made him the target of their calumnies and detraction. He was talked about, his motives were openly questioned, his integrity was suspected, and because he was important, people accused him of being ambitious and proud. As Abbot he would find that the ingratitude or the stupidity or the stubbornness or the eccentricity of some of the members of his community would give him plenty of opportunity to practice the patience and meekness which were so prominent in his dowry of virtues.

Even physically, the Abbey of Rievaulx had become a very impressive place. Many of the monastic buildings had now been completed; thanks to the energetic labor of the large community the construction had been unusually rapid. In scarcely fifteen years since the foundation of the monastery the huge bare nave of the monastic church had been finished. It was the first large Cistercian church in Britain, and was extremely powerful and severe, raising up its nine bays of plain, pointed arches and its clerestories of round-headed windows, and its barrel vaulting. No doubt the transepts and choir were nearly finished when Ailred took over the abbotship of Rievaulx. During his lifetime the monks would be working on the chapter house, which was already probably well under way, the "dorter" or dormitory, the "Frater" or refectory and all the other regular places around the cloister, which was finished in Ailred's prime because he speaks of it. The whole great Abbey was probably finished by the time of Ailred's death.

When Ailred rode down into the valley on his journey from Revesby he saw a far more impressive Rievaulx than the cluster of wooden cottages which had attracted him so powerfully a dozen years before. The clean stone of the new buildings stood out stark white against the dark green foliage of the woods that piled up on the hillside behind them. Green meadows sloped rather sharply down to the banks of the Rye, so that the abbey clung to the hem of the woods and was not orientated, as Cistercian abbeys usually were. The site did not permit it and the church ran north and south.

Otherwise the buildings followed the traditional Cistercian arrangement. The monks' dormitory was built as a prolongation of one of the transepts of the church, and was reached by stairs that led directly down to the choir. In the cloister was an *armarium* or small library and the Chapter House, the meeting place of the monks, where Ailred would preach to them on the *Rule* and on Scripture, where faults against the *Rule* were publicly acknowledged and punished, where sacramental confessions were also heard. Next to the Chapter Room was the *locutorium*, the place set aside for speaking. The Cistercian rule of silence, though not absolute, was very strict. Monks only spoke to the Abbot and Prior.[78] Speaking was never allowed in the cloister or in most of the other regular places. Work was distributed in the *locutorium* and if a monk wished to consult one of the major or minor superiors he would have to bring him there. There was generally another *locutorium* set aside for the Cellarer. Otherwise the superiors had no offices of their own.

Under the day-stairs to the dormitory was a dark, heavily vaulted little room which may have been the treasury at Rievaulx. This room under the day-stairs is generally found in all

78. "*tribus solum hominibus et hoc rarissime et vix de necessariis loquimur*" (*Speculum Caritatis* 2.17 [*PL* 195, col. 562D]).[XCVI] These words are spoken by a novice. The "third" to whom he could speak would be his novice master. The Cellarer could speak to the laybrothers.

Cistercian monasteries of the time and in many of them it served as a prison for monks who had to be excommunicated according to the provisions of St. Benedict's *Rule*.[XCVII]

Past the day-stairs to the dormitory was a passage leading from the cloister to the infirmary, which traditionally belonged outside the main group of buildings, at the "southeast" corner of the monastery. Due south, prolonging the eastern arm of the cloister, was a wing set aside for the novices who were kept apart from the professed monks during their time of probation. Along the "south" side of the cloister were the refectory and warming room (*calefactorium*). Here the monks found a big fire after the night office in winter time, and they could take refuge from the cold during short intervals, although they were still supposed to do their reading in the open cloister.

The ruins of Rievaulx have remained to stir the imagination of poets and painters and archeologists for centuries: but they tell us relatively little about the life of the community that flourished there under St. Ailred. For this we have to go to the saint's own writings.

Abbot William and the founders from Clairvaux had bequeathed to the third abbot of Rievaulx a remarkable community. It was, to begin with, a very large one. Already in 1142 the total had reached something like three hundred, as Ailred himself tells us.[79] With the passage of five years we can assume that it had grown considerably. The majority of the vocations were laybrothers and these did not all live at the abbey itself. They were scattered abroad in groups of two, three, half a dozen or more, at the granges or outlying farms which the Abbey maintained. Some of these were over twenty miles away. The brothers all came down to the Abbey for the big feasts, wearing their brown cloaks, and then Walter Daniel says that the far end of the nave, which was reserved to the laybrothers' choir, was so crammed with brown that it seemed to be swarming with bees.[XCIX] Before Ailred's death there were some six hundred laybrothers at Rievaulx.

But if the community of Rievaulx was large, it was, above all, fervent. The rich new life that was springing up everywhere in the Order and which flourished so powerfully in every part of

---

79. *Speculum Caritatis* 2.17 (*PL* 195, col. 563B).[XCVIII]

the Christian world was particularly strong in Yorkshire and at Rievaulx. The monks lived their hard and simple *Rule* and loved every detail of it. They embraced the fasts, the hard manual labor in the fields and on the construction gangs, the silence, the poverty, the long hours of prayer, the rough clothing, the subjection and obscurity, because they knew from experience that Christ was most generous in repaying those who were generous with Him. They had discovered the meaning of the Psalmist's words, "taste and see that the Lord is sweet," "*gustate et videte quoniam suavis est Dominus*."[80]

The secret of Rievaulx was the intensely supernatural spirit with which the monks had stripped themselves of proprietorship over everything that could stand between themselves and God. Above all, they had had the simplicity to abandon their own wills and give themselves entirely to the "Rule and the Abbot," as befitted those who, in St. Benedict's words, "no longer have power over their own bodies or their own wills."[81] Ailred's novice, in the dialogue which is set down in the *Speculum Caritatis*,[82] confesses that they have all willingly become as beasts of burden,[C] going without complaint wherever they are led and bearing without a murmur whatever burdens are placed upon them. The fruit of this strict regularity is that there is no place left for selfishness and no time for idleness and dissipation: *Propriae voluntati nullus locus: otio aut dissolutioni nullum tempus*.[CI]

Under these conditions – as St. Benedict had foreseen – the monastery became a paradise of order, harmony and peace in marked contrast to the world outside and even to the great feudal abbeys where more room was left for human nature to satisfy its appetites for pleasure and for power.

The twelfth century was astonished and edified at the democratic character of the early Cistercian monasteries where no attention was paid to wealth or titles and where the class distinctions of the world were abolished and lay buried under the unbleached wool of the Cistercian cowl. Rievaulx, when St. Ailred was writing his *Speculum*, was enjoying an altogether re-

80. Psalm 33[34]:9.

81. "*quippe quibus nec corpora sua nec voluntates licet habere in propria potestate*" (*Rule* c. 33 [McCann 84/85]).

82. *Speculum Caritatis* 2.17 (*PL* 195, cols. 561D-566A).

markable immunity from lawsuits and from all worldly disputes. And here, as the novice in the dialogue points out,[83] you heard nothing of the cries and complaints raised against rich, monastic landowners by tenants and serfs, for St. Alberic, in the first days at Cîteaux had swept away all the sources of income which would allow monks to support themselves on the labor of the poor instead of the work of their own hands.[84] If we are to believe the Benedictine historian, Orderic Vital, St. Robert had bitterly complained at Molesme that the monks were "living on the blood of other men,"[85] and this thought had been one of the main reasons for the secession to the marsh of Cîteaux. Everywhere in the monastery there was peace, tranquillity and the sense of liberation from the multiple tensions and conflicts of life in the world – a *mundalium tumultuum mira libertas*.[CIII] One of the things that most impressed the men who came to find peace of soul in this cloister was the thoroughness with which the common life was lived. Here personal poverty was absolute. No one owned anything for himself. Everything was held in common and this was not merely an economic figment, a pleasant abstraction. The fruit of their common labor was distributed among the monks and brothers (not to mention the guests, visitors, pilgrims and the poor of the district), according to each one's needs and not according to rank or ability or personal taste. And the greatest wonder of all was that in this vast household there seemed to be but one mind and one will because the judgment and desires of the abbot immediately became the thought and desire of the whole community. The monastery then was a miniature Mystical Body, and it fulfilled, in its harmony, the ideal that is the very heart of Christianity and for which Jesus had prayed to His Father on the night before His Crucifixion: "That they may be one, as thou, Father, in me and I in thee, that they may be one in us, that the world may believe that thou hast sent me."[86]

---

83. *PL* 195, col. 563A.
84. *Exordium Parvum* c. 15 (*Nomasticon* 62), tells in detail what reforms were made in this matter by St. Alberic. The monks renounced the income from tithes, serfs, manorial farms and public mills, as well as revenues from parishes.
85. Ordericus Vitalis, *Historia Ecclesiastica* (*PL* 188, col. 637B).[CII]
86. John 17:21. Ailred writes (*Speculum Caritatis* 2:17 [*PL* 195, col. 563AB]): "*Inter fratres tanta unitas, tantaque concordia ut singula videantur omnium et omnia singulorum. Et quod me miro modo delectat, nulla*

And that, as we have said, was the principal attraction which the Cistercian monasteries exercised over the men of their time. One felt that here, in the common life of the cloister, with all its poverty and labor and humility, was to be found the perfect form of Christian asceticism, and an ideal of Christian living which contained the essence of the perfection that was taught in the Gospels and in the writings of the Fathers and exemplified in the lives of the old monastic saints.

That such harmony and such concord were truly found in the huge Cistercian communities of the Order's golden age was, indeed, something of a moral miracle, because the White Monks were not very difficult about accepting vocations and they admitted all sorts of men into their cloisters, confident that the grace of God would make up for any human frailty or natural defect. Charity did, indeed, fuse a hundred different types and temperaments into a unified and peaceful organism and reduced the apparently irreconcilable oppositions between characters into a fruitful and harmonious unity where instead of conflicting with one another they complemented and completed one another.

Of course, it was not invariably so. The heroic spirit of faith with which St. Ailred could accept blindly every postulant who presented himself at Rievaulx without turning away a single one was all very well in a community that had a rich leavening of saints. But soon enough the proportion of saints became so small and the Order so huge that monks were no longer willing – or morally able – to pay the high price of heroism that was required to make a success of such a venture. When the fire of charity burned low and natural motives regained the ascendancy, Cistercian monasteries became, in their turn, the theaters of distressing scenes of violence and conflict which present a dark contrast to the bright picture of St. Ailred's Rievaulx. And even at Rievaulx, we shall see there were some extraordinarily difficult characters. It required the charity and patience of an Ailred to absorb them.

---

est personarum acceptio, nulla natalium consideratio. Sola necessitas parit diversitatem, sola infirmitas disparilitatem. Quod enim in communi laboratur ab omnibus distribuitur singulis, non ut carnalis affectus, aut privatus amor dictaverit, sed prout cuique opus fuerit. Quam illud quoque mirandum quod trecentis ut reor hominibus unius hominis voluntas est lex, adeo ut quod semel ex ejus ore elapsum fuerit tanta cura servetur ab omnibus ac si in id omnes conjuraverint, vel ab ipsius Dei ore audierint."[CIV]

Ailred himself speaks somewhere of the multitude of different types who came to his monastery. There were the intellectuals, as we have seen, with their subtle perplexities and doubts. There were also simple men who could neither read nor write, even among the choir monks. Some were sinners who had come to the monastery to break away from their old habits, and who had the whole campaign of the spiritual life to fight out, before them. Others came to the cloister in unstained innocence and appeared to be already saints – like Ailred's friend Simon. Some had been brought up in easy circumstances, and were used to comfort and good food and recreation. Others had had a hard life from the cradle. Some were quick-tempered, others naturally patient and quiet. They all had to be studied and treated according to their needs. For some, particular employments constituted a menace to their spiritual lives: you cannot wisely give a miser the job of cellarer, or put an impatient man in charge of the novices. Then, in spite of the high Cistercian ideal of charity, the price of peace would often be a prudent arrangement which would keep certain characters wisely apart at work or in the monastic choir. Some would need to practice fasting, others would have to be restrained and moderated in an unwise ardor for penance. Some would be called to quiet and contemplative prayer, others would need to work hard at laying the intellectual foundations for a sound interior life; some would profit most by vocal prayers, still others would need to spend time in meditation. The Abbot had to study them all and direct each one not only along some path that was good in itself, but along the right way for that particular person.

The sanctity of Ailred of Rievaulx was planted and rooted and grew into his being and bore fruit in the common life, and in the direction of souls. The Holy Ghost formed Ailred's particular sanctity by using him as a free instrument in the formation of other men to the spiritual life and Ailred's spiritual life was nourished above all by nourishing others. The soul of Ailred is the soul of a Father, a Physician, a Judge of spiritual problems. It is the soul of a Pastor, but in the particularly intimate and perfect sense in which an Abbot is the Pastor and Father and guide of souls that have been chosen by God for the highest of vocations. Ailred was to be sanctified by no common charity, but by the perfect charity which is capable of making its own every trial, every problem, not only of ordinary Christian life but of the perfect Christian life. His soul had to embrace and comprehend the deepest and most searching difficulties of the interior life, and he had to become "all things to all men"[CV] in a contemplative monastery where God draws men into the darkness of the most terrible of spiritual trials in order to purify them for immediate union with Himself.

Chosen for this terrifying task, Ailred realized the extent of his own helplessness to accomplish it without special graces and gifts from God. But in carrying out the work appointed to him courageously and patiently for twenty years he entered more and more deeply into the abyss of God's love and God's mercy, for he was able to contemplate, in the growth and transformation of the souls entrusted to him, something of God that He could never have experienced in any other way, even in the depths of the most perfect contemplative union with Him.

The *Oratio Pastoralis*[CVI] is one of the most beautiful and profound meditations ever written, and it searches the heart of Ailred's vocation as a director of souls. It shows to what extent he himself had become identified with the crucified Redeemer, for in the *Oratio* Ailred says nothing of a mere theoretical and impersonal guidance of men in the ways of the spirit. Far from merely passing judgment on moral problems and giving practical solutions, Ailred's conception of an Abbot's vocation was to spend himself entirely, pour himself out and give himself utterly to his community. He was to form saints not by merely talking to them in chapter, but by living and dying for them as Christ had lived and died for men. He understood the terrifying truth that is at the heart of the priesthood, in so far as the priest is a shepherd of men – a truth which a modern Pastor stated almost brutally when he defined the priest as "a man who is devoured." *Le prêtre est un homme mangé.*[87] "May my thoughts and my speech, leisure and labor, my acts and reflections, my prosperity and my adversity, my life and my death, my health and sickness and whatsoever else is mine: that I exist, that I live, that I feel, that I understand: let all be devoted to them and all be spent for them, for whom Thou Thyself didst not disdain to spend Thyself."[88]

---

87. Words of Père Chevrier, a French priest who worked among the poor in the slums of Lyons in the late nineteenth century.[CVII]
88. *Oratio Pastoralis* 7 (Wilmart, *Auteurs Spirituels* 294).[CVIII]

And there is more still. The ideal is not merely negative. Ailred is not simply allowing himself to be used up by his community as a martyr might have abandoned himself to the claws and fangs of the lions in the arena. Ailred did not merely look upon his monastery as a huge nuisance designed to sanctify his soul by preying on his mind and body twenty-four hours a day. It is hard for us to conceive how much St. Ailred loved his monks. True, there is something of this instinct in human nature itself and no inhumanity can wipe it out entirely. There are officers in armies who love their men; there are employers who love the workmen employed by them, and are loved by them in return – a state of affairs which is intensely embarrassing to those whose interest it is to have workmen hate the men they work for and which is gradually becoming impossible, in any case, under the stress of modern conditions. But Ailred loved his monks with an affection that was altogether unique. It was something born of grace. It transcended the natural order. And yet at the same time, it raised up all that was best in Ailred's nature along with it, and so it managed to be at the same time supernatural and most perfectly human. It was a love in which nature was not destroyed but intensified, ennobled and perfected by grace. And that is precisely what grace is meant to do. There is, therefore, an intensely human tenderness and warmth in Ailred's affection for his community. He can dare to speak of his love with expressions that confound us. They are a bit stark for our age which has reduced all talk about love to the narrow limits of two conventions: the one a sentimental one concerning mothers and children, the other more frankly passionate and concerning men and women. Outside these limits we see to it that love remains formally and conventionally – even melodramatically – speechless.

Ailred did not have our conventions to worry about, and in any case, this deep and consuming affection for the chosen flock confided to him by Christ was his vocation as it was to be his sanctity.

If he loved them all tenderly, Ailred was also to find certain ones in his community who, because they could meet him on a common intellectual ground and were capable of more fully sharing with him the fruits of the spirit, could be called in an even stricter sense his friends. Some of these had even been his intimates in the world. When he returned to Rievaulx to accept the abbatial crozier he found there one who had been his closest companion at the court of Scotland.

Waldef, we remember, had become an Augustinian Canon at Nostell in Yorkshire several years before Ailred entered Rievaulx. The Augustinian *Rule* was far less austere than that followed by the White Monks and it seems to have suited Waldef admirably well. He plunged deep into the interior life, and soon came to have more than a taste of mystical experience. At the same time, there was plenty of outlet for his talents. The Augustinians appreciated him very highly. He was appointed prior of Kirkham and when the time came to elect a successor to Archbishop Thurstan of York, Waldef was considered a very promising candidate.

Perhaps his very success among the Augustinians prompted him to turn to another Order in which he hoped he would manage to be hidden and obscure, in which he would have silence, solitude, and enjoy more freedom to pray and meditate and to rest in the silent companionship of God. But Waldef, of all Ailred's friends, was one of the most subject to doubts and hesitations. The decision to change from one Order to another was something he could not arrive at without torture, and once it had been made, he had to pass through a whole series of more terrible interior conflicts in order to stick to his resolution.

He wanted to embrace the austere life of a Cistercian but he seriously doubted whether his health would be able to stand such a life. In 1144 he consulted Ailred about the problem and it was decided that he should enter Wardon, the first foundation of Rievaulx, in Bedfordshire. The climate was milder there. The monastery was under the direction of Abbot Simon, who had been Ailred's Novice Master at Rievaulx. Another advantage was that it was further away from Kirkham. The Augustinians were deeply distressed at losing so promising a subject and they did not mean to let him go without a struggle.

However, there were other obstacles to his vocation. Waldef had relatives in Bedfordshire. A certain Count Simon, his cousin, was so enraged that he threatened *cum juramento terrifico* to descend upon Wardon and burn the place to the ground unless Waldef were sent away.[89] Such threats were by no means to be

89. "*Quod audiens, comes Simon germanus ejus ira totus incanduit et*

taken lightly in the Middle Ages.[90] It was at this very time that Fountains, in the north, was attacked by a party of men from York, followers of Archbishop William who had just been deposed through the efforts of St. Bernard and by order of Eugene III. They descended upon the abbey with drawn swords demanding the blood of Henry Murdac, the Abbot, whom they considered mainly responsible for the trouble that had befallen their Archbishop. Murdac managed to escape with his life but the Abbey suffered considerable damage. Besides, according to Jocelyn of Furness, Count Simon's character was well known at Wardon and no one at the little abbey seems to have had the slightest doubt that he would carry out his threat. The Abbot's private council had a meeting and decided that Waldef had better make for Rievaulx, which was out of Count Simon's reach. Meanwhile the Augustinians had brought their case to court contending that Waldef, as Superior of a monastery, had no right to walk off and join another Order. They held that he was obliged to remain with the community entrusted to him. However the case fell through and Waldef settled down to the life of a Cistercian novice.

He settled down, but not peacefully.

Waldef's first months of noviceship at Rievaulx were extremely difficult. He found the food disgusting, the clothing irked him, the work exhausted him, the Cistercian method of chanting the psalms seemed to him to be inordinately heavy and lifeless. The chant was exceptionally slow and grave and the pauses were drawn out to great length so that at the mediant of every psalm verse the monks kept silence long enough to say an *Ave Maria* or even a *Pater*. It made the night vigils long and, to the uninitiated, very tedious.

On the whole Waldef began to have intellectual doubts about the whole value of the Cistercian vocation. His problem did not merely present itself to him in the crude form of a desire to return, as the saying goes, to the fleshpots of Egypt. It was much more subtle. He began to ask himself if, after all, the discreet

---

illum sibi et cunctis amicis suis annuntians perditum, totique coenobio de Wardonia cum juramento terrifico consumptorium, si illum ulterius retineret, minabatur incendium" (Jocelyn of Furness, *Vita Waltheni*, *Acta Sanctorum Bollandiae*, Aug. 1, 258).[CIX]

90. See Knowles, *Monastic Order in England* 269-71.

Rule of the Augustinians, which knew how to temper austerity to the weakness of nature, was not a far better instrument for the salvation of souls. His problem seems to have been the same as that of Ailred's novice in the *Speculum* dialogue.[91] After all, he reflected, when he had been following the milder *Rule* of St. Augustine his mind had been more alert, his faculties had not been crushed under the burden of labor and fasting and he had consequently been able to pray better and think more intelligently and lead what seemed, on the surface, to have been a more fruitful and productive spiritual life. He had enjoyed greater freedom and tasted more consolations at prayer, while here he was travelling in a spiritual desert in which his mind was half-starved and his will was dying of thirst.

Ailred was far away at Revesby and could not explain to him the real nature of the problem which, in his case, probably contained generous elements of passive purification. The torment reached its crisis, however, and Waldef threw himself entirely upon the mercy of God, after which the strong tide of the Spirit carried him forward without difficulty through all the tight places that would be landmarks on his Cistercian journey.

Ailred found Waldef at Rievaulx when he arrived there as Abbot in 1147. But he did not enjoy his company there for long. In 1148 the Abbot of Melrose, Rievaulx's Scottish daughter house, had to be deposed and replaced. He had been too severe with his monks. Ailred could not think of a better Abbot to replace him than Waldef.

Then there was Walter Daniel, Ailred's biographer, than whom no one was closer to the Abbot, especially in his declining years. Walter Daniel figures in the dialogue on Friendship, and his peculiarly restless nature lends a little color to the discussions. He was to be Ailred's infirmarian in the Abbot's last illness, and Ailred finally died, not in a grim solitary struggle on straw and ashes but with his head in Walter Daniel's hands, the disciple having lifted him up tenderly to give him a little ease.

Walter was not one of Ailred's novices; Ailred brought him back to Rievaulx around 1150 after one of his expeditions to Durham, in the first years of his abbotship. Walter's father, Daniel

91. *Speculum Caritatis* 2:17 (*PL* 195, cols. 561D-566A).

senior, was already a monk at Rievaulx and a priest. He was a fairly important member of the community since Ailred sent him to Swineshead with a party of monks to teach that community how to live the Cistercian *Rule* when it came over to the Order from Savigny.

Walter Daniel was one of Ailred's precocious intellectuals. Professor Powicke is also inclined to think he was of knightly origin. Walter somewhere refers to his own father as "Dominus Daniel" which implies a secular social distinction. Professor Powicke goes into a charmingly incomprehensible genealogy of Walter Daniel, explaining that the name really meant Walter the son of Daniel, and he believes that Daniel, the father, was really Daniel the son of Walter of the Balliol fief in Cleveland, Yorkshire. This other Walter the father of Daniel and, as is abundantly clear, the grandfather of Walter, was in the company of the "great Bernard of Balliol, Lord of Balliol-en-Vimieu in Picardy, of Bywell in Northumberland, of Marwood, later Barnard Castle in Teesdale, and of Stokesley in the Cleveland district of Yorkshire."[92] Having progressed this far, Professor Powicke proceeds to cover our confusion by smearing Daniels all over us, exhorting us to remember that nothing was more common than Daniels in twelfth-century Yorkshire and calling to life a host of them from medieval cartularies. Finally, to cap his achievement, he tells us that there was another Walter Daniel, a contemporary of our own, who lived and flourished in Cumberland.

Walter Daniel was not a "Dominus" like Daniel Walter his father. He was a "Magister." That is to say he had been through the schools. He was a learned man and had received the licence to teach. He had compiled a book of *Sentences* but that must not be construed as one of those commentaries on the *Sentences* of Peter Lombard which were the usual prelude to the Master's degree in the thirteenth and fourteenth centuries. It is possible that Master Walter had received his degree at Oxford or even Paris, but Professor Powicke considers it quite sufficient to suppose that he acquired all his learning at some cathedral school like York or Durham.[CXI] Even there, he says, there was enough sophistication to account for Walter's familiarity with Porphyry and Isidore, Aristotle and Pythagoras.

---

92. Powicke, "Ailred of Rievaulx and His Biographer Walter Daniel" 314.[CX]

Walter's learning was not hidden under a bushel at Rievaulx. He wrote voluminously and probably taught theology. Leland, cataloguing the writings of the great men of England up to his own sixteenth century, gave careful attention to the volumes of Walter Daniel preserved at Rievaulx, until the dissolution. He calls Walter "almost the equal of Ailred" in learning.[CXII] He wrote books of theology and philosophy but they lack all the life and unction of Ailred's writing. His interests were those of his abbot, at least to the extent that he wrote a treatise of his own on Friendship. His interests were Cistercian, too, to the extent that he wrote on the Virginity of Our Lady and engaged in the controversy over the Immaculate Conception, replying to Nicholas of St Albans.[CXIII]

Master Walter also left a volume of letters, a treatise on one of the "burdens" of Isaias, after the manner of Ailred's own homilies on those obscure passages of the prophet. The most important surviving work of Walter Daniel, besides, of course, his life of Ailred, is the *Centum Sententiae*, a curious and rather pedantic compilation of texts and tropes and "flowers of speech" from Scripture, the Fathers and other approved sources. There is a show of systematization: the weighty thoughts are grouped together in twos, threes and fours under the most curious and fanciful titles which prove that there was no system at all and that the whole thing was an encyclopaedia of texts, arbitrarily grouped together perhaps in order to provide preachers with handy points of reference for their sermons. Some of the chapter headings read as follows:

> "There are three kisses. Of the first it is said: let him kiss me with the kiss of his mouth. Of the second Isaac saith to his son: Give me a kiss my son. Of the third, our Lord to Judas: dost thou betray the Son of Man with a kiss?"

> "There are three special kinds of dove: first and principally the dove which descended upon Jesus in the Jordan; second, that which brought to Noah, in the ark, a branch of olive; third that whose wings David sought after, saying: who shall give me the wings of the dove?"

> "There are three kinds of man. There are men who are prudent without the simplicity of innocence and there are simple men without prudence. There are also some who are simple and prudent together."

> "One Hebrew woman made great confusion in the house of King Nubugodonosor."[93]

Walter Daniel contrasted St. Ailred's intellectual and spiritual personality with that of the average scholar. He might perhaps have been drawing an unconscious comparison between Ailred and himself. He had the formal education and the acquired science which were mostly lacking to Ailred, but he seems to have enjoyed none of the infused and experimental knowledge of divine things that Ailred enjoyed. Walter Daniel seems not to have been a contemplative in the highest sense of the word. The mind of Master Walter was a busy and active and inquiring one, eager to get to the nature of things, and impatient of all obstacles to a clear understanding of the truth. His character was impetuous and sensitive, apparently not tempered by deep gifts of prayer which might have calmed something of his natural ardor which his own efforts were not altogether able to control. Ailred himself has left us a living picture of Walter Daniel at the beginning of the second book of the dialogue on Friendship. This second book was Walter Daniel's idea. He suggested that Ailred complete the short record of his answers, given years before to the questions of Yvo on the nature of Friendship, by some more thoughts on the qualities and advantages of Friendship. Ailred introduces the discussion by telling exactly how the thought was broached to him. He sketches the scene.[CXV]

The Abbot is engaged in conversation with secular visitors who have come to the Abbey on some business or other. These impulsive and powerful Norman soldiers or Saxon knights can be of great help to the monks, or can do them great harm. They must be treated with diplomatic consideration. One would like,

---

93. Powicke, "Ailred of Rievaulx and His Biographer Walter Daniel" 323, 325, 326.[CXIV] The *Centum Sententiae* is preserved at the John Rylands Library, Manchester, England, Latin ms. no. 196.

no doubt, to cut the conversation short and return to one's true vocation, the consideration of spiritual things. But this is not altogether possible. It is the "evil of the day," the *malitia diei* that St. Bernard lamented,[94] and which so often tears the Abbot from his monks or from the silence of contemplation.

Off in a corner sits Walter Daniel. He wants to see the Abbot. He has something on his mind and he is fuming with impatience at the delay. He turns his eyes this way and that. He frowns at the ceiling, vigorously rubs his forehead with his hands, scratches his head and twists his fingers around one another in a torture of impatience. He is bursting with an idea which seems to him to be of the highest importance and urgency. It is a plan which, if put into effect, will be, he thinks, of incalculable spiritual benefit. And here the Abbot, who is supposed to be the Father of the monks and therefore at their disposal, is whiling away his time with the stewards of Pharaoh. What is worse, Ailred seems to be distressingly, almost insultingly cool about it all. He does not seem to care about his monks. Perhaps he even prefers the company of these men of the world. In any case he is in no hurry to get rid of them.

It would be possible to read too much into the character of Walter Daniel, to attach too much importance to the gently humorous sketch of him drawn by Ailred. The effectiveness of such a sketch demands that certain features be slightly overdrawn and the surface defects of a monk, which often remain to plague him all his life, are not necessarily incompatible with real interior sanctity. Surely, if they had been so in Walter's case, Ailred would never have set them down on paper.

Walter Daniel's writing bears out Ailred's portrait. The *Vita Aelredi* was certainly the work of an impetuous, imaginative, enthusiastic mind, ardent and impatient, always ready to overtax words with a burden of meaning that words cannot seem to convey. Walter's style is tense and surcharged, and in his anxiety to make his statements carry conviction he is all too likely to exaggerate. Sometimes the pace becomes so rapid and the tone so shrill that the story turns into a parody of itself and the author is forced to account for its disproportions by becoming explicitly

94. *De Diligendo Deo* 10.27 (*PL* 182, col. 990D).

humorous. But he soon recovers himself and carries on with the same vehemence and energy.

In any case, we know that Ailred loved him, and even that he was one of those that the Abbot cherished with a special kindly affection. The quick, brilliant, impulsive character of this intellectual was also warm and loyal and affectionate and responded better to friendliness and kindness and sympathy than to any other treatment. Ailred loved such ones as these because he knew that they, above all others, needed friendship for their sanctification. If they were forced back upon themselves they would only become neurotics. Ailred realized that such types would not be taught peace by precept or tranquillity and recollection by sermons and admonitions. He wisely relied far more on friendly and informal contact which would permit them to absorb, unconsciously and without effort, the tranquillity and peace and calm which he himself possessed because it filled his own gentle and contemplative soul to overflowing. Ailred knew that it does no good to talk *at* some characters: it only upsets them to be constantly told what is wrong with them. What they need is to be listened to. And where you will only throw them into a greater turmoil by telling them that they ought to be more recollected, you will quickly pacify and calm them if you will listen to them peacefully and calmly yourself and show that you have some appreciation for the way they feel about things.

Ailred may have been criticized for being over-indulgent with his monks. But he was a wise Abbot. If he allowed a great latitude in the matter of silence, for instance, it was because he had a very deep appreciation for the real values of the spiritual life. He was called by God to form contemplatives: but he knew that you cannot force all men into a mould and clamp down the lid of the *Rule* and let them solidify under pressure.

There was no laxity in the actual observance of the rule of silence at Rievaulx, but Ailred seems to have been quick to dispense from that rule when his young monks gathered around him in dozens to talk of spiritual things and of the Cistercian life in particular. These gatherings seem to have been more or less general recreations in which everybody talked to everybody and no subject was barred except such filthy or uncharitable or unholy speech as is forbidden to every Christian.

Of course, one of the main reasons why Rievaulx was so big was that St. Ailred never refused anybody admission. He certainly did not look upon the Cistercian vocation as something restricted to a few "special souls." No one was too weak, too far gone, too much of a sinner, to be unworthy of the religious habit, and Rievaulx became the Abbey of which Walter Daniel said that "its greatest strength was its toleration of the weak."[95] He considered neither bad health nor bad habits an obstacle to admission. Candidates who had been refused by every other Order and every other monastery were accepted without question at Rievaulx. And they came from everywhere, even, as Walter Daniel says, "from foreign nations and from the farthest ends of the earth."[CXVII] Some even got in without Ailred's knowing about it, but he seems to have raised no more difficulty about them than about anyone else. Walter Daniel adds that in the seventeen years of his own religious life under Abbot Ailred, he never knew him to expel anyone outright – and with his community there must have been many opportunities for doing so. Only four monks, says Walter, returned to the world, more of their own volition than at the abbot's injunction. Of these, three came back to the monastery. One remained impenitent, outside.

It should not be necessary to say that no Cistercian abbot could get away with this in the present century. No matter how much he might want to expand the monastery's capacity to shelter the unfortunate, there is Canon Law to be taken into account, and not even Americans can get dispensations from every article in the Code! The mind of the Order in our day is much stricter than it was in the Golden Age or in the time of de Rancé.[CXVIII] The Cistercian Order is no longer the world-movement it became under St. Bernard of Clairvaux. It is, therefore, no longer regarded as a haven to which all Christians may and should fly to save their souls. More emphasis is being placed on the contemplative character of the Order, from which it should follow, at least theoretically, that very special qualifications are expected in anyone who tries to get into a Trappist monastery. A member of an austere penitential Order is normally expected to have good health and a fair physique. If he is a choir monk he ought to have enough brains to understand Latin and philosophy and theology and enough voice

---

95. "*Hic ergo domum Rieuallem fortissimam reddidit ad tolerandos infirmos*" (Powicke, "Ailred of Rievaulx and His Biographer Walter Daniel" 506).[CXVI]

to render an account of himself in the choir. Above all, contemplative monasteries have to be careful to weed out nervous or neurotic candidates who might be likely to crack under the strain of intense, silent, penitential community life. These problems do not seem to have been such a source of concern in St. Ailred's day: but they are in our own, and no matter how much one might like to imitate St. Ailred experience forces us to admit that the Cistercians, though by no means so exclusive as the Carthusian hermits, have a rather special and restricted vocation which is neither morally nor physically accessible to everyone who comes along.

There were monks at Rievaulx who did not hesitate to complain of Ailred's kindness. Sometimes they lost their patience with the less perfect monks, who were the fruit of so much mercy. Ailred would have none of this. He reproached the dissatisfied monks with his usual gentleness. "Brother," he would say, "do not kill the soul for whom Christ died. Do not drive our glory out of this house! Remember that we too are pilgrims on this earth, as all our fathers were, and that this is the supreme and singular glory of Rievaulx, that she has learned more than all other monasteries to bear with the weak and to compassionate with other men's needs."[CXIX]

Irresponsible as it may seem – and did seem to so many of his monks – Ailred's kindness was the kindness of the saints and of Christ Himself. It was a kindness, a mercy that went beyond human prudence because it was born of something higher and was regulated by an experience that transcended the arguments of reason. Ailred, the contemplative, arrived at his practical judgments in the government of his Abbey not merely by natural prudence but by a divine prudence which all too often seemed foolishness to the flesh. In the light and the spirit of Counsel, which is a Gift of the Holy Ghost, and under the impulsion of that other Gift, which is Knowledge, Ailred saw the souls of those who came to Rievaulx, seeking salvation, in the tremendous light of God's own mercy. His mystical union with the Holy Spirit had endowed him, as it were, with a higher interior sense which, enlightened by a supreme supernatural charity, apprehended all that these souls really meant to God, saw something of their value in His eyes, while other men could get no further than the outward accidents and peculiarities of human misery and imperfection.

Seeing, then, that these poor wayfarers might well be lost in the world, Ailred could not refuse them the great gift that Rievaulx could give them: that peace and protection and holiness without which they would never come to the vision of God. And Rievaulx became to all men the Mother of Mercy, the living symbol of the undying tenderness of God.

Everything, says Walter Daniel, was doubled at Rievaulx under St. Ailred. There were twice as many monks at his death as at his abbatial blessing. That meant there were close to seven hundred and fifty in the whole community, six hundred of them being those laybrothers who jammed the back of the Nave like bees in a hive on the great feast days. *Post se Rieualli reliquit monachos bis sepcies decem et decies sexaginta.*[CXX] He also doubled the number of laymen employed by the Abbey, doubled the abbey's lands, farms and all its property. But in spiritual things the growth was far greater still. *Religionem et caritatem triplicauit quidem.*[CXXI]

Ailred had to pay for his own kindness by an accident – one of many, no doubt – which was a heroic test for his charity and his faith. In his last years, when he was forced to live apart from the community in a little cottage built onto the side of the monastery infirmary, he spent most of the time in cold weather crouching over a fire. He was so far gone with arthritis and rheumatism and his other various sicknesses that he needed this warmth, not generally allowed to monks, for there were no permanently heated rooms in the monastery except the *calefactorium* where one was only allowed to stay for short intervals.

Walter Daniel gives us a vivid picture of the saint,[CXXII] sitting on a mat in front of the fire place with his head on his knees "like a crumpled piece of parchment."[CXXIII] One day when Ailred was alone, thus with his infirmarian, one of his less wisely chosen vocations came bursting into the cell, fuming with rage. The man was a huge bull of a fellow and was probably not altogether sane. Obsessed with some weird conviction that the Abbot was a hypocrite who pretended to be ill in order to indulge in luxuries that were denied to the rest of the monks, he proclaimed that the time for justice had come. He was sent to set things right, to expose the pharisee, and to carry out the divine sentence. He rushed on Ailred, picked him up mat and all and hurled him into the fire. Walter Daniel, who was no fighter, made a lunge for the giant and seized him by the beard; the maniac turned his attention to Walter the son of Daniel, the Master of Arts, and would have broken his neck without delay if some other monks had not heard the commotion and rushed in to put an end to it.

Ailred, brushing the ashes and sparks from his clothing, would not hear of them punishing his aggressor: he blessed the man and kissed him on the forehead and let him go his way.

8 – *Ailred and His England.*[CXXIV]

The history of St. Ailred's part in the public life of twelfth-century England is the history not so much of his activities as of his friendships. When he became a Cistercian he did not break all his ties with the world or forget those he had loved before he came to the monastery. Nor did he lose anything of the powerful attachment to his race and native land which made him so conscious of his English heritage. Ailred's love of England remained a force that dominated and molded his life and although he had given up all desire to play an active part in politics he found himself, as soon as he was abbot, in a position to exercise a very definite influence in the nation where he had become, almost in spite of himself, an important figure.

Yet we never feel that Ailred was a politician, even in the sense in which some of the great saints, who were statesmen, also had to be politicians. We do not even feel that he went out to battle, like Bernard, in favor of a definite policy, religious or otherwise, as the result of a preordained plan of action. Ailred's influence was above all religious, and it seems to have exercised itself more or less spontaneously. It was something that was radiated through the medium of friendship. It was a moral influence that he exercised on those he met in the course of the journeys imposed upon him by duty. It was part of the atmosphere he carried with him, not a conscious doctrine which he went about pumping into people. But it was nevertheless an influence.

Ailred had a definite attitude about English national affairs. It was an attitude that had been bred in him with the Christian faith and was so inextricably wound up with the religious instincts and convictions in which he had grown up, that his patriotism entered into his interior life. His love of England became another aspect of his love of Christ, and his "politics" became part of his life of contemplation.

This is not as fantastic as it sounds. For Ailred, as we have said, ceased to be a courtier and a politician in the strict sense when he entered Rievaulx. Nevertheless his well-defined "political attitude" which gave him a very conscious and definite set of ideas about the trend that English public life ought to take, remained with him and even developed and matured as his mind became more immersed in God. Ultimately Ailred's ideal for England was the same as his ideal for himself: an ideal of Christian perfection. His ideal of a free and autonomous and unified England, united under the royal line descended from Alfred and the Saxon Kings, a Catholic England praising God in justice and truth and sending up to Him the sweet incense of adoration from the great shrines of the English saints: all this corresponded to his own aspirations for interior peace and unity, the peace of the triple sabbath that delivers man from sin by asceticism and unites him to his neighbor in charity and leads to his absorption in God by contemplation.[CXXV]

Love of his nation and an active concern with the progress of its social and political life were therefore a harmonious element in the many-sided life of this English contemplative. It is true that he occasionally speaks of the distractions which unsettle the minds of monks in choir when they are too busy with the news and battles of the world: but here it is a question of mere restless curiosity about worldly events. The saint is discussing three types of profitless interior activity which can come under the technical heading of "concupiscence of the eyes"[CXXVI] and which make contemplation impossible. The first of the three is an inordinate love of secular literature. What he means by "inordinate" is quite clear from the examples he gives: it means preferring Horace, Virgil and Cicero to the Scriptures. This, of course, fills the mind with images which are not of great assistance in the contemplative life. The second form of vain curiosity is an inordinate concern with the conduct of the other monks and brothers in the monastery. A contemplative should know how to mind his own business. If he does not, he will pay for it dearly in rash judgments and interior restlessness. Finally, an undue curiosity about the news of the world will keep the monk's mind full of battles and politics when he should be engrossed in the psalms he chants in choir.[96] From these three sources, as well as from many others which he discusses at length, arise the useless interior activity, the "labor" and unrest which are the bondage of the children of Israel in the land of Egypt and are incompatible with the peace of the "Sabbath" – of mystical contemplation.

All this does not exclude a rational love of one's own nation. Ailred, like Bernard, found it impossible to embrace a life of contemplation that ignored and excluded the interests of Christian society in the world at large. The love of God does not exclude every other love; it is the summit of an order which includes and sublimates the love of one's friends, family, and nation and even of one's enemies and all mankind.

Ailred was never a politician in the sense that he became engrossed in policies of the moment, in movements and drives that involved the interests and ambitions of a few. But he was a politician in the broad sense in which every Christian not only may but even must associate himself with the political life of the world in which he lives: he was vitally concerned with the common good of his nation, with the preservation of the rights and benefits which ought to belong to the whole of society. Ailred never ceased to strive and pray for the peace and social unity upon which so largely depend the rights of individuals, of families, the rights of the Church, the rights of God Himself. These things must always be desired and fought for because they are the foundation of all social benefits and there is no order, no justice, no prosperity and no widespread social happiness without them.

Ailred does not theorize about the love of one's country in the third book of the *Speculum* in which he lays out the order of charity, and explains the relation of our love of friends, relatives, strangers and so on to the love of God. But the theory of his love of England is implicit in his theory of friendship and, as a matter of practical fact, Ailred's friendships and his politics and his religion were all part of the same whole and formed a unity that was, in practice, indivisible.

---

96. "*Regum praelia, victorias ducum, quasi sub oculis stultissima praesumptione depingimus, omnia regnique negotia in ipsa psalmodia vel orationibus nostris otiosis discursibus ordinamus*" (*Speculum Caritatis* 2.24 [*PL* 195, col. 573D]).[CXXVII]

In any case, and this is a very comforting thought, Ailred stands poles apart from the type of mystic who might evolve suspiciously complicated mystical theories of the "state" or the "nation." There are no wild allegories on this matter in Ailred's writings; his lively interest in the political life of England was always centered on concrete events and persons – above all on events and persons he personally knew. This concrete and practical character of his political attitude derived from the fact that it was all ultimately rooted in love.

Ailred's love of England was something that had been bred in him with his love of his own family. His earliest memories took him back to the days when his own deeply religious soul was awakening to three loves in the ruined shrine of the Saxon saints at Hexham: there was the love of Christ that controlled and dominated the others; there was the love of the people around him – of his family, his friends; and there was the love of England. The last love was not the love of a mere abstraction. It was a spontaneous extension of his love for his father and mother and brothers and sisters and friends, which went on from them to embrace all the others like them in this land that was desperately fighting its way back to peace and order after centuries of devastation. The love of England rejoined the love of God in Ailred's burning devotion to the Saxon saints, the patrons and protectors of England, first the saints of Hexham, then St. Cuthbert the patron of the North, and finally, in his mature years, St. Edward the Confessor, the ideal of English Kingship.

Since those early days when he had awakened to the misery and distress of a land that was still half in ruins and was so slowly recovering from centuries of barbarian invasion, Ailred had believed with unwavering firmness that it was God's will to bring England back to life, to deliver her from invaders and usurpers, strengthen her against her enemies, unite her under an English king, gather her people around His Churches to praise Him in peace and plenty at the shrines of the English saints. And as he had grown up he had seen all this being realized.

The union of politics and contemplation was something that was all the more easily effected in the mind of St. Ailred, as he grew up to manhood, because it had become natural to him to think of sanctity as something one might reasonably demand in a King. He had been brought up at a court which was still feeling the influence of a Queen who was a saint. David himself was a deeply religious King. And then, in the line of the rightful Kings of England, there were Edward and Alfred, saints also. When a man spontaneously turned to his national saints in heaven and expected, as an answer to his prayers, a sainted King and protector to be sent to rule on the earth and deliver England, one would hardly expect him to think of politics and religion as opposed to one another. Although Ailred was just as aware as anyone else of the sad corruption in political life, he was not inclined, as we perhaps are today, to think of politics as an unmitigated evil. He was not, and could not be, the kind of contemplative who feels in his bones that all statesmen are children of the devil and that the halls of government are but the antechamber of hell. In our century the temptation to such pessimism may, at times, be strong. For Ailred of Rievaulx, living in a world that was, for all its evils, more than nominally Christian, this never became a serious difficulty.

Whether his optimism was altogether well-founded is another matter. His political ideal was abstractly sound enough. It rested on principles of faith that cannot be questioned by a believer. But in concrete fact Ailred's politics turned out to be insufficiently realistic. Ultimately they were based on personal friendships. At the center of Ailred's politics was his love for King David of Scotland, one of the dearest friends of his youth. David united in himself the advantages of being one whom Ailred personally loved, and of belonging to the royal line of Kings to which Ailred looked for the salvation of England. The fact that David conferred the order of knighthood on Henry of Anjou, and the fact that Henry stemmed, through his mother the Empress Matilda, from the Queen St. Margaret and through her from St. Edward, made Ailred see in him the hope of England before he became king. And when Henry of Anjou became Henry II of England, Ailred seems to have felt that his dreams were at last coming true. He certainly enjoyed the friendship and confidence of Henry, both as Duke and as King, and he made use of this advantage to urge him, with serene expectancy of success, to follow in the footsteps of David of Scotland and Edward, the saint, his ancestor. He must have known Henry well enough, however, to have had a shrewd suspicion that he would never be another David, but he seems to have had no inkling that this monarch, before his reign was done, would be scourged at the tomb of the martyred

Thomas à Becket whom his henchman had killed. Ailred himself was in the tomb under the stone floor of the Chapter House at Rievaulx before the terrible rift between Church and King tore apart his hopes for a perfectly and peacefully Catholic England.

Meanwhile, when King Stephen of England died in 1154 and Henry of Anjou ascended the throne in his stead, England certainly entered upon years of peace that were a great relief after the chaotic reign of Stephen. Henry was the first English king since the Conquest who could claim direct descent from King Alfred. The Canonization of St. Edward and the translation of his relics in 1163 symbolized the new unity of England, regained in Henry of Anjou in whom the Norman and Saxon lines were joined. Ailred, who had written a Genealogy of the Kings of England[CXXVIII] and dedicated it to Henry of Anjou shortly before Stephen's death, now published his *Life of St. Edward*,[CXXIX] which could almost be said to have had an official character, inspired as it was by Ailred's kinsman, Abbot Lawrence of Westminster. Both of these historical works celebrated the same theme: the union of Saxon and Norman and the rebirth of old England under Henry of Anjou. Ailred had been commissioned, so to speak, to write an official commemoration of these great happenings. He was present at the translation of St. Edward's relics, which had all the characteristics of a great patriotic festival, when the bones of the sainted King were removed to their more splendid tomb in the apse of Westminster Abbey. Ailred preached the sermon in the Abbey, and also played an important part in the Council of Westminster held at the same time.

The Canonization of Edward had been a favor granted to England by Pope Alexander III in return for Henry's official recognition of him as the true pope, against the antipope Octavian. This, too, had been the work of Ailred of Rievaulx. It was his personal influence that had finally swung the king and all England with him, to Alexander. The festival of St. Edward's translation was, then, the high point of Ailred's public career, and it must have been in some sense a personal triumph in which he could taste, three years before his death, deep satisfaction and gratitude in the thought that England and all Europe were at last enjoying religious peace. He could not have realized how short-lived it was all to be. But the prelate who officiated at the translation that day was the new English primate, Thomas à Becket, the king's former chancellor: and his resignation of the chancellorship had been the first evident sign of the differences that had already so deeply embittered the archbishop's old friendship with his King.

As far as Ailred's own part in all this is concerned, he had contributed all he could to the peace and unity of England by keeping the King in union with the true Pope and with the Holy See. This was the crown of a long career as peacemaker. Ailred's public life, outside his own Cistercian Order was a career of arbitration. He was one whom all could trust and appeal to in the settlement of disputes and it is high honor to him as a monk that this should be the place he came to occupy in the world of his time. The tradition of the Fathers has always associated the beatitude of the peacemaker with the wisdom of the contemplative[97] and Ailred's work as a reconciler of differences is a fitting outward expression of the Sabbath of mystical peace which was the atmosphere of his own soul.

We have said that the record of Ailred's achievements in the public life of twelfth-century England is the story not so much of his activities as of his friendships. The secret of his influence is friendship which brought him into contact with so many people who spontaneously thought of him in their problems and turned to him for help and advice. For the rest, his intervention was mostly in religious affairs, and not in those of a purely political character and he acted only when he was called in by others so although he was an influence he cannot be said to have had a public career. And it was precisely because he was so evidently not a man of a career that he was called in to arbitrate in the innumerable difficulties that arose out of the conflicting ambitions of those who were. He was a contemplative and so, essentially neutral.

But if he was a contemplative, how did it happen that he was so often out of his monastery? How did it happen that he knew everybody of importance in the England of his time, assisted at councils, advised the King, visited and consulted with Bishops and Abbots and secular princes and was welcomed and loved everywhere? Why did he not keep to his monastery?

The duties imposed upon a Cistercian Abbot by the fundamental constitutions of the Order made it impossible for Ailred to

97. See St. Augustine, *De Sermone Domini in Monte* 1.3 (*PL* 34, col. 1234).[cxxx]

remain all the year round at Rievaulx. According to the prescriptions of the *Carta Caritatis*[CXXXI] he was obliged to come each year to the General Chapter at Cîteaux. He had to pay an annual visit to his motherhouse, Clairvaux, and he had to visit yearly each one of the monasteries founded from Rievaulx. This meant that some three or four months out of every year, if not more, had to be spent in travel.

When the snow melted on the moors and green buds began to appear on the forest trees and the monks were plowing the fields, Ailred usually started out on horseback, with one or two laybrothers and a monk perhaps as secretary, and headed for his northern foundations. There were two of them. The first was Melrose, where Waltheof was abbot: it was near enough to Edinburgh to involve Ailred in an occasional appearance at the Scottish court. Melrose was the most important Cistercian abbey in Scotland, and was already founding daughter houses all over the land. Ailred was there when Waltheof refused the bishopric of St. Andrews, which would have made him the most important prelate in Scotland. This was in the early summer of 1159. Ailred had urged his dear friend to accept this offer but Waltheof refused because he knew he was shortly going to die which, in fact, he did, on the third of August that same year.

Rievaulx's other foundation in the north was Dundrennan, over in the west in the wild country of Galloway. Dundrennan was always a poor little house, and never poorer than in the early days when Ailred had to visit the monks in the cottages of their temporary monastery and assure himself that they were keeping the *Rule* properly and not sacrificing the spiritual life to the struggle for a material security and progress – always a great danger in new foundations. Although founded in 1142 by King David, Dundrennan was still so poor in 1165 that Ailred slept in a cottage with a leaky roof: and Dundrennan is in a region where the rainfall is high. The bed where Ailred slept was usually drenched, but according to Walter Daniel, although there was a heavy storm the night Ailred slept there, not a drop fell on him.[CXXXII] This immunity from rain is a traditional Cistercian "miracle." Abbot William, the founder of Rievaulx, is accounted, by a legend, to have written a letter for St. Bernard outdoors in a shower of rain without a drop having fallen on the parchment.[98] No doubt Divine Providence decided to spare the rheumatic abbot Ailred this trial since he had so many other troubles as it was.

His relations with his daughter houses were not always of the smoothest. Walter Daniel records that the abbot of one of them came to Rievaulx on his statutory visit and lost his temper with Ailred.[CXXXIII] He proceeded to revile and calumniate him with great bitterness, and on his return home he soon died in a manner which Walter Daniel regarded as a just punishment. This abbot seems to have been Philip of Revesby.[99] The superior of Dundrennan in Ailred's time was another of the numerous Walters we have to contend with in this history. He was the former sacristan of Rievaulx and had been one of Walter Espec's chaplains before entering the monastery.

Ailred probably took in his southern foundations on the way to the General Chapter. That would mean that on his return from Scotland in June he would have a short rest at Rievaulx and then proceed southward along the Great North Road to his own foundation of Revesby in Lincolnshire. From there he would go to Rufford (founded in 1146) and to Wardon in Bedfordshire where his friend Yvo had died and Simon, his former novice master, was also probably buried by now. It was here that Waldef had made his first attempt at the Cistercian life.

By this time Ailred was within range of the English court and the world of affairs at London and Westminster. His passage through the capital would involve him in many visits and interviews, the chief of them being audiences with the King, with the Earl of Leicester, later on with the great Gilbert Foliot, bishop of London, who would have been the logical choice for primate if Henry had not replaced Theobald as Archbishop of Canterbury, by his Chancellor and favorite Thomas à Becket in 1161. Perhaps at London, or between London and one of the channel ports, a whole group of Cistercian abbots would form and travel on together to Burgundy for the General Chapter. There were certainly enough of them on their way to Cîteaux. Besides the abbots of his own monastic family who would almost certainly be trav-

98. See *Exordium Magnum Cistercii, Distinctio* 3.9 (*PL* 185, col. 1061A).

99. Powicke, "Ailred of Rievaulx and his Biographer Walter Daniel" 461.[CXXXIV]

elling with Ailred by now, there was Richard of Fountains, almost as prominent as Ailred himself. Richard's foundations were mostly gathered around him in Yorkshire and Northumbria but he already had a daughter house and a granddaughter house in Norway, and visitations to Norway were to prove something of a problem for the Abbots of Fountains in years to come.[100]

Waverley did not lie exactly on their way to Dover and most of the houses of Waverley's family were in the west. But there were still a score of Cistercian abbots coming in from the Shires and the home counties as well as those of the former Savigniac houses so plentiful in Yorkshire and the north. In Ailred's time, England, Scotland and Wales would send between fifty and sixty abbots to the General Chapter each year.

Many of these Cistercian Abbots were the best friends Ailred had, outside his own monastery. The General Chapters of the Order of Cîteaux can boast, in general, that they have always preserved something of the atmosphere of warm fraternal charity which St. Stephen Harding was so anxious to impart to his new religious family. The meetings of the Cistercian Abbots gathering from all parts of the world, were often so light-hearted in the Middle Ages that the Chapter had to enact a statute prohibiting the abbots from wandering gaily around the nearby city of Dijon arm in arm.[101] It is easy to understand that they were glad to see one another: they were members of a monastic family whose rapid growth had scattered monks from a few monasteries to every quarter of Europe. Men who had been novices together at Clairvaux or Morimond or Pontigny were apt to find themselves Abbots in England, Italy, Norway, Spain, Germany, Belgium, Switzerland, or even as far afield as Hungary and Silesia and Palestine.

---

100. Fountains founded Lysekloster in Norway in 1146. In the following year Kirkstead, a daughter house of Fountains, in Yorkshire, also sent a colony from Yorkshire to found Hovedo. The Abbots of both monasteries were penanced by the General Chapter for failure to visit these foundations in person. See *Statuta* 1210[CXXXV] and Knowles, *Monastic Order in England* 658.

101. J.-M. Canivez, ed., *Statuta Capitulorum Generalium Ordinis Cisterciensis ab Anno 1116 ad Annum 1786,* 8 vols. (Louvain: Bureaux de la Revue d'Histoire Ecclésiastique, 1933-41) 1.88 [1181.5].[CXXXVI]

For such as these, Cîteaux was the scene of very happy reunions. Ailred was naturally on very intimate terms with the other Cistercian abbots of Yorkshire. He had a deep respect for Henry Murdac, the former abbot of Fountains who had become Archbishop of York and when Henry died in 1153 Ailred was quite willing to attribute miracles to his intercession. However it is not likely that Ailred's relations with this stern disciplinarian and austere reformer of churches and monasteries were as warm and intimate as was, for instance, his love for Waldef. A much deeper bond of sympathy must have united him with the profoundly contemplative Abbot Gilbert of Hoyland, or Swineshead, the only other English Cistercian whose writing measures up, with Ailred's, to St. Bernard's high standard. When Ailred died, Gilbert of Hoyland interrupted his mystical commentary on the Canticle of Canticles to praise the great Abbot of Rievaulx.[CXXXVII] Gilbert's eulogy is not a mere formality. It is written in the accents of deep personal affection and esteem. Gilbert had observed Ailred's qualities at close range, for he had frequently been present at those altogether unique sessions in the dying Abbot's *turgurium*, when the monks had gathered about him to talk of spiritual things. He had been overwhelmed by the contrast between Ailred's poor broken body, dried up by suffering, and the calm, rich vitality of his soul. He had seen, above all, the mighty peace which elevated this contemplative above the agitation of his eager disciples, the supreme simplicity and humble self-possession which marked him out as different from all the rest – as one who breathed a higher spiritual atmosphere. He had heard Ailred's pure and impassioned eloquence as he spoke of the love of Christ and urged his Cistercian monks on to the perfect detachment which opens the door to contemplation.

Not all the Cistercian abbots in England would have been able to enter into the spirit of these rather original gatherings with the same readiness as Gilbert of Hoyland. Henry Murdac, for instance would probably have numbered among those rigid characters who disapproved of the free and easy way in which the young monks crowded into Ailred's cell and piled on his bed "like children gathering around their mother"[102] or sat about on the floor wherever they could find a few inches of space.[CXXXIX] Of

---

102. Powicke, "Ailred of Rievaulx and his Biographer Walter Daniel" 508.[CXXXVIII]

course, Murdac had died before Ailred was confined to his own little infirmary.

Closer to Rievaulx than Gilbert's Lincolnshire abbey, was Byland, and here too was an abbot who had the reputation of a saint. Roger the founder of Byland was one of Ailred's closest friends. He was present at Ailred's death and must have been close to him in life. Roger of Byland has left to posterity a reputation for great devotion to the Cistercian *Rule*. He clung tenaciously to the strict ideal of poverty laid down by St. Alberic at a time when the pressure of benefactions was leading, almost everywhere, to relaxations. Abbots everywhere were beginning to neglect the letter of the *Instituta* and to accept all the prohibited sources of income which were to put the abbeys of Cîteaux on the plane of the powerful Benedictine houses – a plane from which Alberic and Stephen had struggled so hard to remove them forever. Byland was one of the few abbeys in Yorkshire that did not succumb, early in the second half of the twelfth century, to the enticements of benefactors who offered them tithes, parish churches, villages, serfs, manorial mills, common pasture lands.

Richard, the second of that name, abbot of Fountains, was another friend of Ailred's. He was called the "Sacrist" because he had been Sacristan at St Mary's, York, before the migration to Fountains. Although he was of a retiring and contemplative disposition he had been forced to enter into the dispute about the York election. Another Cistercian who had begun life as a Benedictine, first at Whitby, then at St. Mary's, York, was Robert, Abbot of Newminster in Northumberland.[CXL] He was one of the Fountains pioneers, a stern ascetic and, like Ailred, a peacemaker in the troubled north. A third Richard, of Fountains, was present at Ailred's deathbed. This one had been cantor at Clairvaux and had been summoned to Yorkshire by Henry Murdac, when the latter was archbishop of York, to replace Abbot Thorald of Fountains, whom Murdac deposed. Ailred never knew one of the greatest Abbots of Fountains, Ralph Hageth, who combined Ailred's gifts of contemplation and action and indeed seems to have penetrated much deeper into the mystical life than Ailred himself.

It must not be supposed that because the Cistercians differed with the Benedictines on the observance of St. Benedict's *Rule* there was necessarily enmity between the Black and White monks. True, ever since the secession of St. Robert from Molesme and St. Bernard's controversy with Cluny there had been some ill-feeling between monasteries of the two observances and St. Bernard himself observes that those who did not have the right monastic spirit, on either side, took advantage of this situation to lose their time in contention and rivalry which did not help any of them to be better monks.[103] Although Ailred took his own part in the controversy over the two observances in the abstract,[104] he nevertheless remained, as did St. Bernard himself, on the best of terms with the Benedictines themselves.

St. Bernard's sister Humbeline[CXLII] died as a Benedictine nun in the convent of Julley where the spiritual directors came from Molesme – a fact which clearly bears out Bernard's statement that he, and the rest of the Cistercians, had nothing against other branches of the Benedictines observing their own interpretations of the *Rule*, provided the White Monks were permitted to follow theirs.[105] So, too, Ailred's father Eilaf died in the habit of a Benedictine at Durham Abbey.

Durham, the shrine of St. Cuthbert, to whom Ailred had such great devotion, was perhaps of all the Benedictine Abbeys the one to which he was united by the bonds of closest union. The first recorded mention of Ailred as Abbot of Rievaulx occurs in 1147[CXLIII] when we learn that he was present at Durham, on the thirtieth of November, to settle one of those difficult problems of precedence that were always coming up in the rather complicated internal polity of the great Black Monk houses. This time the dispute concerned the appointment of the Prior. The mere fact that Ailred was invited to arbitrate in this question is proof that he was held in high esteem at Durham and that the community liked him and would peacefully abide by any decision emanating from him. They trusted him because they knew he loved them.

---

103. "*Sunt quidam de ordine nostro ... qui aliis ordinibus derogare dicuntur, et suam justitiam solam volentes constituere, justitiae Dei non sunt subjecti: quos profecto ... nec nostri nec cujuspiam esse ordinis verius dixerim, quippe qui etsi ordinate viventes, superbe tamen loquentes, cives se faciunt Babylonis, id est confusionis; immo filios tenebrarum ipsiusque gehennae, ubi nullus ordo sed sempiternus horror inhabitat*" (Bernard of Clairvaux, *Apologia* 5.10 [*PL* 182, col. 905A]).[CXLI]

104. *Speculum Caritatis* 3.35 (*PL* 195, cols. 608B-613B).

105. Bernard of Clairvaux, *Apologia* 4.7-8 (*PL* 182, cols. 903A-904C).

Ailred had many close friends among the Benedictines at Durham, religious who shared something of his sanctity and interior life and who also had some of his natural gifts and interests. The Benedictine writer, Reginald of Durham, wrote a life of St. Cuthbert at Ailred's instigation,[CXLIV] and he also wrote a biography of their mutual friend the hermit St. Godric of Finchale, whom Ailred is recorded to have visited once in the company of a young monk of Durham.[CXLV] It was also when Ailred was visiting St. Godric that the old hermit learned, in a vision, the death of St. Robert of Newminster. Godric was, himself, an ex-monk of Durham who had retired to a hermitage after having made pilgrimages to Rome, Jerusalem and Compostella. He was not the only Durham monk who became a hermit. One former Prior of the great monastery, Bartholomew, became a hermit on the island of Farne. He was joined there in 1163 by another Prior, Thomas. So evidently the active life of a prior in a big Benedictine community often ended in a reaction which sent distracted monastic officers into the woods looking for silence and peace and time to get their breath again!

Durham had been one of the first fruits of the northern monastic revival. William of St. Carilef, a monk from France, had been appointed bishop of Durham immediately after the Norman conquest. He was a prelate of the stamp and intelligence of a Lanfranc, and had set about rebuilding the shrine of St. Cuthbert. He repopulated the cathedral priory with monks from Wearmouth and Jarrow in 1083. Ever since that time Durham was a remarkably fervent and strict Benedictine house, and retained a spirit of simplicity which was unusual in the houses of the Black Monks at the time.

Hermitages were common in Yorkshire in the Middle Ages as indeed they were in most parts of England and the rest of western Europe. Men retired to the woods or the hills to live in solitude, building themselves small cabins under the forest trees by some spring. They lived what was necessarily a simple life, but not altogether a destitute one. Godric of Finchale, for instance, had his garden and his cow. Friends and clients would bring small offerings of food and clothing when they visited the hermit, who was generally the object of respect, if not veneration. They often made their way to his cell to consult him about spiritual problems and ask his prayers.

Women who felt drawn to the solitary life did not generally retire to the woods. This was not altogether safe for them. Instead, they became recluses. They would take some little cell, generally built near a church or even abutting on the wall of some church building, and there, with more or less formality, they would be officially immured. A mason came along and walled them in while a priest or perhaps a higher church dignitary said appropriate prayers. There they lived their lives in prayer, carrying out simple tasks when they were not praying. The recluse was not always immured and in any case she could communicate with the outside through a window which permitted conversations. From the writings of the time we can see that sometimes these conversations became so extensive that the recluse, despite the walled-up door of her cell, was likely to be little more than a common gossip.

Ailred's own sister was a recluse and she had grown old in such a cell as this. The fact that Ailred, at her request, wrote her a *Rule*[CXLVI] when she was well on in years does not imply that she had allowed herself to degenerate into one of these relaxed recluses whose cell was a kind of official news-agency for the whole village. We shall consider Ailred's *Rule* for his sister on a later page.

Ailred's father Eilaf had brought in Augustinian canons to care for the ancient shrine of Hexham. Ailred's devotion to the saints of Hexham never died and it kept him in constant relation with the Augustinians there. When, in 1155, the relics of the saints were translated, the Canons invited Ailred to be present and to preach on the occasion. It gave him an opportunity to express the deepest feelings of his heart in a festival which was in a special way his own, and the matter for the sermon was later expanded into his little tract on the saints of Hexham.[106] Needless to say, this sermon on the translation of the saints of Hexham was something of more than merely pious significance. The intimate connection between the veneration of these saints and the love of Northumbrians for their own land, of which the saints were the protectors, gave it a patriotic and social character, and Ailred's presence was dictated not only by his personal connection with

106. Aelred of Rievaulx, *De Sanctis Ecclesiae Hagustaldensis*, in *The Priory of*

the priory, nor by his prominence in the religious sphere, as Abbot of the greatest Cistercian house in England, but above all by his position in public life. The combination of all these qualities made him the logical choice for the occasion.

After 1157, when Ailred was allowed certain mitigations by the General Chapter on account of his failing health, his activities did not become less intense. Although he was supposed to be confined, to some extent, to a sort of recluse's cell of his own, where he might have a chance to rest, he was neither confined nor did he live as a recluse and he took very little rest. Although he could not observe all the details of the monastic life his interest in his monks was by no means suffered to diminish. As for the external duties of his office as abbot, the journeys imposed on him as visitor to his daughter houses continued, and he attended the General Chapter, although he may have been permitted to space his journeys to Cîteaux over two- or three-year intervals, instead of being compelled to go to France every year.[107]

It was in 1159 that Ailred was forced, by his charity and his love for the unstained Bride of Christ to undertake the most important mission of his life. It was the kind of mission that had fallen to the lot of St. Bernard and to many other Cistercians in the twelfth century, so much so that one feels that one of the peculiar functions of the Cistercian Order in the Middle Ages was to preserve the unity of the Church in an age when the ambition of secular princes was conspiring at every turn to tear the seamless garment of Christ into a hundred pieces.

During the papacy of the only Englishman who ever sat on Peter's throne, Adrian IV (Nicholas Breakspear), the Emperor Frederick Barbarossa was finding it increasingly difficult to reconcile his aggressive Italian policy with his duties to the Holy See, and it was clear that at Adrian's death the Church was likely

---

Hexham, ed. J. Raine, Surtees Society 44, 46, 2 vols. (Durham: Andrews & Co., 1864-65) 1.173-203.

107. The strictness of this rule that imposed a yearly visit to the General Chapter can be judged by the fact that today the Order of Cistercians of the Strict Observance does not demand that American abbots be present at Cîteaux each year although the journey is far less difficult and takes much less time than did the trip from Yorkshire to Burgundy.[CXLVII]

to be torn by another schism like the one which St. Bernard had healed twenty years before. At the death of Adrian in 1159 the majority of the College of Cardinals elected Ronaldo Bandinelli who became Alexander Ill. Three Cardinals dissented, and breaking away from the rest, elected one of their number, by two votes, to succeed Adrian IV as Pope. This was Cardinal Octavian, who took the name of Victor IV. The previous schism had grown out of a papal election concerning which it was possible to have doubts: this election was manifestly clear. There could be no question that Alexander III was the validly elected Pope. The minority party, however, were partisans of the Emperor and relied on his power to establish their claims. The Emperor intervened in the affair, convened a Council at Pavia, declared that Octavian was the true Pope and excommunicated Alexander. This decision was not even accepted with full submission within the borders of the empire and outside Frederick's Dominions it carried even less weight with the bishops and clergy. The secular princes withheld their decision for political rather than religious motives. It was necessary to arouse their consciences to action.

On the continent, the Cistercian Cardinal Henry of Pisa, a former monk of Clairvaux, was one of the many who approached the King of France and urged him to give his support to the rightful Pope. Meanwhile St. Peter of Tarentaise,[CXLVIII] one of the greatest Cistercians of his age, was preaching and pleading the cause of Alexander in Franche-Comté and Alsace and even as far south as Italy. The sanctity of this archbishop of an obscure Alpine see had earned him a reputation and influence second only to those of St. Bernard in his own time. Yet he had tried with all the means in his power to escape the dignity of archbishop and what he considered the dangers of the active life. Ordered to leave the monastery which he had founded in a high alpine valley at Tamié, in Savoy, he had accepted his archbishopric only to attempt escape, incognito, to another small Cistercian monastery near Bâle, where he did not succeed in remaining unknown.

By far the most influential Cistercian to advance the claims of Alexander in France was the Brother of King Louis VII. Henry of France had become a monk at Clairvaux but had not succeeded in remaining in the obscurity of the cloister. He was now bishop of Beauvais. It was his influence that most of all prompted the French king to speak out in favor of Alexander III.

Meanwhile, in England, Ailred had approached Henry II in London and it seems that his influence, together with that of Bishop Arnulph of Lisieux, finally decided the King to throw in his lot on the side of Alexander. The two Kings of France and England then met at the Council of Toulouse, in the spring of 1160, and solemnly declared that they recognized and supported Alexander III as the rightful Pope. This at least ensured that the greater part of Christian Europe was united under the true Pope and the life and work of the Church could continue without being too badly disrupted, at least in these countries.

The schism itself, however, was far from being over. Nor was there any peace in Italy where Frederick Barbarossa ranged freely up and down the peninsula with his armies, after having himself crowned by his creature, Octavian, in St. Peter's. Alexander rarely had access to Rome in the course of a troubled pontificate that lasted twenty-two years.[CXLIX] Even the position adopted by the Kings of England and France was not to remain altogether firm. Henry II, after the death of Ailred, and under the stress of his quarrel with Thomas à Becket, wavered in his loyalty to Alexander, but after the murder and canonization of the Primate Henry did not refuse to perform an ecclesiastical penance that was certainly terrible enough to have prompted a complete revolt against the Holy See if he had been another Barbarossa.

The history of the schism need not detain us any longer. It is enough to say that its final settlement was the work of two other Cistercians. St. Hugh, abbot of Bonnevaux,[CL] and Ponce, archbishop of Clermont, former Cistercian abbot of Grandselve and of Clairvaux, were the ones who finally brought Frederick Barbarossa around, induced him to enter negotiations and finally to make his peace with the Holy See in 1177. A third influence in these negotiations was a Carthusian of Silve Benite, called Thierry.[108]

Since we are speaking of Ailred's friendships, it is time to say a word about Henry II, on whom Ailred had centered such high hopes. We have seen the reason for those hopes. They were based not on Henry's virtues or character so much as on his descent from the English Kings. When Ailred got to know the King

---

108. For a more detailed account of the work of the Cistercians in healing the

better he probably realized that there was not enough in common between them to satisfy his own strict rules on the choice of a friend. In any case, Ailred was not enough of a courtier to enjoy the King's presence in more than an occasional audience as he passed through London.

To be the friend of such a King, one had to be, as Becket had been, ready to share in his parties and his amusements, and to flatter his love of power. And when Becket entered upon a state of life that demanded, as his conscience told him, the highest sanctity, intimate friendship with Henry II ceased to be altogether possible. Henry of Anjou was a man of some culture and social gifts, intelligent, or perhaps, better, shrewd; he was ambitious, selfish, avid for power and for wealth. There was a deep vein of violence in his character – a trait no more surprising in a medieval King than in a modern dictator. He was subject to violent and sudden fits of rage in which he would throw things at his courtiers, or, worse still, fly at them and beat them or try to tear out their eyes. When he came into conflict with Becket, the man he had once considered his best friend, over the rights of the Church in England, he pursued the archbishop into exile with the most vindictive of measures. Becket, in his flight to France, had sought refuge at Pontigny, a Cistercian Abbey. Henry threatened to burn down all the Cistercian houses in England if Pontigny continued to shelter the "traitor." To protect them, Becket left Pontigny.

It is clear that Ailred's friendship with this King was something more or less abstract. We do not know what effect the Becket affair had upon him. He did not live to see its issue, but the storm was gathering and Becket was already in exile when Ailred lay at death's door. He must have seen, then, that his hopes for a peaceful and Catholic England under Henry of Anjou were shot through with illusion.

If there was any peace in Catholic England during the last quarter of the twelfth century it was due not to any wisdom in the government of Henry, but to the blood of the martyr whose shrine at Canterbury became something far more, to England, than the shrine of St. Cuthbert or of the Confessor had ever been.

---

schism, see *Saint Hugues de Bonnevaux, de l'Ordre de Cîteaux (1120-1194)*, par un Moine de Tamié [Anselme Dimier] (Grenoble: Impr. St. Bruno, 1941) esp. 153-58.

It is interesting to speculate on the relations between St. Ailred and this great archbishop of Canterbury whose strange history ended in his becoming the one who, above all others, stood for the unity and the faith of England and became the symbol of the ideal Ailred had always dreamed of and lived for. It is almost certain that Ailred never suspected that Henry's former chancellor concealed such potentialities. Ailred was certainly acquainted with Thomas à Becket – since he preached at the translation of St. Edward, where Becket was the officiating prelate – but he almost as certainly had little to do with him. The differences between the two characters were so vast that some historians[109] think Ailred must have found Becket antipathetic and that, in the early stages of the controversy, at least, he may even have sided with Henry rather than the primate, on the grounds that Becket was only upsetting the precarious peace of England by his impulsive and apparently bungling defense of the rights of the Church.

Ailred's views on this subject were probably contained in his lost correspondence, especially his letters to Robert Earl of Leicester who tried to act as mediator between the King and Thomas.

It is true that Becket was impulsive, that there were traits in his character which seemed extravagant and even theatrical[110] and above all that his mishandling of the Constitutions of Clarendon[CLIII] was so uncanonical that it upset all the mature and experienced canonists who were concerned in the affair. Becket, to tell the truth, was just the kind of man who would be calculated to upset a first-class canonist or any prelate of the balance and experience of a Gilbert Foliot. Thomas à Becket combined in himself just the right amount of brilliancy, impetuosity, inexperience and earnest idealism to make his movements seem wild in the eyes of those whose lives were dominated by an overwhelming respect for the right method of procedure.

Becket's procedure at Clarendon was in every respect what they would call wrong. The King, having drawn up a series of rights which, he alleged, fell to the crown over the Church in England by reason of custom, Becket first accepted them, then

---

109. See Powicke, "Ailred of Rievaulx and His Biographer Walter Daniel" 351.[CLI]
110. I quote these epithets from Powicke "Ailred of Rievaulx and His Biographer Walter Daniel" 351.[CLII]

realizing his *faux-pas* rejected them and on top of it all imposed on himself the penance of not saying Mass. He clearly succeeded in making himself look erratic.

Are we to suppose that this was sufficient to turn Ailred against him? Or shall we grant that Ailred's charity, combined with his zeal for the interests of the Church, put him rather on Thomas's side?

Whatever the answer may be, in 1164, the very year of the Constitutions of Clarendon, Ailred dedicated his volumes of sermons on Isaias, *De Oneribus Isaiae*,[CLIV] to the Bishop who was the leader of the King's party and the chief opponent of Thomas à Becket. The letter of dedication is a document that goes so far to express friendship in the technical language Ailred liked to use on the subject, that it almost astounds us today. If Ailred meant half what he said, and he surely meant all of it, and if, at the time of writing, he had in mind what was going on in politics, he could hardly be said to have sided with Thomas à Becket.

Here, then, is the incredible language of Ailred's dedication of his sermons to Gilbert Foliot, the bishop of London:

> Having heard, most blessed Father, that among the innumerable occupations which are imposed upon you either by the authority of his royal majesty or by the necessity of your pastoral office, you remain nevertheless a devotee of wisdom, a friend of quiet and a lover of spiritual sciences, that you are fond of reading and that along with the sweet delights of prayer you temper the heat of pressing cares with the meditation of sacred Scripture, I have become so attracted to you that I aspire not only to the notice of your serenity, but even, I speak foolishly, to your friendship. Forgetting at the same time your sublime station and my own lowly rank, I rely only on the laws of love, for which there is nothing lofty and nothing low.... My soul, moved by the impulsion of my love, passing through everything which is yours but is not you, seeks to penetrate the very depths of your soul to make my affection one with your

> affection, my thought one with your thought, my spirit to your spirit, that by participating in your spirit, my own may be renewed, from the light of your thought, my own mind may borrow science, and that my own love may be nourished by the sweetness of your love.[CLV]

The first words we have quoted prove that Ailred is writing not to one who is already a close friend but only to a chance acquaintance. Later on in the dedication we learn that his real purpose is to make some return for kindnesses shown to him by the bishop in his recent passage through London. And we must admit at once that such talk, which, today, one would look for only in a schoolboy's parody of a renaissance love-letter, was in common currency in the society of the time. It was a way of paying one's respects. It was Ailred's letter of thanks for something or other, perhaps the bishop's hospitality in London for a day or two. Nevertheless, it was not a mere formality. Ailred was sincerely trying to convey the fact that it had been a real pleasure for him to meet his Lordship and he wanted to get to know him better. Where, in our time, one would simply take care of such a situation in a few plain sentences and invite the good bishop down for a week-end, Ailred turned out this highly romantic document with which the bishop was probably well-pleased. In any case, it does not imply than Ailred was a firm partisan of Thomas à Becket.

Gilbert Foliot was perhaps the most prominent member of the hierarchy in England at the time. By many he was held in higher esteem that Becket ever was, because he was a prelate of much wider experience, more learned and more capable. But unfortunately Gilbert Foliot was not a saint: only a canonist and a statesman.

He was a Cluniac monk, professed at Cluny itself and early deputed to the diplomatic elite selected from the personnel of this greatest of all Benedictine Abbeys to be groomed for responsible posts in every part of Europe. He was early appointed Prior of Abbeville. From Abbeville he moved to Gloucester, and was made Abbot in 1139. In 1148 he was appointed Bishop of Hereford by Pope Eugene III. He became the spiritual director of Henry II and, at the death of Theobald, Archbishop of Canterbury, he was without question the greatest prelate in England. In fact, but for Henry's favoritism, Foliot would have been the logical choice for archbishop of Canterbury. When Becket himself was forced to accept the perilous honor of the primacy, he arranged that Gilbert Foliot be appointed Bishop of London, hoping to soothe him with this consolation prize.

The gesture did not do him much good. Relations between them grew strained with every fresh step that Becket's converted conscience began to dictate and when the rupture fully developed between Becket and the King, Foliot assumed the leadership of the King's party and made no attempt to conceal his feelings against the inexperienced primate.

"You are a fool," he told Becket, "and you have always been a fool."[CLVI] The very natures of the two men made such a conflict almost inevitable under the circumstances.

Though jealousy and frustrated ambition may well have had their part in Foliot's detestation of Becket, the bishop of London was not so small a character as to be guided by passion. A zealous and rigid Churchman, he lived by a high moral standard and doubtless sincerely believed that Becket was an incapable and erratic character who would only end by plunging England into ruin with his ignorance of law and his theatrical appeals to the populace. Foliot was a distinguished canonist, a refined and well-bred character, a man of great discipline and moderation, upright and even ascetic. Not only that, but he cherished enough spiritual pretentions to compose a commentary on the *Canticle of Canticles* and to do that, at any time, but especially in the twelfth century, was avowedly to dabble in mysticism. There was nothing very mystical about Foliot's commentary *In Cantica*.[CLVII] It was a cold and correct exercise, typical of the man.

Here, then, was a man who was solid, zealous, self-possessed, guided by clear notions of law and policy, with a clean-cut attitude on Church discipline and definite policy on the relations of Church and State. Becket, at the beginning, seemed to be nothing more than a confused and incompetent upstart. Placed at the head of the Church in England by an utterly undeserved accident of royal favor, instead of letting himself be guided and shaped by those who were capable of directing policies wisely, he plunged into a fantastic "conversion" and proceeded to set in motion a series of impulsive and clumsy policies which made a great noise and impressed the people and antagonized the king and threatened to set England on its ear.

When, on top of all that, people began to think of Becket as a saint and to speak of his self-sacrificing devotion to the Church, Foliot's impatience and disgust knew no bounds.

What had happened then had happened before and would happen again. A rigid and correct and solid character who knew all the rules and followed the correct procedure was suddenly thrown up against a saint. And saints sometimes fail to measure up to the correct standards laid down in books, during their lifetime. It is only after the saint is dead that the thought processes of the rigid and correct manage to catch up with him, put him in his proper abstract pigeonhole and acknowledge him as "saint." Gilbert Foliot naturally expected a really saintly archbishop would turn out to be something along the lines of Gilbert Foliot, only much more efficient, much more rigid, much more ascetic, much more spiritual and much more humble. When this ignorant and blundering and theatrical upstart appeared on the scene, still so obviously burdened with the weaknesses of human nature, and yet so painfully sincere about doing his duty in his own queer way, for all his own obstacles, Foliot was taken completely by surprise. He failed to realize what was going on. He did not grasp the fact that a really vital issue had arisen and that it was something that could not be fixed by a statesman like himself.

In the end, there was violence. Becket was murdered in his own Cathedral and died with an *éclat* that must have made Gilbert Foliot finally burst with rage. But when the smoke had cleared and passions had somewhat subsided the sanctity of Thomas à Becket emerged like the golden towers of Canterbury rising out of the Kentish mists on a May morning, and it was seen by all for what it was: not the prudence of this world, not the planned sanctity of a too human asceticism, but the work of God and the fashioning of the Holy Spirit, done in a way marvelous and incomprehensible to men and perfected in the furnace of calumny and hatred and tribulation.[CLVIII]

I. Because this essay was not edited by Merton for publication, the procedure used here is somewhat different from that found in the other contents of the present volume. Except for some minor typographical adjustments, the text proper, unless otherwise noted, remains as Merton wrote it, including the alternative spelling of its subject's name, which Merton regularly used at the time of composition and which he explains in a note. To make the material more reader-friendly, however, the often fragmentary bibliographical information provided in his footnotes has been regularized and expanded to conform to citations found elsewhere in this volume. Any additional material, however, such as translations of Latin quotations, is found in the supplemental notes.

II. On Robert see *Valley of Wormwood* 143-53.

III. See Teresa of Avila, *Life* c. 27, in *The Complete Works of Saint Teresa of Jesus*, trans. and ed. E. Allison Peers, 3 vols. (New York: Sheed & Ward, 1946) 1.177.

IV. On Alberic see *Valley of Wormwood* 37-52.

V. On Stephen Harding see *Valley of Wormwood* 262-77.

VI. *Nomasticon Cisterciense, seu Antiquiores Ordinis Cisterciensis Constitutiones A.R.P.D. Juliano Paris* … Editio Nova, ed. Hugo Séjalon (Solesmes: E Typographeo Sancti Petri, 1892) 68-81; J. P. Migne, ed., *Patrologiae Cursus Completus, Series Latina* [*PL*], 221 vols. (Paris: Garnier,, 1844-1865) vol. 166, cols. 1377A-1384B; on the *Carta Caritatis* see *Charter, Customs, Constitutions* xvi-xxi, 1-14.

VII. "Then they are truly monks when they live by the labor of their hands as our fathers and the apostles did" (*The Rule of St. Benedict in Latin and English*, ed. and trans. Justin McCann, OSB [London: Burns, Oates, 1952] 110/111-112/113).

VIII. "[to live] poor with the poor Christ" (c. 15 [*Nomasticon* 63; *PL* 166, col. 1508A]).

IX. "Inspired by the grace of God, they very often amongst themselves spoke and complained and lamented about the transgressing of the *Rule* of St. Benedict the Father of monks, seeing that they and the other monks who had promised at their solemn profession to observe this *Rule* had kept it minimally."

X. "Love overflows itself; when love has come it draws all other affections into itself and captures them."

XI. "God is Truth, and looks for such seekers as search for Him in spirit and in truth."

XII. "Simple nature seeks out simplicity of heart."

XIII. "These Cistercians have renounced everything save the art of good writing; each and all of these hardy ascetics carried in his bosom a humanist who by no means wanted to die" (Étienne Gilson, *The Mystical Theology of St. Bernard*, trans. A. H. C. Downes [New York: Sheed & Ward, 1940] 63).

XIV. On William, see *Valley of Wormwood* 327-37.

XV. On Helinand, see *Valley of Wormwood* 65-69.

XVI. On Foulques, see *Valley of Wormwood* 430-36.

XVII. Merton almost certainly found this reference [which does not include mention of Cicero] in Jean Leclercq, OSB, *The Love of Learning and the Desire for God: A Study of Monastic Culture*, trans. Grace Misrahi (New York: Fordham University Press, 1961) 191: "In the one year for which we have any information as to the Cluny monks' Lenten reading, we know that six of the sixty-four members of the community were given works on history to read: Josephus, Orosius, Bede's Chronicle, and even Livy."

XVIII. "pathless and waterless land" (Ps. 62[63]:3).

XIX. "I rejoice that you are of this school, truly the school of the Spirit, where you learn goodness and discipline and knowledge."

XX. "school of divine service" (*Rule*, Prologue, which reads: "*dominici* [the Lord's] *schola servitii*" [McCann 12/13]).

XXI. "But, as we progress in our monastic life and in faith, our hearts shall be enlarged, and we shall run with unspeakable sweetness of love in the way of God's commandments" (McCann, 12/13).

XXII. "[Then, when all these degrees of humility have been climbed,] the monk will presently come to that perfect love of God which then casts out all fear; whereby he will begin to observe without labour, as though naturally and by habit, all those precepts which formerly he did not observe without fear: no longer for fear of hell, but for love of Christ and through good habit and delight in virtue. And this will the Lord deign to show forth by the power of his Spirit in his workman now cleansed from vice and from sin" (McCann 48/49).

XXIII. "[Scripture] speaks in our own words of the wisdom hidden in mystery; it brings God into our affections as it images Him; it offers to human minds the unknown and invisible realities of God by known comparisons to sensible things, as though what is precious is given in common drinking cups."

XXIV. Genesis 1:26.

XXV. "God is Love" (1 Jn. 4:8).

XXVI. Text reads "Frederico".

XXVII. *PL* 184, cols. 379C-408B.

XXVIII. *PL* 184, cols. 365A-380B.

XXIX. *PL* 182, cols. 895D-918A; for a discussion see *Cistercian Fathers and Their Monastic Theology* 139-57.

XXX. *PL* 182, cols. 1049A-1072D; for a discussion see *Cistercian Fathers and Their Monastic Theology* 179-82.

XXXI. *PL* 180, cols. 205A-248D.

XXXII. *PL* 184, cols. 307A-364B.

XXXIII. Blessed Columba Marmion, OSB (1858-1923), Irish-born monk who became abbot of the Belgian Benedictine monastery of Maredsous, best known as author of *Christ, the Life of the Soul*, *Christ in His Mysteries* and *Christ, the Life of the Monk*; he was beatified in 2000.

XXXIV. For a discussion see *Cistercian Fathers and Their Monastic Theology* 50-68.

XXXV. On Amadeus see *Valley of Wormwood* 52-55.

XXXVI. *PL* 206, cols. 17A-860D.

XXXVII. On Alan see *Valley of Wormwood* 55-57, 277-81.

XXXVIII. The Abbey of Stella (L'Étoile), near Poitiers, of which Isaac became abbot in 1147, is not to be identified with the monastic foundation on the Isle of Ré where Isaac lived part of his later monastic life. For an overview of Isaac's life and works see the opening chapter of Bernard McGinn, *The Golden Chain: A Study in the Theological Anthropology of Isaac of Stella*, Cistercian Studies [CS] vol. 15 (Washington, DC: Cistercian Publications, 1972) 1-33.

XXXIX. *PL* 194, cols. 1875B-1890A.

XL. *PL* 194, cols. 1889B-1896A.

XLI. *PL* 204, cols. 251B-401A.

XLII. PL 205, cols. 559C-828B.

XLIII. Anselme le Bail, "L'Influence de Saint Bernard sur les Auteurs Spirituels de Son Temps," *Saint Bernard et Son Temps*, 2 vols. (Dijon: Association Bourguignonne des Sociétés Savantes, 1928) 1.205-15.

XLIV. I.e. Peter Monoculus: see *Valley of Wormwood* 371-79.

XLV. I.e. Otto of Friesing (d. 1158), son of the Duke of Austria, uncle of Frederick Barbarossa, monk of the Abbey of Morimond, which he entered in 1132 and where he briefly served as abbot in 1138 before becoming Bishop of Freising that same year; in a journal entry of December 11, 1962, Merton writes: "Otto of Freising was so convinced that Constantine had finally inaugurated the Kingdom of God, that he spoke at last only of *one city* in his history of the 'Two Cities.' When the Emperor became Catholic, then Christendom = the Kingdom of God, i.e. the Christian politico-religious world is the kingdom of God. Hence there is no more to be done, but to preserve the status quo of the kingdom, if necessary by violent repression, coercion rather than apostolate. The apostolate of united coercion!! And as the genuine Christian spirit must *necessarily* resist the identification of the Kingdom of God with a limited human society, then the focus of 'Christendom' did in fact tend to repress those movements which tended to genuine development, thrusting them outside the 'city' where their evolution became distorted and unhealthy. Hence another Cistercian, Joachim of Fiore, rises up against Otto of Freising's Constantinian theory with an apocalypse of the 'Spirit.' He was in fact expressing the stirrings that were to bring about the birth of a new age and break down medieval society. Two temptations, then: to evade the responsibilities of a Christian in history by saying that the kingdom has arrived and medieval Christendom is/was the kingdom, or to do the same by saying the kingdom will arrive only at the end of, or outside of time" (*Turning Toward the World* 273-74).

XLVI. *PL* 184, cols. 879B-950A; typescript reads: "Ogler".

XLVII. On Gertrude see *Valley of Wormwood* 401-11.

XLVIII. On Mechtilde see *Valley of Wormwood* 411-17.

XLIX. "The brothers of Waverley, who up until now had, as it were, lived in a corner unregarded, having become known because they were of the same Order, also added to the number of Cistercian monasteries."

L. On William see *Valley of Wormwood* 295-97.

LI. "Upon examination it was displeasing because both the music and the texts were found to be corrupt, excessively disordered and almost contemptible throughout.... Finally it lost the support of our brothers and the abbots of the Order and it was decided that it should be revised and corrected."

LII. *Instituta Generalis Capituli* 12 (*Nomasticon* 215).

LIII. On Waltheof [Waldef] see *Valley of Wormwood* 295-303.

LIV. "O how well it is for him!"

LV. *Speculum Caritatis* 2.23 (*PL* 195, col. 572A), quoting *Confessions* 10.33.

LVI. "*maxime nodus cuiusdam amicitiae, dulcis mihi super omnes dulcedines illius vitae meae*" (*Speculum Caritatis* 1.27 [*PL* 195, col. 532D]).

LVII. See Walter Daniel, *The Life of Ailred of Rievaulx*, ed. and trans. F. M. Powicke (New York: Thomas Nelson, 1950); the fact that Merton did not make use of this edition is further evidence that he wrote his text in the late 1940s, before its publication.

LVIII. Powicke, "Ailred and His Biographer Walter Daniel" 493; *Life of Ailred* 3-4 [c. 2].

LIX. See Powicke, "Ailred and His Biographer Walter Daniel" 471; *Life of Ailred* lxxxii.

LX. "*vox tubae similis*" (col. 703D).

LXI. "*interrogauit quendam suorum, uocabulo amicum, utrum uellet descendere ad abbathiam et plenius quod pridie conspexerat*" ("he asked one of his servants, whom he called his friend, if he would like to go down to the abbey and learn something more than he had seen the day before") (*Life of Ailred* 15 [c. 7]).

LXII. *Rule* of St. Benedict c. 2 (McCann 18/19).

LXIII. Both the century and the founding date were left blank in the typescript but were provided in the periodical version by editor Patrick Hart, who also altered the date in the footnote from 1178-79 to 1181.

LXIV. "Women, hawks and dogs, except those ready barkers, used to drive away thieves from houses, do not enter the gates of their monastery" (*Life of Ailred* 15 [c.7]).

LXV. Powicke, "Ailred and His Biographer Walter Daniel" 486; *Life of Ailred* 72-73 ("Letter to Maurice").

LXVI. *Constitutions of the Order of Cistercians of the Strict Observance* (Dublin: M. H. Gill & Sons, c. 1924) 37 [n. 159].

LXVII. "my son in age, my father in holiness, my friend in love."

LXVIII. "And so, finding almost nothing exterior by which he was delighted, he had withdrawn himself into the interior solitude of his mind, sitting alone and silent, yet not lethargic in his stillness. For he wrote or read or secretly turned to meditation on the scriptures, toward which his mind was certainly alert. Even with the prior he scarcely spoke of necessities. He went about not hearing, as though deaf, and like a mute person, not opening his mouth.... Truly if anyone, finding an opportunity, met him with any word, such gentleness soon wafted forth in his speech, such cheerfulness appeared in his expression, without any carelessness, that both his manner of speaking and his humility in listening made clear how free of bitterness and full of sweetness was his silence.... Divine affection looked upon you alone so that it transferred that tranquil and peaceful soul with all calmness from the miseries of this life to the fatherland you longed for, and with you scarcely aware of it, dissolved the fetters of bodily life with such ease that not even a little fear of death might bother a soul loved by Him."

LXIX. Powicke, "Ailred and His Biographer Walter Daniel" 499; *Life of Ailred* 22 (c.14).

LXX. This refers to Merton's original intention, never fulfilled, to append a selection of texts by Aelred to this introductory essay.

LXXI. "Certainly food is scantier, clothing is rougher; drink is from a spring, sleep is frequently on a book."

LXXII. For Merton's later, more positive view of Abelard, see *Cistercian Fathers and Their Monastic Theology* 167-96.

LXXIII. "*plus anxia quam periculosa*" (*PL* 184, col. 308A).

LXXIV. "he had been given, as he retained, natural capacity to a high degree" (*Life of Ailred* 26 [c. 18]).

LXXV. "These acquire from their teacher a hazy idea of Aristotelian forms and the infinite reckonings of Pythagorean computation; but he, by the rapidity of his genius flying through the world of numbers and transcending every figure of speech, both real and feigned, knew in the Scriptures, and taught, Him who alone has immortality, where there is no number, and dwells in light inaccessible where there is no figure but the very truth which, rightly understood, is the goal of all earthly knowledge" (*Life of Ailred* 26 [c. 18]).

LXXVI. "*Qui non fucos quesiuit assumere uerborum in assercione sua, que dignitatem sensus magis onerant quam honorant, nam amputant a uero indicium ueritatis dum post se trahunt quod aliena declinacione non indiget et in hoc ducunt quod ueritas dedignatur. Se sola enim ueritas contenta est nec uerbis indiget ad deprecandum compositis uel intelligendum*" ("He never sought to involve his speech in the deceitful trappings which burden rather than enhance the value of its sense, because they rob truth of its meaning by digressions which it does not require and by additions which it disdains. For truth is self-contained; it needs no verbal artifice to explain and drive it home") (*Life of Ailred* 26 [c. 18]).

LXXVII. "preferred the pure, undiluted truth" (*Life of Ailred* 27 [c. 18]).

LXXVIII. "In this the love of God should be believed to stand."

LXXIX. Source reads: "… into the will of God, which will of God is likewise …"

LXXX. "To join one's own will to the will of God so that the human will may consent to whatever the divine will requires, and so that there may be no other reason why he wills this or that except that he realizes that God wills it: this is to love God completely."

LXXXI. "This happens when the Holy Spirit, Who is particularly the will and love of God, and is God, brings and pours Himself into the human will; raising it from a lower to a higher level, He transforms it completely into a dimension and quality of Himself, so that joined to Him by an inseparable bond of unity, one is made one spirit with Him."

LXXXII. Powicke, "Ailred and His Biographer Walter Daniel" 482; *Life of Ailred* 67 ("Letter to Maurice").

LXXXIII. While this is the term used in "Ailred and His Biographer Walter Daniel" 499, it is "*secularis clericus*" ("secular clerk") in *Life of Ailred* 24 (c. 15).

LXXXIV. "'*Nolo,' inquit ille, 'licet michi dederis omnes diuicias domus huius*'" ("'I would not stay,' he replied, 'though you gave me all the wealth of this house'") (*Life of Ailred* 31 [c. 22]).

LXXXV. "*Nam accedens subcellerarius ad eum, proximus uidelicet eius secundum carnem, dicit 'O tu quid facis, excecans oculos tuos pro miserrimo illo? Insuper et uotum fecisti ut te fame occidas si non redeat ille?' Et sanctus: 'Quid ad te? Noli queso dolorem dolori meo addere, nam crucior in hac flamma et ecce morior nisi subueniatur filio meo. Quid ad te?'*" ("For the sub-cellarer, his nearest kinsman, comes to him and says, 'Why on earth do you cry out your eyes for that wretched creature? And is it true that you have vowed to starve yourself to death if he does not come back?' The saint, 'What is that to thee? Do not, I beseech you, add sorrow to my sorrow, for I am tormented in this flame and, unless help comes to my son, I die. What is that to thee?'") (*Life of Ailred* 31 [c. 22]).

LXXXVI. "*de supradicto uidelicet fratre cuius exitum per portam in seculum prece sua retardauit*" ("the brother mentioned above, whose departure through the gate into the outside world he prevented by his prayers") (*Life of Ailred* 35 [c. 28]).

LXXXVII. "*homo uultu uenerabilis ... ille tuus monachus*" ("a man of venerable appearance … that monk of thine") (*Life of Ailred* 35 [c. 28]).

LXXXVIII. See *Life of Ailred* 36, n. 2: "Walter Daniel is not using the word *hospes* in a precise sense."

LXXXIX. See the discussion of this point in *Charter, Customs, Constitutions* 196.

XC. Powicke, "Ailred and His Biographer Walter Daniel" 503; *Life of Ailred* 32 (c. 23).

XCI. Typescript reads: "8".

XCII. "*secundus Beda*" ("both in life and learning he alone could be compared with Bede") (*Life of Ailred* 33 [c. 25]).

XCIII. See F. M. Powicke, "Maurice of Rievaulx," *English Historical Review* 36 (January 1921) 20; none of these works are extant.

XCIV. "*Quis scit quecunque fuerit hominum intentio de promotione tua, nisi propterea primam tibi sedem hujus insule concesserit deus ut appareret zelus tuus modo pro domo israel nec lateret industria?*" (Powicke, "Maurice of Rievaulx" 28).

XCV. "he resigned his stewardship after two years and preferred to resume his seat in the cloister" (*Life of Ailred* 33 [c. 25]).

XCVI. "We speak only to three persons, and this very seldom and only concerning necessities."

XCVII. *Rule* of St. Benedict cc. 23-27, 44 (McCann 72/73-76/77, 104/105-106/107); no mention is made in the *Rule* of actual incarceration.

XCVIII. "*Quam illud quoque mirandum, quod trecentis, ut reor, hominibus unius hominis voluntas est lex*" ("How wondrous it is that for three hundred men, as I reckon, the will of one man is law").

XCIX. Powicke, "Ailred and His Biographer Walter Daniel" 507; *Life of Ailred* 38 (c. 30).

C. "*Vere ut iumentum facti sumus*" (*Speculum Caritatis* 2.17 [*PL* 195, col. 563A]).

CI. *Speculum Caritatis* 2.17 (*PL* 195, col. 563A) ("There is no place for self-will, no time for idleness or dissipation").

CII. "*Sic nimirum sanguine hominum vescimur.*"

CIII. *Speculum Caritatis* 2.17 (*PL* 195, col. 563A) ("a wonderful freedom from the upheaval of worldly affairs").

CIV. "Among brothers there is such unity and such concord that each thing seems to belong to all and all things to belong to each. And what delights me in a marvelous way is that there is no regard for rank, no consideration of birth. Necessity alone causes diversity, weakness alone causes inequality. For what is produced by all in common is distributed to each, not as fleshly affection or private love would have determined, but to each according to their work. How wondrous it is as well, that for three hundred men, as I reckon, the will of one man is law, so that once it has come forth from his mouth as much care is taken by all as though they had all sworn an oath about it, or had heard it from the mouth of God Himself."

CV. 1 Corinthians 9:22.

CVI. André Wilmart, OSB, *Auteurs Spirituels et Textes Dévots du Moyen-Âge Latin* (Paris: Bloud et Gay, 1932) c. 10: "L'Oraison Pastorale de l'Abbé Aelred" (291-96).

CVII. Blessed Antoine Chevrier (1825-79; beatified 1986). Jacques-Melchior Villefranche, *Vie du Père Chevrier: Fondateur de la Providence du Prado à Lyon* (Lyon: Librairie Emmanuel Vitte, 1895) 394: "Il faut devenir du bon pain; le prêtre est un homme mangé – Chrétien pour soi, prêtre pour les autres" ("One must become good bread; the priest is a man consumed – Christian for himself, priest for others").

CVIII. "*Sensus meus <et> sermo meus. Ocium meum <et> occupatio mea. actus meus et cogitatio mea. prosperitas mea et aduersitas mea. mors mea et uita mea. sanitas <mea> et infirmitas mea. quicquid omnino sum. quod uiuo. quod sentio. quod discerno. totum impendatur illis. et totum expendatur pro illis. pro quibus tu ipse non dedignabaris expendi*" (Wilmart, *Auteurs Spirituels* 294).

CIX. "Upon hearing this, Count Simon his kinsman became completely enflamed with anger, and proclaiming his loss to himself and all his friends, threatened with the terrifying oath of destroyers to set fire to the entire monastery of Wardon if it kept him there any longer."

CX. *Life of Ailred* xiv.

CXI. Powicke, "Ailred of Rievaulx and His Biographer Walter Daniel" 315; *Life of Ailred* xv.

CXII. "Leland saw the Rievaulx manuscripts shortly before the dissolution, and his account of Walter and his writings deserves careful attention. Walter Daniel, he says, was worthy of his master and, almost his equal in learning, wrote on the same philosophical and theological subjects" (Powicke, "Ailred of Rievaulx and His Biographer Walter Daniel" 317; *Life of Ailred* xvii).

CXIII. Powicke, "Ailred of Rievaulx and His Biographer Walter Daniel" 319; *Life of Ailred* xix.

CXIV. "XLV. *Tria sunt oscula: de primo dicitur: osculetur me osculo oris sui; de secundo dicit Ysaac filio suo: da mihi osculum fili mi; de tertio est illud domini cum Juda: osculo tradis filium hominis.* XLVII. *Tres sunt specialiter columbe: prima et principaliter est que descendit super Jesum in Jordane; secunda que ad Noe in archam attulit ramum olive; tertia cujus pennas petiit David dicens: quis dabit mihi pennas sicut columba.* LXXXIX. *Tria hominum genera sunt. Sunt enim homines prudentes sine simplicitatis innocentia et sunt simplices sine prudentia. Sunt autem simplices et prudentes.* LXXIII. *Una mulier hebrea fecit confusionem in domo regis Nubugodonosor.*"

CXV. *PL* 195, col. 669AC.

CXVI. "He turned the house of Rievaulx into a stronghold for the sustaining of the weak" (*Life of Ailred* 36 [c. 29]).

CXVII. "*ex exteris nacionibus et remotis terre finibus*" ("from foreign peoples and from the far ends of the earth") (*Life of Ailred* 37 [c. 29]).

CXVIII. Armand-Jean Le Bouthillier de Rancé (1626-1700), reforming Abbot of La Grande Trappe; for a discussion of de Rancé and the Trappist reform, see *Waters of Siloe* 32-49, 303-308.

CXIX. "*'noli,' Alredus inquit, 'noli, frater, occidere animam pro qua Christus mortuus est, noli effugare gloriam nostram a domo ista, memento quia et nos peregrini sumus, sicut omnes patres nostri, et hec est suprema et singularis gloria domus Rieuall' quod pre ceteris didicit tollerare infirmos et necessitatibus compati aliorum'*" ("do not, brother, do not kill the soul for which Christ died, do not drive away our glory from this house. Remember that 'we are sojourners as were all our fathers,' and that it is the singular and supreme glory of the house of Rievaulx that above all else it teaches tolerance of the infirm and compassion with others in their necessities") (*Life of Ailred* 37 [c. 29]).

CXX. "Hence it was that the father left behind him at Rievaulx … one hundred and forty monks and five hundred [*conversi* and laymen]" (*Life of Ailred* 38 [c. 30], which reads: "*decies quinquaginta*" rather than "*decies sexaginta*" [six hundred], the reading in Powicke, "Ailred of Rievaulx and His Biographer Walter Daniel" 308, which includes a footnote stating that "The original reading was apparently 'decies quinquaginta'"; a note in the *Life* points out the correction).

CXXI. "Indeed he trebled the intensity of the monastic life and its charity" (*Life of Ailred* 38 [c. 30]).

CXXII. This incident (*Life of Ailred* 79-81) is related not in the *Vita* proper but in the appended "Letter to Maurice" in which Walter defends the accuracy of his portrait of Aelred.

CXXIII. "*quasi membrane folium*" ("like a leaf of parchment") (*Life of Ailred* 79).

CXXIV. Typescript reads: "9".

CXXV. "*Sit ergo homini dilectio sui Sabbatum primum; dilectio proximi sit secundum; Dei autem dilectio, Sabbatum Sabbatorum. Est ... Sabbatum spirituale requies animi, pax cordis, tranquillitas mentis*" (*Speculum Caritatis* 3.2 [*PL* 195, col. 577C]) ("Therefore for a human being love of self is the first Sabbath; love of neighbor the second; love of God the Sabbath of Sabbaths. The spiritual Sabbath is the rest of the mind, the peace of the heart, the tranquility of the soul").

CXXVI. 1 John 2:16.

CXXVII. "With the most mindless presumptuousness we picture the battles of kings and the victories of dukes as if taking place before our eyes, and we arrange all the business of the king with idle daydreams in the very midst of our psalmody or prayers."

CXXVIII. *PL*195, cols. 711D-738A.

CXXIX. *PL* 195, cols. 737B-790B.

CXXX. "*Postremo est septima ipsa sapientia, id est contemplatio veritatis, pacificans totum hominem, et suscipiens similitudinem Dei, quae ita concluditur: Beati pacifici; quoniam ipsi filii Dei vocabuntur*" ("Finally the seventh is wisdom itself, that is, the contemplation of the truth, pacifying the whole person and bringing about the likeness of God, which thus is summed up: Blessed are the peacemakers, for they shall be called children of God").

CXXXI. Chapter 3 (*Nomasticon* 70-71).

CXXXII. See Powicke, "Ailred and His Biographer Walter Daniel" 487; *Life of Ailred* 74-75 ("Letter to Maurice").

CXXXIII. See Powicke, "Ailred and His Biographer Walter Daniel" 511; *Life of Ailred* 44-45 (c. 37).

CXXXIV. *Life of Ailred* lxx.

CXXXV. J.-M. Canivez, ed., *Statuta Capitulorum Generalium Ordinis Cisterciensis ab Annum 1116 ad Annum 1786*, 8 vols. (Louvain: Bureaux de la Revue d'Histoire Ecclésiastique, 1933-41) 1.375-76 (1210:33, 35).

CXXXVI. "*Apud Divionem quando veniunt ad Capitulum vel redeunt abbates, omnino caveant ne manibus se invicem tenentes*" ("At Dijon when abbots are coming to the chapter or returning, let them beware above all of holding hands together").

CXXXVII. Gilbert of Hoyland, *Sermo* 41 *in Cantica Canticorum* (*PL* 184, cols. 214A-219D). In his novitiate conferences on *Liturgical Feasts and Seasons* (currently being prepared for publication), Merton writes of this sermon: "Commenting on the Canticle of Canticles, in Sermon 41 Gilbert introduces a passage in praise of Ailred, recently dead: (a) he praises the purity of his life and the purity of his doctrine; (b) he speaks especially of his great sufferings, accompanied by clarity of mind and peace of heart, due to his great charity; he was consumed by his love for God, even in the midst of his sickness, and he praised God always, with great fervor; (c) his bearing was always tranquil; he was slow to speak, modest and patient in his talk (some of the monks around him were impetuous); Gilbert speaks of him as *opportune loquens et opportune silens* ['speaking when appropriate and keeping silent when appropriate']; (d) he does not call him even 'slow to anger,' because there was no anger in him at all; (e) speaking of the great sweetness of his spirit, Gilbert says it came entirely from the fact that he was a completely spiritual man, living entirely in hope of heaven; (f) he kept the sweetness of his spirit by avoiding controversies and sterile disputes; he was *prudens eloquii mystici* ['skilled in spiritual speech']; he excelled in consoling the little ones and aiding them to rise up to heavenly things; his sermons were easy to understand but full of fervor."

CXXXVIII. "*ut paruulus confabulabatur cum matre sua*" ("as a little child prattles with its mother") (*Life of Ailred* 40 [c. 31]).

CXXXIX. See Powicke, "Ailred and His Biographer Walter Daniel" 508; *Life of Ailred* 39-40 (c. 31).

CXL. On Robert see *Valley of Wormwood* 199-204.

CXLI. "There are certain members of our Order … who are said to disparage other orders, and wishing to set up their own justice alone, are not submissive to the justice of God. I would say that these truly belong neither to our Order nor to any other, even if living according to the *Rule*, yet speaking so proudly they make themselves citizens of Babylon, that is, of confusion; or rather they are sons of darkness and of Gehenna itself, where no order but everlasting horror dwells."

CXLII. On Humbeline see *Valley of Wormwood* 77-84.

CXLIII. Powicke, "Ailred and His Biographer Walter Daniel" 478; *Life of Ailred* xci.

CXLIV. See *Reginaldi Monachi Dunelmensis Libellus de Admirandis Beati Cuthberti Virtutibus*, Surtees Society Publications (London: J. B. Nichols, 1835) viii, 4.

CXLV. See Reginald of Durham, *Libellus de Vita et Miraculis S. Godrici Heremitae de Finchale*, Surtees Society Publications (London: J. B. Nichols, 1847) 176-77.

CXLVI. *De Institutis Inclusarum* (*PL* 32, cols. 1451-1474; published as "*De Vita Eremitica*" under the name of St. Augustine). Merton does not, of course, include excerpts from this work in his text, as originally intended.

CXLVII. In his note in the periodical text, editor Patrick Hart points out that this is no longer the case.

CXLVIII. On Peter of Tarentaise see *Valley of Wormwood* 169-81.

CXLIX. Left blank in the typescript, the proper length of the pontificate was added by editor Patrick Hart in the periodical publication.

CL. On Hugh of Bonnevaux see *Valley of Wormwood* 119-28.

CLI. "I imagine that the sympathies of Ailred – Cistercian though he was – lay with King Henry rather than with the archbishop" (*Life of Ailred xlix*). For a thorough discussion of the complicated involvement of the Cistercians in the Becket controversy, see McGinn 34-50.

CLII. "There were capricious, theatrical, extravagant traits in the archbishop's conduct which could not but repel him" (*Life of Ailred* xlix).

CLIII. The sixteen articles promulgated by King Henry II in January 1164, intended to curb the power of the Church, which led to the conflict between the king and his archbishop.

CLIV. *PL* 195, cols. 363A-500D.

CLV. "*Audiens te, Pater beatissime, inter innumeras occupationes, quas tibi vel regiae maiestatis auctoritas, vel curae pastoralis imponit necessitas, ut cultorem sapientiae, quietis amicum, spiritualis scientiae studiosum, lectioni operam dare, et inter suaves orationum delicias, irruentium curarum molestiam sanctarum Scripturarum crebra meditatione solari; ita tui avidus effectus sum ut non solum ad tuae serenitatis notitiam, sed etiam, quod in insipientia dicam, ad ipsam audeo aspirare amicitiam. Tam enim tuae sublimitatis, quam meae humilitatis oblitus, legibus amoris innitor; cui nihil humile, nihil sublime est; ... Animus proinde meus amoris impetum sequens, omnia, quae tua sunt, non tu; omnia, quae circa te sunt, quae nec tua sunt, nec tu; spirituali quodam motu pertransiens, ipsam etiam corporis molem sui subtilitate traiiciens, in ipsum tuae mentis sinum se totum infundit, affectum affectui, sensus sensui, et spiritum miscet spiritui, ut ex spiritus tui participatione meus spiritus renovetur, ex tui sensus lumine lumen sibi scientiae meus sensus mutuetur, meus insuper affectus, tui affectus dulcedine foveatur*" (*PL* 195, col. 363).

CLVI. "In a moment of passion he told Becket that a fool he was and a fool he always had been, and in a long letter to the exiled archbishop in which the measured sentences, like points of steel, are driven home by the intense feeling of the writer, he travelled over the whole dispute" (Knowles, *Monastic Order in England* 294); see *Epistola* 194 ("*Multiplicem nobis*") (*PL* 190, cols. 892A-905B) written to Becket by Foliot in September 1166; for a discussion of the authenticity of this letter, see David Knowles, *The Episcopal Colleagues of Archbishop Thomas Becket* (Cambridge: Cambridge University Press, 1951) 171-80: Appendix VII: "The Letter *Multiplicem*."

CLVII. *PL* 202, cols. 1147A-1304D.

CLVIII. Following a page of handwritten notes on Gilbert Foliot, now in the archives of the Thomas Merton Center at Bellarmine University, Louisville, KY, that clearly served as the basis for Merton's discussion here, there is a further page, also handwritten, headed "Cistercian background of Ailred's last years," drawing particularly on Knowles, *Monastic Order in England* for key events affecting particularly the economic situation of Cistercian monasteries in England. This is a clear indication that Merton had intended to continue his discussion of the life of Aelred to its conclusion, but there are no extant notes or text directly pertaining to the final stage of Aelred's career or to his death.

Aelred of Rievaulx on Prayer, Memory and Identity – Conferences

On March 22, 1964, Merton completed a long series of Sunday conferences on pre-Benedictine monasticism that he had begun in January 1963 (see *Pre-Benedictine Monasticism* 3-208). Before turning in mid-June to a study of early Syrian monasticism that would initiate a second extensive series of these pre-Benedictine classes, continuing all the way until August 1965 (see *Pre-Benedictine Monasticism* 209-337), when he resigned his position as master of novices to take up full-time residence in his hermitage for the final three years of his life, Merton presented a number of "stand-alone" Sunday conferences, "one or two little things that I'd like to use up," as he describes them. Two of these conferences (Gethsemani recordings 102.1 and 114.1), presented on April 26 and May 7 (Ascension Thursday), transcribed and printed here for the first time, focus on some ideas of Aelred on prayer, memory and identity. This was evidently not the first time that Merton had spoken to his novices about Aelred in his classes: included among the extensive series of conferences on "Liturgical Feasts and Seasons" (currently being prepared for publication) is a presentation for his feast (February 3) entitled "Saint Ailred – *Cistercian Life in His Time*," drawing on the *Life of Ailred* written by his disciple Walter Daniel and on the encomium his fellow Cistercian abbot and author Gilbert of Hoyland, delivered in a sermon at the time of Aelred's death; an undated outline of points on "St. Ailred's Marian Sermons" is also extant (see *Cistercian Fathers and Their Monastic Theology* 425-27 for a transcript), as well as a more detailed set of notes entitled "*Cistercian Easter Sermons – Spiritual Sense of Scripture*" that discusses of two of Aelred's sermons "*In Die Paschae*" along with two Easter sermons of Isaac of Stella (to be included in an appendix to Merton's conferences on Cistercian History, currently being prepared for publication). But the pair of spring 1964 conferences are the only ones that were presented subsequent to late April 1962, when Merton's talks to the novices began to be recorded (see *Cassian and the Fathers* xlvii). Merton draws specifically on Aelred's *De Institutione Inclusarum*, or *Rule for Recluses*, composed for his sister, on the *Mirror of Charity* (*Speculum Caritatis*) and on a couple of sermons. The pastoral nature of these presentations, intended not just for the intellectual instruction of the novices but for their monastic formation, is clearly evident in Merton's approach to the material. He highlights the contemporary relevance of Aelred's understanding of sacred art by linking it to the crucifix painted by Merton's friend Victor Hammer that hung in the novitiate chapel, provides an extensive exploration of the meaning of the Augustinian and Cistercian sense of *memoria* as true self-awareness rooted in the awareness of the interior presence of God, and presents amusing but pertinent reminiscences of his own struggles as a novice with distracting memories from his pre-monastic life. He emphasizes the pedagogical role of both scripture and liturgy in forming the monk and bringing forth in him the divine image. He draws on his own interest in interreligious dialogue by making apt comparisons between the Prodigal Son story and the Mahayana Buddhist parable of the king's son who is unaware of his true identity, as well as between the Buddhist perception of ignorance (*avidya*) as the root of all illusion and the similar perception found in Aelred and Adam of Perseigne. He concludes as he began, with a focus on the redemptive meaning of the cross as the authentic gateway to knowledge of and union with the Trinity, for Aelred, as for his master Augustine, mirrored in the memory, understanding and will of the human person. He is much less interested in presenting Aelred's teaching as a subject for scholarly inquiry than as a stimulus for his young students to undertake an examination of their own identity and of their own vocation.

1.

I'm going to get around to the *Regula Magistri* and all that stuff sooner or later[I] – later maybe! For the time being I've got one or two little things that I'd like to use up: for example a bit from St. Aelred on prayer: there's some rather useful points on prayer from him. There's a little-known thing from one of the Greek texts of sayings of the Egyptian desert fathers which are quite interesting.[II] Then we get into something on the Syrian Fathers,[III] because they're very good. But meanwhile, just these few points of St. Aelred on prayer, for today and maybe the next time we meet. This is partly from the letter to his sister, who was a recluse,[IV] and is partly from his other works.[V] It centers especially around a very important concept from St. Augustine, of the memory in the spiritual life – the Augustinian idea of the memory, which is very important to get, because the spiritual life is to a great extent a question of your consciousness. What are you conscious of? Your consciousness depends a great deal on your unconsciousness, and all this is lumped together in the word *memoria* by St. Augustine.[VI]

First let's start with a very simple external aid to prayer, namely the cross. Think of the novitiate chapel, and think of the cross we've got behind the altar there. Now that is exactly the kind of cross that St. Aelred said you should have in the chapel of the recluse.[VII] That isn't why it's there. A lot of people don't like this cross. All the aesthetes around here think it isn't very good. Actually it's excellent – it's really excellent for the purpose. It's not a great work of art or anything like that, but it's absolutely suitable for its purpose. How we got this cross is, this one was done for a private chapel of a house of some people who are friends of Jacques Maritain and a Dominican group who live outside of Strasbourg. The chapel's about the size of our chapel, and it was designed by this man who lives down here in Lexington,[VIII] and he did the cross just exactly for that little private chapel, which is the same kind of chapel, and then took it all the way over there and saw that it didn't quite fit. So when he was over there he did another one, and then brought this one back, and we've got it – it's sort of providential!

St. Aelred says that in the recluse chapel you should have this particular kind of cross, and of course this fits the Cistercian ancient rule[IX] that you never had sculptured figures in any form whatever in a Cistercian church or chapel, until the decadent period. All you had were crosses with the figure of the Crucified painted on flat – not a figure in the round or anything like that. But what is particularly different about this cross that we have up there, what makes it slightly different from other ones – it certainly isn't a realistic picture of Our Lord's suffering or anything like that. It's not meant to be realistic. It's a picture of Our Lord. What would you say would be the characteristic of the figure on the cross? There's not too much indicating glory openly, but serenity. There's a big, a great serene figure, and I think the thing that strikes you most is the outspread arms. Actually I don't know where Victor Hammer got all these ideas. He's a very traditional person. He's about 85 years old now. He's an old artist who lived in Vienna until Hitler came along, and Hitler threw him out because he wouldn't do propaganda art for the Nazis, so Hitler chased him out. But he lived in Vienna, which is a very cultured city, and he knew a lot of people, and he's got this European tradition of sacred art pretty much in his bones.

What St. Aelred says about this is that in this kind of cross, besides having outstretched arms, straight and so forth, giving a sense of openness and expansiveness and all-embracingness, you've got two figures there: you've got St. John and the Blessed Virgin. Now the way St. Aelred handles this – he makes a great point of this – when he gets through describing this cross, it becomes not just a picture of the crucifixion. It is a kind of expression of the whole transfiguration of the cosmos in Christ, because in Mary and John you have the whole of creation included in the form of masculine and feminine. You see how deep an idea that is, because that goes back to some of these oriental concepts – the Chinese concept of creation, for example: the inner constituent of all being is this division between yang and yin, positive and negative, masculine and feminine and so forth, and the interchange between them. In St. Maximus the Confessor,[X] you find the center of St. Maximus' idea is that in Christ you've got these dualities reduced to unity. He runs through all the different dualities that are reduced to unity in Christ, and one of them is the duality of masculine and feminine. Aelred brings this out here, and so the meaning of this particular kind of cross is, first, you've got this all-embracing, wide-open gesture of the figure on the cross, calling all men to Him, and this all-embracing unity. It's the idea of all things coming to unity through the cross, which is a very deep contemplative idea, and you can see what that means.

The recluse is locked up in a little hutch and never sees the world at all or never sees anything outside this little hutch, but the whole world is supposed to be before the recluse depicted in this form, and so you find writers in the tradition of St. Aelred talking about this cross as the figure of truth. Christ on the cross in this form is the figure of truth painted on the cross, so that actually what is supposed to be contained in this kind of crucifix is all truth. This is an expression of all truth: historical truth, metaphysical truth, theological truth – all truth coming to a point in this particular kind of cross.

Aelred says this is the model for all sacred art. This is his basic point for sacred art that he makes here – that all images should be for you incentives to love, and not *spectaculum vanitatis*. Now *spectaculum* – a spectacle – is something that you look upon: *incentivum* and *spectaculum* – he balances these two words,[XI] and actually in English we use Latin words like this, words of Latin derivation, having lost the original sense of their meanings. So we say "incentive" and "spectacle": an incentive to charity and a spectacle of vanity. If you translate this that way you don't get the meaning! What is included in "incentive" if you think in terms of the Latin word? The idea of fire is in there, and in *spectaculum* is the idea of *spectare*, just simply looking. So there is the alternative, then, of the purpose of good art. It should contain fire; it should be a source of fire and not just a source of looking, so that the function of art is to make you burn within and not just simply to satisfy your desire to see. This is all very important. If you get the feeling of terms like this, you understand what these Cistercian Fathers are talking about. You understand their view of things. Then he says, "Hence from all images it is necessary that you ascend to the One, for One is necessary, and there is this One which is found only in the One, with the One, by the One, with Whom there is no change or shadow of alteration."[XII]

Where have you heard that phrase before? Today's epistle of St. James – from the lesson (you can't call it the epistle any more

– it's got to be called a lesson!) from St. James today.[XIII] "He who clings to Him becomes one spirit with Him."[XIV] Of course this is almost the motto of the Cistercian Order! Where does that come from? It comes from St. Paul, but it is all over the place in every page of St. Bernard:[XV] he who clings to the Lord is made one spirit with the Lord. This is the idea of the Cistercian life – to become one spirit with the Lord. In this is a basically Trinitarian theology: to become one spirit with the Father in the Son, and what that really means – this is sort of shorthand for the whole spiritual ideal of the Cistercians: *transiens in illud* – "passing through to that One which is always the same and whose years never fail."[XVI] So this is the purpose of all sacred images and if they don't fulfill that purpose, then we don't have them. That's what they're for, and of course this is basically a kind of platonic idea.

St. Aelred had great devotion to the cross, and he had also devotion to the name Christ in English, which he kept saying in English. When he was dying he kept saying the name of Christ in English, because it had more meaning to him, and his disciples brought to him the figure of truth painted upon the cross, and he was saying the name of Christ when he was dying.[XVII] This is typical of his spirituality. His meditation, it was said, centered upon the cross and went through the cross to the Father. It's said that his meditation was like a thread in a needle,[XVIII] but his mind was the needle and the thread was the intention of his meditation – not just an abstract intention but the movement of his meditation. It passed through Christ and reached the Father, and of course a thread and a needle – you don't just pass through – it unites: a thread is to sew two things together, so that he was sewed together with the Father by the thread and needle of his mind and his thought. So this is a sort of typical medieval presentation.

Now you want to get down to the real meaning of this – is this idea of memory and presence. We've had this before, but we want to keep going at it because it's very important – a big Cistercian theme – memory and presence – and actually sometimes they contrast the two and sometimes they unite the two. For example it's contrasted in the hymn *Jesu Dulcis Memoria* – "Jesus, Sweet to the Memory."[XIX] Where does that come in the liturgical year? Feast of the Holy Name of Our Lord.[XX] It's supposed to have been written by St. Bernard – probably wasn't, but it's certainly a Cistercian hymn, anyway. The contrast there is: "O Jesus, how sweet it is to have You in the memory; what will it be to have you fully present?"[XXI] and so forth. But other Cistercians don't make that contrast. They run the two together: memory *is* presence. For us, memory usually is referred to the past. We speak of the memory as a faculty which remembers things which were past. For the Cistercians and St. Augustine, it isn't the past; it's the present. Memory is the faculty of the present and not of the past. It only refers to the past in so far as it makes the past present. For us it's the other way around: the memory is that which makes the present past. We get out of the present and go into the past. But for them it was the contrary: that we bring the past into the present. *Memoria* is the faculty of presence. This is the basic thing: for St. Augustine and the Cistercian Fathers, memory is the presence of being to itself, and you could translate it then not "memory" but "awareness." So it's awareness or consciousness, so to speak. It's being conscious of itself, and this is characteristic of man, that he is fully conscious of himself, conscious of his being. The thing that is important about this is not just that *memoria* is the presence of my being to itself, but it's also what's more important than that. The really important thing there is the presence of God as the source of my being, in my being, so that the real idea of Augustinian *memoria* and of Cistercian *memoria* is not just an awareness of myself, without God. On the contrary, that's exactly what it isn't, what it shouldn't be, so that if we are wasting our time thinking of ourselves and being conscious of ourselves with a consciousness that does not make us at the same time conscious of God, we are doing something contrary to our monastic state. This is exactly what we should not be doing. We should develop in the monastic state a consciousness of ourselves which is simultaneously a consciousness of God, and which tends to be such a consciousness of God that we're not conscious of ourselves. This is the real meaning of *memoria*, and this is very important indeed, so that for the Cistercians the great thing is the purification and restoration of our memory.

Now this ties in very well with this whole concept. If you read that thing on St. Augustine and psychotherapy[XXII] that was on the board there a few weeks ago, that was developed very very clearly – that the holiness and balance of the health of the soul is centered on this concept of memory and the restoration of the memory and the healing of the memory. Now this is purely and simply what genuine psychoanalysis does. Fake psychoanalysis does all sorts of other things, but genuine psychoanalysis is like healing of man's inmost consciousness, and a bringing together of consciousness and reality and purifying out of all sorts of unrealities from the consciousness.

To understand this[XXIII] you have to go back to the beginning, and in the beginning Adam was Adam; and for Adam, consciousness and perfect happiness were the same thing. To be conscious was to be happy.[XXIV] Now for us that's sometimes true and a lot of times it's not true. One of the great problems of modern man is that as soon as he becomes conscious of himself he becomes unhappy, because when he's conscious of himself he's conscious of an unhappy being. Now this is perfectly normal. This is our present state. This is a good thing. This is a gift of God to fallen man. That his consciousness of himself should be an unhappy consciousness is a gift, because if we were happy when we're fallen, we would be like people who had a mortal wound and didn't feel it, and therefore didn't do anything about it; whereas the unhappiness makes us, reminds us, that we are a wounded being and consequently we have to do something about it. Now for Adam it was different. As soon as he remembered he was Adam, he was happy, because in remembering that he was Adam he immediately remembered that he was the child of God, and he was aware of God in himself. So memory was happiness. Memory is taken to cover the whole spiritual, interior consciousness of Adam. It's broken up into the three faculties of memory, intellect and will. By his memory he was inseparably present; God was inseparably present to him. That is to say, he never could be separated from God, and this is the work of the Father – it's attributed to the Father. In the depths of one's soul, in the depths of one's memory, is the Father as a primordial presence, of Whom one is basically aware. Now from this deep inner presence of the Father comes forth knowledge in the intellect, unerring knowledge of the Father, and where does that come from? the Son! Fill up the picture now: the will – what's in the will? Where does it come from? Love: it comes from the Holy Spirit. This is the way a man is supposed to be; this is the way he's supposed to function; this is the way we're made; this is the way Adam was.[XXV]

This is the way we are not, and this is what we're trying to be – that our consciousness is basically a consciousness of the Father and not a consciousness of ourselves. If we're conscious of ourselves, we're not conscious of the Father, because if we're conscious of ourselves, we go far enough down so that our self is the root – the root or ground or whatever these Eckhart people call it[XXVI] – if as far as it goes, you take your elevator down and get down in the cellar of your own self, and it's just you, and I get down in the cellar and that's me, that's the ground, and then out of that comes knowledge – of who? of me! From this *memoria* and knowledge of myself, what is born? love – of who? of me! Net result: total unhappiness, because that is the way a man is *not* supposed to be, and that is the way we are, so that the function of the Cistercian life is a healing of this whole being, and it starts with the healing of the memory. It doesn't start with the healing of love! That's where we go wrong. We start working on this end of the thing, but if the root is simply an awareness of myself and not an awareness of God, then I can tinker all I want with the will but it's not going to work.

2.

I ran across a little section of a poem here that a lay woman wrote to somebody who was thinking about religious life. I'll just read you a little bit of this poem. It's quite good: "I hope that you are certain / For if you are not / You will be a baby playing with matches / And may burn up your whole world / Soon you will find that the cross is less often of wood than of air / And that the nails are the winds whistling through the holes in your heart." I think that describes some of the problems of religious life pretty well: "Soon you will find that the cross is less often of wood than of air / And that the nails are the winds whistling through the holes in your heart." If you've got a few holes in your heart, why think of that, because that is what it is. That's what St. Aelred is trying to get away from with this *memoria* idea of not having holes in your heart, or at least if the holes are made in your heart, it's for a purpose: so that you will get down to this real memory of God.

About that memory of God – you mustn't think of it on too superficial a level. Don't think of it just as – well, what would be the superficial level? The superficial level of this memory is: I remember God the way I remember a book, or a person, or something that happened ten years ago or something like that. That is to say, I call to mind an object among other objects, and this object is God, and so I set aside objects like automobiles and TV and other things like that. I move these objects out and I move the object God in, so that I've forgotten TV and I've remembered God. Well, this is alright. There's nothing wrong with this, but it means more. When Aelred and these people talk about it, it means more than that. In what way does it mean more than that? How much deeper does it go? It isn't just in the head, of course. It is a personal relationship. But is there even more than that? Is it just like them coming into the room and being in the presence of somebody else?

Your whole being is transformed by this presence, and actually your whole consciousness of yourself is transformed by this presence. It isn't you remaining the same. For example, I've got these two objects here – this and this, and I'm looking at this. When I take my mind off this one and I look at this one, nothing much happens to me. I just look from this one to this one. But this memory of God is that instead of looking from this object to this object to this object and then to God, all of a sudden instead of seeing objects, I am aware of God. This doesn't necessarily cut out the objects at all. It doesn't block out the awareness of objects. It means that it transforms my awareness of everything. Put it this way: it has to do partly with our awareness of who we are, and we are sons of God.

In many religions, in Buddhism and Christianity and so forth, you get this parable of the son who doesn't know who he is. It's like the parable of the prodigal son[XXVII] – the prodigal son, he knows where he comes from, but in this other one,[XXVIII] I think he doesn't know who he is. He is the son of a king, and all of a sudden, at a given moment, his identity as the son of a king is revealed to him. What does that do? What does the son think? Immediately his whole relation to everything is changed, because he knows himself as someone different. That's what this memory of God means. It does not mean that I, just being who I am and without any change, suddenly called to mind God as an object. It means to say that in acquiring this awareness of God I recover a totally different sense of my own being, and my relation to everything changes, and my awareness of everything changes. For example, if I'm the son of a king, and the king owns everything that's around, and I have thought of myself as a beggar on this property, liable to be chased off at any minute, and all of a sudden I realize that I'm the son of the king who owns it and that nobody's going to chase me off it, and that this is mine, I have a totally different view of the thing. So it is with us in the world, with the Christian in the cosmos. In a certain sense he is a stranger, and in a certain sense he isn't. He knows that this all belongs to his Father, and his relationship to it changes completely. If you understand this, you'll be saved from making some mistakes about this memory of God – mistakes in the order of shutting out everything in order to put in a concept of God, which isn't what it is. It's rather having a new awareness of oneself, and then consequently having a different awareness of everything.

How does he work this? What did we say last time about this? You got one of these three-fold setups; now he's got a lot of these. The one we had was about Adam's happiness consisted in having God the Father present in his memory, which was not just remembering that there is somebody called God the Father up there. It is an immediate presence of the Father in the memory, so that the memory is almost, so to speak, identified with the Father, so that in the deepest root of one's being, what one finds is not himself but the Father. Now this is a big order. This isn't just a question of a thought. This is in the order of mysticism. In the intelligence is the Son, and in the will is the Holy Ghost. This is a standard setup. This you get in St. Augustine all the time, and Aelred runs this through countless times in different forms. When you get this kind of thing, what's important is not just to remember that he said it this way. It's to be able to compare the different times – he runs this three-fold thing numerous times. Every once in a while, every few pages, he takes you though this and the important thing is to note the differences.

Very often it's almost the same, but sometimes there are significant differences, and here's one of the significant differences:

here's the same three, the same subject and the same three, but a significant difference. Adam is now the fellow that's wounded by the robbers on the road from Jerusalem to Jericho, and Christ is the Good Samaritan.[XXIX] That's a standard patristic approach. Adam was in Jerusalem. What's Jerusalem? the city of peace. What follows from this – he's got a three-fold rundown on this peace: peace in the intellect, peace in the will, so forth, so forth.[XXX] So Jerusalem (*pax*) – and peace in the will – with what? with charity. What'll be the next one? peace in the intellect – with what? knowledge, truth, understanding, wisdom – something like that – I forget exactly what's he got here: *ratio*, *veritas* – truth; *ratio*, *intellectus* – it doesn't make too much difference – truth. What's the one we have left? Memory, but he doesn't say memory this time; this time he says: in the nature. This leaves you sort of hanging in midair! What's he getting at? Where are we now? This isn't the same three. This is a funny business here, and you probably can't guess what it is that establishes peace in our nature. He says: "eternity" – it's funny, huh? So here, on these two, he practically hasn't changed, and in this one, there's apparently a very big change. Instead of *memoria* – and of course this is referring to the three Divine Persons, the Holy Spirit, the Son and the Father. In this one, instead of memory, he now says: nature, and instead of what was the memory happy with – presence. So there isn't that much difference actually, after all, because eternity and presence go together. The thing that Adam had in Jerusalem, in Eden, in the vision of peace, was that the Father was unchangingly present to his memory. Here he pushes it even further and says: to his nature. Now that's extremely deep. That's something, if you can really think about that a little bit, because what does that mean? That means that in Adam's own being, the Father was always present; the Father was eternally present to his being, so that in the depths of his own being was the Father.

Why do you suppose that we all respond to this just like that? We do! Why do we? It isn't really our nature, because if you put this into theology after St. Thomas, you get into an awful lot of trouble, because it isn't our nature – it's supernatural. This is the way we're supposed to be, and he actually says – when you say nature in the terms of St. Thomas, you're getting into this abstract nature versus supernature, and it's a totally different question. But he's talking in the concrete, and he says that the reparation of the memory and of the nature is a recovery in the hidden depths of our own spirit of what we actually are – that is to say, in the mind of God, what God has intended us to be, so that actually, the reparation of the memory is simply a recovery of what's there. The Father *is* present in the depths of our being. That's the point, and the reason why we respond to this is because we know that that's the way it ought to be. There is something in us that says, how can it be that the Father isn't present, and we go around – we're prodigal sons who are wandering around far from the Father's house when we're there all the time, so that the most important thing is this reparation of the memory, which brings one down into the depths to realize that although we are, on a certain level, alienated from the Father, in the depths we're united to Him.

But this is not natural. This is supernatural, and it requires the Son and the Holy Spirit. It can't be done without the Son and the Holy Spirit, so that therefore another thing is very necessary here. It's not just the memory of the Father, but now you have to bring the redemption into it, and of course this messes up the threesome. What else have you got to remember – we're now in the order of redemption, of the supernatural – to make this thing really redemptive? Put it in terms of theology: the cross, Christ and the cross.[XXXI] Therefore for St. Aelred, actually the important thing isn't so much that we go straight to this idea of the Father present in us, but we go to the cross. In this memory of the cross, theologically speaking, this reconciliation takes place in the depths of our being, because actually we're not capable at all times of just all of a sudden sitting down and saying, the Father is present in the depths of my being. Sometimes we are, sometimes we aren't – some more than others. But we are capable of thinking the Father has given his Son to die for me on the cross, because this is something that everybody can remember. This is simple, and it's also concrete, and it's something that you can latch onto.

That's a liturgical reminder but he comes to this in a second; maybe we'll get to this. He does bring it to this; actually he is in a minute going to talk about this liturgical memory because the liturgy is supposed to revive this spiritual memory. The liturgy repairs the memory and hence the *anamnesis* in the Mass is a reparation of the memory. So remember what he's talking about.

When you say the reparation of the memory, it means a deepening of this consciousness of the Father with Whom we are reconciled through the sacrifice of the Son. Therefore it is in remembering the cross that we are able to open up the inmost depths of our being so this sort of primordial memory of the Father is able to come out. It is through the cross that we get there. You don't go directly into the depths of your heart. Of course *we* do, to a great extent, but that's because we're receiving the sacraments all the time, and we're hearing the word of God all the time, and we're surrounded at all times by the grace and mystery of the cross, so that in our life here we don't have to think that explicitly of the cross at all times, because we are brought by the cross into the context of this deeper mystery. But nevertheless there is this – it has a part in our life too.

The next thing he says that repairs the memory (before he gets on to the liturgy) is scripture. What it is doing is *reparans memoriam* (he uses the word *documentum* – I don't know how to translate that or make anything relevant out of that).[XXXII] He just says that the scripture is there repairing your memory, bringing you to the consciousness of the Father through these mysteries of Christ. Then he comes to the liturgy, and he explains how all the liturgical feasts are renewals of this deep memory of the mystery of the redemption, bringing us into contact with the Father. He even says the feasts of the saints have this effect too. Here's what he says: "The Christ, my dear brethren, visits us by his servants the saints, or by his most dear Mother, or what is better, in person."[XXXIII] These are in the liturgical feasts. "What are all these feasts of saints that we celebrate so often if not visits of the Lord, and because it was expedient that we should always have in memory the benefits that His corporal presence brought to us."[XXXIV] With Our Lord, again, this *memoria* is repaired, especially by this idea of gratitude. It is not just a question of remembering a fact, remembering the Passion as a fact. It's a question of total gratitude for the Passion. What he's trying to do all the time is to get things that are going to open us up inside, and the mere memory of a fact doesn't open up anything much. It has to be a question of gratitude, of love, of response, which opens us up inside, so that we go down into the depths of our being there because we should remember these things and because He knows that our memory is corrupted by oblivion. Our memory is corrupted by forgetfulness of realities. That is to say that we are remembering other things, and what do we remember? What have we got in our minds all the time – good heavens! What nonsense goes through – all this stuff!

Our memory is corrupted, and one of the functions, one of the first things in the early Cistercian training, is to get the novice soaked in scripture so that his mind is absolutely full with all kinds of scripture images and the scripture images have pushed out everything that he brought in from the world. This is, ideally, what it's supposed to be, what it should be, but we still do get a lot of other images anyway, but still that the idea that scripture should fill our minds – this is the first thing that should happen, that because you know that one of the first trials – at least it was with me and I think it is with most novices – is this disorder of the memory that comes when you enter the monastery. What happens is that you start remembering all sorts of wacky things – at least I did – not necessarily at all things that are attractive or anything, things that are absurd that keep popping back into your mind. I remember the first day I went to work. It was awful! To begin with I was trying to say the rosary on my fingers, raking the préau.[xxxv] My idea was, I was going to get the rosary in every day during the afternoon work, on my fingers. I'd soon find out how you can do that! But every possible idiotic thing that I'd forgotten would start coming back into my mind, and this went on for a long time. I think with a lot of people it's like that. So the first thing is to get something else in our memory that's going to have a function of helping us get deep inside. He knows that our memory is corrupted by oblivion. He willed in His goodness that these benefits should not only be recalled to us by scripture, but they should be represented to us by certain spiritual actions, and that's of course the liturgical mysteries, so that actually what we do is, we relive the mysteries of Christ in the liturgy, and this of course is much more than just recalling them to mind. In reliving them, our whole being enters into the mysteries.

So today we relive the Ascension. The grace of today is the grace of the Ascension, and we relive this grace. Our prayer today is somewhat colored by the grace of the Ascension. If we're really mavericks and are meditating on Christmas or something today, that's all right too, but the characteristic grace of today is the grace of the Ascension – although, who knows, anything's liable to happen, and why not? You may get the grace – it's in the lives of the saints of the Order. One of the great visions of St. Gertrude was in Advent. She was going along in Advent and all of a sudden a responsory of the Third Sunday after Easter hit her,[XXXVI] and the whole thing opened up. It was a responsory of David with the singers dancing in front of the ark – your guess is as good as mine! But this hit her – so fine! no loss! When He gave the sacrament of His body and blood He said, "Do this in memory of me."[XXXVII] It is for this reason that these feasts have been instituted in the Church.

So that gives you some idea of what he's driving at and how important this is. This is the foundation of contemplation in our Order, this deepening of religious consciousness by meditation on the mysteries of Christ, by scripture, by liturgy. Everything that goes on in our life is supposed to be deepening this religious consciousness and driving out this secular consciousness, so that we don't have secular minds. The secular mind is the mind that is lost in forgetfulness of who we are, and it is a consciousness of ourselves as we are not, a consciousness of a secular self. What is a secular self? It's a self that wants to assert itself, wants to get somewhere, wants to have pleasure, wants to satisfy its ambition, and all these things. This is the self that we're struggling with, and what we have to do is recognize the fact that when we are in the grip of this self we are in delusion; we are not ourselves; we are deluded. We're mad! This is madness, and this is what you get.

Adam of Perseigne has got this whole setup that he gives on formation, and the first thing that one has to do is to realize that when you're thinking like a secular, you're nuts! He says it's *amentia*: you're crazy.[XXXVIII] This is a crazy way to think. The sane way to think is to get down to this awareness of who we really are. We're amnesia victims! This is the old platonic idea – people wandering around, not knowing who they are. You pull them into the police court: "Who are you?" "I dunno." Well it's the same thing. So we have to remember who we are. We're children of God. We're not the people that we think we are. We're children of God and we have to get down to this. The basic thing that he's shooting at is ignorance, he says, and this of course brings him very close to Buddhism, because that's the basic thing in Buddhism.[XXXIX] The basic root of all evil in Buddhism is ignorance – not ignorance of facts – the ignorance of the truth about our own being, and this is absolutely fundamental. This is a big thing. This is great, for every approach to contemplation is going to be helped by this kind of thing. It's not a question of responsibility. It's not ignorance in terms of responsibility. It's ignorance in the sense of alienation from reality. All sin proceeds from this – because the Buddhists aren't too much concerned with responsibility, not in the sense that we are. They're very much concerned with it in another sense, because with them every cause has effects.[XL] You can't do anything without paying the price. Anything that you do that is the fruit of ignorance, you have to undo it. They're much tougher than we are! See, we do all these things and then Our Lord undoes them for us, but they: "*You* do it!" You've got to undo it. Everything, every knot you tied, has got to be untied, so that's quite an order.

I. Merton originally intended his conferences on pre-Benedictine monasticism to focus on the *Regula Magistri* (*Rule of the Master*) (J. P. Migne, ed., *Patrologiae Cursus Completus, Series Latina* [*PL*], 221 vols. (Paris: Garnier, 1844-1865) vol. 88, cols. 943-1052) and its textual relationship to the *Rule* of Benedict (see *Pre-Benedictine Monasticism* xvii-xx, 6) but in fact the series of conferences moved in a different direction and he never did return to this text.

II. Merton spends a couple of conferences at this time looking at a pair of dialogues from the Egyptian Desert Fathers on distractions in prayer.

III. On June 21, the week after the second of the conferences on distractions, Merton begins his set of conferences on Syrian monasticism that will continue for more than a year, until his retirement as novice master to become a full-time hermit on August 20, 1965 (see *Pre-Benedictine Monasticism* 213-337).

IV. *De Institutis Inclusarum* (*PL* 32, cols. 1451-1474; published as "*De Vita Eremitica*" under the name of St. Augustine).

V. Merton will also draw on the *Speculum Caritatis* and a couple of the *Sermones Inediti*.

VI. It is likely that Merton is relying here on the discussion in the section "Memoire et presence" of the Introduction to Aelred de Rievaulx, *La Vie de Recluse; La Prière Pastorale*, ed. and trans. Charles Dumont, Sources Chrétiennes vol. 76 (Paris: Éditions du Cerf, 1961) 19-20, which mentions the influence of Augustine along with other aspects of the topic that Merton will touch on below. Dumont cites Étienne Gilson's *Introduction à l'Étude de Saint Augustin* (Paris: J. Vrin, 1931)

130 as his source for the idea of *memoria* in Augustine. See also 52, n. 3, which relates the theme of *memoria* to ancient monastic tradition. On the same topic see also Étienne Gilson, *The Mystical Theology of St. Bernard*, trans. A. H. C. Downes (New York: Sheed & Ward, 1940) 81-82, citing chapter 3 of the *De Diligendo Deo*.

VII. *De Institutione Inclusarum* 26 (Dumont 104/105; *PL* 32, col. 1463).

VIII. The cross was painted by Merton's friend Victor Hammer and came to the novitiate in the circumstances described here. In his Foreword for the Catalogue accompanying the Hammer Exhibition at the North Carolina Museum of Art in 1965, Merton writes of the version finally hung in the Grunelius chapel: "The content of Victor Hammer's religious paintings is at once concrete, spiritual, and individual. And though he generally uses traditional iconographical styles and patterns, his religious art is not *Art d'Église*. His rood Cross painted for the chapel of Alexandre and Antoinette de Grunelius at Kolbsheim, in Alsace (a replica of the same Rood hangs in the chapel of the novitiate at the Abbey of Gethsemani), is simple, noble and even in some sense mysterious, though this judgment might surprise the artist himself. But the adjective is chosen by one who worships daily before this Rood, and he has the right if not the duty to make the impression known. Aelred of Rievaulx wrote in the twelfth century that the Rood Cross was the proper kind to have in the chapel of an anchorage, that is to say in the chapel where a recluse (his sister) was to spend her life of prayer. The rood, with the figures of Mary and John by the Crucified, is in fact a cosmic as well as redemptive symbol, and it has the deepest eschatological significance (the 'recapitulation of all in Christ'). The anchorage needs to contain in its heart this picture of the World not as it is in itself, but as it is in Christ. Aelred was not familiar with the modern concept of psychological archetypes, though he was deeply imbued, as were all his contemporaries, with Biblical typology. It is the archetypal and typological quality of Victor Hammer's religious paintings that make them so arresting and, I might add, sometimes so enigmatic" (*Letters of Thomas Merton and Victor and Carolyn Hammer* 301-302 [Appendix B]). Details concerning the creation and eventual acquisition of the novitiate chapel cross are found throughout the Merton-Hammer correspondence proper (see 43, 47, 50, 85-86, 130, 159, 215, 254-55, 311 n. 13). See also the photographs of the Kolbsheim Chapel and of a replica of the Kolbsheim rood cross following page 174.

IX. See *Instituta Capituli Generalis* [1134], c. 20: "*De Sculpturis et Picturis, et Cruce Lignea*" ("Concerning Sculptures and Pictures, and the Wooden Cross"): "*Sculpturae vel picturae in ecclesiis nostris seu in officinis aliquibus monasterii ne fiant interdicimus, quia dum talibus intenditur, utilitas bonae meditationis vel disciplina religiosae gravitatis saepe negligitur. Cruces tamen pictas quae sint ligneae habemus*" (J.-M. Canivez, ed., *Statuta Capitulorum Generalium Ordinis Cisterciensis ab Anno 1116 ad Annum 1786*, 8 vols. [Louvain: Bureaux de la Revue d'Histoire Ecclésiastique, 1933-1941] 1.17) ("We forbid sculptures or paintings to be in our churches or in other rooms of the monastery, because while attention is directed to such things, the advantage of good meditation or the discipline of religious seriousness is often neglected. However we do have painted crosses, which are of wood").

X. See Merton's summary of the vision of Maximus in *Introduction to Christian Mysticism* 127-28: "*Without theoria physike*, which penetrates to the inner *logos*, and {its} orientation to unity and simplicity and wholeness, nature and law tend to disintegration, separation and conflict. With the understanding of the *logoi*, in love and in the light given by God, they fulfill their true purpose and tend to unity, {to} recapitulation in Christ."

XI. *De Institutione Inclusarum* 26 (Dumont 106; *PL* 32, col. 1463).

XII. "*Hinc enim omnibus ad unum necesse est ut conscendas, quoniam unum est necessarium. Illud est unum quod non invenitur nisi in uno, apud unum, cum uno, apud quem non est transmutatio, nec vicissitudinis obumbratio*" (*De Institutione Inclusarum* 26 [Dumont 106; *PL* 32, col. 1463]).

XIII. James 1:17: "Every best gift and every perfect gift is from above, coming down from the Father of lights, with whom there is no change nor shadow of alteration."

XIV. 1 Corinthians 6:17.

XV. *De Consideratione* 5.12 (*PL* 182, col. 795B); *In Dedicatione Ecclesiae* 1.7 (*PL* 183, col. 521D); *In Festo Omnium Sanctorum* 3.3 (*PL* 183, col. 470); *In Festo S. Michaelis* 2.4 (*PL* 183, col. 454A); *In Psalmum Qui Habitat* 8.11 (*PL* 183, col. 215D); *Pro Dominica I Novembris* 5.2 (*PL* 183, col. 354A); *Sermones de Diversis* 80.1, 92.1 (*PL* 183, cols. 699A, 714C); *Sermones in Cantica Canticorum* 8.9, 26.5, 31.6, 59.2, 61.1, 71.6, 83.6 (*PL* 183, cols. 814D, 906C, 943B, 1062C, 1071B, 1123D, 1184C).

XVI. "*transiens in illud unum quod semper idem est, et cuius anni non deficiunt*" (*De Institutione Inclusarum* 26 [Dumont 106; *PL* 32, col. 1463]).

XVII. Walter Daniel, *The Life of Ailred of Rievaulx*, ed. and trans. F. M. Powicke (New York: Thomas Nelson, 1950) 59-60.

XVIII. *Life of Ailred* 19.

XIX. *PL* 184, cols. 1317-1320.

XX. January 3.

XXI. "*Quam bonus te quaerentibus! / Sed quid invenientibus!*" (col. 1317).

XXII. Martin Versfeld, "St. Augustine as Psychotherapist," *New Blackfriars* 45 (March 1964) 98-110.

XXIII. Merton is evidently relying here on the opening chapter of the original French version of Amédée Hallier, OCSO, *Un Éducateur Monastique:*

Aelred De Rievaulx (Paris: J. Gabalda, 1959) 29-47, for the English translation of which he would provide the Introduction (*The Monastic Theology of Aelred of Rivaulx* [Spencer, MA: Cistercian Publications, 1969]; see the following essay, pages 392-400).

XXIV. See *Speculum Caritatis* 1.3.8-9: "*Quod homo ad imaginem sui Creatoris conditus, et beatitudinis capax sit*" (*PL* 195, cols. 507C-508A) ("That the human person is created in the image of the Creator and has the capacity for happiness").

XXV. "*Tria haec memoriam dico, scientiam, amorem, sive voluntatem. Aeternitatis quippe capax est memoria, sapientiae scientia, dulcedinis amor. In his tribus ad imaginem Trinitatis conditus homo, Deum quem memoria retinebat sine oblivione, scientia agnoscebat sine errore; amore complectebatur sine alterius rei cupiditate. Hinc beatus*" (cols. 507D-508A) ("I say these three are memory, knowledge and love, or will. Memory has the capacity for eternity, knowledge for wisdom, love for sweetness. In these three the person was made in the image of the Trinity, God, whom the memory held without forgetfulness, whom knowledge recognized without error, who was embraced by love without the desire for anything else. Thus he was happy").

XXVI. On the "ground" in Meister Eckhart and John Tauler, see *Introduction to Christian Mysticism* 200-206.

XXVII. Luke 15:11-32.

XXVIII. *Lotus Sutra* 4 (*The Sacred Books of the East*, ed. F. Max Müller, 50 vols. [Oxford: Clarendon Press, 1879-1910] 21:98-117).

XXIX. "*Sermo in Ascensione Domini de Raptu Helye*," *Sermones Inediti B. Aelredi Abbatis Rievallensis*, ed. C. H. Talbot (Rome: Apud Curiam Generalem Sacri Ordinis Cisterciensis, 1952) 101.

XXX. "*Ierusalem interpretatur visio pacis. Cuius pacis? Pax tibi Adam in eternitate, in veritate, in caritate. Eternitas pacificabit naturam, veritas rationem, caritas voluntatem. Pax erat in natura, quam eternitas servabat ab omni corruptione. Pax in ratione, quam veritas servabat ab omni errore. Pax in voluntate, quam caritas servabat ab omni cupiditate. Ex caritate erat voluntas recta, ex veritate ratio luminosa, ex eternitate substantia incorrupta*" (*Sermones Inediti* 101) ("Jerusalem means vision of peace. Whose peace? Your peace, Adam, in eternity, in truth, in love. Eternity will pacify nature, truth will pacify reason, love will pacify the will. Peace was in nature, which eternity preserved from all corruption. Peace was in reason, which truth preserved from all error. Peace was in the will, which love preserved from all false desire. Rightly ordered will was from love, luminous reason from truth, uncorrupted substance from eternity").

XXXI. *Speculum Caritatis* 1.5.14: "*Quod post Salvatoris adventum Dei in homine renovetur imago: et quod non hic sed in futuro speranda sit ipsius renovationis perfectio*" (*PL* 195, col. 509AC) ("That the image of God in the human person was restored after the coming of the Savior; and that the perfection of this restoration will not be here but in the future to be hoped for").

XXXII. "*per Mediatorem Dei et hominum hominem Christum Iesum ... reparatur tandem memoria per sacrae Scripturae documentum, intellectus per fidei sacramentum, amor per charitatis quotidianum incrementum. Perfecta imaginis reformatio, si memoriam oblivio non interpolet, scientiam nullus error obnubilet, amorem nulla cupiditas interpellet*" (col. 509B) ("Through the Mediator between God and men, the man Christ Jesus … at last the memory is restored through the book of the holy scriptures, the intellect through the sacrament of faith, love through the daily increase of charity. The reformation of the image is perfect if forgetfulness does not obscure the memory, if no error clouds knowledge, if no cupidity blocks love").

XXXIII. *Sermo* 23, *De Omnibus Sanctis* 2: "*Aliquando, fratres charissimi, visitat nos per aliquem servorum suorum, aliquando per* plures [sometimes through one of his servants, sometimes through many], *aliquando per charissimam matrem suam, aliquando, quod plus est, per seipsum*" (*PL* 195, cols. 339D-340A).

XXXIV. "*Quae sunt enim istae festivitates Sanctorum, quas tam saepe celebramus, nisi quaedam visitationes, per quas visitat nos Dominus noster, et confortat? Quia ergo expediebat nobis, semper memores existere beneficiorum eius, quae nobis per praesentiam suam corporalem exhibuit*" (col. 340A).

XXXV. The central open space surrounded by the monastic cloister; see *Monastic Observances* 19: "The cloister with its 'préau' or 'garth' should normally then be a place of (1) silence; (2) light; (3) peace; (4) shelter; (5) delight ({an} enclosed garden)."

XXXVI. "*Decantabat populus Israel alleluia: et universa multitudo Jacob canebat legitime: Et David cum cantoribus citheram percutiebat in domo Domini, et laudes Deo canebat, alleluia, alleluia*" (*Breviarium Cisterciense*, *Pars Vernalis* [Westmalle, Belgium: Typis Cisterciensibus, 1935] 340) ("The people of Israel sang alleluia: and the entire multitude of Jacob sang properly: and David struck the lyre with the singers in the house of the Lord, and sang praises to God, alleluia, alleluia"). Merton's source for this information is unknown. According to St. Gertrude scholar and translator Alexandra Barratt (personal communication), there is apparently no such incident recorded in the authentic works of St. Gertrude.

XXXVII. Luke 22:19; 1 Corinthians 11:24.

XXXVIII. Adam of Perseigne, *Epistola* 11 (*PL* 211, col. 615AB); see below, pages 427-28.

XXXIX. See *Zen and the Birds of Appetite* 82: "Buddhism and Biblical Christianity agree in their view of man's present condition. Both are aware that man is somehow not in his right relation to the world and to things in it, or rather, to be more exact, they see that man bears in himself a mysterious tendency to falsify that relation, and to spend a great deal of energy in justifying the false view he takes of his world and of his place in it. This falsification is what Buddhists call Avidya. Avidya, usually translated 'ignorance,' is the root of all evil and suffering because it places man in an equivocal, in fact impossible position. It is an invincible error concerning the very nature of reality and man himself. It is a disposition to treat the ego as an absolute and central reality and to refer all things to it as objects of desire or of repulsion. Christianity attributes this view of man and of reality to 'original sin.'"

XL. This is a reference to the Buddhist teaching of karma.

Introduction to *The Monastic Theology of Aelred of Rievaulx*

On September 3, 1968, just a week before leaving for his trip to the West Coast and on to Asia, from which he would not return, Thomas Merton wrote in his journal: "Yesterday I finished the preface to Hallier's *Aelred*" (*Other Side of the Mountain* 163). The reference is to his introduction (vii-xiii) to the English translation of the French Cistercian Amédée Hallier's study entitled *The Monastic Theology of Aelred of Rivaulx* (Spencer, MA: Cistercian Publications, 1969). The possibility of Merton's providing a preface had first been raised by Hallier a decade earlier when he was preparing to publish, in French, what had originally been his doctoral dissertation (Amédée Hallier, OCSO, *Un Éducateur Monastique: Aelred de Rievaulx* [Paris: J. Gabalda, 1959]; see Roger Lipsey, *Make Peace Before the Sun Goes Down: The Long Encounter of Thomas Merton and His Abbot, James Fox* [Boston: Shambhala, 2015] 116-17), but evidently nothing was composed by Merton until the English translation was being readied for publication. This final look at Aelred takes an explicitly post-conciliar perspective, emphasizing the movement of *ressourcement* that enabled a renewed awareness of the riches of patristic and medieval monastic theology in their own right, not merely as somewhat inadequate, unsystematic predecessors of scholasticism, but as "the fruit not of a special kind of speculation but of a deeply lived experience of the mystery of faith." Merton identifies the "humanism full of psychological insight with plenty of relevance for our own day" of monastic theology generally and Aelred in particular, with his emphasis on a theology of community and of friendship, on the divine image as a creative openness to love and the defacing of that image by a narcissistic misuse of freedom as a kind of Sartrian "bad faith," and on monastic life as an education in "authentic freedom by loving and creative consent" to the Word and the Cross of Christ. He finds an unexpected yet profound compatibility between Aelred's "monastic pedagogy" and the "worldly" Christocentrism of Dietrich Bonhoeffer, the Lutheran theologian executed for his resistance to Hitler. "Aelred," Merton concludes, "would agree perfectly with Bonhoeffer: 'Whoever sees Jesus Christ does indeed see God and the world in one. He can thenceforward no longer see God without the world or the world without God.'" Summarizing the entire period represented by the authors discussed in the present volume and their contemporaries, Merton writes: "the monastic theology of the Cistercian and Benedictine writers of the eleventh and twelfth centuries is highly concrete, existential, biblical, imaginatively rich, full of esthetic as well as mystical intuitions, and deeply rooted in the everyday life of the time. It is concerned above all not with abstract ideas about God but with the living relationship of man with God in Christ." Such testimony is a fitting summation, a little over three months before his own death, of Merton's more than two decades of ongoing engagement with his medieval monastic predecessors.

The postconciliar era is favorable for the rediscovery of monastic theology. Not only have monks been urged to return to their sources and rethink their vocation in terms both of the original charism and of present needs, but also pre-scholastic theology can now be seen in much better perspective. As long as scholasticism occupied the entire Catholic theological landscape, blocking out everything else, with the Bible and the Fathers seen only in relation to its all-embracing system, there was small chance of the monastic theologians getting due attention. They were regarded as obscure and irrelevant scribes who had nothing original to add to the predecessors they merely copied. St. Bernard was of course respected in the domain of "spirituality" (whatever that was) and St. Anselm was mentioned in textbooks as an abbot with a flair for dialectic who had made a pass at scholastic thinking and missed. But by and large the theology of the west between St. Augustine and Peter Lombard was regarded as a wasteland.

It was not until the nineteen forties and fifties – largely with the work of Dom Jean Leclercq[I] – that the real value of the post-patristic writers in the monasteries of the west began to be rediscovered. Where we had assumed there were only trite catalogs of allegory we found again a literature rich in biblical culture, a genuine theology and a humanism full of psychological insight with plenty of relevance for our own day.

However, this does not mean that "monastic theology" has yet come into its own in America. The Middle Ages are still regarded with understandable misgivings because in America the word "medieval" refers in fact to the pseudo-medieval mishmash of romanticism, conservatism and authoritarianism whose epiphany was the pseudo-Gothic parish church in an ethnic ghetto, giving itself the airs of a cathedral though dwarfed by the surrounding factories.

Even in monasteries, where people might be expected to know better, the monastic theologians of the twelfth century have been honored rather than studied and have thus become part of the discredited medieval myth.

Studies like the present one of Fr. Amédée Hallier now make it possible for us to get an entirely new view of medieval monasticism and we can understand why M.-D. Chenu, still one of the best modern theologians, insists that a knowledge of pre-scholastic theology is necessary to balance "a certain spiritual and apostolic pragmatism"[II] in current thinking.

Let us be quite clear that the monastic theology of Aelred is not a partisan "theology of monasticism." It is not an apologia for the life of the monk, not a kind of gnostic system organized to prove some supposed superiority of "the contemplative life," urging a flight to ineffable convulsions.

A "monastic theology" is the fruit not of a special kind of speculation but of a deeply lived experience of the mysteries of faith. The aim of medieval monasticism was not simply to gain heaven by rejection of the world (for after all history shows how deeply involved the monks were in the world of their time) but a positive witness to the presence of Christ in the world. The monastic witness was not so much ascetic as eschatological. Not so much a denial of man and the flesh as an affirmation of the Word made Flesh, taking all created things to himself, in order to transform and fulfill them in himself. Hence the monastic theology of the Cistercian and Benedictine writers of the eleventh and twelfth centuries is highly concrete, existential, biblical, imaginatively rich, full of esthetic as well as mystical intuitions, and deeply rooted in the everyday life of the time. It is concerned above all not with abstract ideas about God but with the living relationship of man with God in Christ. And this of course meant an overriding concern with the love of man for man – that love by which we are known as Christ's disciples, without which there is no "life in Christ" and therefore no union with God.

Aelred's pedagogy centers on the formation of the whole man, not as an individual but as a member of a community. Monastic theology is before all else a theology of community. It implies a certain definite concept of man which it would be well to sketch out here.

Man is in his basic structure *capax Dei.*[III] He is an openness, a capacity, a possibility, a freedom, whose fulfillment is not in this or that isolated object, this or that circumscribed activity, but in a fullness beyond all "objects," the totality of consent and self-giving which is love. God is Love. Man is an openness that is fulfilled only in unconditional consent to an unconditional love. This openness, this freedom, which is at the very core of man's bring – and which imperiously demands that he transcend his being – is what the monastic theologians call the image of God in man. The capacity for freedom and love is the image of God because God himself is pure freedom and pure love. The image in man – the openness that demands to transcend itself in love – seeks to attain a perfect likeness to its original by loving as it is loved. It cannot of course attain this by its own nature. But God has given his own Son that we may be sons in him. The coming of the Word to take our freedom to himself turns the "image" into "likeness." When the Word loves the Father in us, then our freedom is transfigured in and by his Spirit, and our love becomes identical with his love. This implies perfection of pure consent, and the monastery is a school where men devote their lives to learning and practicing this consent. *Consentire salvari est*,[IV] said St. Bernard in his tract on Free Will and Grace, and his whole theology of love is a theology of *consensus*, like-mindedness, unity of hearts and wills, first on the communal level and then in that mystical community of persons where the Christian (individually and ecclesially) is caught up into participation with the triune inner life of God himself. Perfect consent in the visible and everyday life of the monastic community – a life of work in close contact with matter and nature, a life of prayer and praise rich in biblical symbol and human art – makes possible an epiphany of the invisible redemptive presence of God, in whom Three Persons are One inexhaustible consent. The visible Christian community (to realize which is the life work of the cenobite) is the fulfillment of Christ's high-priestly prayer: "May they all be one in us, Father, as you are in me and I am in you, so that the world may believe that it was you that sent me" (John 17:21).

The image of God in man – the openness to love, the capacity for total consent to God in himself and in others – remains indestructible. But it can be buried and imprisoned under selfishness. The image of God in man is not destroyed by sin but utterly disfigured by it. To be exact, the image of God in man becomes self-contradictory when its openness closes in upon itself, when it ceases to be a capacity for love and becomes simply an appetite for domination or possession: when it ceases to give and seeks only to get. In such a case, man becomes his own god and instead of loving others he uses them for his own purposes – to gratify his own narcissism as we would say today. The early Cistercians had some very refined insights into the regressive, sado-masochistic evasions by which men disguise and justify their infidelity to the inmost truth in themselves. The real root of sin, as they saw with Augustine, is close to Sartre's "bad faith"[IV] in its actual structure: it is a lying misuse of one's own freedom, turning it against itself and sabotaging it while pretending to affirm it. In monastic terms: the inclination to love, which is at the core of man's very nature as a free being, is turned in on itself as its own object and ceases to be love. When an individual freedom seeks to be its own sufficient reason for existence it ceases to be free (and here we might explore the ambiguities of freedom in the context of a loveless existentialism!).

The purpose of monastic education is, in plain terms, the education of authentic freedom by loving and creative consent. Since man is made for love, his love has to be liberated, guided, educated, directed not to objects which end in blind alleys but to *other loves* which in their free and creative response call forth more love in ourselves. In other words, love is educated by other loves, freedom by consent to, consensus with, other freedoms. At first this implies a certain difficulty and constraint. There is need of monastic discipline because the spontaneous freedom of love has been lost: egotism and narcissism have corrupted our "taste" for freedom. What we "experience" as freedom and as love is too often selfishness and self-involvement, masking as love for others. Not only must consciences be formed but one must learn to experience, to "taste" the difference between freedom and unfreedom, love and selfishness. We might mention that this "discernment of spirits" is very important in the actual working out of problems in monastic renewal today. We all know that merely authoritarian and legalistic solutions are no longer adequate. But on the other hand we have been so long held up by authoritarian structures that many of us have no idea of how to function without them. Hence, though there is much talk of freedom and love, there is in fact a great deal of infantile and narcissistic authoritarianism at work precisely where everything claims to be most open-minded and most free. The only way to guard against this is by a really serious and patient discipline of love. Aelred writes about that discipline, which alone can restore that intimate "taste" for true freedom and authentic love, the *sapor boni*[V] which is essential to wisdom and to "contemplation."

The thing that is most characteristic of Aelred's monastic theology is its emphasis on friendship. His doctrine is not simply a theology of community but a *theology of friendship*. The Christian life is, for Aelred, simply the full flowering of freedom and consent in the perfection of friendship. Friendship with other human beings as an epiphany of friendship with God. In this, surely, he is quite modern. "To live without friends," he says, "is to live like a beast."[VI] For this very reason – we must dare to admit it – he was for a long time regarded as "dangerous" in certain monasteries. Not so long ago, some of Aelred's books were kept under lock and key in Trappist libraries – just as John of the Cross was kept locked up in some Carmels.

It is significant indeed when a writer who has gone to the very heart of the monastic vocation has to be kept out of the hands of monks lest they be "troubled" by his insights!

For Aelred, the monastic community life is simply a life of friendship. The monastic discipline is an education in friendship. Contemplation is not an individual gnostic exploit arrived at by turning away from everybody else to God: it is a sharing in the friendship of God. The love of the monk for his brothers is the ground of a common contemplative experience of Christ. Friendship is then not an obstacle to some supposed "spiritual perfection": friendship itself is Christian perfection. But it has to be true friendship, not a fake.

The natural basis for this theology of friendship is of course the indestructible inclination to love which is the divine image in us. But we have seen that this inclination tends to frustrate and to caricature itself by unconscious bad faith, selfishness, narcissism, inauthenticity and pretense. The seriousness of this danger cannot be overestimated and no amount of psychotherapy or sensitivity sessions can entirely overcome it. We must of course take advantage of all the psychological and sociological instruments at our disposal, but ultimately, as Aelred says, our love is healed and redirected only in Christ. Only in him is the divine image, our freedom, restored to likeness in authenticity and truth – *in veritate caritatis*.[VII] He alone gives the true gift of community. Friendship is not the flowering of our inborn needs: it is God's creation. An entirely new creation in Christ. Our wounded and broken love is inclined to hate even when it thinks it loves. This brokenness and ambivalence can be healed only in the Holy Spirit. Our healing comes from the Cross. It is the gift of the Risen Savior. All this Aelred makes plain. And we must not forget it in a day when the temptation to be satisfied with an entirely horizontal dimension in theology may only compound our troubles instead of getting rid of them.

We might close by quoting a modern evangelical theologian whose name is so often invoked in favor of this "horizontal" theology, concerned only with man's relation to man. People easily forget that Bonhoeffer was well aware of man's brokenness and of his need for grace. He said: "God and reality are torn apart except where they come together in Christ."[VIII] The statement echoes Aelred's description of true friendship.

Aelred's monastic pedagogy is anything but a training in blindness and rejection. It is a training in openness and consent, a training in outgoing acceptance. But he demands acceptance first of all of Christ and his Cross. It is in Christ, and only in him, that the world makes sense. But once we have surrendered to Christ and to his saving Word, then Aelred would agree perfectly with Bonhoeffer: "Whoever sees Jesus Christ does indeed see God and the world in one. He can thenceforward no longer see God without the world or the world without God."[IX]

I. See in particular Jean Leclercq, *The Love of Learning and the Desire for God: A Study of Monastic Culture*, trans. Catherine Misrahi (New York: Fordham University Press, 1961; rev. ed. 1974).

II. "dont la théologie ecclésiale a grand besoin pour son plein équilibre, face à un certain pragmatisme, spirituel ou apostolique" (M.-D. Chenu, *Points de Vue Actuels sur la Vie Monastique* [Montserrat: Abbaye de Montserrat, 1966] 64) ("of which ecclesial theology, faced with a certain spiritual or apostolic pragmatism, has a great need for its full balance").

III. "having the capacity to receive God".

IV. "to consent is to be saved" (Bernard of Clairvaux, *De Gratia et Libero Arbitrio* 1.2 [J. P. Migne, ed., *Patrologiae Cursus Completus*, *Series Latina* [*PL*], 221 vols. (Paris: Garnier, 1844-1865) vol. 182, col. 1002B]).

IV. See Merton's references to the idea of "bad faith" in *Dancing in the Water of Life* 71, 108, 176.

V. See Bernard of Clairvaux, *Sermones in Cantica Canticorum* 85.9 (*PL* 183, col. 1192B): "*Beata mens, quam sibi totam vindicavit sapor boni, et odium mali*" ("Blessed the soul which a taste for the good and a hatred for evil completely vindicates").

VI. "*sine amico inter mortales nihil fere possit esse iucundum: et homo bestiae comparetur, non habens qui secum collaetetur in rebus secundis, in tristibus contristetur*" (*De Spirituali Amicitia* 2 [*PL* 195, col. 671A]) ("Among human beings, it is nearly impossible to be happy without a friend: a person having no one to rejoice with him in favorable circumstances or mourn with him in sad ones is comparable to a beast").

VII. "in the truth of love".

VIII. See Dietrich Bonhoeffer, *Ethics*, trans. Neville Horton Smith (New York: Macmillan 1955) 8: "No man can look with undivided vision at God and at the world of reality so long as God and the world are torn asunder. Try as he may, he can only let his eyes wander distractedly from one to the other. But there is a place at which God and the cosmic reality are reconciled, a place at which God and man have become one. That and that alone is what enables man to set his eyes upon God and upon the world at the same time. This place does not lie somewhere out beyond reality in the realm of ideas. It lies in the midst of history as a divine miracle. It lies in Jesus Christ, the Reconciler of the world."

IX. *Ethics* 8, which reads: "… henceforward …"

Isaac of Stella
(c. 1110–c. 1178)

Isaac of Stella: An Introduction to Selections from his Sermons

On October 21, 1963, Merton replied to a letter from his English Anglican friend, Canon A. M. (Donald) Allchin, who had inquired if Merton might be willing to write an introduction to selections from the sermons of the twelfth-century English Cistercian abbot Isaac of Stella, translated by the British Anglican nun Penelope Lawson. "I find the proposal to do an introduction on Isaac for Sister Penelope irresistible," Merton wrote, "though I am making firm resolutions to stop all prefaces. But no, not this one. I certainly want to do it, if I can; and the fact that there is no hurry is a big help. How much space do I have? And I would like to see some of the translations. Glad they will be for the layman!" (*Hidden Ground of Love* 25). Merton's deep admiration for Isaac was expressed in a journal entry for December 5, 1960, almost three years earlier, in which he considers a sermon of Isaac for Easter: "Magnificent light in the lapidary sentences of Isaac of Stella. Fire struck from stone: but how marvelous! His Easter sermon – deep, deep intuition of faith as a resurrection because it is an act of obedience to God considered as supreme life. What matters is the act of submission to infinite life, to the authority of Creative and Redemptive Life, the Living God. Faith is this submission." This connection of faith and obedience is seen by Merton as being at the heart of the new life brought by the risen Jesus, a self-gift that is a response to God's gift of that very self in Christ. "The interior surrender of faith cannot have its full meaning except as an act of *obedience*, i.e. self-commitment in submission to God's truth in its power to give life; and *to command one to live*. Hence faith is not simply an act of choice, an option for a certain solution to the problem of existence etc. It is a birth to a higher life, by obedience to the giver of life, *obedience to the source of life. To believe is to consent to a creative command that raises us from the dead*" (*Turning Toward the World* 72). Merton also discusses this and another Easter sermon of Isaac (along with two sermons for the feast by Aelred of Rievaulx) in "*Cistercian Easter Sermons – Spiritual Sense of Scripture*" (to be included in an appendix to Merton's conferences on Cistercian History, currently being prepared for publication), where he notes that Christ's own obedience is both model and source of human obedience that is inseparable from faith: "His obedience was such a perfect union with life that He lived even when soul and body were separated." Merton also writes briefly on Isaac's Third Sermon for the Assumption in an appendix to his conferences on *The Cistercian Fathers and Their Monastic Theology*, where he notes Isaac's criticism of monks who have ostensibly renounced self-will in entering religious life, yet whose behavior in the monastery clearly shows that such renunciation was superficial at best (311-13). He briefly discusses Isaac's traditional three-fold anthropology in the context of the story of Adam, Eve and the serpent in a conference to the monastic community from November 1965, three months after becoming a full-time hermit, while he was beginning work on his introduction for Sr. Penelope (joking about her name that "it takes an Anglican nun to get away with that one"). The translations had not actually arrived until that fall (see Merton's September 21, 1965 journal entry, where he says they "seem … very good indeed," though he adds "I have not read them carefully" as yet [*Dancing in the Water of Life* 298]). His October 17, 1965 letter to Sr. Penelope (*Hidden Ground of Love* 478-80) gives evidence of the meticulousness with which he compared her English versions with the original Latin, focusing particularly, as he would in his conference comments, on the composition of the human person in the context of creation and fall: "the structure of man is a paradise in which you have man (the *mens*), woman (the *anima*) and the serpent (concupiscence of the body in its fallen state).… The *anima* is that in us which responds to beauty, to warm human affection, to pleasure (good or otherwise), to instinct on a higher level. The *mens* is that which is contemplative, intellectual, which enjoys the higher intuitions of the incorporeal, which makes the ultimate decision on which our whole destiny depends, and which, commanding the *anima* and the *caro*, is in immediate dependence on the will and word of God. It is the *mens* which contemplates Him and submits entirely to him, bringing with it the *anima* and the *caro*. These others cannot go to God except when brought to Him by the *mens*. This is the old Cistercian picture of man" (479). He writes in his journal on October 29 of finding in Isaac's teaching "a metaphysic of being and nothingness … an unquestioningly deep and austere intuition, and very modern. But deeply mystical," and as having "Profound implications for my own prayer and solitude" (*Dancing in the Water of Life*

309) and he notes later in the year that the "coherence" and "solidity" of Isaac's language provided for him a steadying influence (*Dancing in the Water of Life* 338). The following July he writes to Sr. Penelope that he was "about ready to do the introduction," calling her translation "an excellent job, very readable, very lively," and adds: "I think it will really make a charming book" (*Hidden Ground of Love* 480). He had finished the introduction before the end of the month, as he tells Sr. Penelope in a July 27 letter (*Hidden Ground of Love* 480), but when no publisher could be found for the volume, the introduction appeared by itself the following year in *Cistercian Studies* 2 (1967) 243-51 as "Isaac of Stella: An Introduction to Selections from his Sermons." Merton notes Isaac's more speculative theological perspective, less influenced by St. Bernard than were other early Cistercian Fathers; the difference between the medieval worldview articulated by Isaac, in which the all-encompassing presence of Christ is found everywhere in scripture and in creation, and that of modernity; Isaac's strongly anti-militaristic stance, contrasted with that of St. Bernard; and the specific setting of Isaac's monastery on the island of Ré in the Atlantic off the west coast of France, which gave to his sermons a particular element of solitude and exile, an emphasis on austerity, simplicity and honesty and on the necessity for trust in the Word in the midst of trial.

The twelfth-century Cistercian school, led and inspired by St. Bernard of Clairvaux, produced some of the finest literature in the mystical tradition of Western monasticism. Isaac of Stella, an English monk and abbot of a community in France, is not the least interesting of the Cistercian writers. If he seems to stand somewhat apart from the others, and if he is considered at times more "mysterious" than they, it is because he is a more independent thinker and less subject to the dominant influence of St. Bernard. The other great Cistercian writers of the time all more or less sat at the feet of Bernard like a circle of disciples. William of St. Thierry was one of Bernard's closest friends. Guerric of Igny was a monk of Clairvaux, drawn to the monastery from Flanders by the preaching of St. Bernard, and later Abbot of Igny, a daughter house of Clairvaux. Even Ailred of Rievaulx though he lived in distant Yorkshire, was a friend of Bernard's, closer to him and to his teaching than Isaac.

Isaac of Stella had a speculative mind trained perhaps in schools to which Bernard was not well-disposed: one wonders at times if he were a former student of Chartres[1] and perhaps a friend of Gilbert de la Porrée, Bishop of Poitiers, near Stella, whose teaching was attacked by St. Bernard. The metaphysical speculations of Isaac are perhaps one reason why he is still something of a mystery. The Sexagesima sermons[II] remind us at times of Eckhart in their tone, and they are not represented in this selection because they might be somewhat puzzling to the average reader. They were indeed found a little obscure by the monks of Isaac's own time, who nevertheless responded to his philosophy as to a challenge and an inspiration. Bouyer considers him one of the most *living* of the Cistercian authors.[III]

The texts from the sermons which are to be presented here are less mysterious and more typical not only of the Cistercian manner, but of the whole medieval monastic spirit. This is the traditional biblical and symbolic approach to *sapientia*, contempla-

---

1. In his 19th sermon (2nd sermon for Sexagesima) Isaac makes a statement that "everything that is, is because it is numerically one,"[I] which echoes, with one slight modification, a declaration of Thierry of Chartres. *Omne quod est ideo est quia unum est*. Franz Bliemetzrieder believes Isaac probably belonged to the School of Anselm of Laon, while admitting also that he has elements of the teaching of the school of Chartres (*Recherches de Théologie Ancienne et Mediévale*. IV 1932, p. 158).

tive wisdom, so familiar in the West since St. Augustine and St. Gregory the Great. One must add that this is an approach which is singularly out of favor today, since it seems us, in our age of scientific criticism, to have very little to do with actual revealed truth and the literal sense of the Bible. But we must remember how the men of the middle ages regarded theological wisdom. It was precisely a *sapientia* or, according to a well-used but perhaps fanciful etymology a *sapida scientia*,[IV] a knowledge based on the experience of life and of love, which embraced the whole of life and indeed synthesized the whole of knowledge in transcendent religious experience, expressed in traditional symbols which were common currency in the monasteries and schools.

Thus, for example, when commenting on the parable of the Good Samaritan,[V] Isaac does not attempt to find out who the victim of the robbers might have been, or why there were robbers on the road to Jericho, or where the robbery might have been most likely to happen – the sort of questions that, for some reason, intrigue moderns. No, he already knows that the victim of the robbery is Adam, the robbers are the devils and the Good Samaritan is Christ. Also he knows that the victim has seven wounds, the seven deadly sins. These are suppositions which far from intriguing moderns, antagonize them. And it all seems at first sight to be quite arbitrary, until we realize that the approach of Isaac is not scientific but aesthetic. Not aesthetic in the sense of "arty," but in the deeper sense that it grows out of a response of one's whole being, and especially of the "heart" (the seat of wisdom), to a world which has been redeemed and transformed by the presence in it of the Living Word of God.

What seems to us a rather cavalier treatment of revelation was for the men of the twelfth century merely a more profound respect which saw *everything* penetrated through and through by the revelation of divine love, so that the whole world and all of life became or could become, not only a commentary on the word but an epiphany of the Living Word. Of course, to appreciate this, we have to share their sense of awe and delight at the cosmic order as they conceived it: and their conception was totally different from ours.

The Newtonian cosmos (which still forms the idea of the universe held by the common man) was a machine governed by law. The medieval universe – though also a *machina* – was governed rather by love, by hidden "sympathies" and connaturalities that made things seek to agree with other things that were "like" themselves or "of one kind" with themselves. Hence the medieval instinct to seek out these hidden "likings" and the "likenesses" which expressed them. Indeed the very core of medieval anthropology is that man is made in the image and likeness of God, so that by his very nature he cannot rest save in God – and God, in his turn, is led by love to seek man, his lost image. Only when we grasp this medieval view of the world of nature and of grace as a vast system of affinities, sympathies, likenesses and loves, can we understand the true meaning of their "allegorizing" and their symbolism. But once we are prepared to meet medieval men half-way, and enter into their view of things, we find there is a singular spiritual consistency in the contemplative harmony between the world and the creative and redemptive designs of God, the pilgrimage of man, following Christ, carrying the Cross, out of this world to the Father. It is, in one word, a view of the entire life of man and of all history illumined and transformed by the *Pascha Christi*, the descent of Christ into the realm of matter in order to overcome death, transfigure man and through him the world, and raise man up with him to glory at the right hand of the Father. In such a context, it is quite natural for Christ to be considered as the "true Jacob's Ladder," a concept which might appear to us slightly quaint and even a bit silly: but it represents the same kind of imaginative and plastic vision which went into the building and decorating of the cathedrals.

Another difference between this world-view and ours lies in its basic assumption that everything has now been said. God has spoken. The structure and purpose of the cosmos is now transparently clear not in itself but in the redemptive work of Christ. Everything is therefore to be understood by being *transposed* into the language of biblical symbolism. The symbol does not teach us something new, but gives us access to what is already there. It gives us a new light, a new intuition and religious appreciation of the mystery of Christ, ever old and ever new, manifesting itself in new aspects but always essentially the same. Only such presuppositions as these could justify the liberty with which the medieval writers allegorized and sought out curious poetic resonances between symbol and symbol, or between objective mystery and subjective experience: all of this in Isaac, is centered in one vast and admirable vision of Christ on earth in his Mystical Body, the Church. For Isaac is one of the great medieval singers of the mystery of the Church.

This poetic wisdom is at once biblical and monastic. That is to say it represents the fruit of concrete and actual meditation on biblical texts as they had been chanted and proclaimed in the monastic liturgy and glossed by monastic theology since the sixth century.

To read these sermons is, then, to enter into the mentality of the medieval monk. We find this mentality imaginative, indeed perhaps fanciful, basically rather simple, solid and practical in a medieval sort of way. The whole concern, after all, is with *attaining an end*. Not just any end, but the whole end of man's life. That, surely, demands a somewhat practical spirit. But of course the practicality will be first of all theological. If we are to attain an end which is beyond our knowledge, in God, then we must listen to God's own teaching about how to attain it. To be precise, we must live as disciples of Christ. We must seek in order to find what he has promised, knock in order that God's door may be opened. We must hear and obey the word of Christ, we must meditate upon his teaching in order to put it into practice, and above all we must live out the teaching of the Beatitudes and of Calvary. Though the middle ages knew as well as any other age, perhaps better, that all Christians were called to follow the way of the Beatitudes, still the monastic life was professionally dedicated to this above all. The monk was *par excellence*, the man of the Beatitudes, and Isaac's sermons for All Saints[VI] form a kind of miniature treatise on the monastic ascesis – an ascesis of authentic poverty in imitation of Christ. It is, in fact, poverty that is the proof of the sincerity of our "seeking" for the invisible and eternal reward promised by Christ.

The monk is one who has abandoned everything for Christ. Indeed, he goes so far as to abandon even some things that might seem to be necessary for the effective living of his monastic life. Books, for instance. This does not mean that the Cistercians were necessarily hostile to study, but some monasteries could simply be so poor that there were very few books available in the cloister *armarium*, beyond a few copies of the Scriptures and some volumes of St. Augustine, St. Isidore and Venerable Bede. This was evidently the case in Isaac's small island monastery of which we shall speak in a moment.

Poverty, which receives great stress in Isaac's sermons as it does in all the ascetic writings of the Cistercians, is positive rather than negative. It consists, of course, in genuine deprivation even of some necessities. It demands severe and strenuous dedication to manual work, since the monk has to make his own living. Isaac does not try to gloss this over, and we find plenty of evidence in the sermons that this was the way he and his monks actually lived. But monastic poverty was more than "doing without." It was a matter of stripping oneself, casting off all surplus baggage, in order the more easily to follow Christ. It also implied a liberation from undue concern with material possessions that might lead to litigation and even violence in order to preserve them. Speaking of violence, it is interesting to notice that Isaac had scant respect for the combination of knighthood and monastic life which St. Bernard was promoting in the Knights Templars.[VII] He calls the "fifth gospel of the new chivalry" simply a "new monstrosity."[VIII] "If heaven is promised to the poor and earth to peacemakers," says Isaac in a sermon on the Beatitudes, "what is left for fighters?"[IX] The monk is a "poor man of Christ" and by that he is also one who has generously embraced the Cross of Christ. These traditional themes are quite emphatic in the sermons of Isaac since he considers genuine renunciation an essential element in that true wisdom which effectively seeks to attain blessedness in Christ.

To put it in another way, though Isaac does not speak much of "contemplation," the monastic ascesis of poverty clears the way for a life of prayer, reading, meditation, the steps by which one ascends to a contemplative knowledge of Christ by love. Isaac is not afraid to speak of that mysterious Cloud which an English mystic was later to call the "Cloud of Unknowing":[X]

> The soul that seeks to see that which is wholly incorporeal must pass beyond not only every body or likeness of a body, but also the whole whirling complex of its thoughts. This is no matter for surprise. You pass beyond the things we have called clouds by watchfulness of mind and

> by a purity of heart that goes beyond words and even beyond thought. When you have done that, another cloud will eventually appear, a clear cloud, a shining cloud, not stormy now or dense, a cloud of wisdom, not of ignorance. For there is darkness in light, and in great light the darkness is proportionately darker. This is because when the light is directed on to its own incomprehensibility, or on to its own unapproachability in which it dwells, and lastly on to its own peace that passes understanding, it then deprives our hearts of light itself. And the consequence of that is that what you do learn about light you learn not by contemplation but by revelation, as did the apostles from the white-robed men who stood beside them on the Mount of Olives.
>
> The soul begins with what it apprehends by means of its bodily senses, goes on from that to imagination or the forming of mental images, and after that in turn to reason, intellect, and lastly understanding. Thus it ascends Mount Tabor, the mount "exceeding high," and there its eyes see Jesus transfigured, glorified, the glory of His flesh infusing His very clothes with light. Yet it is not able to see the face of Him who is co-equal with the Father, incorporeal, invisible, incomprehensible; for, before that Face, reason, intellect and understanding all fall down and fail.[XI]

It was considered entirely traditional and appropriate to speak of this incomprehensibility of God in commenting on the beatitude of the pure in heart. But it is interesting to see that Isaac brushes aside the idea of contemplation, preferring the light of revelation in Christ. In other words he is not satisfied with a neoplatonic intellectualism baptized by Christian authorities, but goes directly to the divine light which is manifested in Christ. In fact, it is the light of Tabor which he grasps by faith. Beyond that, in divine inaccessibility, the Face of God is known by unknowing. In this respect Isaac is closer to Cassian than to Pseudo-Dionysius, by whom he was nevertheless somewhat influenced.

There are, of course, in Isaac, as in all the Cistercians, themes that have a familiar Platonic resonance. It is standard to speak of man's exile in the flesh as a banishment to the "region of unlikeness" (*regio dissimilitudinis*[XII]). Man's exile is like that of the prodigal son in a far country, for he is alienated from himself by attachment to the world of matter perceived as a source of true and ultimate happiness, which it can never be. Each man must seek wisdom by returning within himself and ascending above himself. He must find wisdom in rest, and make it his true business (*negotium*) to be at leisure (*otium*) free from all material cares.[XIII] This sounds aristocratic if you like, but at least the monk's freedom from care is earned with much labor and self-denial. He is not born with contemplative leisure like a silver spoon in his mouth.

It is natural that with this emphasis on leaving the world, on renouncing material things, on poverty, on contemplation, Isaac should attach great importance to monastic solitude. And in fact, though he was not a hermit, he and his monks evidently lived very solitary and lonely lives in a small Cistercian monastery which was struggling to maintain itself in existence.

It is generally thought that this monastery must have been a foundation of Stella (L'Étoile) on one of the islands in the Atlantic, off the west coast of France, possibly the island of Ré. At any rate, Isaac speaks impressively of the island solitude which he and his followers have chosen. It is a rugged and lonely life on this "last outpost of land" in the ocean beyond which, as far as they knew, there was absolutely nothing.

Their life of solitude was not merely interior and intentional. It was a physical reality, and Isaac considered this island life of "exile" a further step into the "desert" beyond the more secure, more comfortable and better established cenobitic community from which they have come and which was well provided with books and other necessities. They were definitely not hermits, since they followed the Cistercian customs and lived in community. Yet Isaac did not hesitate to describe their life as in some sense eremitical. It was not unusual to speak, in those days of a small, poor, isolated cenobitic community as an *eremus*. In fact, the foundation of Cîteaux is referred to in the *Exordium Parvum* as eremitical, in this special sense.[XIV] The word *eremus* occurs several times in the *Exordium*, precisely in contrast with the established and well-to-do community of Molesme from which Cîteaux was founded. *Eremus* in this sense has strong connotations of monastic poverty as well as of solitude.

The small island community of Isaac was one where the monks had to work hard, and their Abbot worked with them. Because they had a very poor library, the Abbot tried to make up for the lack of books by discoursing to the brethren, and a number of the sermons were delivered during the usual break in the manual labor, when the monks recited an hour of the office, then sat down to rest and to listen to their spiritual Father. Nor did they merely listen, for we are told that they asked questions, and evidently there was some discussion of the points raised. This was the traditional *collatio* or monastic conference.

We see from Isaac's twenty-seventh sermon[XV] that for him the Cistercian life might consist of two conversions: one from the world to the monastery, another from the well-established cenobium to the poor and lonely island foundation which could be described as an *eremus*. In this, he was perhaps echoing the traditional meaning of the Apothegm of St. Arsenius, the Desert Father, who asked how he should be saved and was told first, "Fly from men and thou shalt be saved" – at which he retired from the imperial court to the monastic life at Nitria. Having asked this same question again, he was told, "*fuge, tace, quiesce.*" "Fly, be silent, rest (in prayer)."[XVI] At which he fled to the completely solitary life of the desert. Though Cistercians rarely and exceptionally obtained permission to be hermits in the twelfth century, the legitimate aspiration for poverty and solitude was fulfilled in these smaller and more remote monasteries. Isaac is a witness to this aspect of Cistercian monasticism.

Their island life of poverty and labor was no game. The monks were in fact struggling to keep alive. This was the price they paid for the advantages of solitude and "exile." They were truly on pilgrimage out of the visible world to the Father. Yet at the same time they neglected no opportunity to do good to their fellow pilgrims.

Isaac compares their island monastery to a little boat out in the stormy sea. This frail wooden barque is to them a piece of the cross. If they cling to it steadfastly they can be saved from drowning.

> How readily, how willingly, therefore, should I accept this cross, this little ship whereon the Savior mounted when He set death apart from us, or us from death, when He rescued and freed us and plucked us apart from the world, the flesh, and the devil! He "went up" into the ship, the gospel says. He went up into it, not as unwillingly, not as coerced, but of His own free will. He went up to the cross, and there he gave himself to the Father – He, who is Himself both priest and sacrifice. As Scripture says, "He was offered because He willed it." He hastened to the conflict that was ordained for Him with joy. He laid down His life when and as He willed, and for as long.
>
> I think we can quite reasonably call this life of ours, here in this place, a cross. For here the practice of obedience separates you from yourselves, just as the outward loneliness cuts you off from other people. No pleasures are allowed you here; you have nothing that you may call your own, not even your own body; you cannot choose your work, nor can you rest when you like. This dependence on another's will in everything, what is it but a climbing up on to the cross of Christ, along with Christ?
>
> Consider then, my brethren, how great our Lord Christ is, and how safe it is to sail for him and with him in his ship, to suffer and to die with him, so that "the full tale of his afflictions still to be endured for the sake of his Body the Church" may be fulfilled in us who are his members.[XVII]

Hence having read in holy books of the "strength there is in solitude, the fruit that comes of quiet and the grace of poverty,"[XVIII] they have now come into solitude itself where Christ is their book, "written inside and out."[XIX] He will be their chief and indeed their only study, and in Him they will find the way to the meaning of everything else. If they can "read" Him they will learn that all things form "books" that tell of Him. Abbot Isaac tells his monks where to look for these "books." First of all there is their own soul, an accurate copy of the Word, the Image of the Father. Then there is creation itself, a *liber obscurus*[XX] for those who have no inner vision. Even the poorest monastery has the Old and New Testaments, and above all the Gospel which brings us Christ Himself, *sapientia palpabilis*,[XXI] and His Flesh and Blood are our food and drink in the Sacrament of the Altar. Thus brought into direct contact with the Word, the monk enters into the darkness where he sees the "invisible light"[XXII] (Sermon 21, quoted above). This direct contact with the Word is the purpose of all reading and meditation. When one has found Him one can lay aside the book and commune with Him in silent, adoring love. In this "silence of the monks one speaks to the Lord in a sweet whisper, face to face, as a man talks to the one who is closest to him" (Sermon 37).[XXIII]

But the life of solitude also has special demons of its own which are always at work, filling the minds of the monks with fear, anguish and discouragement. Indeed many have not persevered, and even the Abbot himself admits that he sometimes feels himself fainthearted, almost surrendering to discouragement, so that he begs the brothers for their earnest prayers. He even thinks that he has his own peculiar demon who tempts him with rambling and discouraging thoughts. He knows that the monk must keep his serenity of heart in pure faith and that disgust and *acedia* mean loss of the fruit of one's active virtue and incapacity to find the light of contemplation (Sermon 25, col. 1774).[XXIV]

But on the other hand, this last outpost of the world, is, he feels, a kind of springboard from which they will take off for the other world, and for the heavenly Jerusalem, provided only that they listen to the Word of God, obey in humility and in the fear of the Lord, and persevere unto the end in spite of all their trials.

To sum up Isaac's character and his teaching: we find in it a singular consistency, a coherence in variety, an austerity with sensitivity, a certain daring curiosity, an impatience with half-measures and an ardent poetic fervor, and above all a deep love for Jesus Christ. Some of these elements were peculiarly Cistercian and one finds them reflected, for example, in the simple and bare honesty of twelfth-century Cistercian architecture which is always at once simple and original. It is a pleasure to present to modern readers these few samples of Isaac's thought, so engagingly done into readable English by Sister Penelope, who has truly caught the spirit of the mysterious Cistercian and has, thereby, made him much less mysterious after all.

I. J. P. Migne, ed., *Patrologiae Cursus Completus, Series Latina* [*PL*], 221 vols. [Paris: Garnier, 1844-1865] vol. 194, col. 1753D, which reads: "*Omne enim quod est, ideo est, quia unum numero est.*"

II. *Sermones* 18-26 (*in Sexagesima* 1-9) (*PL* 194, cols. 1749D-1777D).

III. "[T]his practically unknown thinker, at times the most abstract of the Cistercian school, in the few pages of Migne where all that is left of him is to be found, more than any of his contemporaries gives us the impression of being remarkably alive" (Louis Bouyer, *The Cistercian Heritage*, trans. Elizabeth A. Livingstone [London: Mowbray, 1958] 161).

IV. "a knowledge that is tasted"; see *Seasons of Celebration* 74: "Man lost the taste, the experiential knowledge, of divine things (*sapida scientia*) in the fall."

V. *Sermo* 6 (*in Festo Omnium Sanctorum* 6) (*PL* 194, cols. 1708D-1713A).

VI. *Sermones* 1-6 (*PL* 194, cols. 1689A-1713A).

VII. Bernard of Clairvaux, *De Laude Novae Militiae* (*PL* 182, cols. 921A-940A); the reference is probably not directly to the Templars but to another monastic military order, the Spanish Order of Calatrava, that was organized by the Cistercians and officially associated with the Order in 1164 (see Bernard McGinn, *The Golden Chain: A Study in the Theological Anthropology of Isaac of Stella*, Cistercian Studies vol. 15 [Washington, DC: Cistercian Publications, 1972] 3).

VIII. "*cuiusdam novae militiae obortum est monstrum novum, cuius, ut lepide ait quidam, Ordo de quinto Evangelio est, ut lanceis ac fustibus incredulos cogat ad fidem; et eos qui Christi nomen non habent, licenter exspoliet, ac religiose trucidet*" (*Sermo* 48 [*in Nativitate Sancti Ioannis Baptistae* 3] [col. 1854C]) ("the new monstrosity of a certain new chivalry has arisen; as someone has charmingly said, it is the Order of the fifth Gospel, to force unbelievers to the faith with lances and clubs, and to freely despoil and religiously slaughter those who do not have the name of Christ").

IX. "*Coelum pauperibus, terra mitibus: quid relictum est contentiosis?*" (*Sermo* 2 [*in Festo Omnium Sanctorum* 2] [*PL* 194, col. 1694A]).

X. See Merton's discussion of *The Cloud of Unknowing* in *Mystics and Zen Masters* 137-40 and in the Foreword to William Johnston, *The Mysticism of the Cloud of Unknowing* (New York: Desclée de Brouwer, 1967) ix-xiv.

XI. "*sic nimirum qui ad pure incorporeum cernendum aciem mentis erigit, non solum omne corpus, vel corporis similitudinem, sed etiam cogitationum universam volubilitatem transcendat, necesse est. Quid miramini? Cum omnes has quas diximus nubes, vigilantia mentis et cordis puritate, silente, imo postmanente omni cogitatione, pertransieritis, apparebit tandem nubes clara, nubes lucida, non iam turbida, non densa, non iam ignorantiae, sed sapientiae nubes. Tenebrae enim sunt in lumine, et multo magis in multo lumine: quod ipsam lucem, cum ingreditur suam incomprehensibilitatem, suam inaccessibilitatem, in qua habitat, suam denique pacem, quae exsuperat omnem sensum, suscipiat ab oculis nostris: ut deinceps revelatione potius quam contemplatione de ea quidquam discatis, sicut sancti apostoli a viris, qui astiterunt iuxta illos in vestibus albis.... Propter primum incorporeum discernendum in intellectus soliditatem surgat, ob secundum incorporeitatis genus intuendum in intelligentiae igneum candorem ascendat, tanquam in montem Thabor, excelsum valde, ut tertium et invisibile videat incorporeum: sicque transfiguratum, sic glorificatum Iesum oculis cernat, vestimenta propter gloriam carnis, qualia non potest fullo facere super terram (Marc. IX): faciem vero ob incomprehensibilitatis, incorporeitatis, invisibilitatis simplicem formam, in qua Patri manet aequalis, non sustineat, imo in faciem suam ratio, intellectus et intelligentia cadant*" (*Sermo* 4 [*in Festo Omnium Sanctorum* 4] [*PL* 194, cols. 1701C-1702A, 1702C]).

XII. "the land of unlikeness": see *Sermo* 2 (*in Festo Omnium Sanctorum* 2) (*PL* 194, col. 1695D): "*Itaque in semetipsum homo reversus, sicut iunior ille prodigus filius, ubi se invenit, nisi in regione longinqua, in regione dissimilitudinis, in terra aliena, ubi sedeat et fleat, dum recordetur patris et patriae?*" ("Therefore the man returns to himself like that younger son, the prodigal, when he finds himself, but in a far country, a land of unlikeness, an alien land, where he sits and weeps while he recalls his father and his fatherland"); see also St. Bernard, *Epistola* 8.2 (*PL* 182, col. 106A); *De Gratia et Libero Arbitrio* 32 (*PL* 182, col. 1018C); *De Diversis* 40.4, 42.2 (*PL* 183, cols. 649A, 661D); cf. chapter 2 in Étienne Gilson, *Mystical Theology of Saint Bernard*, trans. A. H. C. Downes (New York: Sheed & Ward, 1940) 33-59, which has this phrase as its title and considers the loss of likeness to God as the result of the Fall, and 224-25, n. 43, which discusses in detail the source and meaning of the phrase in Augustine (*Confessions* 7.10.16 [*PL* 32, col. 742]) and the Platonic tradition.

XIII. See St. Bernard, *Sermo* 72 *in Cantica Canticorum*: "*in operibus obedientiae, ubi omne negotium otium*" (*PL* 183, col. 1129C) ("in the works of obedience, where all business is rest").

XIV. *Exordium Parvum*, c. 3: "*eremum quae Cistercium dicebatur*" (*Nomasticon Cisterciense, seu Antiquiores Ordinis Cisterciensis Constitutiones A.R.P.D. Juliano Paris* … Editio Nova, ed. Hugo Séjalon [Solesmes: E Typographeo Sancti Petri, 1892] 54-55) ("the desert that is called Cîteaux"); in *The Silent Life*, Merton writes: "In the *Exordium Parvum* Cîteaux is spoken of as an hermitage (*eremus*)" (98) and goes on to quote Isaac: "For this reason, my dearly beloved, we have led you all away into this remote and arid and vile solitude; and we have done it wisely, in order that here you may be humble, and *never be able to become rich*. Yes, here in this solitude, cast far out into the sea and having almost nothing in common with the rest of the world, destitute of all human and worldly consolation, you have become totally silent from the world. For indeed, here, look where you will, you see that you have no world left at all except this poor little island, the last extremity of the earth" "(Isaac de l'Etoile, *Sermon xiv*, (2nd Sermon for the IVth Sunday after Epiphany), Migne, P.L. 194–1757)" (98-99).

XV. *Sermo* 17 (*in Dominica Quinquagesimae* 1) (*PL* 194, cols. 1777D-1780D).

XVI. *Verba Seniorum* 2.3 (*PL* 73, col. 858B); *Wisdom of the Desert* 29 (n. xii); see *Cassian and the Fathers* 77.

XVII. *Sermo* 15 (*in Dominica IV post Epiphania* 3) (*PL* 194, cols. 1738D-1739A, 1739B, 1739D): "*Ipsam ergo crucem, naviculam libenter acceperim, in quam Salvator ascendit, ubi mortem a nobis, vel nos a morte discrevit: a mundo, carne, et diabolo, abstraxit, separavit, liberavit. Ascendit, inquit. Non invitus, non tractus, sed volens. Ascendit, voluntarie sacrificavit Patri, sacrificium et sacerdos, ipse oblatus quia voluit. Animam quando, quomodo, et quandiu voluit, posuit, qui ad propositum sibi certamen cum gaudio cucurrit.... Ego hanc disciplinam professionis vestrae, et abditam eremum non immerito crucem dixerim: ubi sicut vos solitudo separat ab aliis, sic disciplina obedientiae a vobis ipsis: quibus nihil, quod libet, licet; quibus nec substantiae, nec corporis proprietas, nec operis, nec quietis libertas. Quid est hoc, obsecro, nisi quibusdam obedientiae clavis alienae iussionis rigori affigi pro Christo, crucifigi cum Christo? ... Consideremus ergo, fratres, quantus sit iste, et quam tutum sit pro ipso ac cum ipso navigare, eique compati, ac commori, ut ea quae desunt passionum eius compleamus in nobis, membris videlicet eius.*"

XVIII. *Sermo* 18 (*in Sexagesima* 1) (*PL* 194, col. 1749D): "*Edocti enim a libris sanctis sanctae solitudinis virtutem, quietis fructum, paupertatis gratiam.*"

XIX. *Sermo* 8 (*in Dominica infra Octavas Epiphaniae* 2) (*PL* 194, col. 1719B): "*Hic ergo, hic fratres mei, unus sit vobis magister Christus, hic etiam liber vobis scriptus intus et foris*" ("Here then, my brothers, is your Master Christ alone, here the book written for you inside and out"); *Sermo* 9 (*in Dominica 1 post Octavas Epiphaniae* 1) (*PL* 194, col. 1719D): "*Sequitur vero liber tertius, corporea videlicet et visibilis creatura, etiam ipse scriptus intus ac foris*" ("There follows then the third book, the bodily and visible creature, written both inside and out").

XX. "obscure book" (*Sermo* 9 [*in Dominica 1 post Octavas Epiphaniae* 1] [*PL* 194, col. 1719D]).

XXI. "a palpable wisdom" (*Sermo* 9 [*in Dominica 1 post Octavas Epiphaniae* 1] [*PL* 194, col. 1720D]).

XXII. *Sermo* 22 [N.B. not 21] (*in Sexagesima* 5) (*PL* 194, col. 1763A): "*Sicut enim nihil videndo tenebras invisibiles videmus, et inaudibile silentium nihil audiendo audimus: sic nimirum superabundantem et intolerabilem lucem non videndo nec tolerando, videmus invisibilem, non quidem caeci, sed a lumine superati*" ("Thus we see the invisible shadows in seeing nothing and we hear the inaudible silence in hearing nothing: thus of course we see the invisible light, superabundant, unbearable, not blind but overwhelmed by the light").

XXIII. *Sermo* 37 (*in Dominica II Quadragesimae* 5) (*PL* 194, col. 1815A): "*Ista est, quae in silentio monachorum suavi susurro ore ad os loquitur ad Dominum, tanquam vir ad proximum suum.*"

XXIV. *Sermo* 25 (*in Sexagesima* 8).

Adam of Perseigne
(c. 1145–1221)

The Feast of Freedom: Monastic Formation according to Adam of Perseigne

In an August 19, 1956 letter to Fr. Charles Dumont of Scourmont Abbey in Belgium, editor of the Cistercian Order's official magazine, Merton writes that he is "pleased and grateful to have you as my translator, in the article on Adam" (*School of Charity* 96). The reference is to an article on monastic formation as presented in the letters of Adam of Perseigne that Merton had submitted to the journal. Son of a serf who became a Cistercian abbot in Normandy and a highly respected counselor and spiritual director, for King Richard I of England among numerous others, Adam was the latest of the major early Cistercian writers who attracted Merton's attention. Among the many projects Merton had listed in his letter to the 1946 Cistercian General Chapter (along with his biography of Aelred) was a proposal to translate Adam's Marian writings, for which he is best known. On May 1, 1949, Merton had written in his journal of "marvelous things in Adam of Perseigne about Mary being 'the way,'" commenting, "She is that. Through her we come quickly to – everything" (*Entering the Silence* 307). The translation was never made, but while serving as master of scholastics in May 1952, Merton did present conferences on Adam's *Mariale*, focused on finding Mary as the surest way of meeting her Son and as the model of the hidden life of silence and humility. When he became master of novices in 1955, Merton evidently found Adam's reflections on monastic formation particularly helpful in carrying out his own duties, which presumably led to his writing successive versions of an article on this topic, the first of which was that referred to in his letter to Dumont, which appeared some months later, in French, as M. Louis Merton, "La Formation Monastique selon Adam de Perseigne," trans. Charles Dumont, OCSO, *Collectanea Ordinis Cisterciensium Reformatorum* 19 (January 1957) 1-17. Master of novices before becoming abbot, Adam is described by Merton as not only a theologian and a master psychologist with a profound knowledge of the human soul but a person of genuine spiritual depth. Adam's fundamental insight was that an entrant into the Cistercian life came from a deformed world and therefore needed to be transformed by monastic ascesis to become a new person in Christ. He needed to reject the "*spiritus fictionis*," the inauthentic self and its illusions, a process which for Adam took place particularly under the guidance of Mary, the special patroness of the Order, but also through the guidance of the novice master, whose approach was above all that of encouragement, support and friendship rather than arbitrary or demeaning humiliations. The "*dura et aspera*" of the Benedictine life, its difficulties and trials, would come of their own accord rather than being imposed artificially from without. Humility was essential, but it was in essence a participation in the humility of the Christ who emptied Himself of His glory in the Incarnation, so that the novice is taught humility above all in the "school of the Christ Child," as well as in the ultimate self-gift of the Passion – in both of which the Mother of God played an essential role. This instruction in obedience, humility and sweetness, Merton concludes, leads to a purity of heart and freedom from care that brings peace and a tranquil heart, a "sabbath of innocence" that foreshadows the rest of eternal union with God. Five years after this initial publication, an expanded version of this study appeared in English as "Christian Freedom and Monastic Formation" (*American Benedictine Review* 13 [September 1962] 289-313). For most of its length the presentation was essentially the same, though the ten numbered subheadings were reduced to four ("The New Life," "Christ Is the Way," "The Blessed Virgin and the Cistercian Life" and "The Sabbath of Contemplation"), and most of the specific references to Cistercians were altered to the more general terminology of monks or monastic life, as befitted its appearance in a Benedictine journal. But toward the end of the article the "Sabbath" section was considerably expanded, adding four full pages just before the final two paragraphs that focused on the seven gifts of the Holy Spirit as the foundation of the mystical life that is the full flowering of the Sabbath of contemplation. "The seven gifts, or seven spirits, are simply seven different aspects of that superabundant love of God by which the Holy Spirit celebrates in the soul the mystical festivity of its marriage with the Word." Adam refers to them as seven feasts, or seven Sabbaths, and shows how each is a participation in the ultimate feast of perfect freedom. These festivals, above all the feast of wisdom, bring about not only communion with the divine Bridegroom but a deeper, more nourishing community with other people. "Friendship, and the radiation of spiritual love, is not only no distraction from the contemplation of God, but forms an inseparable part of the contemplative life as he conceives it.... Indeed it is obvious that such friendship should exist as the normal fruit of our participation in the Eucharistic banquet." Like Aelred, "Never for a moment does Adam consider that this friendship in Christ is a distraction or a disturbance to his life of prayer." It is an integral dimension of participation in the mystical body of Christ. Thus this revised version of the article both broadens and deepens the understanding of the Sabbath of contemplation according to Adam, further articulating the working of the Holy Spirit in both its mystical and its communal dimensions, and perhaps reflecting some of Merton's own experience in working with his novices during the period separating the two publications. There is one final version of the article, now renamed "The Feast of Freedom: Monastic Formation according to Adam of Perseigne" and thus highlighting the new material it shares with its immediate predecessor. This text appeared posthumously as an introduction to *The Letters of Adam of Perseigne*, vol. 1, trans. Grace Perigo, Cistercian Fathers, vol. 21 (Kalamazoo, MI: Cistercian Publications, 1976) 3-48, and is the one included here in edited form. It is nearly identical to "Christian Freedom and Monastic Formation," restoring some though not all of the explicitly Cistercian terminology and containing some relatively minor additions, deletions and alterations that do not substantially change the message of the text. The one significant addition is the extended quotation from Gerard Manley Hopkins' poem "The Blessed Virgin Compared to the Air We Breathe," which Merton cites as sharing a common theme with Adam's view of the incarnation as bringing about an immersion in the new spiritual world of divine love in which all the faithful are united in Christ and "enveloped together in the mother-love of Mary," and so empowered by the Spirit to become themselves new Christs, united in Him to the Father, a point already made in the very first version but only recognized as having a striking similarity to Hopkins' poem in this final stage of the text's evolution. It is worth noting that at the monastic conference in Thailand on the very last day of his life, in his presentation on "Marxism and Monastic Perspectives," Merton returns to this material, citing Adam as exemplifying the early Cistercians' understanding of the period of formation as "a kind of monastic therapy" in which the novitiate is seen as "a period of cure, of convalescence," making possible "the education of the 'new man'" in selfless love that is "the whole purpose of the monastic life" (*Asian Journal* 333).

At the end of the twelfth century and the beginning of the thirteenth the Cistercian Abbey of Perseigne in Normandy had for its abbot a man of learning and sanctity who, like so many other Cistercians of his day, played an important part in the religious life of the age. His reputation for learning and holiness gradually won him an ever-increasing influence first in other monasteries of the Order, then in abbeys of the Benedictines and in various Charterhouses. At the same time his advice in spiritual matters was sought on every side, and he became what we might call today the "spiritual director" of many great secular and ecclesiastical personages, the most famous of whom was Richard Coeur de Lion.[I]

This future director of kings was himself a man of very humble social origins. The son of a serf of the Count of Champagne, he had been born somewhere around the time when the monastery of Perseigne was founded (1145). We do not know where he acquired his considerable store of education – probably in one of the cathedral cities of Champagne: Troyes, Rheims or Sens. He was ordained to the secular clergy and found himself early in favor in the court of Champagne where he shone, among other things, as a poet writing in the vernacular. He was the chaplain of the Countess of Champagne.

Although the details of Adam's life are very uncertain, we know from his own avowal that he had passed from the secular clergy to a monastery of Canons Regular, thence to the Black Monks (or Benedictines) and finally to the Order of Cîteaux. We do not know the reason for these wanderings, except that he was looking for a life of complete renunciation and prayer, and that he finally chose the Cistercians because of their special devotion to the Blessed Virgin Mary. It is thought that he entered the Order at Pontigny.[II]

By 1188, or perhaps even 1183, Adam had become abbot of Perseigne, in Normandy, the monastery where the famous Abbé de Rancé was to make his novitiate, in the seventeenth century, before assuming his office as regular abbot of La Grande Trappe.

Although Adam of Perseigne was not another Bernard of Clairvaux either in his contemplation or in his activity, he was nevertheless destined to live a life reminiscent of the great saint who dominated the twelfth century. The needs of the Church called him frequently forth from the silence of the cloister. Perseigne, being in Normandy, was under the protection of the Plantagenets, the reigning house of England. Several charters remain to bear witness to the friendship of Henry II and Richard I (Coeur de Lion) for the monastery, and it was in this way that Adam became a trusted advisor to the second of these kings.

One of the most important missions with which Adam of Perseigne was entrusted by the Church was that of handling the "difficult case" of Joachim of Flora.[III] Joachim, a Cistercian abbot in Italy whose doctrines came under censure after his death, was a powerful and doubtless disturbing influence in the Church at the end of the Middle Ages.[IV] His doctrine of the coming of a New Age, the "Age of the Holy Ghost" started one of those "prophetic" movements characteristic of the time.[V] We do not know precisely what Adam was supposed to do with Joachim, or to what extent he succeeded. He was in Italy in 1195, and was back again in France the following year.

In the hard years of famine that closed the twelfth century, Adam of Perseigne joined the great crusade of charity led by Foulques de Neuilly[VI] to feed the poor and to convert souls. In 1200, his name is among those designated to help preach a less metaphorical Crusade. Like St. Bernard, Adam sent men off to fight the Holy War for Jerusalem. It is doubtful whether he embarked with the Crusaders, and he is not mentioned in Villehardouin's *Chronicle*,[VII] though other Cistercian abbots went with the expedition. In 1208, Adam was charged by the Holy See to negotiate peace between Philippe Auguste and John Lackland.[VIII] During the last years of his life, at his own request, he was spared such missions as these and was permitted to remain more often and for longer periods in the peace of the cloister. One of the few events of his declining years was the foundation of a convent of Cistercian nuns under his tutelage. The abbess was a nun who had been for a long time under his direction and who had received many letters from his hand. One of the last recorded events in his history was that he was penalized by the General Chapter of 1218 for allowing laypersons to he buried in the church of Perseigne. He had also been penanced once before for an "excessive" spirit of hospitality when he had allowed cheese and eggs to be served to his guests on a Friday![IX] He died about 1221.

Not all Adam's writings have yet been published. There can be found in Migne's Patrology [*PL 211*][X] a representative selection of letters and his *Mariale*, a collection of homilies on the Blessed Virgin which rates a high place in the Cistercian literature of the Middle Ages. A volume of his letters has recently appeared in the French series, *Sources Chrétiennes*.[XI] Adam's doctrine is typical of the school of St. Bernard, but is not without a character and vitality of its own.[XII] The pages that follow,[XIII] without pretending to be an exhaustive study of the theme of monastic formation as it was developed by him, will nevertheless provide an introduction to his thought and to his "spirituality."[XIV]

Like so many of the Cistercian Fathers, Adam was a penetrating observer of life[XV] and possessed a profound intuitive knowledge of the human soul. But he was also and above all a theologian who knew God in his revealed word. His knowledge of the Scriptures, far from being mere piety or dry pedantry, entered deeply into the very substance of his everyday life so that, like St. Bernard, Adam viewed and experienced everything in a scriptural atmosphere. He heard God's word in everything that happened.[XVI] He was one who saw all things, and particularly the monastic life itself, centered in the mystery of Christ. Because of this unity of outlook, Adam's theology of the spiritual life is not merely a collection of devout abstractions or a synthesis of ideas: it is a *sapientia*, a wisdom which is rooted in life. His theology is centered in the knowledge of Christ living in the Church and exercising his divine action upon souls through the Holy Spirit. Hence when Adam speaks of the formation of Cistercian novices he does not merely talk about the acquisition of virtues or exterior discipline (although these also find their place in his theology), he speaks of life in Christ, life in the Spirit, Christ living in us. He speaks of "the new man who is created according to God in justice and the sanctity of truth."[XVII]

Truth,[XVIII] light, holiness, grace – all these are manifestations of Christ living in our souls. To form a Cistercian novice is then to draw out the inner spiritual form implanted in his soul by grace: to educate – that is to say, to "bring out" – Christ in him. It is not a matter of imposing on the novice a rigid and artificial form from without, but to encourage the growth of life and the radiation of light within his soul, until this life and light gain possession of his whole being, inform all his actions with grace and liberty, and bear witness to Christ living in him.

Adam's view of the Cistercian life is, then, characterized by its sanity, its breadth of view, its depth, its organic wholeness. It ignores and rejects nothing that is good. It takes account of the whole man, called to find his place in the whole Christ. It is realistic, simple, supremely spiritual, that is to say, attuned to the inspirations of the Holy Spirit.[XIX] It is based on the great and fundamental truths of the Christian life – our union with Christ in his mysteries, through the mediation of Our Lady. The asceticism of Adam of Perseigne is based, like that of St. Benedict,[XX] on silence, humility, obedience, and love. It is an asceticism in which the virtues are not just virtues but are, precisely, the virtues of Christ in us. We acquire them not by seeking virtue so much as by seeking him.[XXI]

The New Life

The most characteristic of the monastic vows is the vow of conversion of manners (*conversio morum*, or *conversatio morum*[XXII]). This vow, which contains implicitly the obligations of poverty and chastity, is something more than a promise to tend to perfection. It is at once more concrete and more all-embracing. It is an irrevocable consecration to a *new life* in Christ, by which one leaves behind the "old man" by responding as far as he is able, within his own limitations, to the action of the Holy Spirit in his life.

The "monastic formation" is then not simply the superimposition of a few religious routines upon a subject who remains unchanged: it means the transformation of the monk himself – his transformation in Christ. And this is a matter of "life" – that is to say of an immanent spiritual principle. To give oneself over to this new life is to "do penance" in the full sense of the word, that is to say, to "change" (*metanoiein*) completely from within. Such is the traditional concept of the monastic vocation, and it is on this concept that Adam's teaching is based.[XXIII]

The postulant who knocks at the monastery gate comes from the world deformed. He is spiritually "sick" and needs to be "healed" by grace. This deformity of the old man must give way to the "splendor" of the new man, a new form, the likeness of Christ. A novice is truly what his name implies only if he labors to "take off the old man" and to be "formed with the splendors of the new life" – *novae vitae splendoribus informentur* [*PL* 211:584[XXIV]].

The *splendor novitatis* is symbolized by the white habit of Cîteaux. Adam's vivid expression contains all the optimism of the Cistercian spirit – a spirit related to the "mysticism of light" of the Greek Fathers and influenced by St. John's "Gospel of Light." The white monk is clad in a wedding garment. His cowl is a *vestis nuptialis*, a sign that he is invited and admitted to the wedding feast of the Lamb.

The true novice is one who is filled with the *sanctae splendor novitatis* – the "splendor of holy newness." The splendor of the new life consists especially in three things: chastity, love, and discipline. The function of discipline is to give to our lives an exterior splendor and elegance which manifest the interior love and purity of our hearts. "… the splendor and elegance of discipline; which, being blamelessly observed outwardly, is seen to be a sign of the interior condition of purity and love" [587]. Hence we see how Adam relates exterior and interior perfection. In exterior perfection alone there is no splendor, no beauty. It is dead. It is a body without a soul. It can only be brought to life by the splendor of Christ. Love of the risen Christ and virginity are the two sources of contact with "the Life which is the light of men."[XXV]

The novice is reformed "unto the beauty of the new man" by the "study of a stricter Life" – *studium correctioris vitae*. The idea contained in *correctior* is not only "stricter" but "truer" – more according to the mind of Christ. The *splendor novitatis* in our "new life" gives glory to the Lamb – the new life is a radiance that proclaims his sanctity and his love for us – *splendor est et gloria novitatis* [*Ibid.*].

What is the deformity of the old man that has to be put away? It is a kind of madness – the *insania vanissimae vetustatis* [615] – irrationality, vanity, deformity of the soul, the madness of an insane love – *amentia insani amoris*. As St. Paul says, it is the condition of a soul "corrupted by the desire of error" [Eph. 4:22]. To become a novice is therefore to seek "therapy" for this *amentia* – this condition of soul which makes us love what is unreal.

> Let him who desires to become a novice turn his heart away from the great vanity of the old man; unless, the madness of this insane love having first been removed, he shall have become sound of mind, he will not otherwise be able to engage in the new study of wisdom. [*PL* 211:615]

Like St. Bernard, Adam wishes first of all to restore to man the natural purity and balance of his soul before elevating him to union with God. This restoration is of course the work of grace. It makes us able to enter the *schola Christi* – the school of Divine Wisdom.

The first thing the Cistercian life must do to us is to bring us to our senses. If it does not do this, then all our apparent progress in asceticism and prayer will be deformed by the *amentia* of the old man, and the "insanity" of his love for what is vain and unreal.

This restoration of our "senses" is brought about by *faith*, *love* and *obedience*. According to Adam these are not possible unless we first resolve to forget the world we have left behind [*Ibid.*]. Contempt of the world is the beginning of our return to ourselves and to God; it precedes the second step which is entrance into the monastery and contempt of the flesh. Then comes the third step – *timor Dei*. The fourth is *confessio* – the complete acknowledgement of the truth and the final giving up of all defence of falsity in ourselves [cf. 621].[XXVI]

The "new man" is "created according to God in justice and the holiness of truth" [Eph. 4:24]. The Holy Spirit is himself the Spirit of Truth. The Cistercian life is a life based on that interior freedom which the truth alone can give us: "The truth shall make you free" [Jn. 8:32]. Original sin, on the other hand, was the work of the "father of lies."[XXVII] It is pride, which is based on a lie by which, in one act, man becomes untrue to himself by becoming untrue to his God. This pride remains with us, and St. Bernard has in many places studied its subtle work: but in all its various ways of leading us away from God, pride is always a lie. It always brings us to the feet of a false god, which is our own inordinate self-love. We cannot return to God, we cannot become new men, except in so far as we renounce this lie in ourselves.

But to give up the falsity that is in us we must see that it is false. No man will cling to something that he manifestly believes to be unreal. No one will defend the evil that is in himself unless for some reason he views it as a good. We have to see that what our pride believes to be good is, in fact, a very great evil. And this is very difficult. Hence the constant need to be honest with ourselves, and to grapple with the "spirit of fiction" that is in our very blood itself, always ready to deceive us in the disguise of an angel of light.

Adam is, like so many other monks of his time, a very acute psychologist and we are often astonished by the "modern" ring of many of his statements. True, he does not explicitly set out to explore man's unconscious mind. But he certainly recognizes that there is a deep vein of unconscious falsity in us which must become conscious, must be seen for what it is, before we can get free of its all-pervading influence in our lives.[XXVIII] We not only have falsity within us, but we instinctively prefer it – we defend it against grace. One of the chief characteristics of the old man is his "hypocrisy" or duplicity, the "spirit of fiction" which prevents the light of truth, the splendor of the new life,[XXIX] from shining through in our souls.

It is of the greatest importance to get rid of the *spiritus fictionis*, otherwise one will be a monk in appearance only. The *spiritus fictionis* destroys the whole value of our conversion and entrance into the monastery. Some monks, says Adam, are holy only in their exterior acts. In their interior they still follow the spirit of the world – a spirit of ambition, revenge, self-complacency, love of comfort, of praise, of possessions. They are content to change the outward appearances and remain centered on themselves within.

> Having the reputation of being alive, they are dead within, for while they appear outwardly to be poor and modest, interiorly they aspire to the glory of transitory praise or to the degrees of various dignities. [*PL* 211:618]

The evil spirit, cast out by contempt of the world and monastic conversion, returns to find his house swept and garnished and enters in with seven worse than himself [*Ibid.*]. This is what grieves the Holy Spirit [*Ibid.*], that while pretending to be guided by him, we allow ourselves in reality to be moved by his enemy, established secretly within our souls.

> O supreme unhappiness, under the form of the new man to conform oneself totally to the old.… [619]

We must not imagine that it is easy altogether to avoid something of the "spirit of fiction." The very structure of the religious life, with its innumerable external ceremonies, and observances – with the temptation to please brethren and superiors by "conforming" – can bring falsity and insincerity into our lives without our realizing it. To guard against this, we must not be content with our renunciation of the world by our vows, but in the fear of God we must guard the door of our hearts against the entrance of the spirit of fiction [*Ibid.*].

Self-custody is, then, a "most vigilant doorkeeper" who humbly and faithfully ministers to love. In Adam's own words, this intuitive, sincere awareness of our real motives acts as a guard "who keeps out of our soul all things which might disturb the banquet of love" – *ut nihil omnino quo amoris festivitas perturbetur, admittat* [*Ibid.*]. Self-knowledge is necessary to see through fiction. But it is a grace, a special gift. It cannot be merited *de condigno*[XXX] by any act of ours.[XXXI] We must desire it and pray for it. We must try to deserve it at least by accepting the evidence of truth when it flashes upon us, not resisting and evading the accusation that we fear to face.[XXXII]

Falsity begins with an inordinate care of the body – seeking more than is necessary to keep us living reasonably. The traditional ascetic norms of the monastic Fathers, the *discretio patrum* [616], teach us that we must not deny the body what it needs, and not pamper it beyond its needs. Extreme asceticism is just as dangerous as softness and self-indulgence.[XXXIII]

If discretion is ignored, falsity entrenches itself in the soul by the habit of sin – *usus peccandi* [618]. This in turn gradually blinds the conscience and perverts one's whole sense of values until evil takes on the appearance of good.[XXXIV] Thus falsity takes complete possession of the soul which defends its own sins – *defensio peccati*. Hence the special importance of self-restraint, humility, self-knowledge, and obedience, in order to defend the soul against the spirit of illusion.[XXXV]

But above all, the monk who has entered the monastery to seek the truth in Christ must truly and irrevocably renounce all affection for "the world" which is the realm of falsity and illusion, under the sovereignty of the Prince of Liars. Unless a man has really given up "the world" in its bad sense, he cannot gain that capacity for spiritual enlightenment and love which are necessary for the purification of his heart. Desire of worldly things and desire of the things of God are absolutely incompatible and they cannot reign together in one heart. One or the other must go [648]. Hence the necessity for an honest and uncompromising asceticism, above all for that chastity which renders the heart sensitive to spiritual love and capable of tasting the joys of contemplation.

> All impurity must be cast out from our heart in order that it may be able to taste the sweetness and only joy of oneness. Let the truth of chastity (*veritas castitatis*) cast out the desires of the flesh; let the concupiscence of the eyes be kept far away by the seriousness of discipline and by the desire of inner purity. Let love of poverty and contempt of honor destroy the pride of life. [646][XXXVI]

We shall see later the part played by Mary and Jesus in this work, but it is necessary at this point to observe that all this purification is not achieved by mere will-power and human effort. It is a work of divine grace, accomplished through God's love.[XXXVII] All takes place under the eyes of God and the Blessed Virgin Mary and with her guidance.

To acquire the *mira novitas* of the new life is to share in the divine infancy of Jesus, and that means to have Mary for a mother. To avoid the "spirit of fiction" and all the other pitfalls of life, we must dwell entirely in the love of Our Lady and receive from her love[XXXVIII] the light of the new life which is the splendor of truth. She is all-pure. There is in her no stain of falsity or evil. What comes to us through her love is therefore pure. It purifies our souls while forming them in the Christ-life.

Adam puts all this in a graphic and concrete form. As Jesus, the infant, had to be nourished by Mary's milk, so we who are infants in the spiritual life must also be nourished by it, and it is for this that we hunger [636].

What does he mean? The "milk" with which Our Lady nourishes our lives is actual grace: light to distinguish good from evil, strength to do God's will. These we receive through her. In the order of grace we are as dependent on Mary as an infant is dependent on his natural mother. If this is true of all Christians, it is particularly true of the monk.[XXXIX]

Adam's teaching[XL] is characteristically Cistercian in its concreteness and its positive emphasis on the happiness of our life in Christ.

> O happy newness, O new festivity which is celebrated not at the banquet table of this world but in the heaven of the pure soul. [619]

The life of the soul that has renounced all is a joyous banquet of Wisdom in which the mercy and love of God keep holiday. Here we may draw a comparison from St. John of the Cross, *Living Flame*, Stanza i. (He is speaking of transforming union, but *mutatis mutandis*, and with due proportion, the same is true of lower degrees of the spiritual life.)

> When this soul is so near to God that it is transformed in the flame of Love, wherein the Father and the Son and the Holy Spirit commune with it, how is it a thing incredible that it should be said to enjoy a foretaste of eternal life .... The delight caused in the soul by the flaming of the Holy Spirit is so sublime that it teaches the soul what is the savour of eternal Life .... The effect of this flame is to make the soul live spiritually in God, and experience the life of God, even as David says: My heart and my flesh have rejoiced in the living God....
>
> Inasmuch as this is a flame of Divine life, it wounds the soul with the tenderness of the life

> of God …. The office of love is to wound, that it may enkindle and cause delight, so it is ever sending forth its arrow-wounds, like most tender sparks of delicate love, joyfully and happily exercising the arts and wiles of love….
>
> These wounds, which are the playing of God, are the sparks of these tender touches of flame which proceed from the fire of love.
>
> This feast of the Holy Spirit takes place in the substance of the soul, where neither the devil nor the world nor sense can enter …. The more interior it is, the more abundantly and frequently and widely does God communicate Himself…. [*Living Flame* i, ed. A. A. Peers 3:120-22[XLI]]

Adam does not stress the passivity of the soul, he is not speaking of purely mystical experiences. He does not speak of the feast being merely in the substance of the soul. He is not speaking only of contemplation, but also of virtuous action.[XLII] But the virtuous life, the interior life, is for Adam a "feast" of God in the depths of the soul, in which the soul is called to rejoice with God in a banquet of light and grace and peace far from the cares and deceptions of the world.

To be a monk, then, is to embrace a life in which all is designed to make us enter into this joyful and secret festivity with God who has loved us and united us to himself in Christ.

> The splendor of wisdom are those virtues of the soul through which the feasts of love are continually celebrated in the secret recesses of the pure heart … to feasts of this kind are invited the novices, whose interior celebration is so much the more joyful, the more carefully holy fear guards the entrance to their hearts. [*PL* 211:619]

The monastic ideal is therefore one of interior purity and solitude and silence in which we celebrate our new life in the Spirit and praise our heavenly Father for the mystery of our redemption in Christ.

The most important elements in this "newness of life," he says, summarizing his thesis in Letter One, are: faith, by which we are rescued from the shadows of ignorance and incorporated in Christ; holy fear, which helps us do penance and protects our soul against the incursions of the *spiritus fictionis*; and love of wisdom, which draws us on to enter deeper into the secret life of joy with Christ.[XLIII]

The novice does not enter into the banquet of the interior life merely by his own good will and initiative. He needs someone to guide him in the ways of virtue and of grace. He is placed under the care of a "Spiritual Father" whom he must obey in a spirit of faith, seeing in him the representative of God.[XLIV]

The Father Master must take care to prove the spirit of the novice, to see if he is really zealous for the Work of God, for obedience and humiliations, as St. Benedict requires.[XLV] But the Master does not expect to find these qualities already formed in the novices. It is up to him to encourage their development. He must inspire fervor in divine praise (the *Opus dei* or choral office of the monk[XLVI]) – especially attention to what is sung. He must make sure that the novice does not become a monk who honors God with his lips alone. With his love for truth, Adam holds this in abomination; it is hypocrisy to say what one does not mean.

The Master of Novices must teach love of obedience and humiliations. Concerning the latter Adam says:

> He who loves his brethren out of charity, and denies himself out of humility,[XLVII] is not much concerned when reproaches are heaped upon him; but rather crucifying himself with Christ, rejoices to unite himself with the ignominy of his Cross. [586]

The spirit of prayer, the love of obedience and true humility are what St. Benedict demands above all of the novice. They are the surest indication that he has come to the monastery to seek God,[XLVIII] and not just to escape[XLIX] from the responsibilities and difficulties of life in the world. The novice who is obedient proves that he wants to give up his own will and do the will of God. The novice who is humble gives evidence that he is not deceiving himself in trying to seek his own glory by self-exaltation in the spiritual life.[L]

A most important element in the formation of the novice is the spiritual direction, given in an atmosphere of friendliness and love, by the Father Master: "Friendly and frequent conversation concerning spiritual things or the regular observances" [*Ibid.*]. Adam keeps repeating the word "friendly" – *amica*. The direction session is a friendly conversation, marked by a "praiseworthy familiarity." The aim of this friendliness and sympathy is to guard the novice against discouragement and *acedia*.[1] The atmosphere of direction must then be one of unaffected simplicity and spontaneity, completely informal and even somewhat merry.[LII]

What is talked about in direction? The mysteries of Scripture; examples of virtue in the lives of the saints; the reward promised us in heaven, how this reward is to be gained by good works; the pains of hell and the vices which lead there; but above all, the trials and hardships of the monastic life – the *dura et aspera* (hard and painful things) [*RB* 58:8]. In this matter Adam makes it clear that the Master must warn and admonish the novice concerning the *dura et aspera*. But he must avoid inflicting harsh trials and punishments on him. Adam does not recommend arbitrary and fictitious humiliations. It is the Master's duty: "not indeed to *inflict* but to preach the *dura et aspera* through which one goes to God" [*Ibid.*]. What the Father Master should do is to show, demonstrate to the novice, from the Scriptures and from living examples, how it is necessary to pass through trial, suffering, and hardship in order to get to heaven, and how our love of Christ demands we renounce ourselves completely and abandon ourselves entirely to the way of obedience and self-denial. Real progress in the way of sanctity depends on a right understanding and a true practice of self-renunciation – a renunciation[LIII] which does not destroy our will or our nature but liberates them and consecrates them entirely to God that we may serve him fruitfully and with joy.

---

1. *Acedia*. This complex ascetic term is not sufficiently well translated if we call it only "spiritual sloth." It is a kind of enervation and depression that comes when one "goes stale" in the ascetic life, and all spiritual things tend to become repugnant and hateful. Cf. Cassian, *Institute* X.[LI]

Finally, and this is most important, inseparable from the teaching of the *dura et aspera* is the teaching that CHRIST IS THE WAY. In other words, the negative content of this ascetic teaching is merged with the positive content which is more important: Jesus himself is with us, leads us, helps us, and sustains us in the difficulties of life. To seek them is to seek him. In finding the Cross, the love of him, we find Christ himself.

If we find Christ in our difficulties, we find joy, liberty, consolation. Hence it is that the only true hardship, the only suffering that is without fruit and which is to be avoided, is the suffering of those who travel the way of self-seeking amid self-satisfaction, and who are always frustrated, never at peace, because they are not united with Christ. Those who find him are liberated from frustration and sterility. They become fruitful and are able to develop freely. Hence they are happy. In these few points Adam has outlined for us a whole directory of the Cistercian life.

CHRIST IS THE WAY

The only way to bear trials and sufferings is to find Jesus in them. What does this mean?

1. By his love, by the action of his Spirit, Jesus enters into our hearts in the midst of our trials and takes away the love of worldly things, delivers us from self-love which is the obstacle to our progress and the real source of our suffering.

Hence his action liberates, heals, and alleviates. It brings joy and strength. The inner strength which comes from Christ is something we could never attain without him. It is therefore his, it comes to us as a gift from him. Yet also it is ours, for he has given it to us, it operates in us, it is ours to use and to enjoy.

2. Jesus also and above all produces in us his own dispositions and his own love, so that doing all and suffering all as he himself does, we shall experience his victory and share his love of his Father.

Adam here remarks that the Spirit of Christ produces in us the "three liberties" of which St. Bernard speaks in the *De Gratia et Libero Arbitrio*:[LIV] freedom from sin, from necessity, from misery (Adam gives them in that order [587]).

3. The action of Christ produces in our souls a true love of heavenly things. This love unites us to Christ as our Head. "Christ is our Head. The 'sense' that is in this Head is the love of heavenly things." *Caput nostrum Christus est. Cujus capitis sensus est amor coelestium* …. [Ep. 16; *PL* 211:640].

4. Letter 18 to the monks of Perseigne is a treatise on this action of Christ in our souls. In it, Christ appears above all as the *magister humilitatis*, the Master of Humility, not only by his teaching and example in the Gospels but by the interior action of his grace.[LV]

Christ is the fountain of living waters – the inexhaustible source of grace and wisdom.

But these waters flow only into the valley of humility. It is therefore only by humility that we learn his wisdom and acquire his virtues and fruitfulness. Humility is indeed the close friend of wisdom and of all the virtues. All our virtues must be learned from Christ. But if we do not have humility, we cannot learn any of them.

> How intimately related to heavenly Wisdom is humility, how productive of virtue, how rich in merits, how able to grasp heavenly secrets …. [643][LVI]

Because humility is a channel always wide open for these living waters, it purifies the soul from every stain. It nourishes us and gives us strength for the ascetic life. It disposes our hearts for contemplation.

> Happy therefore is humility which merits to bathe in these waters lest any stain of defilement appear or remain in it. It merits renewed strength so that in every struggle it remains steadfast …. [644]

Hence we must learn humility from Jesus:

> Learn, O children, to be humble, and learn from him who is the effective teacher of this discipline, Christ. [645]

We learn to be humble from him who is humble, by imitating him, and the result is that we find peace for our hearts.

> The art therefore which the Christian must learn .... the art indeed which makes the disciple of Christ is called meek humility and humble meekness. [*Ibid.*]

Humility, being the companion of wisdom, is also the guardian of discretion and of all the other virtues. Without humility we cannot avoid making all kinds of errors of judgment. But when we are humble (that is, when we distrust our own wisdom) our judgment is sustained and directed by the truth of Christ.[LVII]

Humility is all the more secure in proportion as it is more secret – *tanto securius quanto secretius cordis disponit officia*. Not seeking to be seen and praised by men, it judges all things secretly and interiorly by the light of God's truth [Ep. 11; *PL* 211:619].

> The less one thinks of oneself, so much the more abundantly do graces overflow. [*Ibid.*] Charming and gracious humility builds their dwellings in the soul for each and every virtue, arranges the duties of each, and nothing is done either in the bodily senses or in the affections of the soul which is not subjected to the control of this God-fearing humility. [620]

Like St. Benedict, Adam considers humility not so much in its narrow meaning as in the broad sense of a climate in which all the monastic virtues flourish, a climate of complete and trusting dependence on the grace of God.[LVIII]

Humility, then, guarantees right intention. It governs the passions, leading them into right channels; anger is converted into zeal for God, concupiscence is transformed into charity. Passion is sublimated and transfigured in the crucible of selflessness, over the fires of humility.[LIX] Humility leads to peace, and it is the only way to contemplation. If the monk lacks humility, he can know by this sign that he is without Christ. No matter how great may be his zeal, his energy, his apparent generosity, all is empty and sterile without humility.

In a word, to summarize the Cistercian life of virtue[LX] in Christ, it can all be contained in the word *humility* as it is understood by the Benedictine tradition. Humility in this sense is something much greater than mere modesty and self-depreciation. It is a permanent disposition to live in complete submission to the deepest spiritual realities and to renounce one's own judgment at all times in order to follow the will of God. This is what it means to be taught by Christ in the Cistercian "School of Humility."[LXI]

But the School[LXII] of Christ is especially and before all else the School of the Infant Christ. In the "emptying" of the Word in the Incarnation Adam contemplates the humility of God.

> In the meanwhile let all our philosophy be concerned with the infancy of the Incarnate Word, and the love of God toward us which this study shows us to some degree, let us strive faithfully and as far as we are able to reciprocate. [Ep. 16:636]

Life in the cloister is a spiritual participation in the mystery of the divine infancy. The swaddling bands with which he is bound are the monastic rules – *Fascia qua stringitur in cunabulis, sanctae est religionis districto, cujus institutione religamur in claustris* [635]. As we meditate on the way in which he humbled himself for us we are filled with desire to be humble for love of him. As we come to understand with what great love he gave himself to be the nourishment and the life of our souls, we begin to see something of the unfathomable mystery of God's love for us. We are filled with fear, piety, strength, and all the other gifts of the Holy Spirit by the contemplation of Christ poor and helpless in the manger at Bethlehem [635].

The totality of his gift of himself to us in the cradle gives us a deeper understanding of the totality of his sacrifice for us on the Cross, and inspires our hearts to give themselves completely to him in return:

> The entire deity poured itself out into man, all his soul it gave over to obedience. Its whole body it committed to death, even to the death

> of the cross, thus has the Almighty completely loved us, and it is not enough if we give back in return all that we are, all the little that we are. [636]

The *Magister Christus*, who teaches us in his school of charity, desires by his teaching to lead us to that height of perfection which is the wisdom of the Cross, the wisdom[LXIII] that consists in giving ourselves totally and completely for love of him.

The fruit of this wisdom is a union of hearts with the Incarnate Word. Here we see that Adam prepared the way for devotion[LXIV] to the Sacred Heart, a devotion which is deeply rooted in the Cistercian mysticism of the twelfth and thirteenth centuries. Adam teaches us that in emptying himself, in his incarnation, the Word Incarnate, coming forth from the heart of the Father, opened to us his heart in order to give us his humility, in order to show that he came to dwell in our own hearts, and therefore in order to win our hearts for himself.

> He opened his heart to us, when he emptied himself, in order to teach us by the example of his humility. He sought our heart for himself, when he showed himself to be the One who loves and dwells in our hearts. [Ep 18:646]

A few lines later, he shows how this indwelling of Christ in our own hearts is what gives meaning to our whole spiritual life[LXV] and especially to our asceticism:

> If therefore you are men of heart (*viri cordati*), if you desire to feel within you Jesus who dwells in hearts, you must guard your hearts with all care. [*Ibid.*]

A *vir cordatus* is a man who has a heart, who has a strong heart – courageous and tender because it is humble. The monk, then, is *cordatus* not only because he has a man's heart, but because in his heart also beats the heart of Christ.

The presence of Christ in our hearts is kept alive by the memory of his sacred passion, and this constant thought of Jesus crucified, is intimately connected with the practice of *custodia cordis*.[LXVI] The light of humility and holy fear plays ever in the recesses of our soul, lighting up our actions to compare them with the sufferings and the love of Jesus. Thus we continually strive to make our lives conform to the model of his love, and in so doing we find happiness, we discover the "freedom of devotion" with which we are always able to partake in that interior festivity, where we celebrate our union with God in the splendors of his wisdom.

> O happy soul, for whom fear has barred the paths of vice, so that with free devotion it may keep festival in these splendors of wisdom. [Ep. 11:623]

This fear has nothing to do with servile anxiety. It is a form of love which makes our conscience delicate and tender.[LXVII] It is a purely filial fear – the dread of being separated, even for a moment, from Christ crucified dwelling in our hearts.

The Blessed Virgin and the Cistercian Life

At the end of Letter 11, after speaking about[LXVIII] the constant memory of Jesus on the Cross, Adam turns to Our Lady. He recognizes that it may prove to be too difficult for us to fix our gaze at all times on the Cross, and follow Christ Crucified without respite. In order to make this possible, he would have us look rather at Mary, who will be the source of our strength.

> If the resolve to follow this path which we have undertaken should seem difficult, let us fly to the aid of Our Virgin …. [623]

Our union with Christ becomes at the same time a union with Mary, and this implies the reproduction of her virtues in our lives. Indeed, it is her purity that lives in us when we are pure, her fecund love that is fertile in good works in our own souls when we are zealous in the service of God.

> Let us gain for ourselves the whiteness of her lily-like innocence through our purity of conscience, nor will there be lacking to us the per-

> sistence of fruitful work together with that purity of the flesh which adorned the virginal fruitfulness. [*Ibid.*]

Since the whole spiritual life is the life of Christ in us, then Mary, the mother of the incarnate Word, is the mother of our spiritual life. Our strength in Christ depends on our confidence in Mary. Our confidence in her should be without limits. We should never cease to praise her, no matter how unworthy we may feel. We must constantly give thanks to her for bringing us Jesus. We must seek the mercy of God in and through her. In her we find peace, because in her we find the Truth, the Incarnate Word whom she brings to us. She gives us strong faith and by her intercession defends us against every form of sin. She is the great "sacrament" of God, so to speak, containing within herself all the abundance of his graces, *charismatum universitas* [635].

Seeking Jesus through Mary is, for Adam, not so much a matter of thinking about Mary and then advancing, by a series of logical steps, to Jesus her Son. It does not mean thinking first about Mary and then about Jesus. It means finding Jesus in and with Mary, Mary in and with Jesus. It means also finding ourselves in them. It means finding that deep spiritual life – the life of God in us – in which we are one with Jesus, in and through the Virgin Mother.[LXIX]

Adam expresses this by saying that we find Jesus and Mary by receiving the life which she has earned for us, by her prayers. We become companions of Jesus, playing with the infant Christ at her feet, nourished with him at her breast (*collactanei* [636]), embraced with him in her arms. We see Mary exclusively and completely with the eyes of the Infant Christ. We are united to her in him, we are identified with him in her mind, she sees him in us, and us only in him. Hence we must see her as he does also, we must come to her as he did, with his trust and his dependent love. Grace created this love in our hearts.[LXX]

Our life of dependence on Mary in the order of grace is the simplest and purest expression of our life in Christ.

To seek Christ, therefore, and to seek him through Mary, it is not necessary that we "rise above" Mary, or somehow exclude her. It is not necessary that we rationalize our relation to Christ and to his blessed mother.[LXXI] It is only necessary that we unite our poverty and helplessness with the poverty and helplessness of the Infant Christ,[LXXII] and abandon ourselves to our mother. In this way we find Mary and Jesus together. They are inseparable. But what strikes us[LXXIII] first of all is Mary's love and mercy, her mother's love for us. We go on from there to realize more clearly that this is the same love she lavished upon Jesus, and that in this love of hers we are one with him. This love of hers makes us her children by drawing us to her heart with the divine Infant. And it is Christ present in us who makes her love us as her sons.[LXXIV]

It is clear to Adam that we do not have to "climb" or "ascend" to find Jesus. He has descended to our level in order to give himself completely to us. In his poverty he stands in the midst of us as one whom we know not. To recognize him, we need only love our own nothingness, and see that he has embraced our own poverty for love of us. But if we are devoured by spiritual ambition that resents our own lowliness and seeks to be exalted above our own poverty then we will never find him.

> How delightful it is, how innocent to play together with this infant, to make oneself small to enter his cradle, to speak softly in answer to his infant cries! O how happy is that infancy, which joins its stammering speech with that of such an infant, and wraps itself in his swaddling clothes. [635]

It is here that Adam goes on to explain that monastic rules and observances are the "swaddling clothes" with which we are wrapped together with the Infant Christ, by his blessed mother. He takes a very positive view of the restrictions and self-denial of the monastic life – he does not regard them merely as painful and humiliating restraints upon human nature, hut above all as means of uniting ourselves with Jesus and plunging ourselves into the love with which he was embraced by Mary.

The love of Our Lady for us does not thereby become an end in itself. The whole organic reality of Mary's love for us and our union with Jesus her Infant, is the concrete and total expression of God's love for us in the Incarnation. Hence we return to that great central thought: the Incarnation is for Adam not something abstract, but a concrete mystery, which is grasped when we plunge into the very midst of it, when we, too, become infants with the Incarnate Word, and are embraced, with him, by the love of his Virgin Mother.

The Incarnation, then, in its most concrete expression in the life of the monk, is the whole surrounding element of divine love, the new spiritual world in which he lives and moves and is contained, a world made up of Jesus and Mary and of all the souls who are one in Christ enveloped together in the mother-love of Mary, that love in which the mysterious and infinite power of the Spirit works secretly to bring forth new Christs and unite them to the Father.

It is the theme developed in Gerard Manley Hopkins' poem "The Blessed Virgin Compared to the Air We Breathe":[LXXV]

. . . I say that we are wound
With mercy round and round
As if with air: the same
Is Mary, more by name.
She, wild web, wondrous robe,
Mantles the guilty globe,
Since God has let dispense
Her prayers his providence:
Nay more than almoner,
The sweet alms' self is her
And men are meant to share
Her life as life does air.

If I have understood,
She holds high motherhood
Towards all our ghostly good
And plays in grace her part
About man's beating heart,
Laying, like air's fine flood,
The deathdance in his blood;
Yet no part but what will
Be Christ our saviour still.
Of her flesh he took flesh:
He does take fresh and fresh,

Though much the mystery how,
Not flesh but spirit now
And makes, O marvelous!
New Nazareths in us,
Where she shall yet conceive
Him, morning, noon, and eve;
New Bethlems and he born
There, evening, noon, and morn –
Bethlem or Nazareth,
Men here may draw like breath
More Christ and baffle death;
Who, born so, comes to be
New self and nobler me
In each one and each one
More makes, when all is done,
Both God's and Mary's Son. . . .

So God was god of old:
A mother came to mould
Those limbs like ours which are
What must make our daystar
Much dearer to mankind;
Whose glory bare would blind
Or less would win man's mind.
Through her we may see him
Made sweeter, not made dim,
And her hand leaves his light
Sifted to suit our sight.

Be thou then O thou dear
Mother, my atmosphere;
My happier world, wherein
To wend and meet no sin;
Above me, round me lie
Fronting my froward eye
With sweet and scarless sky;
Stir in my ears, speak there
Of God's love, O live air,
Of patience, penance, prayer:
World-mothering air, air wild,

Wound with thee, in thee isled,
Fold home, fast fold thy child.[LXXVI]

The Sabbath of Contemplation[LXXVII]

We have now considered in Adam of Perseigne the elements of the monastic life, as it was seen by the Cistercian Fathers, the disciples of St. Bernard. We have seen the structural elements of a deep mysticism. There is no room, within these perspectives, for a merely ascetical view of the monastic life. That is to say, there is no place for the idea that the monastic life is simply a collection of observances and "things to do" which will improve our souls and gain merit for us, so that eventually we will be able to confront Christ as our Judge and receive from him a favorable verdict. Our intimate knowledge of the mystery of Christ is not something reserved only for heaven.[LXXVIII]

God has already entered deeply into our earthly lives with all the splendors of his wisdom and all the radiance of his eternal joy. The fire of God is playing in our souls, enlivening and transforming them. All our monastic observances are shot through with the flames of this mystical wisdom, and with the transforming power of the Holy Spirit, which is charity. The power of this "new life" – this *felix novitas* – is ever busy correcting and purifying the traces of sin left in our nature by the "old man" who has been cast out by our conversion to the monastic life. By his direct action, and through the medium of human agents, particularly the novice master, the Holy Spirit is exorcizing the *spiritus fictionis* in our souls and refashioning our lives according to the pattern of God's own Truth, manifested in Jesus.

Jesus himself is the Master in the school of charity and humility which we have entered, and we have learned that the whole new life, the whole *festivitas* of our new existence in Christ, is simply the concrete expression of the Incarnation, in our own monastic lives. This means that in practice and in the concrete, we can say that Mary is our very life itself, because the new life was brought into the world by her faith and her love, and is kept alive in the world by her constant mediation and her maternal care for all whom she knows and loves in the Infant Christ.

It now remains to round out this brief survey of the Cistercian life by considering that life in its mystical perfection – the "Sabbath" of the soul resting in Christ, and mystically united to him.

The mystical life is the work of the Holy Spirit in the soul of which he has taken full possession by the action of his seven gifts. Here Adam follows the common teaching of the Western Fathers which was later taken up and systematized by St. Thomas Aquinas. There is however nothing rigid or systematic about Adam's presentation of the doctrine. The seven gifts, or seven spirits, are simply seven different aspects of that superabundant love of God by which the Holy Spirit celebrates in the soul the mystical festivity of its marriage with the Word.

Adam refers to the gifts as "seven solemn feasts" or seven holy days, seven sabbaths of rest, "in which the soul is liberated by God from every servile work in order that it may occupy itself exclusively with him" [590]. His emphasis, as is usual in the Cistercian Fathers, is upon mystical union as a supreme manifestation of liberty: the liberty of God in choosing the soul for his spouse and the liberty of the soul in responding to the choice. Mystical union is then a feast of supreme freedom, the feast of Truth himself rejoicing in the soul whom he has made free with his own freedom.

Even the gift of fear is, for Adam, a feast of freedom: it is the custodian of the banquet, who dismisses all turbulent and distracting thoughts and enables the soul to feast freely upon divine things [594]. The fear of the Lord is thus considered not so much as something that makes us attentive to the danger of sin, but rather as an experience of "loathing for the labor of making bricks without straw"[LXXIX] which Pharaoh (the devil) imposes upon the citizens of "this world."

Piety is a feast of sincerity – a feast of truth in God's service, in which love for God's will makes us serve him with joy and self-forgetfulness, and thus drives out of our hearts the "noise and confusion of evil inclinations" [590]. Piety, says Adam, "is worship of God and compassion for the neighbor, a feast in which we taste the beginning of that rest and silence which the prophet called the cult of justice" [Cf. Is. 32:17]. It is also the "silence in heaven"[LXXX] during which Michael battles with the devil, for in our mystical ascent to God we must face a fierce battle with the spirit of darkness. All the same, this battle does not alter the fact that the soul rests and celebrates in silence the joy of being united with God.

The "feast of knowledge" illuminates the mind to enable a man to know God and to share his knowledge with others. And so, as we shall see repeatedly, the festivity of silent and solitary union with God by no means excludes good works and fraternal union with others. On the contrary, in proportion as our love of God is purified, so also is our love for our brothers and those are most closely united to their brothers who are at the same time most closely united to God. This is one of the basic principles of Cistercian mysticism and it is strongly emphasized in the letters of Adam of Perseigne.

In the "feast of fortitude" we find again the paradoxical union of joy and suffering, peace and combat in the soul united with God. The gift of counsel brings the soul under the direct guidance of Christ "The Angel of Great Counsel"[LXXXI] but at the same time gives us the ability to direct others in the ways of God's will. The same pattern seems to repeat itself in Adam's descriptions of these various gifts, which shows that his distinctions are not meant to be too clear-cut or absolute.

In the "feast of understanding" the bride of Truth enters into the banquet of the angels. Purified of all images of external things it rejoices in the contemplation of invisible realities that have no bodily image or representation. It is a feast that is "all splendor" (*tota est splendore*), a feast of spiritual light, and he who is invited to it becomes equal to the cherubim. But he who attains to the "seventh feast," the feast of Wisdom, reaches the pure and perfect sabbath of charity. This is a feast not of light but of fire, a feast of total transformation, the ultimate goal of the monk's vow of *conversatio morum*. The monk now knows God as perfectly as man in this life can know him – by being consumed in the flames of God's own love. Here he is no longer himself, and yet is most perfectly himself. Having died to himself he finds himself perfectly in God.

One of the most striking things about the mysticism of Adam is the parallel growth of love for God and love for men. The mystic who is transformed by the fire of love in the "feast of wisdom" is by that very fact brought closer to other men and becomes for them a source of inspiration, drawing them powerfully along the way to the same union. This is done not only by example and teaching, but by a direct communication of the same vehemence of love. The fire of Christ's love leaps from one soul to another, and does so all the more quickly in proportion as they are united in intimate friendship with one another.

Indeed, the Fathers of the Church and the monastic writers of the Middle Ages seldom if ever talk of souls in the abstract and colorless way that we find in a certain type of modern spirituality. There exists today a concept of the apostolate that treats men as objects and numbers rather than as persons. The apostle is regarded almost as if he were an inert instrument, and this instrument is used to "make converts" in greater or fewer numbers. What seems to matter is not the persons themselves who are converted, their happiness, their growth in Christ, hut simply the "souls" who, without identity and without special features have become eligible for inclusion in statistical estimates of the Church's "growth." This is simply an effect of the universal disease of materialism, the worldly reverence for quantity and number. Such things are not so common in the spirituality of earlier centuries.

Although, as we have seen, Adam himself took part enthusiastically in an apostolic movement of vast dimensions, that of Foulques de Neuilly, he seldom speaks of apostolic radiation except in terms of a contact between friends. The communication of love from soul to soul is, for Adam, a communication from friend to friend. When one Christian becomes a saint, his sanctity of course raises the level of sanctity in the whole Church. But what Adam is concerned with is the fact that this sanctity communicates itself to *his immediate circle*: to those with whom he lives, and especially to those with whom he is united by special bonds of friendship. And in this he resembles many of his contemporaries, most of all Aelred of Rievaulx, author of a classic treatise on *Spiritual Friendship*.[LXXXII]

The fact that the monk is a "solitary," and "flees from the multitude .... leaving the labors of Martha" for the life of contemplation poses not the slightest problem for Adam. Friendship, and the radiation of spiritual love, is not only no distraction from the contemplation of God, but forms an inseparable part of the contemplative life as he conceives it. Of course, we have to admit that the term "contemplative life" is itself somewhat alien to Adam. Certainly he seldom uses it in its modern, more or less juridical, sense. For him, it is simply the monastic life, which is a life of love. And wherever there is love, there is sharing of the good gifts which God showers upon those who love him. Most of all, there is union and cooperation in the greatest work of all, the work of seeking God and finding him by love. Hence paradoxically love is always at rest, always in silence, always at peace, and yet never idle. *Revera amor numquam est otiosa* [*PL* 211:596]. As St. Bernard said somewhere, the very leisure (*otium*) of love is its business (*negotium*).[LXXXIII] And since the nature of the good is to communicate and share its goodness, love cannot help sharing itself with friends.

A good example is the beautiful sixteenth letter, written to one of Adam's close friends, a Benedictine abbot, and through him to his community. Here we have a typical example of that frank, spontaneous and warm affection which is so often found among the medieval and early Christian saints and which seems to have vanished into oblivion in our day, at least in spiritual writing. The thing that is most striking about this open expression of deep spiritual friendship is its patently eucharistic character. Indeed it is obvious that such friendship should exist as the normal fruit of our participation in the eucharistic banquet.

> Let us love Christ and in Him let us love one another for nothing is happier in this life than to love faithfully and to be loved [640]. Break your bread [says Adam] break your bread to your begging and hungry friend; for in this you will prove yourself a friend if you will allay your friend's hunger with your bread. Your bread is Christ. Your bread is your love. Your bread is your prayer. Your bread is your compunction of tears with which you wash away not only your own sins but also those of your friend. [594]

An exclamation in a letter to his Benedictine friend sums it all up: "All that I have to write to you is about love." *Tota mihi tecum est de amore materies* [632].

Never for a moment does Adam consider that this friendship in Christ is a distraction or a disturbance to his life of prayer. But how is this possible? Only because his love itself is so eminently simple, strong and pure. It is completely free from worldliness, from falsity, from the *spiritus fictionis* which seeks its own selfish satisfaction under the cover of lofty spirituality. Here is no disguise, no pretense, no hidden selfishness. Certainly there is satisfaction and joy. But they are pure, and the love of his friends has become, in all truth, one and the same thing with his love for Christ.

In one word, this true love is not and cannot be unhealthy because it is the fruit of his union with Christ. Christ is the head of the mystical body, says Adam, and a love that is ruled by Christ the head of the body must inevitably be normal and healthy and free. It is perfectly "sane." But worldly love only gets into us by separating us from Christ our head. Such love then, does not come from our "head" and therefore it is an "insanity" [640].

This then sums it all up. Love is the answer to everything for Adam as it was for St. John and for Christ Himself. "God is charity, and he who remains in charity remains in God and God in him" [I John 4:16].

This love is the soul's bond with God as the source of all reality, and therefore such love is itself the triumph of truth in our lives. Hence it drives out all falsity, all error. To remain in love is to remain in the truth. All that one has to do is to continue loving, in sincerity and truth, and seeking before all else the will of God. Everything else follows. Life is then a perpetual "sabbath" of divine peace.[LXXXIV]

When the soul of the monk has arrived at perfect union with the will of Christ, so that there is no longer any discrepancy between them, the light of holy fear and compunction no longer discovers anything to reproach, and the soul tastes perfect peace and contentment. It rests in the interior silence of a pure heart in which Christ is present. The soul is perfectly tranquil because it is in harmony with the supreme Truth of God himself, in Christ.

> Peace prepares a chamber of rest for a man in the testimony his conscience gives him, to whom justice more sweetly offers its kiss, the more it takes away every wound of sin by the proposal of truth. [*PL* 211:620]

Humility, meekness, and obedience have played the most important part in producing this interior peace. How? By bringing the soul into complete dependence on Christ, and total freedom from every other influence [See Ep. 18; PL 211:645]. Liberated from all cares, because free from every other desire than the desire of pleasing Christ, the soul is delivered from the tyranny of sensual attractions and from all interest in the things of the world. It tastes already the joys of eternity in the "sabbath of innocence."

> Within there takes place the sabbath of innocence keeping festival in days of eternal peace. [*Ibid.*]

The light of perfect charity has risen in the pure heart, the orient star which brings us, like the Magi, to the true King [Ep. 16; 637]. This is the star of peace, the star of love, whose rays are the splendor of the divine festival in the depths of our soul. Under the rays of this star, the soul enters the *cella vinaria*[LXXXV] and tastes the sweetness of contemplation. Now the monk no longer knows the labor of learning or the toil of discipline. The soul rests in the arms of the Spouse, and sings the nuptial song of union with Him Who alone is her glory and her joy [Ep. 18; 648]. This is the full and perfect flowering of the monastic life.[LXXXVI]

I. I.e. King Richard I of England (1157-1199).

II. Along with Clairvaux, La Ferté and Morimond, one of the first four daughter houses of the Abbey of Cîteaux.

III. *Letters* text (6) reads: "Fiora"; "Christian Freedom and Monastic Formation," *American Benedictine Review* [*ABR*] 13 [September 1962] 290 reads: "Flora".

IV. See *Introduction to Christian Mysticism* 172-73 for a brief discussion of Joachim (1135-1202) as "*one of the most important figures of the Middle Ages*."

V. This sentence in *ABR* reads: "His doctrine of the coming of a new age, the 'Age of the Holy Spirit,' corresponded to deep aspirations for renewal and prophetic reawakening, and exercised a decisive influence on the Franciscan movement" (290).

VI. French priest (d. 1202) who became a popular and influential preacher of moral reform and was subsequently entrusted by the pope with the task of preaching the Fourth Crusade, though he died before its scandalous conquest of Constantinople in 1204.

VII. Geoffrey de Villehardouin (d. c. 1218), *The Conquest of Constantinople*: see Joinville and Villehardouin, *Chronicles of the Crusades*, trans. Margaret Shaw (New York: Penguin, 1963) 27-160.

VIII. I.e. King Philip II of France (1165-1223) and King John of England (1166-1216).

IX. This sentence is followed in *ABR* 291 by: "We may be permitted to take a kindlier view of his 'laxity' than did the contemporary Cistercians!"

X. J. P. Migne, ed., *Patrologiae Cursus Completus, Series Latina* [*PL*], 221 vols. (Paris: Garnier, 1844-1865); marginal notes in *Letters* have been inserted in the text in brackets.

XI. Adam de Perseigne, *Lettres*, trans. Jean Bouvet, Sources Chrétiennes vol. 66 (Paris: Éditions du Cerf, 1960); *Letters* text (7) omits "recently" as found in *ABR* 291, presumably because that volume was no longer recent when this version was published, and adds a marginal note: "*SC 66 – on which this translation is based.*"

XII. Instead of the preceding material, the first version of the text ("La Formation Monastique selon Adam de Perseigne," trans. Charles Dumont, OCSO, *Collectanea Ordinis Cisterciensium Reformatorum* [*COCR*] 19 [January 1957] 1) reads: "Adam, Abbé de Perseigne, fut, au sein de l'Ordre aussi bien qu'au dehors, un des plus fameux directeurs spirituels de son temps. Il nous a laissé une collection de lettres qui portent la marque de l'esprit de nos Pères et qui restent des témoins de l'âge d'or de l'Ordre. Plusieurs de ces letters traitent explicitement de la formation des novices. Adam avait été Maître des novices à Perseigne; il correspondait avec d'autres Maîtres des novices et des directors spirituels de l'Ordre, comme Osmond de Mortemer et G., le destinataire de la letter 11e, qui était peut-être Maître des novices à Pontigny. L'examen de quelques-unes de ces letters nous fera entrer dans une mine d'idées fort riches dont l'étude qu'on en fait ici, sans prétendre être exhaustive, rendra sans doute service en raison de la valeur pratique de cet enseignement" ("Adam, Abbot of Perseigne, was one of best known spiritual directors of his time, both in the bosom of the Order as well as outside it. He has left us a collection of letters which bears the mark of the spirit of our Fathers and remains among the witnesses of the Golden Age of the Order. Many of these letters explicitly concern the formation of novices. Adam had been novice master at Perseigne; he corresponded with other novice masters and spiritual directors of the Order, such as Osmond de Mortemer and G., the addressee of Letter 11, who was perhaps novice master at Pontigny. An examination of some of these letters will provide entry into a mine of very rich ideas; without pretending to be exhaustive, the study which is made here will undoubtedly provide a service because of the practical value of this teaching").

XIII. Merton draws on the following letters in his presentation: *Epistola* 1, to Osmond (*PL* 211, cols. 583B-589B); *Epistola* 2, to Osmond (cols. 589B-592D); *Epistola* 3, to Osmond (cols. 592D-595B); *Epistola* 5, to Osmond (cols. 595D-597B); *Epistola* 11, to G. (cols. 614A-623D); *Epistola* 16, *ad abbatem de Turpiniam* (cols. 631C-641C); *Epistola* 18, *ad fratres suos* (cols. 644A-648C).

XIV. "study … 'spirituality'": no equivalent in *COCR*.

XV. "observer of life": *COCR* 1 reads: "un psychologue" ("a psychologist").

XVI. "in his revealed word … everything that happened."; *COCR* 1 reads: "dans la révélation qu'Il a faite de Lui-Même" ("in the revelation that He made of Himself").

XVII. See *Sermo III De Partu B. Virginis* (*PL* 211, col. 721A): "*hominem … novum, qui secundum Deum creatus est*" (Eph. 4:24; the final words of this scriptural verse, though quoted here by Merton, do not appear in the text of the sermon).

XVIII. *Letters* text (8) reads: "True"; *ABR* 291 reads: "Truth"; *COCR* 2 reads: "Vérité".

XIX. "that is to say … Holy Spirit": no equivalent in *COCR*.

XX. "like that of St. Benedict": this phrase is not found in *ABR* 292, though its equivalent ("comme celui de saint Benoît") is in *COCR* 2.

XXI. This sentence is followed in *ABR* 292 by: "In a word, Adam is a characteristic writer of the medieval Benedictine tradition, characterized by his sanity, his simplicity, his positive and optimistic view of life, and his truly Benedictine wisdom."

XXII. For a detailed discussion of this vow see *Life of the Vows* 274-314.

XXIII. "The most characteristic … is based": no equivalent in *COCR*.

XXIV. *Letters* text (6) reads: "581"; *ABR* 293 and *COCR* 2 read, correctly: "584".

XXV. John 1:4.

XXVI. "falsity in ourselves": equivalent followed in *COCR* 4 by: "II. Le 'spiritus fictionis'."

XXVII. John 8:44.

XXVIII. "The 'new man' … influence in our lives": no equivalent in *COCR*.

XXIX. "the splendor of the new life": this phrase is not found in *ABR* 295, though its equivalent ("la splendeur de la vie nouvelle") is in *COCR* 4.

XXX. i.e. as deserved, properly earned.

XXXI. "by any act of ours": equivalent followed in *COCR* 5 by: "III. Degrés dans la déloyauté."

XXXII. "We must desire … fear to face": no equivalent in *COCR*.

XXXIII. "Extreme asceticism … self-indulgence": no equivalent in *COCR*.

XXXIV. "This in turn … appearance of good": no equivalent in *COCR*.

XXXV. "spirit of illusion": equivalent followed in *COCR* 5 by: "IV. Marie, Mére de sincérité."

XXXVI. "But above all … pride of life": no equivalent in *COCR*.

XXXVII. "that all this purification … God's love": *COCR* 5 reads: "n'est pas question pour Adam que le moine s'examine ou se dirige lui-même" ("it is not a question for Adam of the monk examining or directing himself").

XXXVIII. *Letters* text (18) reads: "from her"; *ABR* 297 reads: "from her love"; *COCR* 6 reads: "de son amour".

XXXIX. In the order … of the monk": *COCR* 6 reads: "ceci prouve combien en tout nous dépendons d'elle et combien nous lui sommes étroitement unis" ("this proves how much we depend on her for everything and how much we are closely united with her").

XL. "Adam's teaching": preceded in COCR 6 by: "V. Sommaire du noviciat – Vie nouvelle."

XLI. *Living Flame of Love* I.6-9, *The Complete Works of Saint John of the Cross*, ed. and trans. E. Allison Peers, 3 vols. (Westminster, MD: Newman Press, 1949) 120-22, which reads: "when this soul … the delight …. that flaming …. its effect is to make …. this flame is a flame …. the office of love … may enkindle with love and cause delight, so, when it is, as it were, a living flame within the soul, it is ever …. these wounds … which touch the soul intermittently and proceed …. this feast … the more interior it is, the more is it secure, substantial and delectable; for the more interior it is, the purer it is, and the more of purity there is in it, the more abundantly and frequently and widely does God communicate Himself."

XLII. "He is not … action": no equivalent in *COCR*.

XLIII. "joy with Christ": equivalent followed in COCR 7 by: "VI. Le Maître des novices."

XLIV. "The novice does not … representative of God": *COCR* 7-8 reads: "Adam énumère six qualités spécialement requises chez celui qui aura à former des hommes à la 'vie nouvelle' du cistercien. 1) Un foi fervente qui donne l'intelligence des choses spirituelles. 2) La crainte du Seigneur qui naît chez celui qui a le sens de Dieu. Comment pourra-t-il dire si le disciple cherche vraiment Dieu, le Maître qui n'aurait pas lui-même le sens de Dieu? Cette crainte *met fin à toute malice* et fait débuter une vie dans la Sagesse. Le commencement de la sagesse signifie ici: qu'on *évite toute négligence* pour les choses de Dieu. 3) L'amour de la sagesse: un thème qui revient souvent dans ces lettres. Dans le contexte cistercien, cet amour de la sagesse signifie un zèle 'connaturel,' affectif et fervent pour les actes des vertus. Comparez saint Benoît à la fin de son chapitre septième et saint Bernard au sermon

85e *In Cantica*. Amor sapientiae … dum his qui scienda vel facienda sunt ex affectu diligentiam impendit, alacriter justitiam consummat et perficit (585). Cet amour de la sagesse a deux autres effets; en plus de nous faire vivre une vie vraiment juste, il garde notre innocence et nous mène à la contemplation des choses éternelles. Quelqu'un qui possède cette sagesse, dit Adam, peut vraiment s'appeler philosophe (585).… quia dum ei splendor illuminat veritatis, etiam oblectat amor virtutis. 4) Le bon exemple: *Religiosa Magistri conversatio, quae quasi in speculum est adhibenda novitio* (585). 5) Un souci affectueux des âmes. *Pia Magistri circa novitium sollicitudo*" ("Adam lists six qualities especially required of one who will have to form persons in the 'new life' of a Cistercian: 1) A fervent faith that brings an understanding of spiritual things. 2) The fear of the Lord who is born in one who has a sense of God. How could a master who had no sense of God himself say if the disciple truly seeks God? This fear puts an end to all malice and marks the beginning of a life of Wisdom. Here the beginning of wisdom means that one avoids all negligence of the things of God. 3) The love of wisdom: a theme that recurs often in the letters. In the Cistercian context, this love of wisdom represents a 'connatural' zeal, deeply felt and fervent, for acts of virtue. Compare St. Benedict at the end of chapter seven and Saint Bernard in Sermon 85 on the Song of Songs. 'The love of wisdom prompts affectionate attention with regard to what should be known and done, and quickly completes and perfects righteousness' (585). This love of wisdom has two other effects: as well as making us live a truly just life, it preserves our innocence and leads us to the contemplation of eternal things. Anyone who possesses this wisdom, according to Adam, can truly be called a philosopher (585): 'because the splendor of truth illuminates him and likewise the love of virtue delights him.' 4) Good example: 'The religious way of life of the master which should be displayed to the novice as though in a mirror' (585). 5) An affectionate care for souls: 'The respectful care of the master surrounding the novice.'").

XLV. *Rule* of St. Benedict c. 58 (*The Rule of St. Benedict in Latin and English*, ed. and trans. Justin McCann, OSB [London: Burns, Oates, 1952] 130/131).

XLVI. "the *Opus dei* … of the monk": no equivalent in *COCR*.

XLVII. *Letters* text (22) reads: "brethren out of humility"; *ABR* 299 reads: "brethren out of charity, and denies himself out of humility"; *COCR* 8 reads: "ses frères de charité et se renonce par humilité".

XLVIII. *Rule* of St. Benedict c. 58 (McCann 130/131).

XLIX. *Letters* text (22) reads: "not just escape"; *ABR* 299 reads: "not just to escape".

L. "The spirit of prayer … spiritual life": no equivalent in *COCR*.

LI. For a discussion of acedia see *Cassian and the Fathers* 183-90.

LII. "The atmosphere … merry": no equivalent in *COCR*.

LIII. *Letters* text (24) reads: "self-renunciation, in a renunciation"; *ABR* 299 reads: "self-renunciation – a renunciation".

LIV. C. 3: "*Triplicem esse libertatem, Naturae, Gratiae, Gloriae*" (*PL* 182, cols. 1004D-1006C).

LV. "not only … his grace": no equivalent in *COCR*.

LVI. *Letters* text (26) reads: "secrets …."; *ABR* 301 reads: "secrets … (643)".

LVII. "But when … truth of Christ": *COCR* 11 reads: "Avec humilité, nos jugements son protégés par la vérité du Christ" ("With humility, our judgments are protected by the truth of Christ").

LVIII. "Like St. Benedict … grace of God": *COCR* 11 reads: "Après saint Benoît, Adam considère l'humilité comme le climat dans lequel toutes les vertus s'épanouissent" ("Along with St. Benedict, Adam considers humility as the climate in which all the virtues flourish").

LIX. "Passion … of humility": no equivalent in *COCR*.

LX. "the Cistercian life of virtue": *ABR* 303 reads: "monastic *conversatio*"; *COCR* 12 reads: "la vie cistercienne de vertu".

LXI. "the Benedictine tradition.… Cistercian 'School of Humility'": *ABR* 303 reads: "the Benedictine tradition.… monastic 'School of Humility'"; *COCR* 12 reads: "nos Pères. L'école du Christ pour le cistercien, c'est simplement la *schola humilitatis* (645-647) et la *schola caritatis* (632)" ("our Fathers. The school of Christ for the Cistercian is simply the school of humility (645-647) and the school of charity (632)").

LXII. "But the school": equivalent preceded in *COCR* 12 by: "VIII. A l'école du Christ-Enfant."

LXIII. *Letters* text (30) reads: "Cross, in the wisdom"; *ABR* 304 reads: "Cross, the wisdom"; *COCR* 12 reads: "la sagesse de la Croix: la sagesse".

LXIV. "devotion": *ABR* 304 reads: "the Church's devotion"; *COCR* 12 reads: "la dévotion de l'Église".

LXV. "what gives … life"; *COCR* 13 reads: "est la pierre de base" ("is the rock of foundation").

LXVI. "guarding the heart".

LXVII. "has nothing … tender": no equivalent in *COCR*.

LXVIII. "after speaking about": *COCR* 13 reads: "après avoir parlé, ainsi que nous venons de le voir" ("after having spoken, as we have just seen").

LXIX. "in which … Mother": *COCR* 14 reads: "où tout est un" ("where all is one").

LXX. "with his trust … hearts": no equivalent in *COCR*.

LXXI. "It is not . . mother": no equivalent in *COCR*.

LXXII. *Letters* text (34) reads: "poverty and helplessness with the Infant Christ": *ABR* 306 reads: "poverty and helplessness with the poverty and helplessness of the infant Christ"; *COCR* 15 reads: "*notre pauvreté et notre impuissance à la pauvreté et à l'impuissance du Christ-Enfant*" ("our poverty and our helplessness to the poverty and helplessness of the Infant Christ").

LXXIII. "But what strikes us": *COCR* 15 reads: "Mais, par la logique des choses, ce qui nous frappe" ("But, by the logic of things, what strikes us").

LXXIV. "This love of hers … her sons": no equivalent in *COCR*.

LXXV. "The Blessed Virgin Compared to the Air We Breathe" ll. 34-72, 103-26, Gerard Manley Hopkins, *Poems and Prose*, ed. W. H. Gardner (Baltimore: Penguin, 1953) 54-58 ("New Bethlems, and he born / There, evening, noon, and morn – / Bethlem or Nazareth" corrected from "New Bethlehem or Nazareth,").

LXXVI. "It is the theme … *thy child*": no equivalent in *ABR* or *COCR*.

LXXVII. "The Sabbath of Contemplation"; *COCR* 15 reads: "X. Le Sabbat."

LXXVIII. "Our intimate … heaven": no equivalent in *COCR*.

LXXIX. See Exodus 5:6-8.

LXXX. Apocalypse [Revelation] 8:1.

LXXXI. Isaiah 9:6 [Greek Septuagint].

LXXXII. *PL* 195, cols. 659A-702B.

LXXXIII. "*in operibus obedientiae, ubi omne negotium otium*" (*Sermo* 72 *in Cantica Canticorum* [*PL* 183, col. 1129C]) ("in the works of obedience, where all business is rest").

LXXXIV. "and mystically united to him.… divine peace": no equivalent in *COCR*.

LXXXV. "winecellar" (Song of Songs 2:4).

LXXXVI. "This is … monastic life": no equivalent in *COCR*.

Appendix A
Thomas Merton – Writings on St. Bernard

"St. Bernard on Interior Simplicity," in *The Spirit of Simplicity Characteristic of the Cistercian Order: An Official Report, demanded and approved by the General Chapter. Together with Texts from St. Bernard of Clairvaux on Interior Simplicity. Translation and Commentary by A Cistercian Monk of Our Lady of Gethsemani*. Trappist, KY: Abbey of Our Lady of Gethsemani, 1948.

"St. Bernard on Interior Simplicity." *Thomas Merton on St. Bernard*. Cistercian Studies vol. 9. Kalamazoo, MI: Cistercian Publications, 1980: 105-57 (this version does not include Merton's Foreword or Conclusion from *The Spirit of Simplicity*).

* * * * * * *

"Transforming Union in St Bernard of Clairvaux and St John of the Cross," *Collectanea Ordinis Cisterciensium Reformatorum* 9.2 (1948) 107-17; 9.3 (1948) 210-23; 10.1 (1949) 41-52; 10.3 (1949) 353-61; 11.1 (1950) 25-38.

"Transforming Union in St Bernard of Clairvaux and St John of the Cross." *Thomas Merton on St. Bernard* 159-226.

* * * * * * *

Foreword to *St. Bernard of Clairvaux Seen through his Selected Letters*, trans. Bruno Scott James. Chicago: Henry Regnery, 1953: v-viii.

Jubilee 1.4 (August 1953) 32-37 (partial reprint with explanatory note and excerpts from nine letters).

Foreword to Henry Daniel-Rops, *Bernard of Clairvaux*, trans. Elisabeth Abbott. New York: Hawthorn Books, 1964: 5-7 (slightly altered text, omitting mention of the letters).

"St. Bernard." *A Thomas Merton Reader*, ed. Thomas P. McDonnell. New York: Harcourt, Brace, 1962: 315-18 (omitted from 1974 revised edition).

* * * * * * *

"Saint Bernard, Moine et Apôtre." Commission d'Histoire de l'Ordre de Cîteaux, *Bernard de Clairvaux*. Paris: Éditions Alsatia, 1953: vii-xv.

"Saint Bernard, Monk and Apostle." *The Tablet* 201.5896 (23 May 1953) 438-39; 201.5897 (30 May 1953) 466-67.

"Saint Bernard, Monk and Apostle." *Cross and Crown* 5.3 (Sept. 1953) 251-63.

"Saint Bernard, Monk and Apostle." *Disputed Questions*. New York: Farrar, Straus and Cudahy, 1960: 274-90.

* * * * * * *

"Le Sacrement de l'Avent dans la Spiritualité de Saint Bernard," *Dieu Vivant* 23 (1953) 21-43.

"The Sacrament of Advent in the Spirituality of St. Bernard." *Seasons of Celebration*. New York: Farrar, Straus & Giroux, 1965: 61-87.

* * * * * * *

"Action and Contemplation in St. Bernard," *Collectanea Ordinis Cisterciensium Reformatorum* 15.1 (January 1953) 26-31; 15.2 (July 1953) 203-16; 16.2 (April 1954) 105-21 (this version of the essay consists of the second, third and fourth of the five parts included in the expanded version).

Marthe, Marie et Lazare, trans. Marie Tadié. Paris: Desclée de Brouwer, 1956 (expanded version of the article with a new preface).

"Action and Contemplation in St. Bernard." *Thomas Merton on St. Bernard*: 23-104 (includes expanded version but not the preface).

* * * * * * *

Preface to *Marthe, Marie et Lazare. Honorable Reader": Reflections on My Work*, ed. Robert E. Daggy. New York: Crossroad, 1989: 17-22.

* * * * * * *

The Last of the Fathers: Saint Bernard of Clairvaux and the Encyclical Letter, Doctor Mellifluus. New York: Harcourt, Brace, 1954.

* * * * * * *

The Cistercian Fathers and Their Monastic Theology: Initiation into the Monastic Tradition 8, ed. Patrick F. O'Connell, Monastic Wisdom Series vol. 42. Collegeville, MN: Cistercian Publications, 2016.

Appendix B
Bibliography of Books by Merton Cited in This Volume

The Asian Journal, ed. Naomi Burton Stone, Brother Patrick Hart and James Laughlin. New York: New Directions, 1973.

Cassian and the Fathers: Initiation into the Monastic Tradition, ed. Patrick F. O'Connell, Monastic Wisdom [MW], vol. 1. Kalamazoo, MI: Cistercian Publications, 2005.

Charter, Customs, and Constitutions of the Cistercians: Initiation into the Monastic Tradition 7, ed. Patrick F. O'Connell. MW 41. Collegeville, MN: Cistercian Publications, 2015.

The Cistercian Fathers and Their Monastic Theology: Initiation into the Monastic Tradition 8, ed. Patrick F. O'Connell, MW 42. Collegeville, MN: Cistercian Publications, 2016.

Conjectures of a Guilty Bystander. Garden City, NY: Doubleday, 1966.

The Courage for Truth: Letters to Writers, ed. Christine M. Bochen. New York: Farrar, Straus, Giroux, 1993.

Dancing in the Water of Life: Seeking Peace in the Hermitage. Journals, vol. 5: 1963-1965, ed. Robert E. Daggy. San Francisco: HarperCollins, 1997.

Disputed Questions. New York: Farrar, Straus and Cudahy, 1960.

Entering the Silence: Becoming a Monk and Writer. Journals, vol. 2: 1941-1952, ed. Jonathan Montaldo. San Francisco: HarperCollins, 1996.

The Hidden Ground of Love: Letters on Religious Experience and Social Concerns, ed. William H. Shannon. New York: Farrar, Straus, Giroux, 1985.

"Honorable Reader": Reflections on My Work, ed. Robert E. Daggy. New York: Crossroad, 1989.

In the Valley of Wormwood: Cistercian Blessed and Saints of the Golden Age, ed. Patrick Hart, OCSO. Collegeville, MN: Cistercian Publications, 2013.

An Introduction to Christian Mysticism: Initiation into the Monastic Tradition 3, ed. Patrick F. O'Connell. MW 13. Kalamazoo, MI: Cistercian Publications, 2008.

The Last of the Fathers: Saint Bernard of Clairvaux and the Encyclical Letter, Doctor Mellifluus. New York: Harcourt, Brace, 1954.

The Letters of Robert Giroux and Thomas Merton, ed. Patrick Samway, SJ. Notre Dame, IN: University of Notre Dame Press, 2015.

The Letters of Thomas Merton and Victor and Carolyn Hammer: Ad Majorem Dei Gloriam, ed. F. Douglas Scutchfield and Paul Evans Holbrook Jr. Lexington: University Press of Kentucky, 2014.

The Life of the Vows: Initiation into the Monastic Tradition 6, ed. Patrick F. O'Connell, MW 30. Collegeville, MN: Cistercian Publications, 2012.

Marthe, Marie et Lazare. Paris: Desclée de Brouwer, 1956.

Monastic Observances: Initiation into the Monastic Tradition 5, ed. Patrick F. O'Connell. MW 25. Collegeville, MN: Cistercian Publications, 2010.

Mystics and Zen Masters. New York: Farrar, Straus and Giroux, 1967.

The Other Side of the Mountain: The End of the Journey. Journals, vol. 7: 1967-1968, ed. Patrick Hart. San Francisco: HarperCollins, 1998.

Passion for Peace: The Social Essays, ed. William H. Shannon. New York: Crossroad, 1995.

Pre-Benedictine Monasticism: Initiation into the Monastic Tradition 2, ed. Patrick F. O'Connell. MW 9. Kalamazoo, MI: Cistercian Publications, 2006.

The Road to Joy: Letters to New and Old Friends, ed. Robert E. Daggy. New York: Farrar, Straus, Giroux, 1989.

The Rule of Saint Benedict: Initiation into the Monastic Tradition 4, ed. Patrick F. O'Connell. MW 19. Collegeville, MN: Cistercian Publications, 2009.

The School of Charity: Letters on Religious Renewal and Spiritual Direction, ed. Patrick Hart. New York: Farrar, Straus, Giroux, 1990.

Seasons of Celebration. New York: Farrar, Straus & Giroux, 1965.

The Seven Storey Mountain. New York: Harcourt, Brace, 1948.

The Silent Life. New York: Farrar, Straus & Cudahy, 1957.

The Spirit of Simplicity. Trappist, KY: Abbey of Gethsemani, 1948.

Thomas Merton on St. Bernard. Kalamazoo, MI: Cistercian Publications, 1980.

A Thomas Merton Reader, ed. Thomas P. McDonnell. New York: Harcourt, Brace, 1962; rev. ed. Garden City, NY: Doubleday Image, 1974.

Turning Toward the World: The Pivotal Years. Journals, vol. 4: 1960-1963, ed. Victor A. Kramer. San Francisco: HarperCollins, 1996.

The Waters of Siloe. New York: Harcourt, Brace, 1949.

The Wisdom of the Desert: Sayings from the Desert Fathers of the Fourth Century. New York: New Directions, 1960.

Zen and the Birds of Appetite. New York: New Directions, 1968.

Appendix C
Primary and Secondary Sources for Authors Included in This Volume

St. Peter Damian

Letters. 6 vols. Washington, DC: Catholic University of America Press, 1989-2005.

* * * * * * *

McCready, William. *Odiosa Sanctitas: St. Peter Damian, Simony and Reform*. Toronto: Pontifical Institute of Mediaeval Studies, 2011.

Ranft, Patricia. *The Theology of Peter Damian: "Let Your Life Always Serve as a Witness"*. Washington, DC: Catholic University of America Press, 2012.

__________. *The Theology of Work: Peter Damian and the Medieval Religious Renewal Movement*. New York: Palgrave Macmillan, 2006.

St. Anselm of Canterbury

Basic Writings. Edited and translated by Thomas Williams. Indianapolis, IN: Hackett, 2007.

The Letters of Saint Anselm of Canterbury. Edited and translated and with an Introduction by Walter Fröhlich. 3 vols. Cistercian Studies [CS] Series vols. 96, 97, 142. Kalamazoo, MI: Cistercian Publications, 1990-94.

The Major Works. Edited with an introduction by Brian Davies and G. R. Evans. Oxford World Classics. New York: Oxford University Press, 1998.

The Prayers and Meditations of St. Anselm. Translated with an Introduction by Sr. Benedicta Ward. New York: Penguin, 1973.

St. Anselm. Edited and translated by Jasper Hopkins and Herbert Richardson. 4 vols. Toronto and New York: Edwin Mellen Press, 1975-76.

* * * * * * *

Evans, G. R. *Anselm*. Wilton, CT: Morehouse-Barlow, 1989.

__________. *Anselm and a New Generation*. New York: Oxford University Press, 1980.

__________. *Anselm and Talking about God*. New York: Oxford University Press, 1978.

Hopkins, Jasper. *A Companion to the Study of St. Anselm*. Minneapolis: University of Minnesota Press, 1972.

Shannon, William H. *Anselm: The Joy of Faith*. New York: Crossroad, 1999.

Southern, R. W. *Saint Anselm: A Portrait in a Landscape*. New York: Cambridge University Press, 1990.

Ward, Benedicta. *Anselm of Canterbury: His Life and Legacy*. London: SPCK, 2009.

Guigo the Carthusian

The Meditations of Guigo I. Prior of the Charterhouse. Translated with an Introduction by A. Gordon Mursell. CS 155. Kalamazoo, MI: Cistercian Publications, 1995.

* * * * * * *

Mursell, Gordon. *The Theology of the Carthusian Life in the Writings of St. Bruno and Guigo*. Salzburg, Austria: Institut für Anglistik und Amerikanistik, Universität Salzburg, 1988.

Bl. Guerric of Igny

Liturgical Sermons. Introduction and translation by monks of Mount Saint Bernard Abbey. 2 vols. Cistercian Fathers [CF] Series vols. 8, 32. Kalamazoo, MI: Cistercian Publications, 1970, 1999.

* * * * * * *

Morson, John. *Christ the Way: The Christology of Guerric of Igny*. CS 25. Kalamazoo, MI: Cistercian Publications, 1972.

St. Aelred of Rievaulx

Dialogue on the Soul. Translated by C. H. Talbot. CF 22. Kalamazoo, MI: Cistercian Publications, 1981.

For Your Own People: Aelred of Rievaulx's Pastoral Prayer. Translated by Mark DelCogliano. Edited by Marsha L. Dutton. CF 73. Kalamazoo, MI: Cistercian Publications, 2008.

The Historical Works. Translated by Jane Patricia Freeland. Edited by Marsha L. Dutton. CF 56. Kalamazoo, MI: Cistercian Publications, 2005.

Homilies on the Prophetic Burdens of Isaiah. Translated by Lewis White, Introduction by Marsha L. Dutton. CF 83. Collegeville, MN: Cistercian Publications, 2018.

The Liturgical Sermons. The First Clairvaux Collection. Translated by Theodore Berkeley. CF 58. Kalamazoo, MI: Cistercian Publications, 2001.

The Liturgical Sermons. The Second Clairvaux Collection. Translated by Marie Anne Mayeski. CF 77. Collegeville, MN: Cistercian Publications, 2016.

The Liturgical Sermons. The Durham and Lincoln Collections. Translated by Catena Scholarium, Lewis White and Katheryn Krug, edited by Ann Astell. CF 80. Collegeville, MN: Cistercian Publications, 2018.

Lives of the Northern Saints. Translated by Jane Patricia Freeland. Introduction by Marsha L. Dutton. CF 71. Kalamazoo, MI: Cistercian Publications, 2006.

Mirror of Charity. Translated by Elizabeth Connor, OCSO. Introduction by Charles Dumont, OCSO. CF 17. Kalamazoo, MI: Cistercian Publications, 1990.

Spiritual Friendship. Translated by Lawrence C. Braceland. Edited by Marsha L. Dutton. CF 5. Collegeville, MN: Cistercian Publications, 2010.

Treatises and Pastoral Prayer. Introduction by David Knowles. CF 2. Kalamazoo, MI: Cistercian Publications, 1995.

* * * * * * *

Daniel, Walter. *The Life of Aelred of Rievaulx and the Letter to Maurice*. Translated by F. M. Powicke and Jane Patricia Freeland. Introduction by Marsha L. Dutton. CF 57. Kalamazoo, MI: Cistercian Publications, 1994.

Hallier, Amédée, OCSO. *The Monastic Theology of Aelred of Rievaulx*. Translated by Columba Heaney. CS 8. Spencer, MA: Cistercian Publications, 1969.

Sommerfeldt, John R. *Aelred of Rievaulx: On Love and Order in the World and the Church*. New York: Newman Press, 2006.

__________. *Aelred of Rievaulx: Pursuing Perfect Happiness*. Mahwah, NJ: Newman Press, 2005.

Squire, Aelred. *Aelred of Rievaulx: A Study*. CS 50. Kalamazoo, MI: Cistercian Publications, 1981.

Truax, Jean. *Aelred the Peacemaker: The Public Life of a Cistercian Abbot*. CS 251. Collegeville, MN: Cistercian Publications, 2017.

Isaac of Stella

Sermons on the Christian Year I. Translated by Hugh McCaffrey, OCSO. Introduction by Bernard McGinn. CF 11. Kalamazoo, MI: Cistercian Publications, 1979.

Three Treatises on Man: A Cistercian Anthropology. Translated by Benjamin Clark, OCSO, Bernard McGinn, Erasmo Leiva and Benedicta Ward, SLG. CF 24. Kalamazoo, MI: Cistercian Publications, 1977.

* * * * * * *

McGinn, Bernard. *The Golden Chain: A Study in the Theological Anthropology of Isaac of Stella*. CS 15. Washington, DC: Cistercian Publications, 1972.

Adam of Perseigne

Letters of Adam of Perseigne. Translated by Grace Perigo. CF 21. Kalamazoo, MI: Cistercian Publications, 1976.

"With his usual care and diligence, Patrick O'Connell has put together a series of essays and conferences by Thomas Merton on Cistercian Fathers and Forefathers. Even after all these years they fill a need not otherwise satisfied. They are valuable not only to Cistercians, but to all who have an interest in monastic tradition. In them, Merton shows his expertise in presenting these people in a way that is both scholarly and full of human interest."

James Conner
OCSO Thomas Merton's Former Undermaster of Novices

"The more we know about monastic and Cistercian tradition, the more we know Thomas Merton who was preeminently a monk of Gethsemani. Perhaps no living scholar knows more about or has done more to make this material more widely available than Patrick F. O'Connell ... [T]his new collection of Merton's monastic studies ... illustrates Merton's continued conviction ... that the Cistercian Fathers had lost none of their relevance for contemporary Christians:"

Bonnie Thurston
Former President: International Thomas Merton Society,
Editor: *Merton & Buddhism*

New City Press is one of more than 20 publishing houses sponsored by the Focolare, a movement founded by Chiara Lubich to help bring about the realization of Jesus' prayer: "That all may be one" (John 17:21). In view of that goal, New City Press publishes books and resources that enrich the lives of people and help all to strive toward the unity of the entire human family. We are a member of the Association of Catholic Publishers.

www.newcitypress.com
202 Comforter Blvd.
Hyde Park, New York

Periodicals
Living City Magazine
www.livingcitymagazine.com

Scan to join our mailing list
for discounts and promotions
or go to www.newcitypress.com
and click on "join our email list."